1995

HUMAN RESOURCES
MANAGEMENT

FOR THE

HOSPITALITY INDUSTRY

HUMAN RESOURCES

MANAGEMENT

FOR THE

HOSPITALITY INDUSTRY

MARY L. TANKE, PHD

 delmar publishers inc.

Cover photo courtesy of Stouffer Hotels and Resorts.

Delmar staff:

Managing Editor: Gerry East
Associate Editor: Cynthia Haller, Lisa A. Reale
Project Editor: Susan B. Simpfenderfer
Production Supervisor: Larry Main
Design Supervisor: Susan C. Mathews

For information, write:
Delmar Publishers Inc.
3 Columbia Circle, Box 15-015
Albany, New York 12212-5015

Printed in the United States of America
Published simultaneously in Canada
by Nelson Canada,
A Division of The Thomson Corporation

10   9   8   7   6   5   4   3

Library of Congress Cataloging-in-Publication Data

Tanke, Mary L.
      Human resources management for the hospitality industry / by Mary
  L. Tanke.
          p. cm.
      Includes bibliographical references.
      ISBN 0-8273-3590-3. — ISBN 0-8273-3591-1 (instructor's guide)
      1. Hospitality industry—Personnel management. I. Title.
TX911.3.P4T36 1990
647.94'068'3—dc20

89-25716
CIP

CONTENTS

152,841

vi

vii

Human resources management will have a profound impact on the success of hospitality organizations in the 1990s. With the service sector growing by 80%, the traditional teenage work force shrinking and expectations regarding work changing, new human resources skills and practices are required. Hospitality managers that assume human resources responsibilities must be prepared to deal with such issues as AIDS, a subject matter that few have the knowledge base from which to make decisions. Counseling and interpersonal relations skills, motivational techniques and legislative trends all become increasingly important for successful hospitality managers. While marketing, operations and finance have dominated the high-level executive positions in the 1980s, human resources expertise will become equal in organizational stature in the 1990s and beyond. Front-line hospitality managers, regardless of the sector of the hospitality industry they choose or the job function they are hired to perform, will be required to understand sound human resources theory and practice. It is these individuals who seek to accomplish the goals of the hospitality organization through the human resources who actually provide the service. Your company's greatest asset *is* its human resources!

Human Resources Management for the Hospitality Industry was written to fill a void and meet a need for a book that specifically addressed human resources issues in the context of the hospitality work environment. When I was asked to teach a course in human resources management two years ago, I realized that not even a textbook existed that was hospitality-industry specific! In the ten years I have been teaching, I have always found that hospitality students have a greater difficulty assimilating material that is not industry specific. While there are literally dozens of generic personnel and human resources management textbooks on the market, at this time, few deal specifically with the issues of importance to the hospitality industry.

Hospitality and other service-related industries **are** unique and do deserve a book that addresses the entire spectrum of human resources management activities from the perspective of the service sector. The very nature of hospitality and service is people, people, people! The quality of service our guests receive is how our hospitality operations are judged. Our human resources are the critical link between the hospitality operation and the guest. It's service that keeps guests returning.

Take care of your human resources and they will take care of the guests and everything else takes care of itself.

As service industries grow there will be more competition for employees. Restaurants and hotels will not only be competing among themselves for people to fill their job vacancies, but will also be competing against the local grocery and retail stores. This will be compounded by the reduction of the 16–24 year-old age group that is historically where the hospitality industry has obtained a large proportion of its work force. With a serious labor shortage in the near future, a renewed emphasis will be directed towards the recruitment function. It will become increasingly important that the **right** people are hired into your hospitality organization. The first important human resources activity in the 90s will be to attract the right people.

The management of our human resources affects the lives, dreams, goals and ambitions of the individuals we employ and their families. Once quality people have been recruited and hired the functions of training, development, counseling, discipline and evaluating performance come into play. These functions revolve around retention and make retaining the right people the second important human resources activity in the 90s. Each chapter of this book focuses on human resources processes and procedures presented as an integrated picture that will assist the reader in both attracting and retaining a quality hospitality work force. Innovative approaches to such human resources functions as development, counseling, team building, coaching, disciplinary actions and motivational techniques in the hospitality industry have been included. The chapter on employee assistance programs contains a detailed section on AIDS to assist the reader in becoming better educated on this critical issue that is of concern to all management.

The changing demographics will place a new burden on the hospitality manager with human resources responsibilities in "the next chapter." "The next chapter" will be a reference point throughout the content of this book that was written to alert you to the human resources challenges you face in the 1990s. Whenever you see the phrase "the next chapter" used, it should serve as a signal that this is an idea or concept that deserves your careful attention. My suggestion is that, as you read through this book, you make a list of these ideas, challenges and trends. At the book's conclusion you will have a list covering all facets of human resources management that will require your watchful eye.

Industry Contributions

My years of teaching in hospitality administration programs was preceded by twelve years in operations, primarily in the food service sector, and although I make a conscious effort to stay current on what is happening in the industry, I am not naive enough to believe that the world of hospitality management has not changed in the years since teaching has been my primary occupation. The last thing that I wanted to write was an esoteric, highly theoretical text that had little purpose beyond the classroom lecture, discussions and testing. To me, the most serious criticism that a student can make of a text is that it has no "real world" application or value beyond the classroom. To ensure that this was not a deficit in *Human Resources Management for the Hospitality Industry* and that this book would emphasize the pragmatic, I went to the hospitality industry for assistance.

Fourteen of the sixteen chapters in this book have specific input from some of today's leading hospitality industry experts. From presidents and executive vice presidents of hospitality companies to representatives of the National Restaurant Association and members of the American Hotel and Motel Association, from corporate directors to directors of training and development to directors of college relations, and from managers of recruiting to managers of food and beverage operations, fourteen industry representatives served as my advisors on the matter you are about to read. Upon being written, each chapter was sent to one industry advisor for his or her critique and review. They helped me to identify inaccuracies and clarify theory by providing specific industry-related examples, practical common-sense guides and hands-on help based upon their own hospitality experiences. In the Industry Experts Speak portions of each chapter, some of their advice has been highlighted for special consideration. These industry leaders are identified in a special section following this preface. Please take a few minutes to read the abbreviated backgrounds of these industry experts who advised me on the following chapters.

Mention needs to be made of the industry advisement to Chapter 12, "Progressive Discipline, Counseling and Exiting the Organization," because it speaks to the present concern in the hospitality industry over increased government regulations, legislation and litigation involving human resources activities. Four industry representatives from two major hospitality corporations reviewed the material in Chapter 12 and supplied me with much feedback as well as the data I needed to complete the figures and tables in this chapter. While the information was taken directly from company policies and handbooks, legal counsel for these companies felt that the material was too sensitive and left them open to potential litigation in the future. Hence, the names of the individuals and companies who provided me with valuable assistance will remain nameless, at their request. You know who you are and, again, my sincere thanks for all your efforts in making this a valuable chapter in the book.

Features of the Text

To assist the reader in exploring human resources management, each chapter has been preceded by a general discussion of the human resources topic under discussion followed by a list of objectives that you will have accomplished by reading the chapter and a list of key words. At the chapter conclusion, a series of discussion questions has been provided to test your understanding of the chapter material. Case problems have also been included so that the reader may apply the concepts of each chapter to hypothetical industry situations. Last, you will find a list of selected recommended reading chosen for those readers who wish to expand upon the human resources management areas broached by this book.

Acknowledgments

This text could not have been completed without the friendship, assistance and support of numerous individuals. Foremost, my deepest gratitude goes to Dr. Lendal Kotschevar whose patience endured endless questions pertaining to the writing and preparation of a book manuscript. An author writing her first book could not ask for a better mentor, friend and colleague.

To my graduate students, Captain Guy Palumbo, Farhan Lone, and Zoeanne Palumbo who spent countless hours inside Florida International University's library, tracking and locating materials that were invaluable to me. Thank you for finding articles without author's names, uncovering reference information for articles for which I had no idea from where they had come and for searching through miles of microfilm looking for documents I insisted upon having. The staff at University Park library were diligent and thorough in dozens of requests for books and articles on interlibrary loan. I have appreciated your endurance with this project.

I would like to thank my faithful typist, Michaela Lopes, who tolerated my dropping off draft copy all hours of the day and night. Half way through the manuscript she convinced me that I had to stop using my typewriter and learn word processing. I owe special thanks to Richard Ishmael for every time he rescued me from another computer crisis. Dealing with floppy disks instead of paper is a frightening experience for a computer novice. Michaela's and Richie's help and encouragement saved me untold hours of work during the revisionary process. Today I can't imagine writing anywhere but on my computer!

I am especially thankful for the support and help of my industry advisors, who not only made writing this book an enjoyable experience, but an educational one as well. I know you spent time reading chapter drafts between meetings, early mornings and late nights, while commuting and traveling on business, between opening new restaurants and at home on weekends when you undoubtedly had more pleasurable things to do. I am indebted to your kindness and willingness to assist me in the preparation of a useful tool for future and present hospitality managers.

Writing this book has tested the patience and humor of colleagues, neighbors, friends and family who all received the same reply to any request for my time, "I'm sorry I can't; I'm writing." Thank you for enduring with me the pains of writing my first book. I am especially thankful for the prayers and words of encouragement and support from Pastor Neal Greatens and the members of Concordia Lutheran Church.

I owe special thanks to photographer Michael Upwright as well as to Professor Kevin Robson for his assistance in setting up photo shots. I was fortunate to have the special assistance of Mr. T. W. Berry, Vice President, Human Resources, Family Restaurant Division and Far West Concepts and Professor Don Smith, Westin Distinguished Professor, Hotel and Restaurant Administration, Washington State University, who either read chapters or dialogued with me. Don Smith was instrumental in helping me to organize my thoughts in a coherent fashion. In addition to industry input, the following academicians offered insight and suggestions when reviewing the text manuscript. My sincere thanks for your time and efforts:

Toby Strianese, Schenectady County Community College, Schenectady, New York; Eugene Bertog, Oakton College, Des Plaines, Illinois; Robert Edgar Smith, Hilton College, University of Houston, Houston, Texas; John Moonan, Daytona Beach Community College, Daytona Beach, Florida; Pearl Brewer, Purdue University, West Lafayette, Indiana; David Ebert, Tucson, Arizona; Florence Berger, School of Hotel Administration, Cornell University, Ithaca, New York; Matteo Casola, Schenectady County Community College, Schenectady, New York.

And, finally, to all of my students, whose words of encouragement, genuine concern about the progress I was making and supportive notes slipped under my office door: Thank you, you helped make what follows a reality.

Welcome to *Human Resources Management for the Hospitality Industry!*

Mary L. Tanke
Miami, Florida

Dedicated in love and memory of my grandmother, Lillian Lemster, as she would exercise these words from Proverbs 31:30:

"Charm is deceitful and beauty is vain, but a woman who fears the Lord, she shall be praised."

ABOUT THE AUTHOR

Mary L. Tanke, PhD is a professor in the School of Hospitality Management, Florida International University, Miami, Florida. After receiving her bachelor's degree from Florida International, she later went on to complete her master's and PhD degrees from Purdue University. This is Dr. Tanke's tenth year of teaching Hospitality Management, which includes a semester in Switzerland at the Centre International de Glion. She holds a CFBE designation from AH&MA's Educational Institute and is an active participant in the Council on Hotel, Restaurant, and Institution Education where she co-chairs the Accreditation Committee. In 1987 she received the Ryder System, Inc., Award of Excellence in Research/Scholarship for her work on accreditation and Multicultural Management. In addition to this textbook, she recently finished workshop modulars for industry professionals on the subject of Multicultural Management for the Hospitality Industry.

In addition to Dr. Tanke's educational background are 12 years of foodservice industry experience. Starting at Strongbow Turkey Inn in Valparaiso, Indiana as a busgirl, she worked for several different companies, primarily in the back-of-the-house. Her experience includes working chef at the Alabama Hotel, Winter Park, Florida; cook at Valparaiso University; manager of the student lab-cafeteria at Purdue University; banquet chef at Holiday Inn and assistant to the chef at the Depot, Miami, Florida; and as a food specialist aboard Amtrak.

Industry Advisor Biographies

Elaine G. Etess has spent her entire professional life in the hospitality industry. Prior to the sale of the Grossinger Hotel in 1985, she was co-owner and Executive Vice President. Currently she is President of Elaine G. Etess Associates, a hotel consulting company in Boca Raton, Florida, and also serves as executive assistant to the President of American Inn Management Company in Tucson, Arizona. In January 1989, she became the first woman President of the American Hotel & Motel Association.

Growing up in the business, **Michael Hurst** started working during sixth grade in restaurants and now has 47 years of experience. He owns his own restaurant (15th Street Fisheries, Fort Lauderdale, Florida) and is involved in lecturing, teaching (Florida International University) and association work (National Restaurant Association). Previous employers include Michigan State University, Marriott Corporation, Win Schuler's Inc., Don the Beachcomber Enterprises, and others. Being a full-time teacher at FIU, an official of the National Restaurant Association and giving 50 or more speeches a year is surely full-time work for him.

Dr. Geneva Gay is a well-known educator, scholar, author, and national consultant to school districts, state departments of education, colleges and universities, regional service centers and professional associations on what is multicultural education, why is it important, and how to design programs to implement multicultural education and multicultural staff development. In addition to being actively engaged in multicultural teacher preparation and working regularly with a wide variety of educational organizations on issues of ethnic and cultural diversity, Dr. Gay has consulted with the U.S. Army in Europe, the British Institute of Education, and Southwestern Bell Telephone Company on similar concerns.

Joel S. Katz has more than twelve years experience in training, management development, and recruitment. Currently, he is director of Human Resources Development at ARA Services. ARA is a multibillion-dollar diversified services corporation with over 130,000 employees, and is the leader in contract foodservice management. One of Joel's major accomplishments has been spearheading ARA's integrated, competency-based approach to selection, performance management, training and development, and succession planning. Prior to joining ARA, Mr. Katz held a variety of positions in organization and management development at RCA Corporation and a major retail department store chain. His specialty is human resources development in multi-unit service organizations.

David R. Murphy is the former Corporate Director of College Relations with the Marriott Corporation. He has spent the last 18 years with the evolving human resources functions of this giant corporation. During his tenure, the employee base has grown from 25,000 to over 150,000 employees.

Cathy Conner didn't come from hospitality operations. She began in the recruiting field by recruiting women into nontraditional fields (for example, electronics, drafting, airplane mechanics) as part of a sex-equality program in vocational education. After some sales experience in another industry Ms. Conners joined Gilbert/Robinson as a Corporate Recruiter in 1985—a newly created position. Her position has grown and evolved to include managing the entire recruiting function.

Nick Horney directs all training and development activities for Stouffer Hotel Company, including customer service and executive development, from corporate headquarters in Solon, Ohio. Dr. Horney holds a doctorate in industrial/organizational psychology. Prior to joining Stouffer Hotel Company he was director of organizational development for Pizza Hut, Inc. Before that he held a series of training and development posts with the same firm.

Hugh Murphy, former Vice President-Human Resources, Chili's Inc., Dallas, Texas has more than 15 years' experience in the restaurant business. Mr. Murphy has gained an insight into the business that can only come from the ground up. One of the industry's most dynamic personalities, he is a frequent speaker on college campuses throughout the United States.

Richard Ysmael joined Motorola in 1968 and has held a series of increasingly responsible positions. He is currently responsible for 25 Motorola foodservice facilities located in Arizona, Florida, Illinois and Texas, serving over 50,000 employees daily. He acts as liaison for Motorola's domestic subsidiaries and international foodservice operations in Europe, Asia, Pacific, Central and South America; directing a staff of 400 employees with food and vending sales in excess of $20 million in the United States. Ysmael's marketing expertise included the development of a unique identity concept, "Food Works," which has created more of a commercial restaurant atmosphere versus the stereotype company cafeteria. Mr. Ysmael is a 1982 recipient of IFMA's Silver Plate Award and was voted an Ivy Winner for 1985. He is Past-President of the Society for Foodservice Management and a founding board member.

James F. Moore, President of Far West Concepts, is a graduate of Penn State University with a B.S. degree in Hotel and Restaurant Administration. He was with Stouffer Food Corporation for fifteen years in jobs ranging from management trainee to Vice President of Operations. He spent five years with The Henrici Corporation as Executive Vice

President C.O.O. and the last ten years with Host International and the Grace Corporation, which has turned into a LBO under the name Restaurant Enterprises Group, Inc. Far West Concepts is a group of 100 Dinnerhouses including Charley Brown's, Reuben's Steak Houses and Sea Food Grill and Baxter's restaurants.

Jim Tye is the Director of Employment for Furr's/Bishop's Cafeterias L.P., a 160-unit public cafeteria firm. A graduate of Texas Tech University, Tye began his foodservice career working part-time while attending college, and has performed a variety of human resource duties during his 10-year career with Furr's/Bishop's. He is an active member and has held various committee responsibilities within the Council of Hotel Restaurant and Institutional Educators, Southwest Placement Association, and the Rocky Mountain College Placement Association.

Regynald G. Washington is the Senior Vice President of Concessions International, Inc., Atlanta, Georgia. Mr. Washington began his professional career in the food services business in 1974, after receiving a B.S. degree in International Hotel and Restaurant Administration at Florida International University. Since beginning his career, Mr. Washington has been an active participant in several restaurant activities, such as the California, Florida, and Washington State Restaurant Associations. As Corporate Senior Vice President, Mr. Washington controls revenues in the excess of twenty million dollars annually. Operations include Los Angeles, Seattle, Dallas, Orlando, and four joint ventures in Louisville, Hartford, Cleveland and Chicago.

HUMAN RESOURCES

PLANNING

AND

ORGANIZATION

CHAPTER 1

INTRODUCTION TO CONTEMPORARY HUMAN RESOURCES MANAGEMENT

INDUSTRY ADVISORS
Elaine Grossinger Etess, President
Elaine G. Etess Associates

and

Michael Hurst, Vice President
National Restaurant Association and Owner 15th Street Fisheries

"If a man is called to be a streetsweeper, he should sweep streets even as Michelangelo painted, or Beethoven composed music, or Shakespeare wrote poetry. He should sweep streets so well that all the hosts of heaven and earth will pause to say, here lived a great streetsweeper who did his job well."—MARTIN LUTHER KING, JR.

KEY WORDS

behavioral sciences
employees
Hawthorne Experiments
human resources
human resources functions

human resources management
industrial revolution
personnel management
scientific management
Taylor, Frederick W.

INTRODUCTION

How do you get your employees, your **human resources**, to be the best they can be? The best dishwasher, the best front desk clerk, the best bartender, the best bell person, the best prep cook, the best housekeeper? Human resources skills have always been important for the hospitality industry, but from now until way beyond the year 2000 they will be the single most important skill that a manager can have. You will have to have these skills to stay alive.

3

That's what this book is about: staying alive, being competitive and being successful. This challenge means that your people skills must be far greater than those competing against you and certainly better than those of the era of the 70s and 80s.

How important are human resources management skills to you, as you graduate and enter the hospitality work force as a manager? Managing people will be something that you will do every workday. Regardless of the segment of the hospitality industry you choose, the company you plan to work for or start on your own, the job title you are assigned, or the size of the operation you will work in, human resources will affect you and be affected by your actions. We welcome the opportunity to show you, through our own personal experiences in the hospitality industry, how to assist each of you, and the human resources you manage, in being recognized as "a great streetsweeper who did his job well."

At the conclusion of this chapter you will be able to:
1. Describe the important historical influences that led to the development of the human resources focus of management as we know it in the 1990s.
2. Define human resources management and the functions associated with its actions.
3. Distinguish between personnel skills and human resource skills.
4. Discuss the importance of the role of the manager with human resources responsibilities in the hospitality industry.
5. Explain how certain terminology will be used in the remainder of this text.

Defining Human Resources Management

In the hospitality industry all managers are human resources managers, or more appropriately, all managers have responsibilities that include their human resources. Dealing with people is what our business is all about: whether it's our employees or those guests who walk in the front door. When providing services to our guests our primary resource is our people, our workers, our employees. Being such a labor-intensive industry you would think that it would be hard to neglect these valuable resources, but oftentimes we do.

Successful hospitality managers need the ability to work with people. We need to develop a people orientation in our management approach. This text is not about management per se but rather about a singularly important skill of management: human resources management. What's the difference, you ask? A manager with human resources responsibilities is first and foremost a manager of people. As a manager with human resources responsibilities, your concern is those people and how their needs, wants and desires fit into the needs and desires (or rather the organizational goals and objectives) of the hospitality enterprise. We are not talking about your management style or how to manage your human resources but rather the knowledge and skills it takes to effectively use and coordinate your people resources.

INDUSTRY EXPERTS SPEAK	Mike Hurst further emphasizes, "The role of management is changing—overmanagement in the past and underled. Hospitality is based on the gift of friendship—nice people who care. With competition intensifying, capital requirements accelerating, and the dilemmas imposed by an expanding industry and shrinking labor force, it has become imperative in a service society for management to shift its focus—*from profit to people* and its style—*from the back door (office) to the front door.*"

We will define **human resources management** as the implementation of the strategies, plans and programs required to attract, motivate, develop, reward and retain the best people to meet the organizational goals and operational objectives of the hospitality enterprise. The activities or **functions** required by human resources management are what make up the job duties of the manager with human resources responsibilities.

Before reading any further, take out a pencil and piece of paper and write down a list of what you believe are the job duties of a hospitality manager with human resources responsibilities. In other words, just what does a manager with human resources responsibilities do in the course of his or her workday? What does your list look like? Does it include hiring? Interviewing? Job placement? And what about performance appraisals, discipline, termination, development, orientation and training? If these were some of the items on your list, you already have a good idea of the job duties that you, as a manager with human resources responsibilities, will need to be able to perform. Table 1-1 lists the

Table 1-1. Human Resources Management Functions

Planning	Coaching
Analysis	Teambuilding
Recruitment	Performance evaluation
Selection	Compensation administration
Hiring	Benefits planning and administration
Placement	Discipline
Orientation	Counseling
Training	Termination
Development	Labor relations

Figure 1-1. The hospitality industry provides job opportunities for numerous skill levels. Photo A courtesy of Marriott Corporation; photo B courtesy of Michael Upright; photo C courtesy of Strongbow Inn, Valparaiso, Indiana; photo D courtesy of Stouffer Hotels and Resorts

functions of human resources management. The best way to view the functions of human resources management is as the job duties of the manager with human resources responsibilities.

You might have noticed that the listing in Table 1-1 corresponds almost identically with the table of contents for this text. That is not by accident. This book was carefully designed, with the assistance of several industry advisors, to give you a comprehensive overview of the types of activities and programs that make up the field of human resources management in the hospitality industry (Figure 1-1). You will have the opportunity to actually assume the role of a manager with human resources responsibilities as you read through the following pages.

The human resources department (whether it formally exists or not) assists the hospitality organization in meeting its goals and objectives. Elaine G. Etess points out that without the presence, involvement and cooperation of a human resources department (even in an informal structure), the goals and objectives of the hospitality organization will be difficult to reach. Each of the chapters will discuss a human resources function where you will learn the specific duties of the manager with human resources responsibilities in the implementation of that function. "How to's" and the actual forms being used in the hospitality industry today have been generously supplied by a number of industry advisors. It is our hope that this book will not only be useful during your academic endeavors, but will serve as a beneficial guide when you enter the hospitality work force.

7

Human resources management is a relatively new term for what has historically been referred to as personnel administration or personnel management. Let us review the major historical contributions to human resources management that have led us to this important change in terminology.

Historic Changes in Human Resources Management

The human resources managers of the 1990s have earned a place of respect for their contribution to organizational effectiveness. The contemporary role of managers with human resources responsibilities is an important one to any hospitality organization. Most people spend more than one-third of their waking hours at their jobs, and as a manager of human resources you will make decisions that affect and influence the lives, dreams, goals and ambitions of these individuals and their families. A look at the historical development of the human resources profession will show us that this was not always the situation.

Early Employer-Employee Relationships

Practices related to human resources management can be traced back to the Babylonian Code of Hammurabi around 1800 B.C. that provided for an incentive type of compensation plan as well as a minimum wage. From high school history you will recall the institution of slavery, one of the earliest forms of structured employment. When you read the chapter on "progressive discipline," you might recall that one of the reasons for the failure of slavery was the precept of punishment as a motivator. Slaves had no incentive to work harder, and their major achievement was to avoid the whip.

Serfdom followed slavery. This was still an oppressed form of labor since serfs were forced to work for their landowners; however, they fared better than slaves since their income was tied to their productivity. This provided for some of the early forms of incentives.

The guild system, composed of apprentices, journeymen and master craftsmen, is still used, in part, in the hospitality industry in Europe, and to a lesser degree in the United States. This formed the basis for early training and development systems. Since the guild system also required careful selection of apprentices along with a reward system built on retention, you might say that this was the true beginning of human resources management.

The Early Contributions

While not specifically concerned with the management of people in the work place, some of the earlier philosophers, such as Machiavelli, did exhibit a good understanding of how people should be treated. It was in *The Prince* that Machiavelli pointed out that a leader cannot make people love him, but that he can make people respect him. The conclusion, therefore, was that leaders should concentrate on those aspects of human behavior over which they had control, and get their people to respect them.

By the mid-1850s, the United States was experiencing the industrial revolution, which had already occurred in Europe. Robert Owen, a British businessman, was probably the first individual to study the effects of the work environment on productivity. He implemented his ideas in model villages located next to his cotton mills in Scotland. Some of his ideas included the installation of toilets in his factories, shortening the work day to ten hours and eventually abolishing child labor from all of his operations. Mr. Owen's ideas were quite revolutionary for his day!

Scientific Management

Toward the end of the nineteenth century, Frederick W. Taylor began his experiments leading to the birth of scientific management. Taylor believed that workers could receive high wages and that management could keep labor costs down by improving productivity.[1] His arguments to treat workers fairly resulted in the elimination of dismissal without cause and the institution of "just cause" as a standard for termination. While scholars are still not sure of Taylor's motives, the principles of scientific management did take into consideration the welfare of the worker.[2]

It is important for you to keep in mind that working conditions were very bad during the industrial revolution. There was no protection from employers who expected their workers to live and work in unsanitary conditions, suffer long work hours, perform their jobs in unsafe environments and endure great physical fatigue.

Many others picked up Taylor's teachings, and the study of employee productivity became popular. Frank and Lillian Gilbreth, Henry Gantt, Carl Barth and others spent their lives studying how to maximize output while minimizing input. This was the wave of efficiency experts who studied division-of-labor techniques and conducted time-and-motion studies to reduce expending any unnecessary energy when performing a job task. The efforts of these individuals did result in improved training methods, the development of a more appropriate wage system and pointed out the importance of proper selection procedures.

It was during this time, preceding World War I, that individuals started to specialize in personnel management. In 1900, for example, the B. F. Goodrich Company started an employment department.[3] Welfare secretaries or social secretaries were hired to deal with matters involving housing, wages, medical and recreational concerns. The National Cash Register Company, in 1902, established a Labor Department that handled compensation administration, employee grievances, working conditions (one of the first companies to institute a safety function in human resources management), and recordkeeping.[4]

World War I

In 1913, two books were published, first by Munsterberg and then by Gilbreth, that dealt specifically with management behavior.[5,6] Hugo Munsterberg's work in accident reduction led to the development of the first preemployment selection tests. It was Munsterberg's idea that some people are better suited to certain job positions than are other people, an idea that is still used today to improve the quality of the selection and placement decisions. Gilbreth continued the work of her late husband, which discussed the importance of human factors in the work environment. Taking considerable care in matching the right people to the right jobs has lead to vast improvement in job satisfaction and performance.

The need to improve selection and placement decisions during World War I led to further research and test development. Much of this work was conducted by the U.S. Army under the leadership of Robert Yerkes. The committee he headed developed an intelligence test for recruits known as Army Alpha. Later, the Army Beta was developed for use in testing illiterate recruits. Army Beta became even more useful after the war in the psychological testing of immigrants who could not speak English.

During the 1920s, companies continued to add personnel departments, and several colleges and universities began to offer courses in personnel management. The areas of specialization at that time emphasized selection and training needs along with employee welfare. Of special concern was employee health and safety. To this day, health and safety concerns continue to fall under the auspices of the human resources department.

The Hawthorne Experiments

The original intent of the Hawthorne studies was to examine the effect of lighting and ventilation on productivity. The results of these historic experiments, however, indicated that the most important factors affecting productivity levels were the concern and interest of management in their workers.[7] These findings have become the basis for the human relations movement. People finally recognized that the individual workers were really important and needed to be treated with a certain amount of consideration.

After the First World War, the U.S. experienced a period of great prosperity during the roaring twenties. Personnel policies and departments that were established during the war continued to grow, although personnel management was still not fully accepted by all managers.

The 1930s ushered in the Great Depression. What had been so good in the twenties was now reversed. It was during this period that the Roosevelt administration passed several pieces of legislation to regulate personnel management practices. The Social Security Act of 1935 provided for retirement packages, disability and unemployment insurance. The Fair Labor Standards Act of 1938 established a policy for minimum wage and a maximum length for the workweek. Personnel departments were seen as an unnecessary cost of doing business during this period, and the human resources management function suffered a setback.

World War II

The setback encountered during the depression was soon to change with the serious labor shortage that resulted during the Second World War. It is unfortunate, but historically true, that the greatest advances in human resources management were made in the U.S. during periods of war.

The greatest influx of labor into the work place was that of women, as men were called upon to serve in the armed forces. New and more advanced technologies generated the need for specialized training programs and better methods of using the work force that was available. The principles of human engineering were applied to design work spaces and equipment. More effective ways of teaching large numbers of unskilled people how to use the new equipment led to great advances in training and development, and a government-imposed wage structure led to the development of fringe benefits to attract people to the work place.

Training programs for managers at the nation's universities and colleges were encouraged by the government. For the first time, courses were offered in personnel administration and office management. By the end of the war, training at all skill and responsibility levels was commonplace. The development of the computer also occurred during this period.

The Forties and Fifties

After the war, the baby boom began that would lead to the abundance of workers in the 1960s, especially for the rapidly growing hospitality industry. New technologies and occupations had been created because of the war. The government required that businesses hire veterans, a practice that is still regulated today. The role of the business schools at universities expanded, with a number of research centers established specifically to study personnel and manpower problems. The interstate highway system was built, which along with the growth of the automobile industry and the shift from industrial production to service industries, contributed to the rapid expansion of hospitality businesses throughout the United States.

Mike Hurst points out that an increase in leisure time and more disposable income lead to a greater demand for food away from home, and no supply to service it. This was a period of expansion for fast food and the limited menu.

11

The Sixties and Seventies

The personnel manager came of age during this time period. The government passed a series of legislative actions that continue to affect human resources management today. These include the Civil Rights Act of 1960, the Work Hours Act of 1962, the Equal Pay Act of 1963, Title VI of the Civil Rights Act of 1964, the Age Discrimination Act of 1967, the Occupational Safety and Health Act of 1970, and the Equal Employment Opportunity Act and Commission.

The behavioral sciences influenced training and development with the introduction of sensitivity training and programmed learning. The evolution of the computer assisted the personnel manager with an increasing variety of tasks.

Personnel functions during the sixties generally consisted of staffing, training and development, wage and salary administration, labor relations and collective bargaining, and employee benefits and services. The work of the personnel manager was still not widely respected by other managers in the organization. A similar situation was found in the hospitality industry.

The personnel department was seen as a staff function, one that supported the other departments whenever they were in need. Personnel was viewed as an advisory role. The personnel managers could make suggestions and recommendations but did not have the authority or power to implement their ideas.

> "The hotel personnel director commonly is responsible for recruiting and screening new employees, checking unemployment insurance claims and doing a variety of odd jobs that just don't seem to fit any other department's domain. As a result, he tends to have a clerical status rather than the professional standing enjoyed by his counterparts in other industries."[8]

The 1970s expanded the personnel function to also include motivational techniques, organizational development and policy development. For the first time, the role of personnel managers was seen as affecting the outcomes of the organization as a whole, in particular, with an impact on the bottom line. Personnel management was now being referred to, upon occasion, as **human resources management.**

The Eighties

It was during the 1980s that the disparities between the line managers and the human resources managers disappeared as both came to the realization that they shared a commonality of purpose. The human resources department was more than just a place where employees went to be hired or fired. Human resources managers became aware of the needs of their work force and that the satisfaction of those needs was a critical function of their jobs. Human resources responsibilities were seen as a job duty of all front-line managers.

The needs of the hospitality organization also entered into the picture. Selecting human resources that fit into an organization's corporate culture became important. Managers with human resources responsibilities also recognized that it was up to them to make sure that the human resources they selected had all of the tools and knowledge necessary to be successful in their job positions. Career development was seen not just as a path for management, but as a strong retention tool for the hourly human resources as well.

INDUSTRY EXPERTS SPEAK

Elaine Etess, head of Elaine G. Etess Associates relates the following story: "During my tenure as a member of the BOCES (Board of Cooperative Educational Services) Vocational Advisory Board, I hired a 17-year-old high school student to work part-time at our resort. This was part of a work study program for students who were not academically talented. She was taught the necessary job skills to be a powder room attendant. She was pleased to have an after-school job, and particularly one that was school-related and enabled her to earn some money. On the evening of her recognition program, I presented her certificate and also gave her a wristwatch as a personal gift. She was so appreciative. After graduation she worked full time. This was a great help to us as the position was necessary, but difficult to fill. After several months, a position as attendant in the health club became available and we gave her the promotion. Not only did she work exceedingly well accepting the additional responsibilities, she also learned to interact well not only with her peers, but with the guests as well. When the receptionist was off, she was able to fill in to make appointments.

This is a tangible example of an hourly, nonskilled employee becoming a career person. It is interesting to also note that her sister came to work, as did her mother. Her mother had been a long-time welfare recipient and now felt that she was a part of an organization that gave her a feeling of self-worth. We created three loyal and dedicated "human resources." Their skills level was limited, but they were exceptional employees in their areas."

Human resources managers truly began to see the people in the work force as human resources and not as mere employees. We have elected to continue this emphasis in the pages that follow, and refer to the workers not always as employees, but as human resources. Some of you might find this wording awkward at first, but we hope that at the conclusion of this text it will serve to reinforce the importance of having the proper attitude as a human resources manager and manager of human resources. An employee is, after all, a human being first!

INDUSTRY EXPERTS SPEAK

Mike Hurst, owner of 15th Street Fisheries adds, "The perfect labor cost is zero. Just leave your doors locked and get rid of your customers. That will get it for you instantly! On a more serious note, remember that the greatest compliment we can get in this business is, "Where do you get the nice people who work here!"

The Role of the Human Resources Manager

The manager with human resources responsibilities in today's hospitality organization participates in the strategic planning sessions, understands the financial documents and can relate the job they perform to the bottom line. In many hospitality organizations the human resources manager is part of the senior management team. The reactive stance of fire fighting has been replaced with the proactive stance of anticipating the future needs of the hospitality organization.

INDUSTRY EXPERTS SPEAK

Mrs. Etess adds, "The human resources manager must be part of the executive management team. A thorough understanding of the entire operation is a necessity. This knowledge will enable the manager with human resources responsibilities to

> evaluate employees to the fullest for the important program of career development. The philosophy of getting employees to look at our industry as a career, not just a job, must be a part of the human resources manager's job description."

The recognition has occurred that the human resources manager's role is social as well. The new needs of our work force have required some new responses. The changing demographics of our society have created the need for new programs such as flextime, job sharing, child care, flexible benefits and employee counseling. The effects of relocation are being more carefully considered than they have been in the past. The enormous strain that relocation places on the family is sometimes not worth the benefits for either the employee or the hospitality organization.

INDUSTRY EXPERTS SPEAK	Elaine Etess points out that it is important for the manager with human resources responsibilities to have a great sensitivity to the effects of relocation on the family as she relates this story: "I hired a highly professional male executive. When he came for his interviews, his wife accompanied him. We talked candidly regarding the pluses and minuses of small town living versus a large metropolitan city. As she had her own career we also covered the limited opportunities available in her designated field. He accepted the position, was doing an extraordinary job, but resigned after six months because his wife could not find satisfactory employment. The cultural differences and small town limitations were too great for them to adjust to."

As we await the turn of a new century, hospitality leaders in both academia and the industry face numerous challenges and opportunities in the arena of human resources management. Within the context of this text, as we examine these issues, we ask you to put yourself in the role of a manager with human resources responsibilities. It does not matter what segment of the hospitality industry you select, the size of the operation or its location (Figure 1-2). Envision yourself where you would like to be when you graduate, whether it's with a major hospitality corporation or back in your home town in your family's hospitality enterprise.

We will refer to you, the manager with human resources responsibilities, in an applied context. Now we recognize that most of you will not actually hold a title of human resources manager when you graduate. In fact most of you, throughout your entire hospitality career, will not

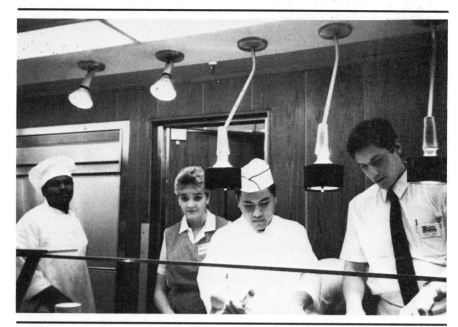

Figure 1-2. Service in the hospitality industry is viewed as a positive experience that can lead to a great career.
Courtesy of Furr's/Bishop's Cafeterias, L.P.

hold that title. But as we have stated before, as a manager with human resources responsibilities, human resources management will need to be part of your skills and knowledge base. The human resources manager is an adjunct to all departments.

Perhaps as assistant food and beverage director the only human resources function you perform will be that of training. Or, as a front desk manager you will select, hire, train, evaluate performance and have the responsibility for initiating disciplinary actions. As a recruiter for a major hospitality company your human resources function might be limited to recruitment and maybe selection, with someone else in your organization doing the actual hiring and placement functions. If you go back to your family's operation or elect to work for an individual proprietor, then your job will likely include every human resources function that we discuss in this text, along with the job of accountant, marketing director, designer, menu planner, purchaser, etc. So no matter if the duties and responsibilities of the human resources manager are a portion of your job or your entire job, it is important for you to begin to think like a manager with human resources responsibilities, and not just as a manager of human resources.

The role of the manager with human resources responsibilities in the hospitality industry is no longer a simple one of filling out paperwork and making sure that the food and beverage director has a dishwasher for the evening shift. The world of today's hospitality manager is filled with complexities, largely due to the changing demographics and increasing legal constraints. These will be pointed out to you throughout this text.

INDUSTRY EXPERTS SPEAK	The hospitality industry is recognizing the need to emphasize people and human resources functions as vital to the success of their organizations. Mr. Hurst emphasizes, "In our service society, the customer is the focal point of the organization. How to insure the 100% and make a salesperson out of your staff is critical. The ten year value of a customer who spends $150.00 a year, sends two friends to your operation who do likewise and repeats this pattern every year is in excess of $1,000,000! A single party of four may be worth more than your whole restaurant. *Think customers, not dollars!*"

Conclusion

You might have noticed that the last chapter of this text is titled The Next Chapter. . . . In it you will find some ideas about where the industry advisors to this text believe human resources management will be in the year 2000. They have also been kind enough to give you some advice that you can use in your own career development. This advice is based upon their years of industry experience.

In the development of the chapters that follow it becomes increasing apparent that "the next chapter" of human resources management must be planned for today. (More of that proactive stance mentioned earlier.) Therefore, you will find those areas pointed out to you. While the specific direction is yet unknown, it is already clear that preparations for "the next chapter" need to be happening now.

Human resources functions such as recruitment, hiring, training and development used to be considered as solely costs that somehow had to be written off. These programs were often deemed unnecessary expenses in times of financial need. Understaffing, terminations and minimal training were commonplace. While saving the hospitality operation money in the short run, these practices destroyed morale and motivation. Career development was unheard of.

The attitude we hold about our human resources has changed. In the 1990s we no longer consider employee programs as unnecessary expenses. Instead we view these programs, such as training and development, as a necessity to both attract and retain the hospitality enterprise's most costly and valuable assets.

Employees have a unique value to our hospitality organizations because they are *human* beings. Our orientation in human resources management is on those people. The change in terminology from *personnel* to *human resources* is more than mere semantics. It is a significant attempt to recognize human needs and their importance in the organizational structure of the hospitality enterprise. It is with this focus that hospitality can overcome the service crisis in America.

"The young men and women entering business organizations have plenty of skill to do their work, but they fail because they do not know how to get along with people." — John B. Watson[9]

17

CASE PROBLEM 1

18

You have just been hired by a hospitality organization as a manager with human resources responsibilities. Since you want to be sure to make a good impression upon arrival at your new job you have decided that it would be a good idea to prepare a list of the duties and responsibilities you might be asked to assume in your new position.

To bring some realism to the situation you are about to put yourself into, *you* decide which segment of the hospitality industry (either food service or lodging) your new job position is in. It can be either. A suggestion would be to place yourself in the "ideal" hospitality manager's job—one in which you see yourself in the future.

In one or two paragraphs describe the operation in which you will be employed. You should provide enough of a description so that the reader has a feel for the type of operation in which you envision yourself. Next, continue to prepare yourself for your new job position by identifying the human resources functions that you might be responsible for. During the job interview process this information was vague and not spelled out specifically. Now you can prepare the list of job duties and responsibilities.

Next identify four or five challenges that you will have to face in your job as a hospitality manager with human resources responsibilities. Which of these challenges do you personally feel will be the greatest? Why do you think so? Defend your position. Which of the duties and responsibilities that you identified will you enjoy the most? The least? Which of these duties and responsibilities are you most familiar with at the present time?

RECOMMENDED READING

Hackett, T. J. 1988. The real role of personnel managers. *Personnel Journal* 67 (3): 70–75.

Luthans, F.; Hodgetts, R. M.; and Rosenkrantz, S. A. 1988. *Real Managers*. Cambridge, Mass.: Ballinger Publishing Company.

Restaurant Hospitality. 1988. The 500 panel. *Restaurant Hospitality* LXXII (6): 140–156.

Rothwell, S. 1988. Management update. *Journal of General Management* 13 (3): 94–101.

END NOTES

1. Taylor, Frederick W., *The Principles of Scientific Management* (New York: Harper and Brothers, 1911).

2. Kakar, Sudhir, *Frederick Taylor: A Study in Personality and Innovation* (Cambridge, Mass.: The MIT Press, 1970).

3. Eilbirt, Henry, "The Development of Personnel Management in the United States," *Business History Review,* 33, (Autumn 1959): 345–364.

4. Eilbirt, Henry, "The Development of Personnel Management in the United States," *Business History Review,* 33, (Autumn 1959): 345–364.

5. Munsterberg, Hugo, *Psychology and Industrial Efficiency* (Boston: Houghton Mifflin Co., 1913).

6. Gilbreth, Lillian, *The Psychology of Management* (1913 Reprint, Easton, PA.: Hive Publishing Company, 1973).

7. Wren, Daniel A., *The Evolution of Management Thought* (New York: The Ronald Press Company, 1972).

8. Lattin, Gerald W., *Modern Hotel Management* (San Francisco: W. H. Freeman and Company, 1966): 98–99.

9. John B. Watson (1878–1958) was both a psychologist and exponent of behaviorism.

DISCUSSION QUESTIONS

1. Over the past century numerous social, political and economic factors have changed *personnel* management to *human resources* management. Trace these changes from the industrial revolution through the 1980s.

2. Identify the major human resources management functions. Are these common to all hospitality organizations regardless of size? Please explain.

3. Compare the functions of human resources management in the 1990s with those of the traditional personnel management models.

4. How does the role of the human resources manager change in relationship to the size of the hospitality organization? In relationship to the segment of the hospitality industry, you might find yourself working in (lodging or food services)?

CHAPTER 2

HUMAN RESOURCES PLANNING

"My interest is in the future because I am going to spend the rest of my life there."—C. F. KETTERING

KEY WORDS

behavior-oriented planning
corporate mission
effectiveness
efficiency
forecasting
forecasting variables
hospitality enterprise
human resources planning

long-range planning
operational objectives
operation-oriented planning
organizational goals
planning
qualitative forecasting
quantitative forecasting
short-range planning

INTRODUCTION

Planning is a topic that is addressed from many perspectives in hospitality management programs. Nevertheless, the subject of planning and its relationship to human resources management is frequently overlooked. And how can this be? As you will soon learn, it is the planning process that sets the stage for all other functions we will be discussing in this first section. It is the purpose of this chapter to assist you, the manager with human resources responsibilities, in integrating the various components of planning and management that you are already familiar with, into a logical framework. The sequence of the material has been carefully planned to lead you through the stages of planning necessary for effective human resources management. The activities appear in the order you would perform them if you were working in a hospitality operation today.

At the conclusion of this chapter you will be able to:
1. Present a conceptual framework that sequences the stages in the human resources planning process.
2. Define planning within the context of human resources management.
3. Describe why planning is necessary for effective human resources management.
4. Interrelate the various components that makeup the human resources planning process.

5. Develop a systematic approach to human resources planning and implementation that can be applied in the hospitality industry.
6. Distinguish between planning, forecasting and determining objectives.
7. Discuss the role of forecasting in the human resources planning process.
8. Determine operational objectives for human resources management.

Why Plan?

Imagine that this is your first day as a manager with human resources responsibilities in the hospitality industry. Perhaps the operation you are in is a fast food restaurant, or a table service restaurant with a high check average. Maybe the operation you are working in is part of the lodging sector of the industry, a property owned and managed by a multinational hotel company or a single operation owned by your family. The operation you are now a part of might serve 1,000 covers a day or 100, it might have 1,000 rooms or 100 rooms. The size of the operation and scope of services offered exist within your imagination.

No matter what the size and scope, you are responsible for the human resources in this operation. If your title is manager or director of human resources your entire job revolves around the people side of the business. If your title is a little more generic, say assistant manager, partner or owner, then your job involves both the production and the people aspects of the business.

Knowing that you are responsible for the people or human resources of your hospitality operation, where should you begin? What is the starting place in human resources management? We have already discussed the numerous functions that occur in human resources management. Which one would you pick to begin? What do you do first? If you are like many managers when asked this question you will respond with "hiring." After all, there is very little you can do with respect to orientation, training, development and compensation until you have hired! Right? Wrong!

If the first thing you do as a manager of human resources is hire, you are just like the production kitchen manager who starts with the designing and construction of the kitchen, and then determines the menu. It is not long before the work flow in the kitchen and types of equipment it contains dictate what the production kitchen manager can include on the menu. Courses in production management teach you that the starting place is with the menu. What is a menu? It is a *plan* that provides guidelines for decision making with respect to work flow and equipment needs.

Just as a good production kitchen manager begins with a plan, so should a good manager with responsibilites for the operation's human resources. The way planning is carried out is largely determined by the way an organization is structured. The types of planning required depend solely on the situation in which that organization finds itself, and on its particular needs. The need for planning, for example, changes and is affected by the age of the operation. A new operation calls for more flexibility and centralization in planning, while a more established operation will be more formally structured and have a tendency to be increasingly decentralized. As the operation evolves, so does planning. While planning must always be conducted in light of the situation in which it is going to be used, there are important reasons why you should begin human resources management with planning.

The Importance of Planning

To begin with, planning increases effectiveness and efficiency. Effectiveness refers to an operation's ability to accomplish its goals and objectives. Efficiency refers to an operation's ability to achieve maximum results with minimum input. Planning also helps keep an operation on track, moving forward. Without something to guide us, how do we know where we are going, or if we have arrived? Do you remember traveling as a small child in the car on a long trip and asking your parents, "When will we get there"? A frequent response was, "When we get there!" Without planning, managers are like small children in a car: never sure of when they will get there.

Planning, or more specifically the results of planning—plans— guide what everyone in the operation does. From the dishwasher to bell captain to maître'd to front desk clerk, plans tell our employees what to expect. Imagine what chaos would occur if our employees, upon reporting for work each day, did not know what was expected of them! Planning can improve productivity and increase human satisfaction.

Morale is also influenced by planning. Morale is extremely important in an environment where people work closely together in a team effort. By the nature of the work in the hospitality industry, our employees work together in decentralized, informal work groups. The dishwashers share a common bond, as do the bellhops, the front desk personnel, the housekeeping staff, the dining room staff in the restaurant and so on. Being a member of these informal groups means that people share ideas and concerns about the operation they work in, and the managers they work for. Have you ever worked for a manager who seems disorganized, who was constantly running around "putting out fires"? The informal work groups in an operation, while quick to rally around a manager they have faith in, will rapidly become disillusioned and unmotivated when they begin to wonder: "How did she or he ever get to be a manager? I could do a better job than that." Planning leads to an improved common understanding of operational objectives, which leads to greater cooperation among departmental work groups. Even managers work better together when they know what to expect.

Planning impacts every function in human resources management. Without planning, performance appraisals are not effective. For how can one evaluate how individuals contribute to the organization's growth? How do you know whom to hire, or how many people to hire? What their skill levels should be? How much you should pay them?

Planning is the *most* important factor in the continuing success of any hospitality operation. All other aspects of management—finance, marketing, sales, production—are planned. Planning is a management function, and to be good managers of human resources you need to know how to plan for your areas of accountability.

Human Resources Planning for Hospitality Enterprises

The hospitality industry has been one of the fastest growing segments of the American economy. Throughout the country an increasing number of dollars are being spent annually for food, beverage and lodging away from home, making hospitality the largest consumer industry in the United States. An industry originally comprised of small chains and independent operators has grown into an industry of multiunit and multiconcept conglomerates.

With such rapid growth you may be asking yourself, "How can we afford *not* to plan?" You are absolutely correct in your conclusion: we *cannot* afford not to. Unfortunately, though, many of you can probably think of places where you worked where management failed to plan. What are the symptoms of these operations? Managers who overworked their good employees because they knew they could depend on them in a pinch. And these managers always seemed to be in a crisis mode of operation: either overstaffed or understaffed, never time to train or evaluate your performance. If raises were given, it was because the manager knew who you were. This is what happens in an operation that does not plan, but instead chooses to simply respond to events as they occur. Managers seemingly averse to planning choose to rely on intuition, experience and chance to get them through their day-to-day operating challenges.

Efficient and effective management of human resources requires planning. Achieving the coordination of human resources in a hospitality enterprise is not an easy task. Yet as a manager, your success depends on your ability to get other people to do work. For your human resources planning to be effective it must meet the needs of the individuals you hire, the groups they become members of and the needs of the formal organization. Which of these three needs is most important? None. To sacrifice any one of these needs is to sacrifice all three.

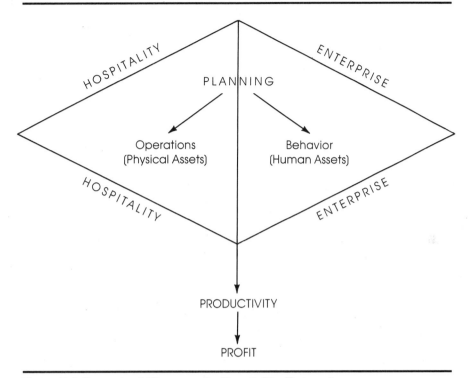

Figure 2-1. Conceptual Diagram of a Hospitality Enterprise.

Let's examine an additional perspective of the hospitality industry. In a service business such as hospitality, the relationships established between employees and customers (your guests) are of supreme importance. More than 50 percent of the people you hire will come into *direct* contact with your customers! Do these employees know what to expect in the performance of their jobs? Without planning, probably not.

Planning in human resources management controls what all people do in your operation. You have to know what positions you need to hire for. You will have to train to develop the skills you need in your personnel, if you cannot find individuals with the necessary skills. Without long-range planning you would not know who you needed or what skills were available. You would live day-to-day, fighting fires, working many extra hours and becoming very frustrated.

Planning human behavior is a feat each of us must conquer to succeed as a manager. The operations side of hospitality management is certainly easier to plan for than the attitudes, behaviors, temperaments and whims of our human resources. But this does not mean that planning has no place on the people side of management. Figure 2-1 sketches this perspective of a hospitality enterprise for you.

Operations-oriented planning, as shown on the left side of the diamond in Figure 2-1, determines the physical assets. In a food service operation this would include, but certainly not be limited to, the menu items to be served, equipment requirements, physical layout of the facility, the china, tableware, glassware and linens to be used, as well as the purveyors who provide you with the products your plans determined you need.

Behavior-oriented planning, as shown on the right side of the diamond, determines the human assets or resources. This includes controlling what people do, what skills they must have, how long they will perform those skills, upon what basis their performance will be evaluated and how they will be compensated for their performance in terms of both money and benefits.

In the management of human resources planning is a process that can give your operation advantages over another operation. Without productivity from our human assets the physical assets have little chance of achieving profitability. As the available labor pool shrinks management needs to plan increases, as other operations within the hospitality industry compete for the same people. Human resources planning provides the framework for accomplishing all this and, as you will learn, much more!

What is Planning?

As a manager with human resources responsibilities you can already see many reasons for becoming more proficient in planning. To do so allows us to direct our future instead of letting the future direct us. So before we do human resources planning, let us first more clearly define what planning is.

Planning has been defined in a variety of ways. Ewing (1968) likes this definition:

> *"A method of guiding managers so that their decisions and actions affect the future of the organization in a consistent and rational manner, and in a way desired by top management."*[1]

Miller and Porter (1985) state simply:

> *"Planning means looking ahead to chart the best courses of future action".*[2]

What these definitions indicate is that planning is foremost a process, or series of actions or behaviors. Actions, such as forecasting and decision making require planning to be a continual process because change is continual. Behaviors such as communication and motivation are necessary to produce the desired outcomes.

For this book **planning** is defined as a process of collecting information that allows hospitality managers to make decisions in order to formulate objectives and determine which actions are most appropriate in achieving those objectives. This definition is one which views planning as a process, hence an activity. It allows managers of human resources to remain flexible, a necessity in a changing environment. The result of planning, the plan itself, is a product of the process. The framework for human resources planning that we will now begin to build will answer the following questions:

- How many people do you need?
- What kind of people, with respect to skills and abilities, do you need?
- Where will you find the type of people you need?
- How will you keep the people you need and prevent them from being hired away by other companies?

Hospitality managers typically have technical competence, but the exceptional managers who want to grow in both ability and achievement possess planning skills. No longer will you have to operate by hunchs and intuition. To plan you must step back, forecast the future, anticipate what will be the desired outcomes and determine how they should be accomplished.

At the beginning of this chapter you were asked to think of a hospitality operation that you might like to work in as a manager with human resources responsibilities. We said that the size and scope of the operation did not matter because the principles of planning we discussed are applicable in any of the situations in which you imagined yourself. There is no one best system that applies in all situations. Hospitality operations differ in their objectives, their complexities, the types and number of services they offer, the environments they operate in and the resources they have available to them. Therefore, the degree to which you can implement the approaches and techniques discussed must be evaluated in light of the situation in which you are operating. There is, however, a *systematic process* of human resources planning that is appropriate to all situations in the hospitality industry. If you understand the process by which a human resources system is developed, you can then modify the system to fit your particular situation.

The systematic process we are referring to begins with **Forecasting,** the next topic.

27

Forecasting

Planning is not forecasting; however, forecasting is one of the activities that make up the planning process. Ewing (1968) points out that:

28

"Equating the two is probably the oldest trap that managers and teachers in business . . . have fallen into."[3]

It is possible for planning to occur without being involved in forecasting. In human resources planning forecasting is where the process begins. It is important for you to recognize the distinction between the terms *planning* and *forecasting*.

What is Forecasting?

Forecasting involves an analysis of the environment to determine what future needs will exist, and what opportunities will there be for us to fill them. On the basis of estimates and predictions forecasting makes assumptions about the future. Forecasts about the future environment enable you, as a manager with human resources responsibilities, to reach assumptions that provide guidelines for all of your planning activities. Forecasting is concerned with the events that occur in a changing world. The hospitality industry is a volatile enterprise and, as such, we must learn to make forecasts and use them in our planning process.

Forecasting will be defined as the task of making assumptions about the future of the hospitality industry, as it affects your operation, formulated on the basis of predictions and estimates that better enable us to plan for a changing business environment. Depending upon your hierarchical position within the company, the scope of your forecasts will vary.

As an example, the chief executive officer (CEO) of a corporation may have a mission for the corporation. That mission may be to become the premier hospitality corporation in North America with an annualized x% return to shareholders and an x% annualized growth rate. The vice president of an operating division may have a goal of being the market leader in his or her business(es) with sales growth of x% and an operating profit of y%. The staff members supporting this vice president then put together functional plans to support the mission and organizational goals. If you were a director of human resources, your forecasts would focus on management and hourly human resources needs and supplies for specific operations and/or geographies. If, on the other hand, you were manager of a specific operation, you would focus on forecasting and determining what your unit human resources needs were and then work towards meeting those needs.

Table 2-1. Forecasting Considerations

- Competition
- Demographic Shifts (both customer & workforce)
- Economic Environment
- Governmental Policies and Regulations
- Technological Advancements/Changes
- Trend Analysis
- Societal and Cultural Differences

There is no one way in which forecasting is applied. The method you select is the one that best meets your needs and your assumptions about the environment in which your unit must operate. In other words, concentrate on the areas of greatest importance by asking yourself, "Which areas will influence our future success in this market?" Table 2-1 is a list of some considerations you must take into account when forecasting.

Determining Human Resources Requirements

Human resources forecasts stem from the operational plans of finance, sales, marketing and production. Predicting the number of employees that you will need to recruit, hire, train, develop, transfer and promote is based upon operational objectives. These predictions are made for a specific period of time, generally on an annual basis. The methodology for determining your human resources requirements depends on whether you are forecasting management or hourly employee needs.

Demand for employees is based upon a combination of variables that are common to all operations. These variables would include the expected productivity levels, the demand factor for your products and services, projected turnover and projected growth rates. Entwined with these variables are the financial performance objectives of your organization. In hospitality the process is further complicated by the fact that the variables differ by job category. Turnover rates, for example, change depending on whether you are forecasting management or hourly needs. And among hourly employees, the turnover rate can further vary between dishwashers and wait persons, between bellpersons and front desk personnel or between any two other job categories you might like to compare.

Forecasting in the hospitality industry is handled typically on a qualitative or intuitive, nonstatistical basis. This is predominantly the case when forecasting hourly human resources needs. To quantify this

Table 2-2. Forecasting Hourly Human Resources Needs			
	Current Year		Projected Year
Job Category	Number of Employees	Percentage of Total Workforce	Number of Employees
Waitpersons	48	40%	64
Hostess	6	5%	8
Buspersons	12	10%	16
Cashiers	6	5%	8
Dishwashers	12	10%	16
Cooks	20	17%	27
Production	16	13%	21
TOTAL	120	100%	160

approach you need to identify the number of employees by job category for a specific period of time. Table 2-2 shows a simplified example of this forecasting approach done on an annual basis.

Once the number of employees per job category is identified (through human resources inventories), the percentage of hourly work force per category is calculated. Forecasts made for the upcoming year would use the same percentage breakdowns as a proportion of human resources needed by each job category. Thus, if sales were projected to increase, the proportion of buspersons needed would still represent 10% of the total work force. Caution: You must be conscious of the fact that these increases may not always follow a simple geometric progression based upon volume. There are in many businesses, threshholds that have some absolute range where a set number of employees can handle a set range of customers(e.g., if the minimum number of wait staff is 2, they can handle 0–40 customers, as opposed to an absolute number).

Management needs can also be forecasted on both a qualitative and quantitative basis. Qualitatively, you could estimate your management requirements as a measure of sales volume and company goals. For example, based upon what corporate management feel needs to be accomplished with respect to quality of service, they want to raise the number of managers per operational unit from two to three. Quantitatively then, with a goal of three managers per unit, it is easy to calculate projected management needs for the next several years. Taking into account planned growth, length of training programs and turnover ratios, you know exactly how many management trainees to hire and when to hire them.

The methods used in forecasting have improved greatly in the past decade with respect to objectivity and reliability. Athough not frequently used in the hospitality industry, the quantitative techniques available do help to increase the accuracy and reliability of predicting human resources requirements.

Forecasting Variables

Forecasting deals with a common set of variables that follow operational lines within an organization. Specifically related to human resources management, manpower planning variables to be forecasted include:

- customers' changing needs
- product demand
- labor cost trends
- availability of labor (unemployment ratio)
- number of employees needed per job category
- need for additional training
- turnover per job category
- absenteeism trends
- government regulations affecting
  - labor costs
  - changes in working hours
  - changes in retirement age
  - social security benefits

Each of these variables must be determined for the particular environment you are working in to identify the skills and people required at both hourly and management levels. Forecasting should be viewed as a tool to improve the decision making surrounding human resources requirements. Good decision making requires having as much information as possible to make accurate predictions about the future.

The Forecasting Function

The techniques we are discussing are largely necessitated by the increasing competitiveness within the hospitality industry. Regardless of the operation size, forecasts play an increasingly important role in the effectiveness of management decision making and performance ability.

Uncertainty is part of forecasting. Your forecasts are only as good as the data and information that goes into their formulation. In hospitality organizations, historical data is typically the basis for forecasting. When historical data is not available, as when you open a new operation, forecasts must rely more on qualitative, rather than quantitative data. Qualitative data includes managerial judgment and good sense, or what may be referred to as subjective estimates.

We have identified the following questions as important to ask when forecasting human resources. But remember, the questions *you* must ask are determined by the areas that are critical to your success. What information is it absolutely essential that you have to continue the planning process? The answer to that question will lead you to developing the appropriate questions for your particular situation.

Here are some suggestions to get you started:

- What is the prevailing hourly wage in your market?
- What are the unemployment statistics? In other words, how discriminating can you be?
- Will you have to train employees to achieve the skill levels you require or will you hire them from other organizations?
- What has been the nature of your labor pool in the past?
- What influences will cause the labor pool to change?
- What will the skill levels of the labor pool be in the future?
- How successful have you been at attracting the skill levels you need?
- What effect will new competition in your market area have on the availability of labor?

Forecasts can serve as a valuable management tool when adjusted to fit the particular needs of your hospitality operation. There is no one correct approach to forecasting human requirements. Approaches differ from company to company, just as demographic considerations vary widely from location to location.

In general, human resources forecasting in the hospitality industry is more qualitative than quantitative. Large corporations do conduct labor productivity studies, and there are numerous, tested quantitative models available to you to assist in forecasting human resources requirements. Examples of statistical procedures used include time-series analysis, regression, and correlation techniques. Just because these quantitative models are not used frequently does not mean they have no value to you; they do. Mastering quantitative forecasting techniques will make you better prepared to face human resources planning. As the hospitality industry grows in sophistication, and computer technology is found in even the smallest mom-and-pop operations, the use of these quantitative methods will increase. The handling of mass quantities of historical data will be as easy as turning on your computer. Hospitality managers in "the next chapter" will be as comfortable with regression analysis as today's managers are with intuition.

The Human Resources Process

Human resources planning refers to identifying and selecting the right person for the right job at the right time. The right person refers to the appropriate qualifications in terms of skills and experience. The right

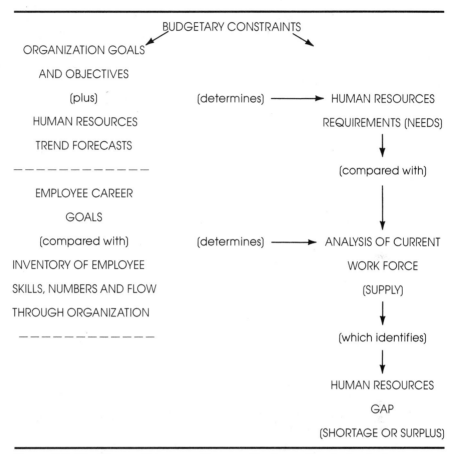

Figure 2-2. The Human Resources Process: Needs vs. Supply Analysis

job implies that a careful analysis has been done to determine what the work requires in both mental and physical energies. The right time would indicate some knowledge of projected needs.

Figure 2-2 presents an overall view of the needs vs. supply analysis through which the human resources process evolves. The human resources process begins with organizational goals and objectives and adds those to the data gathered through your trend forecasts. This determines the human resources requirements for your operation. Next, you need to identify the status of your current work force taking into consideration your employees' career goals, and compare that with an inventory of your current human resources skills and numbers. This comparison gives you an analysis of your human resources supply. A gap between your needs and supply, either as a shortage or surplus, indicates that corrective action needs to be initiated by management. As is true with all human resources planning activities, the entire process is governed by budgetary considerations.

Many of the functions in human resources planning occur simultaneously. When you assume human resources responsibilities in an existing operation, the planning process must occur while products and services are being offered to your customers. You will not have the advantage of having your system planned and in place before the doors open for business. How quickly you will be able to develop your plan will depend largely on how much information about the employees has been kept on a continuing basis.

The remainder of this chapter will be spent on determining objectives. Future chapters will study job analysis and job descriptions along with conducting human resources inventories to identify the gaps between the overall job category requirements and current supply. Plans developed to close these gaps become the decision-making basis for recruitment, assignment and the development of human resources. This, then, begins the human resources planning process.

Goals and Objectives

Planning stems from both the long-range (possibilities of diversification in products and services) and short-range (How many covers do we want to be able to serve tonight?) goals. Long-range goals provide growth and development, short-range goals keep the operation on target.

What will our customers' perceived needs be? This is the first question we must ask. We can then, based upon these needs, make decisions that will determine how we can best achieve customer satisfaction. And that is why we are in the service business: to satisfy customer perceived needs.

To begin with, you must keep in mind that the appropriateness of any objective is contingent on the particular situation in which it must be used. Simply stated, objectives specify what an organization or operation desires to realize. Much literature has been devoted to the topic of goals and objectives, and each author has selected his or her own interpretation of how to define goals and objectives. For our purposes in this text, **operational objectives** stem from **organizational goals,** which are determined by the **corporate mission** (Figure 2-3). Furthermore, in human resources management we are primarily concerned with the operational objectives of our specific arena. Again, since managers with human resources responsibilities do not operate in a vacuum, all other operational objectives both affect and are affected by what we do.

Remember that the lower your position in the organizational structure the more narrow and focused (micro) your objectives become. The higher your position in the organization the broader your objectives (macro). Each level in the organization must take into account the objectives of its superiors when developing objectives for a unit. While incorporation of the corporate mission follows a top-down path, human

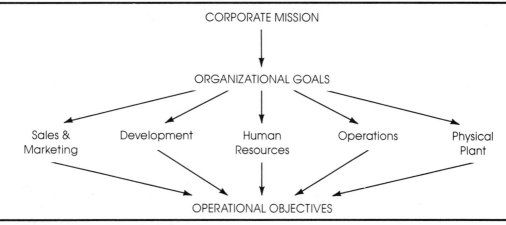

Figure 2-3. Establishing Goals and Objectives

resources objectives must follow a bottom-up path in planning to effectively support the mission statement.

Do you forecast first or set objectives first? They are related. To say that one must follow the other should not imply some greater importance to one than the other. The operation's success is dependent upon each function in the planning process being effectively carried out, but it is helpful to first set your operational and human resources objectives in order to effectively forecast human resources needs.

Determining Objectives. Objectives are stated in terms of actions or activities. Notice the objectives at the beginning of each chapter. The manner in which they are written always states an action that will occur as the result of your participation in the reading material.

A second characteristic of the operational objectives is that they are specific, meaning that they can assist the hospitality manager in his or her decision making process (Figure 2-4). Objectives should also state a time frame in which they are to be accomplished. Without a time frame it is up to the hospitality manager responsible for carrying out the objective to determine if it is to be accomplished within this week, this month, this year or perhaps five years from now. In other words, is this a short-range or long-range objective?

Objectives must also be consistent with each other as well as with organizational goals. This is of particular importance in the hospitality industry where you have several decentralized departments all operating under common organizational goals. The operational objectives of the housekeeping department must complement the operational objectives of the front desk; the operational objectives of the food and beverage department must complement the operational objectives of the sales department; and so on and so forth.

36

Figure 2-4. Planning is a critical human resources function in a hospitality organization.
Courtesy of Gilbert/Robinson, Inc.

Even within departmental units objectives must strive to be consistent. If one objective for the food and beverage department is to increase service quality and another is to lower labor costs, they may well be in conflict. Is it possible to increase quality and at the same time lower costs? Can the manager only achieve one of these objectives at the expense of the other? If objectives do not support a common goal, but rather create a conflict and a sense of frustration, no matter what objective the manager chooses, he or she is doomed to failure.

Objectives for Human Resources Management

Objectives, for managers with human resources responsibilities, state desired outcomes that provide guidance in attracting personnel within a specific time frame. Objectives can be thought of as expectations with respect to evaluating not only operational performance, but human performance (productivity) as well. Objectives for managers with human resources responsiblities are used for defining acceptable performance, determining what kinds of recruitment activities are necessary, reducing turnover (employee satisfaction) and individual development plans for both hourly staff and management.

Remember the earlier example about menu planning? The menu should dictate everything required on the operations side of the hospitality enterprise. Does it? Not always. Should it? Yes. The same analogy can be used in thinking about human resources objectives. The objectives we develop should dictate our human requirements. The number of people currently on the payroll should not form the basis for dictating our human resources needs.

Conclusion

Objectives state the continuing results that must be obtained to meet the human resources goals of your organization. Objectives are what you will accomplish through an effective utilization of human resources. Remember that these objectives are based, in part, upon the information you gathered in forecasting, pertaining to costs and availability of labor in the geographic area you will be operating in. Once the goals and objectives are established, action plans are then developed that identify the decisions and activities that must be taken to meet your objectives through implementation.

All human resources functions develop from planning. Planning therefore should not be viewed as a single exercise for analyzing staffing needs, but rather as a continuing process. People are the most valuable resource in any hospitality enterprise. Planning efforts to better capitalize upon the operation's human resources are critical. The human resources planning function requires that both operational and personnel objectives be combined to meet the goals of the organization. While human resources functions do not include the development of operational objectives, this is one of the numerous occasions where the human resources arena interacts directly with other departments within the organization. Human resources management can not and does not act independently of the rest of a successful organization.

As the number of the people available becomes increasingly limited, we need to become better planners, committed to the efficient utilization of those human resources we have. Established objectives, developed through our forecasts, become the focal point for planning all other human resources functions. It is important, then, that the objectives clearly state the results we need to achieve. The results allow us to determine the jobs necessary to achieve the objectives. Hence, the objectives become the basis of our **job analysis** and determine the job categories that are necessary to accomplish the work activities of our organization.

Use the hospitality operation that you describe in Case Problem 1. Upon arriving at your new job you realize that your initial tasks will revolve around the function of human resources planning. To provide you with a framework to work within, the following conditions exist:

1. The hospitality company, at the present time, is only regionally based with operations in four connecting states.
2. It is a for-profit operation.
3. The company's mission statement reads as follows:
   The mission of XYZ hospitality company is to provide a high level of quality products and services to its guests within a four-state region with plans for expansion to a 20-state area in a 10-year period.
4. Organizational goals include:
   Expansion into four additional states in a three-year period and another four states, bringing the total number of operations to 12, is projected in a five-year period.
5. This hospitality company has been in existence for five years.
6. There are two to five operations in each of the four states, with a total of 15 operations.
7. Human resources management functions have historically been conducted on a operation-by-operation basis.
8. With the projected expansion plans, the company president has recognized the need to centralize the human resources functions.

The company president has asked you, based upon the company's mission statement and organizational goals, to provide a strategic human resources plan.

Part of your job in preparing this plan will be to determine which human resources functions should be centrally managed and which should be managed at the operational level. A transition plan for centralizing those human resources functions will also need to be established. The company's expansion plan will need to be taken into consideration in this transition plan.

The president has told you that more important than meeting organizational plans for expansion, is the maintenance of the high-quality level of all products and services that this hospitality company has based its reputation upon.

Your first task will be to determine which human resources functions should be centrally managed and which should be operationally managed. The second component in your strategic plan should be a timetable for implementation. As the Director of Human Resources, you will eventually have additional staffing requirements. A third component of your strategic plan is determination of staffing needs for the centralized human resources division. (You are a human resources department with one employee—you—at the present time.) Your staffing requirements should be consistent with your plan for centralization. Be sure to include a forecast of your needs for additional staffing. This might require establishing some additional assumptions.

Based upon the information that you prepared for case problem 1, and the previously stated assumptions, prepare a mission statement and two organizational goals for the human resources division. For each of the organizational goals develop two operational objectives. During the preparation of this strategic plan it might be useful for you to keep track of the rationale or logic behind the choices you make. You will be asked to present this strategic plan orally to the president of the company. You will be expected to be able to defend the choices and decisions that you make.

RECOMMENDED READING

Allen, L. A. 1982. *Making Managerial Planning More Effective.* New York: McGraw-Hill.

Bartholomew, D. J. and Forbes, A. F. 1979. *Statistical Techniques for Manpower Planning.* Chichester: John Wiley & Sons.

Ewing, D. 1969. *The Human Side of Planning.* London: The Macmillian Company.

Parson, M. J. 1985. *Back to Basics: Planning.* New York: Facts on Publication.

Vajda, S. 1978. *Mathematics of Manpower Planning.* Chichester: John Wiley & Sons.

Wheelwright, S. C. and Makridakis, S. 1985. *Forecasting Methods for Management.* New York: John Wiley & Sons.

END NOTES

1. Ewing, D. W., *The Practice of Planning* (New York: Harper and Row, 1968): 17–18.
2. Miller, J. E. and Porter, M., *Supervision in the Hospitality Industry* (New York: John Wiley & Sons, 1985): 301.
3. Ewing, D. W., *The Practice of Planning* (New York: Harper and Row, 1968): 16.

DISCUSSION QUESTIONS

1. Where does the human resources process begin? Why?
2. Describe the importance of planning within the context of human resources management.

3. Why don't we do a better job of human resources planning in the hospitality industry?
4. Planning in human resources management controls what all people do in your operation. Comment on this statement.
5. What is forecasting? How does it differ from planning?
6. Are hourly staff and management needs forecasted in the same way? Explain.
7. Identify seven considerations you must take into account when forecasting.
8. Forecasting in hospitality is largely based on historical data kept by the property or operation. What does this historical data consist of?
9. Describe the needs vs. supply analysis in the human resources process.
10. Discuss the top-down and bottom-up approaches in determining objectives.
11. Explain why operational objectives must be kept consistent with each other.
12. Describe the importance of objectives in the human resources planning process.

CHAPTER 3

ETHNIC DIVERSITY IN

THE HOSPITALITY WORKPLACE

INDUSTRY
ADVISOR
Dr. Geneva Gay, Professor
School of Education, Purdue University

"People have one thing in common;
they are all different."—ROBERT ZEND

KEY WORDS

conflict management
culture
ethnic and cultural conflict
ethnic group
ethnicity

ethnic pluralism
Multicultural Manager
Multicultural Management
prejudice
stereotype

INTRODUCTION

Regardless of which part of the United States, or world, that you come from, the ethnic diversity that surrounds you in your daily life is probably more prevalent than it has been in the past. The focus in the chapter you are about to read is on the ethnic diversity that is found today in the United States, and how that diversity affects your job as a hospitality manager with human resources responsibilities. We will not be discussing international management techniques that are important when American business people travel to work abroad. Learning how to negotiate contracts, motivate employees, maximize profit margins and even the appropriate interpersonal etiquette in relating to ethnically diverse personnel and customers can be crucial to your business effectiveness when you work in a different culture and attempt to manage human resources that are socially and ethnically pluralistic.

Our discussion will revolve around the concept of **Multicultural Management** and its related techniques. This is a very new focus in human resources management in the hospitality industry, but one that is essential to your managerial effectiveness, given the increasing diversity of the industry from the perspective of management, personnel and consumers.

At the conclusion of this chapter you will be able to:
1. Define Multicultural Management.
2. Understand concepts related to Multicultural Management such as ethnicity, culture and ethnic pluralism.
3. Explain the importance of cultural awareness to effective human resources management practices in the hospitality industry.
4. Determine how basic human resources functions may be impacted by ethnic diversity in the hospitality work place.
5. Explain how ethnicity and culture can affect your ability to function effectively with different ethnic employees and customers.
6. Define conflict management and determine its relationship to managing ethnic diversity.

Basic Concepts of Multicultural Management

American culture is ethnically diverse. Think for a moment about your own ethnicity. What is your ethnic makeup? Asian? Italian? Cuban? German? Polish? Chicano? French? African? Spanish? Jewish? Russian? Swiss? Indian? If Indian, native or eastern? If native Indian, are you Cherokee-speaking Iroquoian, Seminole from Florida, Apache from the southwestern parts of the United States, or Cheyenne originally from Minnesota or the Dakotas. When we asked you what your ethnic makeup was did you respond, "American"? Unless you are native or American Indian or perhaps North American Eskimo, your answer of "American" was incorrect. Are you surprised? Curious? Offended?

Ethnic group, as we have defined it, relates to a racial or national group that share common origins, experiences and cultural characteristics. Your **ethnic makeup** refers to your background, origins or heritage. The common characteristics shared by members of an **ethnic group** that distinguish them from other groups are part of that group's culture. **Culture** refers to the customs, beliefs, practices, traditions, values, ideologies and lifestyles of a particular ethnic group.

What was your reaction when we told you that unless your heritage was native Indian or Eskimo that your ethnic makeup was *not* American? Were you surprised, curious or offended? Your reaction will give you an indication of your acceptance of the principles of Multicultural Management. Most of you reading this material think of yourselves as Americans, and you are. Multicultural Management does not imply that you are not American, but it does emphasize that in addition to being American our ethnic make-up contains other components. Therefore, people are bi-ethnic or bicultural. Some are biracial and bilingual, too. Thus, American society is ethnically and culturally pluralistic.

You have probably already heard references to African American, Chinese American (or sometimes Chinese-born Americans), Cuban American, Italian American and many others. Members of these ethnic groups, with their strong sense of ethnicity, recognize (and want to have recognized) their dual heritage. Your **ethnicity** is your sense of belonging to a particular ethnic group, a self identity. **Ethnic pluralism** defines a state of co-existence of ethnic and racial groups, an existence that is separate, but equal. For example, it's OK to be both Cuban and American. When ethnic pluralism exists, individuals do not have to shun or deny their Cubanness to be American or their Americanness to be Cuban. They have dual ethnic identities and are bicultural.

Well, you might be thinking, how can one individual be *both* Cuban and American. How does ethnic pluralism operate? We said earlier that members of ethnic groups share a commonality of culture. For individuals with two or more ethnic backgrounds this means an integration of two or more cultures forming their own, oftentimes unique, ethnic make-up. When ethnic and cultural pluralism are accepted and understood, individuals can harmoniously go about their daily life. When there is a struggle and tension, either between ethnic groups within a particular society or within the psychological state of individuals over diverse beliefs, practices, values or ideologies, ethnic conflict is occurring.

Our focus of attention in Multicultural Management is on the potential conflict that can result when ethnic, racial and cultural differences come together in the hospitality work environment without mutual knowledge, understanding and respect. We are particularly concerned about the cultural tensions that may result between managers from one ethnic group and employees from other ethnic groups, and how these tensions may negatively affect work quality, human resources management and service. These concerns give rise to the idea of Multicultural Management.

Multicultural Management is the application of general human resources management principles and strategies within the context of the ethnic and cultural diversity found in your hospitality operation. This approach to human resources management operates on the premise that both the managers' and employees' ethnic identities and cultural orientations, backgrounds and experiences are important influences that affect how both behave in the work place. Multicultural Management also assumes that work habits and attitudes are influenced by culture. Thus, culture matters when managing a work populace that is ethnically and culturally pluralistic. Increasingly, today's hospitality managers are expected to manage cultural diversity, for it is a part of the daily life of both their role functions in the industry, and the hospitality industry itself.

Multicultural Management is *not* a separate human resources function. Rather it is an integral part of all the human resources policies, practices, principles and procedures that we will be discussing in future chapters. It is not something separate and distinct. Rather it permeates all the activities that you as a hospitality manager will have to do each day such as motivating, training, disciplining, assessing the quality of job performance and guaranteeing customer satisfaction. Multicultural Management is a fundamental element of your success as an effective manger with human resources responsibilities in the ethnically diverse hospitality environment and the culturally pluralistic consumer marketplace that the industry serves.

The Impact of Ethnic Diversity in Hospitality Management

Several realities about American society and the hospitality industry indicate that the principles of Multicultural Management will become increasingly significant in "the next chapter." Demographers already know what the populace of the United States will look like in the year 2000. At that time, it is estimated that one fourth of the population will be members of minority ethnic groups. This increase is a result of the phenomenal birthrates among racial minority groups like African Americans and Hispanics, and the changing immigration patterns to the United States. Most immigrants entering the U.S. now come from parts of the world such as Southeast Asia, the Middle East, the Pacific Islands, the Caribbeans and South America, where people and cultures are significantly different from earlier generations of immigrants (Figure 3–1). Even though legal immigration has been regulated, illegal immigration will continue at a rate of three to five million persons per year throughout the remainder of the century.[1] While 47 percent of the work force in the late 1980s was native white males, by the year 2000 that figure will drop by 15 percent.[2] Many of the new immigrants will enter the work force in unskilled positions and in service industries like hospitality.

On the other side of the coin is the growing cultural and ethnic diversity of hospitality consumers. More people of a wider variety of ethnic, social and cultural backgrounds are traveling, eating out and engaging in other leisure activities serviced by the hospitality industry. These multicultural consumers will demand some adjustments in service styles and qualities, just as the ethnic diversity of hospitality employees will require some alterations in traditional human resources management principles to maximize job performance.

The biggest challenge each of you will face as managers in "the next chapter" in the hospitality industry is attracting and retaining a qualified work force. Hospitality has historically depended on the 16- to 24-

44

Figure 3-1. Ethnic diversity is on the increase in all job positions in the hospitality industry.
Courtesy of Marriott Corporation

year-old white males and females to fill it's vacant job positions. This age group among Anglos is declining in size. Service industries are expanding, making competition for a limited supply of qualified workers even tougher. Gone are the days of applicants with a work ethic and cultural style similar to yours knocking your door down to wait tables in your restaurant, manage the cocktail lounge, work at your front desk, train your bellhops, clean your property's rooms, supervise your banquets and catering functions and wash your restaurant's dishes.

Women, racial minorities and ethnic immigrants are the largest untapped pools of labor in the United States today. The Bureau of Labor Statistics reports that by the year 2000, women will makeup two-thirds of labor force growth. More than one-third of those women will be Black or Hispanic. Approximately 29 percent of all labor force growth will consist of Hispanics, with Blacks consisting of 17 percent and Asians 11 percent.

These immigration and work force patterns present some very different challenges to managers in the hospitality industry with human resources responsibilities. Many of the managers will trace their ancestry and cultural origins back to the original immigrants who came to America from Western European countries. The geographic locations, ethnic heritages and cultural traditions of today's immigrants who populate the unskilled labor force from which the hospitality industry draw many of its entry level employees is quite different. Typically, these ethnic group members are undereducated, some even illiterate. For many, English is a second language, or a language that they can not speak at all. Some Americans feel threatened by the new wave of immigrants, not unlike their ancestors who feared jobs would be taken away from them. Racism and ethnic prejudice are as prevalent in the work place in the early 1990s, although somewhat more subtle, as it was at the turn of the twentieth century. As hospitality managers, part of your human resources responsibilities will be to deal with these diversities, fears and injustices in a way to fashion teams of workers that are competent and efficient in their task performances and to ensure that they are treated fairly with regards to their labor rights. In a real sense, your success as hospitality manager with human resources responsibilities will depend largely upon how well you respond to the challenge of ethnic and cultural diversity among your employees and consumers.

Interaction between Ethnic Diversity and Human Resources Management

Because the hospitality industry is labor intensive and service centered, it is a people enterprise. Both the industry's power and potential are nested in the extent to which its multicultural human resources are effectively managed to maximize their productivity. To realize this potential, you as a hospitality manager with human resources responsibilities need to understand how ethnicity and culture affect human behavior in general, and in the work place in particular, along with their influences upon work incentives, work habits, job performance, expectations, satisfaction and motivation. You need to realize the enormous stress cultural and ethnic differences can impose upon efforts to communicate with and manage ethnic employees when these differences are not addressed deliberately in interpersonal relations. You also need to develop skills in how to apply principles and strategies of human resources development within the context of ethnic and cultural diversity.

Unless you understand the behaviors, values, beliefs, customs and traditions of your ethnic employees, and are able to use these to your benefit in your management functions, you will be at a decided disadvantage in providing the leadership required to achieve maximum success in the industry. Of necessity you must learn how to manage ethnically diverse people to service an ethnically and culturally pluralistic industry. Your preparation for this task begins with developing an awareness of and sensitivity to differences in the work values, beliefs and behaviors of your employees from various ethnic backgrounds.

46

The Human Resources Functions

Discussing ethnic diversity so early in the text will allow you to incorporate your understanding of and sensitivity to ethnic, racial and cultural differences into each of the other human resources functions routinely performed by hospitality managers. A further study of the culture of the ethnic groups found in your hospitality organization will provide you with specific information that will assist you in understanding how ethnicity and culture affect human behavior. The depth of your knowledge will affect your ability to successfully manage the ethnic employees in your operation.

Culture is a complex multidimensional phenomenon. It is manifested in numerous ways, some of which are very explicit while others are more subtle. Some cultural expressions surface in the work place while others do not. Examples of situations where culture can influence your behavior and that of ethnic employees in the work place are:

- Communication problem in recruitment
- Policies and procedures such as:
  - Interviewing
  - Disciplinary Actions
  - Rules of Conduct
  - Dress Codes
  - Perceptions of Time
  - Service Procedures
- Motivation for professional development
- Employee counseling
- Work schedule
- Role of women in the operation

The cultural influences that will affect your role as trainer will stem from differences in values, beliefs, work ethic, roles of social decorums, interpersonal relations and patterns of learning, as exhibited by the various ethnic groups. A culturally sensitive hospitality manager knows how to recognize these differences among his or her employees and understand how they affect job related performance and personal behaviors. They can then be used advantageously in the human resources training and development processes. With respect to employee development, the Multicultural Manager has the ability to determine performance levels and assess training needs from a cross-cultural perspective.

The relationships affected by ethnic diversity and the barriers cultural differences may generate are not limited to the interactions between management and employees. Our guests, clients and consumers in the hospitality industry also represent a distinct pool of ethnic, cultural, social, racial and national differences. Any time interactions occur, either **within** or **among** any of these three pools of people, misunderstandings and conflict due to ethnic differences in cultural values, beliefs, experiences and behaviors can, will and do occur. The extent to which you, as a manager with human resources responsibilities, understand these differences and use them to form your leadership style, has a direct effect upon the ultimate success of the industry with respect to its effective operations, quality of service and profit margin.

Personal Cultural Barriers

Our own sense of ethnic identity can become a cultural barrier and in so doing it can effect our effectiveness. Have you ever heard a manager say, "I'll never hire another (you fill in your choice of ethnic group). They are always late, or lazy, or sloppy, or unclean, or slow, or undependable!" Too often an isolated unpleasant experience with one member of an ethnic group leads us to generalize that negative encounter and its related characteristics to *all* members of that ethnic group. This is **stereotyping**.

Sometimes negative attitudes toward ethnic group members exist even though we have had no direct experience or personal contact with that group. This is **prejudice.** How ridiculous it would sound if we said, "I'll never hire another Anglo because they are too ambitious and hard working." Regardless of your ethnic makeup we are sure that you know of at least one Anglo who is not always ambitious or hardworking. You probably even know or have seen a few African Americans and Hispanics who are even more ambitious than Anglos and some Anglos that are lazy, unclean, sloppy and slow.

Ambition, work ethic, time usage, space, cleanliness and methods of conducting business are all affected by cultural values and ethnic backgrounds. When they are defined by standards from our own personal cultural orientation we tend to view them as "good," "proper," "right" and "positive." When they are shaped, however, by another ethnic group's culture, the same values and behavior can become "bad," "inappropriate" and "negative." Perhaps you have seen the cartoon that describes similar characteristics in both a male and female. Whereas the man is ambitious and a disciplinarian, the woman who acts in the same way is pushy and inflexible! This is gender prejudice that is preferential to males.

A major factor in the management of ethnic and cultural diversity lies in overcoming your own misconceptions, prejudices and biases about ethnic and cultural differences. Cultural awareness assists in this process by moving you out of your own cultural orientation and helping you develop a sensitivity to different styles of operation. Instead of viewing the actions of an ethnic employee from your cultural perspective, Multicultural Management creates a culturally pluralistic knowledge base to view the values, beliefs and behaviors in the ethnic context in which they were intended. Each culture differs from the dominant Anglo culture and, hence, deserves to be understood and appreciated for its own value system. This diversity does not need to interfere with the effective operations of the hospitality industry. It can enrich and enliven it when hospitality managers know how to use it as an asset to the business.

Conflict Management

The primary ethnic groups in the hospitality industry today are African American, Asian American and Hispanic American. Great care, however, must be taken whenever you attempt to make generalizations about all ethnic groups because of the differences within the group. For example, among Hispanics there are subgroups whose origins are Puerto Rican, Cuban, Mexican, Spanish and South American. Depending upon the location of your hospitality operation, other ethnic groups will also be prominent in the work place. An examination of some of the core values, attitudes, behaviors and traditions of these ethnic groups explains how these differences may affect the behaviors and performance of individuals from those ethnic groups as they interact in the hospitality industry. Such a study will also indicate potential conflict areas with respect to beliefs, values, practices and ideologies.

Whenever you have people interacting in a work environment the potential for conflict exists. Some people suggest that when individuals merely interact among themselves conflict is inevitable because of differences in perspectives, experiences and values. Others believe that conflict stimulates creativity, and that an environment needs conflict in order to be healthy. Whatever your views on conflict are, one thing is certain. When conflict exists, it must be properly managed. Oftentimes your success as a manager will be judged by how well you are able to manage conflict and turn it into a positive resource and productive energy.

When managing a work environment filled with ethnic diversity the potential exists for the conflict to be the result of ethnic differences, misconceptions or stereotypes by management and co-workers about the ethnic group, language or cultural barriers. As a result of the differences that exist, each side misinterprets or dismisses the viewpoint of the other by failing to understand the cultural framework in which the other operates. When these differences, misconceptions and barriers affect the hospitality organization's ability to provide effective and efficient services to its guests, someone has to have the skills and ability to act as mediator to resolve the conflict. As the hospitality manager who deals with the organization's human resources, this becomes your responsibility.

As a mediator your job is to represent both sides of the conflict fairly so that the differences or tension can be resolved in the best interests of all concerned. As we have already mentioned, it is impossible to represent an ethnic group fairly unless you have an understanding of that group's cultural orientation. In this role of mediator, the principles of Multicultural Management become closely tied to employee relations.

As a manager you can perform more effectively by expanding your understanding of interpersonal and intergroup ethnic relations. Accepting the importance of ethnic understanding and fair treatment in the work place is one thing, but assuring it is quite another. Let's take a moment to examine the principles behind managing employee conflict as they relate to ethnic diversity.

Resolutions to Conflicts

Conflicts occur in hospitality organizations for a variety of reasons in addition to the ethnic diversity factor. Conflicts have historically occurred between the front of the house staff and the back of the house, whether it is the front desk vs. housekeeping or the waitstaff vs. the cooks. The temperamental chef is still a common stereotype even today. The last thing that a hospitality manager needs on a busy day or evening is an open confrontation between two of the operation's employees.

Throughout this text we will point out the importance of open channels of communication. No where is this more important than in the prevention of conflict in the work place. Getting people to know and understand each other before conflict occurs is the optimum solution. The more people understand about other ethnic groups, cultures and behavioral styles, the more likely they are to reach a compromise. Employee communication is part of a sound human resources management plan, not an afterthought.

Unfortunately, a typical management approach to conflict is to ignore the situation, taking the attitude that the parties involved will be able to work out the differences on their own. Ill-managed or ignored conflicts will only fester, and in the long term lower staff morale and job productivity will be the end result. In an era when reducing turnover will become an increasing goal, conflict situations simply cannot be permitted to linger.

Another resolution to conflicts in the work place is to change the structure of the interpersonal relationships by moving your employees around. The logic is that by changing the environmental conditions that created the conflict to begin with, you will diffuse the tensions, and the conflict will be resolved. For those of you with work experience in the hospitality industry, you can see the difficulty in changing employees from one department to another. Skill levels and abilities are seldom identical from job position to job position. And even if moving people around could easily be accomplished, aren't you just setting the stage for another conflict, only with different players? The conflict has not been resolved; the interpersonal relationships involved have merely been shifted from one context or location to another.

For the Multicultural Manager there is another option available when dealing with conflict that is created by the ethnic diversity in the work environment. You act as a culturally sensitized mediator, one who is aware of the conflict points in the routine ways of functioning among individuals from different ethnic backgrounds. You can ease tensions and help employees in conflict understand each others' points of view, thereby facilitating conflict resolution. It is always easier to change a person's behavior than to attempt to change the person. Cultural awareness and sensitivity of the ethnic groups that work in your hospitality operation combined with knowledge of the causes of individual differences can assist you in getting both parties to modify their negative behavior. Misconceptions, misunderstandings, biases and stereotypes about ethnic group members by individuals outside the groups must be corrected. This objective requires that you have a knowledge base of the ethnicity that surrounds you in the work place before you can sufficiently help your ethnic employees to understand and respect their own and each other's cultures, as well as work better with each other. Knowledge of ethnicity is also fundamental to your overall effectiveness as a Multicultural Manager.

Even the most conflict-free multi-ethnic work environments require a system of accommodation and compromise to maintain organizational stability and maximize productivity. The needs of each individual ethnic employee can only be met if the manager with human resources responsibilities has the appropriate knowledge base, understanding and sensitivity to break down the ethnic and cultural barriers.

Conclusion

The existence of a multicultural environment and an ethnically pluralistic work force in the hospitality work place is a reality each of you face in "the next chapter." Understanding cultural and ethnic pluralism and accepting the ethnic diversity must be seen not merely as a necessity, but as a creative potential and positive resource for enriching the hospitality industry's quality and productivity. If you are going to make appropriate decisions as managers, you have to have an understanding of how the value systems of different cultures operate, and how these affect job related attitudes, values, and behaviors. This understanding increases the likelihood of your effectiveness as a human resources developer.

The service industry has historically obtained a significant proportion of its work force from the 16– 24-year-old age group. Taking into consideration the predicted reduction of this age group among Anglos of the mainstream culture, hospitality operations will be forced to seek out some other sources of labor supply to meet their human resources requirements. Increasingly, this resource will be from among groups who are racially, culturally and socially different from the middle-class mainstream of society. It will also include more and more women and recent immigrants.

The United States is becoming increasingly ethnically diverse as is the labor force that supplies the service industries. The populace of immigrants will be, and to a great extent already is, able to assist the hospitality industry in meeting its labor needs.

The increasing diversity of the hospitality work force places a special demand upon managers with human resources responsibilities to communicate with, motivate, attract and retain employees from a culturally different background. Cultural awareness, knowledge and sensitivity are necessary to meet these demands. Becoming a Multicultural Manager requires understanding both yourself and the ethnic groups you are expected to manage. Knowing what cultural factors (values, beliefs, experiences and backgrounds) affect your everyday life can help you understand how ethnicity shapes the lives of the human resources in your operation. A study of ethnic groups and their cultures is really a study of people, and learning how their values affect the way they interrelate in a variety of social and interpersonal contexts, including the work place.

Multicultural Management must be an ongoing, integral part of the hospitality industry operations. It is a process that occurs simultaneously as you go about fulfilling your routine responsibilities as a human resources manager within the context of the cultural and ethnic diversity that characterizes the hospitality industry's settings, purposes, employees and consumers. The diversity of cultures can be an asset, not a detriment, to your hospitality organization. Your ability to manage that diversity is fundamental in your personal success and your organization's effectiveness.

You have been the front office manager of a 100-room property for the past 18 months. A job vacancy for executive housekeeper has been posted and has attracted your interest. One of the reasons you are attracted to this new job is that it will require a greater use of your human resources management skills. The property is located on the outskirts of a large metropolitan area.

In the new job position you would be responsible for a staff of 30 full-time human resources and 10–20 part-time workers. The number of part-time people varies with the occupancy rate that changes at different times of the year.

One of your hesitations in accepting this position is that you have noticed that a great deal of conflict existed between the former executive housekeeper and the full-time human resources employed in the house-keeping department. Since you are current on the topic of Multicultural Management, you suspect that part of the conflict is due to the ethnic and cultural factors that do not exist among your front desk staff.

Are you ready to accept the challenges of becoming a Multicultural Manager and take the job position of executive housekeeper? To accept the challenge you will need to clearly identify the city in which the hospitality property is located. Next, identify the ethnic composition that make up your housekeeping staff. Why do you think that the ethnic and cultural factors play a greater challenge in your role of executive house-keeper than they did as front office manager?

Based upon the ethnic groups that are predominant in your geographic location, what do you feel might be some of the potential causes of the existing conflict? Think of two solutions for resolving or easing the current tensions. Write two goal statements for the housekeeping department that reflect your attitude as a Multicultural Manager.

RECOMMENDED READING   Bryant, J. R. 1987. How to manage employee conflict. *Restaurants USA* 7, (9): 16–19.

de Cordoba, J. 1989. More firms court Hispanic consumers—but find them a tough market to target. *Wall Street Journal* CCXI: 25.

Kroeber, A. L. 1923, 1948. *Anthropology* New York: Harcourt, Brace & World, Inc.

Kuh, G. D. and Whitt, E. J. 1988. *The Invisible Tapestry: Culture in American Colleges and Universities.* ASHE-ERIC Higher Education Report no. 1. Washington D.C.: Association for the Study of Higher Education.

Nicolau, S. 1989. Forging closer ties to Hispanics. *Restaurants USA* 9 (3): 21–23.

Treires, J. J. 1989. Dark side of the dream. *Newsweek CXII* (12): 10–11.

54

END NOTES
1. McKinney, Sally, "Changing Demographics Will Define Destiny," *The Purdue Alumnus,* (July, 1988, 7): 8.
2. Willis, Rod, "Can American Unions Transform Themselves,?" *Management Review,* 77, (1988, 2): 16.

DISCUSSION QUESTIONS
1. Define and distinguish the four fundamental concepts of Multicultural Management.
2. Explain why ethnic pluralism is becoming such a strong presence and force in the hospitality industry.
3. Explain some reasons why Multicultural Management is essential to the effective functioning of the hospitality industry.
4. Explain how culture and ethnicity influence attitudes and behaviors of managers and employees in the work place.
5. Describe and discuss a scenario involving ethnic conflict in the work place that you have experienced, witnessed or heard about. Explain how it amplifies the needs for and principles of Multicultural Management.
6. Explain the relationship between human resources development and Multicultural Management in the hospitality industry.
7. What are potential conflict points created by ethnic pluralism in the hospitality industry?
8. What skills and competencies are necessary to be an effective Multicultural Manager?

CHAPTER 4

ANALYSIS OF THE WORKPLACE

INDUSTRY
ADVISOR

Joel S. Katz
Director, Human Resources Development, ARA Services

**"When you can measure what you are speaking about,
and express it in numbers, you know something about it."**
—LORD KELVIN, 1824–1907

KEY WORDS

bottom-up approach
critical incident technique
duty
element
human resources "gap"
job
job analysis
job description
job incumbent
job inventory
job inventory questionnaire
job-related information
job specification
management inventory
manning table

occupation
position
position guides
skills inventory
staffing guide
staffing table
succession planning
task
task analysis
task and skills analysis
task identification
task inventory
task statement
top-down approach
work

INTRODUCTION

Planning, forecasting and the determination of objectives can be thought of as broad or general human resources activities. As we begin our discussion of job analysis, we begin to narrow the scope to the more specific human resources functions. Our interests in this chapter now turn to the nature of the jobs that we need to successfully run our hospitality operations. A careful analysis of these jobs is essential at this stage in the human resources planning process. All other human resources functions which we will be examining in the future depend upon effectively defining jobs. Can you imagine selection, performance appraisals, promotions, training or even terminations taking place without taking into consideration the jobs that we expect our employees to perform?

The analysis activities which we will be discussing in this chapter will further help you, the manager with human resources responsibilities, to use your knowledge of organizational goals, operational objectives and forecasting to close the human resources gap that is created by an imbalance of human resources need and supply. It is the purpose of this chapter to assist you in understanding the procedures involved in analyzing both human resources needs and supply according to job category.

At the conclusion of the chapter you will be able to:
1. Distinguish between job analysis, job description and job specifications.
2. Use the job inventory approach to determine job tasks.
3. Identify how the results of the job analysis process are used.
4. Determine the job-related information necessary to perform a job analysis.
5. Prepare a job description and job specification.
6. Identify the uses of a job description.
7. Describe the importance of job redesign to human resources managers in the 1990s.
8. Conduct a skills inventory assessment.
9. Define succession planning and explain its importance to the strategic human resources planning process.

Job-Related Terminology

When we discussed planning in Chapter 2, we identified it as a process. In the same way, we now look at the job analysis process that will assist us in turning the operational objectives we have devloped into specific human actions. It is these actions that need to be taken by our employees in order to satisfy the needs and desires of our customers. Even the most creative planning and analysis processes will be of no value unless the needs and desires of of our customers are satisfied. Contemporary management thought suggests that the sole reason for the existence of a business is to *satisfy the needs of customers*. Some say it is to make a profit, but as Joel Katz is quick to point out, you can't do that unless you are meeting customer needs. Effectiveness and efficiency are measured not in terms of creativity, but in terms of guest satisfaction. Before we begin to examine the processes involved in job analysis we must first reach a common understanding of what work is.

Work is the exertion of mental and physical energy to accomplish results. It comes from the Greek word erchon, meaning "to do." It is important to note that not all energy accomplishes results that contribute to the goals of the hospitality organization. For our purposes only, work leading to results that contribute to the goals of our hospitality organization will be considered in the discussions in this chapter. What we are interested in is work that relates to performance. Individuals in the work place can accomplish results through their own efforts (hourly personnel) or through the efforts of others (supervisory or management). The study of human work involves an improved understanding of how to effectively and efficiently get work done. As such, human work is a legitimate area of study unto itself and has made numerous contributions leading to better solutions in dealing with the human problems in human resources management.

Jobs, in the hospitality industry, are designed for the purpose of either producing products or creating services to meet the needs and desires of our customers. In human work terminology, a **job** is a group of positions that have common tasks and responsibilities. A job revolves around a type of work that needs to be accomplished to meet the operational objectives. A **position** is the place or slot that is to be occupied by an individual. A position exists whether it is vacant or filled, and thereby determines your human resources needs or supply. For example, in most food service operations a job that has common tasks and responsibilities is that of a dishwasher. Depending, however, on the size of the operation, the type of service provided, the amount of chinaware used, and other related factors, the number of dishwasher positions required will vary. While each dishwasher, once hired, will perform the same job he or she will each hold a different position within your hospitality enterprise.

In the performance of his or her work your dishwashers will have **duties** and **tasks**. A **duty** refers to a major activity or action required by the job, which may be composed of many tasks. A **task** may be thought of as a subset of a duty, or more specifically a piece of the work that the duty requires. A duty that your dishwashers might have would be to clean the dish machine at the end of their shift. One task that would be involved in completing this duty would be to drain the water from the machine, another task would be to clean out all the food particles from the machine drains. When studying tasks, the work activities are broken into **elements** that are motions or movement required to complete the task. In draining the water from the dish machine the employee must bend to open the drain. The bending motion would be one element, while the movement of turning the drain valve would be a second and standing back up again would be the third element required in just this one task. To clarify the work terminology for you, Figure 4–1 schematically shows these relationships. Elements combined together make up tasks, series

58

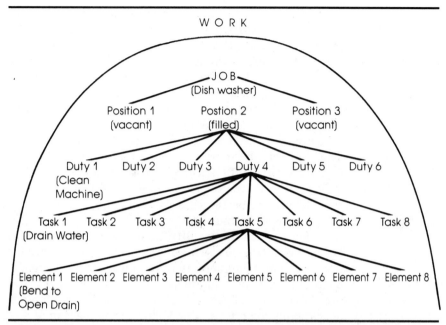

WORK

JOB
(Dish washer)

Position 1   Postion 2   Position 3
(vacant)   (filled)   (vacant)

Duty 1   Duty 2   Duty 3   Duty 4   Duty 5   Duty 6
(Clean
Machine)

Task 1   Task 2   Task 3   Task 4   Task 5   Task 6   Task 7   Task 8
(Drain Water)

Element 1 Element 2 Element 3 Element 4 Element 5 Element 6 Element 7 Element 8
(Bend to
Open Drain)

Figure 4-1. Diagram of the Relationships between Job-Related Terminology.

of tasks are a duty, while a position involves all of the tasks and duties required of one individual. A job includes all positions that perform similar work activities. The **occupation** to which your dishwashers and all other employees belong is that of food service workers.

INDUSTRY EXPERTS SPEAK

According to Joel Katz, "In an effort to get employees to practice more "self-management," many companies (ARA for one) are looking at defining jobs in terms of the *results* they are accountable for. For example, instead of saying that a dishwasher's duty is to "clean the dish machine at the end of his or her shift," we would say that the dishwasher is accountable for the following result: "At the end of each dishwasher's shift the dish machine will be left clean and sanitized to company and regulatory agency standards." If the dishwasher understands the results objective, he or she can have some say in the tasks and elements he or she uses to accomplish the result. If some unexpected or emergency situation comes up that requires a deviation from normal tasks or elements, he or she will have a basis for making decisions on an alternate course of action to achieve the result.

"A better example might be in the area of customer service. We usually tell our customer contact employees that we want them

> to smile. In reality, we don't care if our employees smile: we want our customers to smile (as evidence of their satisfaction). If we tell employees that the result we want is for our customers to smile, they'll likely figure out ways to do this (other than or in addition to smiling themselves)."

Why It Is Necessary to Describe Jobs

Before developing a job description and specification through the job analysis process, it is important to determine what you are going to use the information for. This will determine what information you will need to include in the document and, therefore, the data you will need to collect during the job analysis. Job descriptions and specifications can be used for many purposes in a hospitality operation. Some of those purposes are:

- recruiting
- selecting
- communicating expectations
- doing performance appraisals
- identifying training needs
- making promotional decisions
- identifying development needs
- determining compensation
- human resources planning

Figure 4–2 shows you what the analysis process looks like.

The Job Analysis

The **job analysis** predicts or indicates the job activities of the human resources that will eventually be hired to achieve the operational

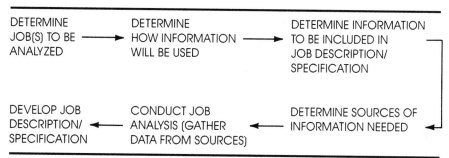

Figure 4-2. The Job Analysis Process
Courtesy of Joel Katz, ARA Services

objectives of the hospitality enterprise. There are two different approaches in conducting a job analysis. The one you use will depend on whether you find yourself responsible for the human resources in an existing operation or if the operation you will be working for is still in the conceptual or preoperational phase.

The **bottom-up approach** is used most frequently when the organization exists and the basis for your analysis becomes incumbent employee behaviors and the job activities they perform. A bottom-up approach may also be used for a start-up organization by analyzing similar jobs in other organizations. If you are analyzing new and future jobs the **top-down approach** is used. Since you don't have employees to study and observe, you must analyze the corporate mission statement, organizational goals and operational objectives to determine what tasks must be performed to achieve the planned objectives. Sometimes you might want to take a top-down approach even when your employees are in place. This will help ensure that people are performing the appropriate tasks and that you are organized and staffed adequately, without making any assumptions. This fresh-start approach—the human resources equivalent to zero-based budgeting—is often used when organization restructuring is being considered.

Where does the job analysis process begin? Before the human resources are hired, and before the jobs themselves actually exist. When the job analysis is used before the operation opens its doors to the first guest, the designing of the job is done to maximize its benefit, not only to the hospitality enterprise, but also to the future employee.

When human resources were plentiful in the 1970s and 1980s very few owners and operators of hospitality organizations took time to think about how the job would impact or affect the employees they would be hiring. It was not uncommon, for example, to have foodservice operations that would close between the lunch rush and the dinner hour. Servers were expected to punch out during that period of time, go home and report back to the operation in time to prepare for the evening customers. While the designing of a job that includes the idea of a split shift maximizes the benefit to the hospitality operation, we think that you will agree that this does not typically reflect the best interests of your employees. In some situations in some operational locations, this practice might be highly acceptable to both the operation and the employee. But in "the next chapter" you will be facing a serious shortage of hourly personnel in many hospitality operations. In situations where human resources are difficult to find, jobs will have to be designed to take into consideration the needs of your future employees. This is where you will use the information you gathered previously in your forecasting.

Job analysis determines the content for each job which is needed to meet the operational objectives. Job analysis in the top-down approach defines the nature of the work activities by determining the appropriate

---

Table 4-1. Items Identified in a Job Analysis

A Job analysis may identify any or all of the following:

1. The *Results* the job is accountable for (ie. specific results or "Key Result Areas" (KRA's).
2. The *Tasks* or the *Behaviors* needed to achieve the Results.
3. The *Knowledge, Skills* or *Attributes* needed to do the Tasks or exhibit the Behaviors.
4. The *Education, Training, Experience* or other *Credentials* needed to acquire the necessary Knowledge, Skills or Attributes.
5. *Performance Standards* (which may include quantity, quality, time or cost measurements.)

Courtesy of Joel Katz, ARA Services

61

tasks that are required by the job, rather than by what the people in the job are doing. It asks what tasks need to be accomplished in order that the objectives are met. It does not look at what work the job incumbent is (or is not capable of) performing.

In addition to determining the tasks, job analysis also defines the skills necessary to do the work and identifies the time in which the job needs to be completed. Table 4–1 lists the various items identified through a job analysis. Knowing the work to be done, the skills necessary and the time frame required, you can outline the human resources needs for the future hospitality enterprise. The recruitment program can then be developed based on a solid knowledge base of how many human resources are needed, what the skill levels will have to be and a good indication of the training requirements. At this point you have identified the number and types of jobs that are needed.

Job analysis can be performed for any job, hourly or management. The top-down approach to job analysis uses the objectives and goals of the hospitality operation to predetermine the jobs that are necessary. Once the jobs are identified, the job duties (along with acceptable performance standards), job tasks and sequence in which the job activities should be completed are defined.

Now that we have discussed what job analysis is and how the process works when applied to a new hospitality operation, we can more clearly present you with a definition. **Job analysis** is the process by which job information is obtained so that the job duties and tasks can be determined. The job duties and tasks will then define the abilities, knowledge, skills and responsibilities that are required for successful job performance.

From our earlier example of the dishwasher used in Figure 4–1, we can apply this definition. A job analysis of the job "dishwasher" would indicate to us that one of the duties of this job was to clean the dish machine. Furthermore, the job analysis would tell us that for the duty of "clean the dish machine" one of the tasks would be to drain the water. The next question you must ask yourself is what abilities, knowledge, skills and responsibilities does a person need to have to "clean the dish machine," the duty and to "drain the water," the task. You can probably already see how useful this job information will be to us in the writing of job descriptions and job specifications.

Job Inventory Approach

The **job inventory** approach is one method of conducting job analysis in hospitality organizations that are doing business. Because you have job incumbents in all, or most, of your job positions, an inventory or audit of all the tasks that comprise their jobs can be collected and organized. This would be an example of the bottom-up approach to job analysis. Job inventories are conducted onsite providing a first-hand account of tasks, the knowledge and skills required for the performance of each task, the time requirements of each task, as well as an identification of where the knowledge and skills were obtained. Did the job incumbent have specialized training or education? Was the training conducted on-the-job or in a classroom setting? What types and how much education does the job incumbent have? One area of particular concern for managers with human resources responsibilities in the hospitality industry is the past experience requirements of the job incumbents. For the majority of hourly personnel in hospitality it is job experience, rather than the educational background, which qualifies them for and makes them proficient at their jobs.

The job inventory approach is referred to by many different names including task analysis, task inventories, task identification, and task and skill analysis. Generally, these terms are synonymous in the job analysis literature, but it is always a good idea to compare definitions just to make sure the author is using the terms in a manner consistent with how you want to use them in your own operations. We will define **job inventory** as a method of obtaining job-related information through an audit of tasks performed by job incumbents.

The job inventory approach focuses on the performance requirements of the job by listing the relevant job tasks. Care must be taken not to look solely at job titles that can oftentimes be misleading. While job content is an important component of any job analysis, the job inventory provides detailed objective information about a job or sets of jobs through a study of jobs and work. Table 4–2 is provided to present you with the information that is commonly obtained from a job inventory. To get the most use from a job inventory, you should modify this table so that it reflects the specific needs of your operation. Can you think of any other information, based on your past work experiences, which we should have included?

Table 4-2. Information Obtained in Job Inventory Approach

The Job Inventory approach provides an audit of:

- Essential Job Content
basis for recruitment, training, development

- Basic Educational Qualifications
basis for selection, placement, development

- Experience Requirements
basis for selection, placement, training, development

- Required Training
basis for content and length of training

- Development Patterns
basis for internal career paths, individual development

Deriving Task Statements

There is no set number of tasks that appear on a job inventory. The number of tasks is completely dependent on the job or set of jobs being inventoried. The first step in conducting a job inventory is to determine the tasks. A **task description** or **statement** of job requirements (what must be accomplished) are descriptors of the work that is performed in target jobs.

Where does the task statement come from? To write a job task statement you need a job information base that may be derived in one of several ways, or through a combination of different approaches. One approach is to have either the job incumbent or the supervisor or both identify what they feel is relevant in completion of the job being inventoried. Another method of deriving task statements might involve a content analysis of written job-related documents such as job descriptions, hiring guides, work flow charts, policy manuals, etc. Oftentimes a job analyst will be hired as a consultant to make observations of job incumbents and supervisors while they work. This observational information is then frequently supplemented with data acquired through individual and group interviews.

A form used to gather job information through the observation method is shown in Figure 4–3. The job analyst would begin by recording the first task in the left hand column, the second task would be recorded on the same row in the right hand column, the third task is recorded in the second row in the left hand column, the fourth task in the second row in the right-hand column and so forth. In some jobs, tasks may have a specific sequence, such as cleaning a slicer, while in other jobs sequence may be irrelevant. This form provides the analyst with a detailed flow of the tasks as the job incumbent proceeds from one task to another. Remember that a task is a specific unit of work with a beginning and an end. The analyst can indicate when a duty has been completed by drawing a heavy line at the end of the last task as indicated by the example shown in Figure 4–3. The amount of time required to complete each task can be recorded simultaneously by the job analyst. Job observation forms may be modified to include additional information which you, as the manager with human resources responsibilities, might be inter-

Job Incumbent's Name _____ Date _____

Job Title _____ Observer's Name _____

Department _____ Page Number _____

TASK	AMT. OF TIME	TASK	AMT. OF TIME
Align box springs & mattress		Center bed pad so it is flush w/head of mattress	
Spread bottom sheet over bed		Tuck sheet accross top of bed	
Miter corners (top)		Place top sheet over bed	
Smooth sheet		Place blanket over bed	
Fold top and cover sheet over top of blanket		Go to opposite side of bed	
Straight top sheet and blanket		Miter bottom corners	
Tuck Sheets & blanket together		Place spread on bed	
Fold top of spread across top sheet		Flip pillows	
Lay pillows on bed		Slide pillowcase over pillow	
Place up spread		Lay pillows beneath spread	
Re-check bed for smoothness		Check telephone	
Wipe clean		Check pad & dialing instructions . . .	

Figure 4-3. Job Observation Form

Figure 4-4. The observational method can be used to gather job related information for your job analysis.
Photo by Michael Upright

ested in for purposes of your specific job analysis (Figure 4–4). One word of caution when using observational methods: care must be taken not to study the characteristics of the job incumbent, but rather the requirements of the job itself.

The job information which you have gathered is then used to develop a list of **task statements**. The actual job task statements are important because the job descriptions that we will be deriving from these statements will reflect their accuracy and thoroughness. The task should be written in a clear and unambiguous manner, brief and to the point. Examples of task statements for a housekeeper, evening turndown job are found in Table 4-3.

The Job Inventory Questionnaire

The list of job tasks that you have identified for each job or set of jobs is then cast in the form of a questionnaire similar to the one shown in Figure 4-5. The job incumbent rates each listed task in terms of how significant, or important, it is in relationship to all the other tasks that need to be performed for that job. The amount of time spent to complete the task is also given.

A variety of judgmental responses can also be included on the job inventory questionnaire that will assist us in the development of job descriptions. Such responses might include the skills required, where

Table 4-3. Task Statements for Housekeeper (Evening Turndown Job)

- Knock on the door and identify yourself.
- Open door.
- Turn on lights.
- Position cart in front of door.
- Remove dirty ashtrays and dishes.
- Remove loose trash.
- Tidy newspapers.
- Replace used matches.
- Move into bathroom.
- Remove soiled linen to linen bag.
- Wipe down sink, mirrors and tub.
- Replace used soap.
- Replace soiled linen with fresh linen.
- Remove bedspread and turn down bed.
- Place mint and card on pillow.
- Close drapes.
- Turn on lamp by bed.
- Turn out light by door and close door.

the job incumbent learned the skills (on-the-job training, brought with them to the job, trade school, etc.), the level of difficulty of the task, or if supervision or if both of them is required. The answers are coded so that they may be analyzed either manually or by the computer. An interview might have to be done to obtain this information for incumbents in lower level jobs.

The job inventory method is based on the idea that the basic source of job information is contained in the on-the-job tasks that are performed. The questionaire is often used as a way to validate what the job analyst has found out in interviews or through observations. The job inventory method of job analysis is used mostly to analyze existing jobs, but it can also be applied to future jobs by using an operation similar to yours, relying on consultants or upon your own experiences to guide you. To assist you with the job analysis process a listing of job-related information that might be of interest for your hospitality operation is presented in Table 4–4. Job inventories as we have discussed them are limited to manual activities. Tasks pertaining to mental activities and thought processes are much more difficult to identify. As a manager with human resources responsibilities you will find the job inventory approach to job analysis to be an effective way to obtain job-related information from job incumbents.

(1) Task List	(2) Task Performed?	(3) Time Spent	(4) Significance to Job?	Skills Required	(5) Difficulty Level	(6) Supervision Required?

(1) Task List-what is done in job-oriented terms
(2) if task is performed
(3) 5 = Great amount; 4 = Above average; 3 = About average; 2 = Below average; 1 = Small amount
(4) 5 = Most significant aspect; 4 = major part; 3 = substantial part; 2 = Minor part; 1 = no part of job
(5) 3 = Hard; 2 = Medium; 1 = Easy
(6) Y = Yes; N = No

Figure 4-5. Job Inventory Questionnaire

Other Types of Job Analysis Methods

There are many variations on the specific job analysis methods described so far in this chapter. Safety implications, job satisfaction levels, demographic factors or all of these may be included on the job inventory questionnaire, depending on the specific needs of your operation, thereby maximizing the amount of information obtained for time

Table 4-4. Job-Related Information

Job analysis should conform to the needs of your operation. The job information listed here is identified to assist you in focusing your job analysis to the area(s) that will help you most.

- work activities (process and activities)
- skills involved
- worker-oriented activities (human behaviors)
- job demands
- working conditions (physical and social)
- equipment, tools and work aids
- work performance standards (error rate and time per task)
- materials used
- services rendered
- products made
- work schedule
- accountability
- personal attributes (personality)
- education and/or training requirements
- work experience background

Once you have decided what information is most beneficial to you, the items are placed together on the Job Analysis Form.

spent. Any job analysis method is time consuming, however the value of the information, and even the process itself, is worth the investment.

While job analysis forms and procedures vary, the process is common in all job analysis methods. The critical incident technique is a method of job analysis that identifies job-related behaviors of incumbents by examining successful (effective) types of behavior or unsuccessful (ineffective) behavior. This can be done through an interview or by observations. The recording of the incident can be made by observers, supervisors or by the employees themselves. One of the greatest values of the critical incident method is as a performance appraisal tool. For job description purposes, this method provides valuable insight to the human qualities necessary for successful performance in a particular job.

Other sources for information for job analysis include:

- incumbent observations
- structured or critical incident interviews with job content experts (incumbents, supervisors, those who interact with the job, those who have been in the job previously)
- work-related documents
- strategic and business plans, mission statements
- individuals in similar jobs in other companies
- questionnaires completed by job content experts and incumbents

The information we have presented on job analysis will provide you with a systematic approach to the processes of gathering and analyzing job data. For the job analysis to be of most benefit to you, i.e., applicable to your situation, the first determination you must make is what types of job-related information you will need in order to achieve your operation's objectives. Then you can select the best method of collecting the necessary job information for your particular work environment.

Job analysis involves collecting and interpreting relevant job data. Although the study and analysis of human work has become more systematic and scientific than a decade ago, the basic outcome of the conventional job analysis has been, and is, the **job description** and **job specification**. The advantages of work simplification, however, can be one of the side benefits of a thorough job analysis.

Job analysis is not a complicated procedure, but it is detailed and time consuming. The importance of the analysis justifies the time. Job analysis can be used for designing new jobs or redesigning existing ones that have been found through job evaluation to be less efficient than what is desired by management, or where tasks have been found to overlap between jobs, creating conflict in the work place. We predict that in "the next chapter" your role as a manager with human resources responsibilities will highly rely on the information obtained in an accurate job analysis. Especially with the labor shortages we will have to:

- make jobs more efficient
- simplify so they can be performed by less skilled or disabled workers

Job Descriptions

The results of the job analysis are used to develop job descriptions. Job descriptions are in turn used as the basis for preparing job evaluations, recruitment procedures, training requirements, and performance appraisals. Job analysis gives management information about the work that needs to be accomplished to meet the operational objectives. Job descriptions tell the employee what job duties need to be accomplished to ensure progressive individual development within the hospitality organization. It is the job description that ultimately becomes the basis for the training plan, as training needs are one of the outcomes.

Job descriptions are also called **position guides.** The type of job description, for hourly workers that Joel Katz has proposed for use at ARA Services would contain:

- Results/Standards that the employee is accountable for
- Physical Tasks
- Interpersonal behaviors

In order to write a good job description both quantitative and qualitative job-related information is necessary. This is where the task data collected through your job inventories are analyzed. The task inventories have provided you with an indication of how many job incumbents in the same job perform various tasks and how much time they spend on the tasks. The quality of the job description that you develop is very much a direct reflection of the quality of job analysis performed.

Preparing Job Descriptions

It is indeed difficult to run an efficient, profitable operation unless every employee knows what his or her job is. In order for this to occur, management needs to first determine what every employee's job consists of. While this sounds like common sense, think of some of the jobs you might have held in the hospitality industry where you were hired, given a job title (such as bellperson, server, or bartender) and told to perform. As you probably learned in a situation like this, titles rarely are sufficient explanations of the roles and tasks that you and other employees like you actually performed. In some cases, job titles can even be misleading, for example a dishwasher whose job title is "sanitary engineer."

Once you have collected complete and accurate information about the job, you are ready to prepare the job description. This will include a job summary, detailed duties of the job and specific job requirements (skills, mental and physical requirements, responsibilities and job conditions). It is of utmost importance that these be both clear and detailed in order to effectively communicate the standards for good performance. A prerequisite to satisfactory performance is a clear understanding by employees of what they are supposed to do, how and when they are suppose to do it and the results that are expected of them. The hospitality industry is full of people—our human resources—who want to achieve results for themselves and the organizations of which they are a part. Job descriptions better enable them to meet these objectives.

We can now define **job descriptions** as an accurate, complete statement of the duties and responsibilities required of a specific job. In a very real sense a job description represents a written contract between the employer and the employee. Employees want, and have the right to know, what is expected of them when they report to work each day, and employers have a need and right to know what tasks they can expect will be performed. A written agreement of expectations is likely to lead to a greater understanding and better relationship between management and employees.

At this point you know that job descriptions are derived from the information obtained and analyzed in the job analysis process. You also know that job descriptions are written for the job incumbent as well as for use by management. More examples of how management uses job descriptions will be presented later in this chapter. Right now think about ways that you could convey information about the jobs in question to the job incumbents so that they will know all that is expected of them in the performance of their jobs.

By identifying the "what," the "how" and the "why" of each job, within the composition of each job description, you will be sure to include all relevant job-related information. The "what" is both the physical and mental activities required to do the job. Physical tasks in a hospitality operation might include such activities as transporting material, cutting, cleaning, delivering, kneading, portioning, folding, wiping, sanitizing, and measuring. Mental activities might include: planning, judging, directing, and organizing. The "what" can be taken from your job inventory, although tasks may need to be rewritten so that the description reads clearly and smoothly. Table 4–5 identifies sample questions that will assist you in developing job descriptions for your own operation.

The "how" includes all the procedures, processes and methods used to do the "what," and again can be divided into both physical and mental actions. Operating machinery, following standardized recipe procedures, and using work simplification methods in routine activities are physical in nature, whereas a mental action would be making calculations to increase or decrease recipe amounts. The "why" is simply the basic purpose of the job. It can be found in the job summary, sometimes stated in the form of a job objective.

The actual job description can be very detailed or very brief, depending on the size and needs of the organization in which it is used. The writing style should be direct and terse, not wordy, and written in the present tense. Typically, the language is easily understandable. The listing of job duties is behaviorally based with each sentence beginning with an action verb. The arrangement of job descriptions is not entirely rigid. With relatively simple jobs a chronological order can be used. For a

---

Table 4-5. Questions to Ask When Developing Job Descriptions

WHAT the employee does:

- What are the tasks performed by the job incumbents?
- What is the frequency with which the tasks are done?
- What is the difficulty of the task as compared with all the tasks done?
- What tasks exist that have not been identified?

HOW the employee performs the job:

- Which tools and equipment are required to perform the job?
- Which materials will the job incumbent need?
- Which processes and procedures are required?

WHY the employee does the job:

- Why does this job exist?

job, such as that of a busperson or bellperson, the description can be arranged according to the general order in which the tasks occur. Job descriptions prepared for supervisory and management human resources require more planning and generalizing with fewer specifics and mechanics.

Whichever format you decide to use, there are certain items essential for a good job description. To start with, there must be an accurate title, one that is descriptive of the work. The title of the immediate supervisor is included, along with a job summary. The job summary is a brief statement that sets forth the purpose of the job. Next comes a list of not only the duties but also the responsibilities of the job. These can be determined by referring to the job inventory analysis. It is often wise at the conclusion of job duties and responsibilities to state "may be called upon at times to perform other related tasks not specifically included in this description." Proper relationships with others in the organization is an important component so that the job incumbent understands the position his or her job plays in the success of day-to-day operations. Table 4–6 is an example of a job description used by ARA Services.

Table 4-6. Position Description

Line Server

Major Goal of Position: To efficiently serve meals while maintaining an appealing presentation of the food and excellent customer relations.

Key Result Areas:

1. Customer Satisfaction
2. Service Efficiency
3. Personal and Line Presentation
4. Product Knowledge/Suggestive Selling
5. Maintenance of Standards (e.g., sanitation, portion control)

Tasks:

Prior to Meal Service:

1. Examine own appearance to make sure you make an excellent personal presentation (e.g., uniform clean and pressed, name badge, no excessive jewelry, excellent personal hygiene, hair restraint).
2. Examine your work station to make sure that heat wells are on and water is at appropriate levels, food is placed in wells in proper sequence, garnishes are in place, spills are cleaned up and clutter is removed from the counter.
3. Ensure that all supplies and utensils are available and in place (e.g., plates; silverware, napkins, condiments, clean towels for spills, spatulas, serving spoons and other utensils, oven mitts to change pans).
4. Check with cook to get product information (e.g., what each item is called, ingredients, what is being called fresh and what is pre-cooked).

(continues. . .)

72

5. Fill all juice machines, make coffee, check fountain soda machines.
6. Examine food warmer for backup products.

During Meal Service:

1. Follow the five Key Principles of Customer Service as described in the "Spirit of Service" training Program:

   - Make a good impression.
   - Listen, ask and respond.
   - Show customers they're important.
   - Know your service.
   - Make the extra effort.

2. Serve quickly to keep line moving, while giving each customer appropriate attention.
3. Follow portion control specifications at all times.
4. Let the cook know your needs. If a certain entree is being heavily selected, let the cook know.
5. Keep the line attractive, clean and neat.
6. Stir casseroles to keep them from drying out. Do not put food up when there are no customers.

After Meal Service:

1. Wipe down serving area and tray slide using specified cleaners and following cleaning procedures.
2. Polish all stainless steel surfaces following specified procedures.
3. Replenish all supplies (e.g., plates, silverware, napkins, condiments) for next meal service.

Courtesy of ARA Services

Uses of Job Descriptions

The importance of the job description to the hospitality industry is often understated (Table 4–7). The information is useful to every area of supervisor-subordinate relationships as it maintains a more closely organized work group based on job duties and responsibilities. Job descriptions that identify job entry requirements are used to aid the interviewer in the selection process. By knowing the necessary job qualifications and skills, training can be more effective.

In addition, job descriptions can be used as a basis for compensation administration, as well as in the creation of development, transfer and promotion programs. Supervisory control, performance appraisals, placement activities, work load evaluations and incentive program planning: the job description provides a source of basic job information that can assist each of these human resources functions. Job descriptions can even help establish organizational charts in their identification of who reports to whom. Using job descriptions to set standards and assign responsibilities can help you eliminate the "but it's not my job" attitude. These

73

are basics. You and your organization are free to use job descriptions to the extent that you want, depending upon your particular needs.

Redesigning Jobs

One last aspect of job descriptions is their ability to be modified for the purpose of employing the mentally or physically challenged, the se-

74

Table 4-7. What to Include in a Job Description/Specification	
Purpose	**Information Needed**
Recruiting	Competencies Education/Experience Working conditions
Selection	Competencies Education/Experience Working conditions Tasks/Behaviors
Communicating expectations	Results Tasks/Behaviors Reporting relationships Individuals/Groups job interacts with Tools/Materials/Work facilities Working conditions
Performance appraisal	Results Tasks/Behaviors
Identifying training & development needs	Tasks/Behaviors Competencies Education/Experience Individuals/Groups jobs interact with
Making promotion decisions	Competencies Education/Experience Working conditions Tasks/Behaviors
Determining compensation	Results Competencies Education/Experience Individuals/Groups job interacts with Working conditions Tasks/Behaviors Degree of autonomy Managerial responsibility for others Consequence of errors
Determining the HR Gap	Competencies Education/Experience

Courtesy of Joel Katz, ARA Services

nior citizen or members of the immigrant populace. As hiring human resources becomes more difficult, the idea of redesigning jobs to meet
people's needs becomes a very real possibility. In some job markets,
knowing what your labor supply consists of (forecasting) can influence
how a job will be structured.

Job entry requirements tend to be reduced when human resources
are hard to find and then increase in periods of unemployment. The
theory behind job redesign is that profits will not be sacrificed and job
performance will not be affected if you are selective in the altering of the
job content. The manager with human resources responsibilities plays a
large role in this process as you attempt to locate the most qualified
persons available for employment. Relaxing job requirements means that
the jobs are redesigned to fit the abilities of the human resources
available to fill them. Reading, writing and arithmetic requirements
may need to be designed out of the job. In many cases, complex tasks
cannot be expected to be completed, so the complex parts of the jobs must
be eliminated by reorganizing the tasks in some jobs to be simpler and
more routine in order that satisfactory performance can be accomplished.

Thus, not every job in every organization possesses the ability to be
redesigned in such a manner (Table 4–8). A relatively high percentage of
the jobs in the hospitality industry, however, could be changed to make
the job less demanding and psychologically frustrating for the many
alternative pools of labor that are available to us in certain markets. A
certain amount of redesigning may even be beneficial to the operation.
Accomplishing work more efficiently always contains the possibility of
resulting in higher profits for the organization.

Job Specifications

While job descriptions concentrate on what the job itself consists of,
job specifications are concerned with the qualifications needed to perform the job. Specifications include such things as education, physical
characteristics, experience, training, personality, skills and the degree
to which each is needed by the employee for every job. We can define **job**

Table 4-8. Attitudes for Job Redesign

Redesigning jobs to meet people's needs

- Flexibility in Management
- People Do Not Always Need to Do the Adapting
- Be Creative in Your Approach to Employee-Job Relationships
- Can Prospective Employees Develop the Qualifications While on the Job?
- Be Goal Rather than Task Oriented

---

specifications as the human requirements and qualifications needed by someone filling the job. Job requirements are translated into human resources requirements. Job specifications provide guidelines for hiring, frequently forming the basis of interview questions. We will discuss this in further detail in the chapter on recruitment and selection.

Caution needs to be exercised so that human resources requirements do not become overly specific or request too much background. Outside of legal ramifications, which can be costly, unnecessary requirements (for example in the amount of work experience) can inflate the wages that your operations must pay. In addition, inflated requirements can give the employee unrealistic expectations of what the job actually contains, causing frustration and eventual job turnover.

Remember also that many of the jobs in the hospitality industry require direct guest contact. Obviously, in our industry, personality characteristics and communication skills become extremely important for both guest satisfaction with our products and services and for employee satisfaction. And almost all jobs in hospitality operations require that our human resources work closely and effectively with their peers. Here, skills in interpersonal relations are equally important.

As we have seen, the concept of developing and using job descriptions is easy to understand. Job descriptions must be flexible enough to encourage growth and change. Once job descriptions are established it does not mean that they will remain stable forever. Organizations in the hospitality industry are under constant change and revision. For this reason job descriptions and job specifications should be reviewed at least once, if not twice, a year to update them. It must be kept in mind also that job descriptions are used as positive tools and as such should encourage greater contributions to the operation by the employee. They should not be used as tools for disciplinary actions or they will quickly lose their usefulness.

In summary, remember that your basic objective in developing job descriptions and specifications is to relate specifically, simply, clearly and understandably to the employee just what his or her job is and what qualifications are needed to perform the job effectively. To be of value they must be accurate, complete, current, and used. The hospitality industry is full of employees from dishwasher to manager that want to achieve results for themselves and for the organization of which they are a part. These human resources tools better enable them to succeed.

Human Resources Inventories

When the hospitality industry was comprised of mostly family owned and operated businesses, little concern was given to who their employees were. It was generally assumed that family members would all pitch in whenever business was better than usual. In the early 1980s the situation was quite different. The hospitality industry had grown and was composed of companies that had numerous operations or companies made up of several individuals who had selected the hospitality business as an investment and really knew nothing about the business. Today, while the family operations still exist along with many successful small chains and entrepreneurs who find hospitality both exciting and challenging, the multinational corporations have changed the size and scope of the hospitality business. The size and diversity in locations makes it difficult for the manager with human resources responsibilities, sitting in a corporate office, to know what talents and skills his or her employees have. With no knowledge of the in-house skills available, it becomes difficult for that manager to replace his or her employees when they retire, quit or are fired.

Skills or human resources inventories, computerized when company size demands, list all of the employees by name along with their respective skills, training, and educational backgrounds, providing necessary data when changes occur in the hospitality organization. Skills inventories, as we will discuss, can and probably should be developed for both hourly and salaried employees.

In addition to providing an inventory of your current human resources with respect to size and skill distribution, the skills inventories also can be used as indicators of turnover rates, productivity levels and wage scales. They present you with an idea of how the people are currently progressing within and through your organization. Replacement charts, succession charts and manning tables are all derived from skills inventory data.

Human Resources Supply Analysis

In order to plan for both the present and the future, you, as a manager with human resources responsibilities need to analyze the abilities, skills, talents and growth potential of the human resources in your operation and organization. This involves the need for both an inventory of internal labor supplies and a forecast of external labor supplies that we discussed earlier in Chapter 2.

We shall define **skills inventory** as a data system which describes the human resources working for the hospitality organization by name, skills, and important characteristics. The skills inventory is a management tool used for assessing the supply and available skills of your human resources. It is an ongoing system which means that it will provide you with a procedure for monitoring the capabilities and performance levels of your work force. Since skills inventories provide a useful way of recordkeeping when retrieving a vast amount of data, they have become a true human resources planning tool. Through **succession planning** they permit a strategy and technique for rationalizing the essentialprocess of filling position vacancies. In addition they assist with structuring career paths for present and future human resources.

Designing A Skills Inventory System

The primary, and most difficult, decision in designing a skills inventory system for your particular situation will be to determine what information the inventory should contain. Remember that you can only access the information you have placed into the system in the way that you designed the system to retrieve the information. Care should be taken to identify the types of information *essential* to your operation. This will provide you with a list of items that your skills inventory must contain. Next, you will want to identify the information that is *useful* to your operation, and make a decision item by item, as to its value in the skills inventory system. You should design your skills inventory system to include the information that is necessary for human resources planning as this is an integral component of the overall process. Table 4–9 is a list of potential items that might be included on a skills inventory. The information you decide to contain in a skills inventory in your operation is dependent upon the specific needs of your operation. That is why no two skills inventory formats will be identical.

Much of what is contained in a skills inventory is determined by how you plan to use the inventory system. When skills inventory systems contain information regarding employees' desires and career goals, pro-

---

Table 4-9. Skills Inventory Checklist

- Incumbent's name
- Date of birth
- Sex
- Current job
- Present location
- Date of employment
- Prior work experience
- History of work experience in organization
- Current and past wage levels; dates of raises
- Membership in professional groups
- Test scores
- Retirement information
- Geographic location preferences
- Education (special courses, i.e., cake decorating)
- Health information
- Specific skills and knowledges
- Foreign languages
- Supervisor's evaluation of job incumbent capabilities
- Job incumbent's own stated career goals
- Potential for promotion
- Amount of training necessary for promotion

---

motions or transfers can be planned that satisfy both organizational and individual development plans. For training purposes, skills inventories are used to identify not only the skills that exist, but simultaneously indicate the skills that need to be present in your work force and are not. For recruitment, these inventories identify the strengths, weaknesses and imbalances in your current work force. Individual development programs (identifying employees for promotion, transfer or training), long-range human resources planning (projection of work force capabilities), turnover reports (present and projected) and EEO compliance updates are some of the potential ways skills inventory data can be used in hospitality operations and organizations. Skills inventories can also be a motivational device, helping employees to reach their full potential. You should recognize at this point that for skills inventories to be effective for any of these intended purposes, an accurate job analysis is essential. If the job tasks, work load requirements, productivity levels and skill needs have not been adequately identified, the procedures involved in inventorying skills are worthless.

The initial information for a skills inventory data base is collected through a questionnaire or interview. While much of this information is probably available in the personnel files in most hospitality organizations, it might not be easily and readily available, or may not be current. Once the information is obtained, the challenge arises of maintaining and updating data. For many operations this is the most difficult aspect of the skills inventory system. Maintaining the information must be part of the human resources planning process, for the data serves no purpose if it is outdated and inaccurate. The frequency with which the inventory should be updated is a function of the size and growth rate of the organization to which you belong. Some operations place update forms in their payroll envelopes on a periodic basis. In a stable operation with very low turnover once a year might be adequate, or in dynamic high growth operation updates may be necessary every quarter.

Remember also that skills inventories cannot select your people. They provide the basis for a list of qualified individuals. Since specific skills may belong to a number of persons, it is impossible solely through this process to select only the one best person for the position. This inventory is only a tool that must be coupled with proper interviewing, evaluating and selecting. It cannot replace good human resources decision making, but may supplement sound human resources practices. As stated by Kaumeyer, "The actual selection decision is made from the list provided by the skills inventory, but the skills inventory does not make the selection."[1]

Management Inventories and Succession Planning

Skills inventories for your salaried human resources are generally called management inventories. Frequently it is desirable to keep different information about your salaried employees than for your hourly employees.

When skills inventories are used to identify individuals for promotion and advancement, they become a key tool in the process of succession planning. We will define **succession planning** as a formal process in which plans are developed to ensure that replacements can be readily identified to fill the key positions in your organization. As part of the overall planning process, succession planning supports the strategic goals and mission of the organization and is supported by the training and development programs. In succession planning, through the use of replacement or succession charts (Figure 4–6) the future supply of management can be forecasted by analyzing the current supply in relationship to the patterns of progression in your organization. Used in this way, skills inventories identify, at any one period in time, the types of individuals with specific skills who are or will be available.

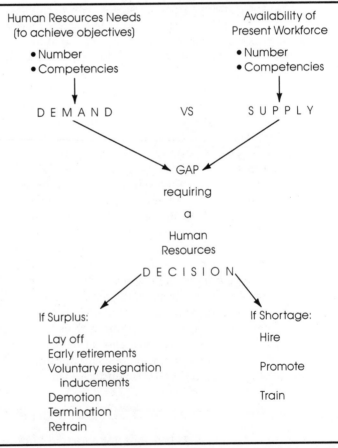

Figure 4-6. Closing the Gap between Human Resources Needs vs. Supply

Succession planning begins with the first level of supervision and operates on a continuing basis. It requires a broad perspective when looking at the organization and not just an up-the-ladder approach to advancement. By tracking the development and preparedness of potential job candidates within your organization, succession planning assists in insuring the availability of the human resources needed to staff your organization. Staffing tables, manning tables, staffing guides and manning charts are all formats for presenting a census of the human resources found within your organization. When determining replacement needs, consideration is given to the effect of expected attrition whether through death, retirement or promotion. Such an analysis of management skills and progression permits a projection of future internal supply.

81

Succession planning assures that development activities are ongoing and relevant for job incumbents as well as providing input to specific training programs. An organization that is known for investing in and developing its own human resources is an organization people want to work for. Succession planning makes obvious the need for effective initial selection of management personnel. In "the next chapter" of human resources management, succession planning ensures the optimum use of a scarce pool of human resources by helping to show current employees that your organization has an interest in their planned development and growth. New meaning can be given to the term human resources planning as identifying qualified individuals, not on a one-time basis, but on a continuing basis.

Closing the Gap

At the beginning of this chapter you learned through job analysis the types and numbers of human resources you need for your particular work environment. The information from your job analysis must now be compared with information obtained through a skills inventory of the human resources presently employed. Recall in Chapter 2 the needs vs. supply analysis (Figure 2–2). We said that the human resources process began by matching organizational goals and operational objectives with the human resources needs developed through your forecasts. An analysis of the current work force would then be conducted to identify the supply of human resources available to us. Any gap between the two would indicate a corrective action which you, as the human resources manager, would need to take. Figure 4–6 also shows how we continue that process in order to close the gap we created.

A gap, or the difference between the future state of affairs and the organizational goals, is what will happen if no new action is taken. Human resources gaps take the form of either a surplus or shortage of personnel or specific skills. It is not enough in the hospitality industry to just have the people, our people must also possess the skills necessary for the operation to meet its objectives. The human resources decisions that you will need to make are all action oriented, meaning that you will need to have a plan developed for each potential decision before you can implement it.

From the information you have already learned to obtain, you can now prepare an estimate of the total human resources needs from external sources. The plans for fulfilling these needs become the basis for recruitment and selection, which we will be discussing in chapters 5 and 6. While you now know how many jobs need to be filled, you will learn how to fill the jobs as we initiate our discussions of the employment process. Promotion and training are involved when the human resources needs are to be filled from within the organization.

Conclusion

One of the most beneficial outcomes of the skills inventory is the ability to effectively match individuals with jobs and in so doing increase both productivity and job satisfaction. As with job analysis, job descriptions and job specifications, the skills inventory is one of the tools in human resources planning that assists both you and your human resources in using and developing their skills to their fullest abilities.

Unless every employee knows what his or her job is, there is a high probability for work left undone, arguments over responsibilities, indifference and a high turnover. In order to avoid this confusion, you must plan your human resources activities. The human resources planning system as we have explained it determines the activities to be done, the method of completion, the human resources involved in the activity and when the activity should be performed.

The tools discussed in this chapter will assist you in answering the following questions:

- what work has to be done
- what tasks comprise the work
- what skills do the employees need to perform the tasks
- how many employees it will take to accomplish the work
- who will perform the tasks
- when will the work be performed
- time and effort required for each task
- what skill levels your present employees have
- the number of employees available to accomplish the work
- the shortages or surplus of employees for each job
- who will be available in the future within your organization to fulfill job needs.

Job analysis identified the essential tasks and who should do them based upon the organizational goals and operational objectives. Job descriptions were then structured to delegate the tasks, responsibilities and relationship of one particular job to all other jobs. All activities in the human resources system indicate that they are dependent upon the job description document and would be ineffective without it. The ineffectiveness of the human resources function would have definite repercussions throughout the entire organization. The human resources manager or department is responsible for the functions of obtaining, maintaining and retaining the human resources of the organization with the job description serving as a connecting thread. This thread is the key to each activity we will be discussing in future chapters. Along with the job description are the job specifications that indicate the qualifications necessary to perform the job.

The skills inventory provides you with information on the skills, knowledge and background of your current employees. The difference between what you have and what you need indicates the gap that must be filled to effectively meet your operational objectives. This indicator of strengths and weaknesses focuses not only on individuals in their present positions, but through succession planning for future positions as well.

The job analysis process as discussed in this chapter determines much of the content for future human resources decisions. Training program content, individual development and organizational development content, recruitment, selection, placement and even compensation and benefits will be based upon the data you have obtained so far. Throughout this chapter we have tried to emphasize that the human resources analysis process must be designed to fit the circumstances of the environment in which you are currently working in or will be working in the future. The larger the organization you work for the more formal each of these procedures and formats will need to be to maximize efficiency. The bottom line for this chapter is to maximize *your* effectiveness in matching people to jobs with respect to skills, abilities and performance levels thus creating organizational human resources efficiency.

As a manager with human resources responsibilities in a large multinational hospitality corporation, you are aware that one of your organizational goals is to achieve maximum productivity through the efficient use of your human resources. To achieve efficiency, you must have a solid organizational structure for each of the required job tasks necessary, identified and then assigned to the appropriate job position. Unless every human resource knows exactly what his or her job entails, there will be work left unfinished, arguments over responsibilities, indifference, and eventually a larger than desired turnover. Thus, the very heart of human resources management is the *job*.

The company that you work for has both hotels, resorts, free-standing foodservice operations and catering facilities. The company is headquartered in the United States, where it maintains over 450 individual hospitality establishments as well as a dozen hotel properties located throughout Europe.

The senior vice-president for development has shown you the following organizational goals: "To expand lodging operations into the economy hotel market within two years, with expansion into a five-state region in the midwest within a period of five years after entering the marketplace."

The vice-president of development is under pressure to prepare a prospectus for the company president in two weeks. Because of your previous experience with job analysis procedures and techniques you have been asked to provide information from which a projected payroll budget could be determined. What will you need to do in order to prepare this information for the senior vice-president of development? (Hint: Remember that it has been stressed that job analysis procedures follow a logical sequence.) The information that the vice-president is requesting from you will become the basis for the long-range plans for the human resources functions of orientation, training and development for this newly proposed chain of lodging properties. In this particular situation, would it be best to use a top-down approach or bottom-up approach for your job analysis? Would the job inventory approach be a suitable method of job analysis in this particular situation? Defend your response.

After you completed the job analysis you determined that one of the job positions that need to be filled is that of laundry room attendant. Develop a job specificaton for this job description. What are the skill levels and educational background that will be required of the individual filling this job position? Could this job position for laundry room attendant be redesigned to accommodate the skill levels and educational background of some nontraditional sources of labor (such as the physically or mentally challenged)? How would you go about redesigning this particular job?

JOB DESCRIPTION   LAUNDRY ATTENDANT

JOB DUTIES:

1. Make sure all linen for rooms is washed and ironed.
2. Make sure all linen for restaurants (including country club) is washed and ironed.
3. Help to sort out all soiled linen.
4. Help to make up the laundry carts when needed.
5. Keep the laundry area cleaned and organized.
6. Keep the machines cleaned.
7. To inform the laundry supervisor when there is any problem with the machines.
8. To separate all stained linen.
9. To do the side work assigned every day.

JOB LIST:

1. Sign-in.
2. Sort linen.
3. Wash linen.
4. Dry linen.
5. Fold guestroom linen.
6. Run restaurant linen through mangle.
7. Re-stock all laundry carts and replenish laundry room shelves with guest linen.
8. Clean all machines.

85

RECOMMENDED READING

Azevedo, R. E. 1977. Missing ingredient in skills inventories. *Journal of Systems Management* 28, (4): 24–29.

Gael, S. 1983. *Job Analysis: A Guide to Assessing Work Activities* San Francisco: Jossey-Bass Publishers.

Gottlieb, L. 1980. A modern job description. *Restaurant Business* 85, (16): 62, 64, 176.

Grant, P. C. 1988. Job description. *Personnel Journal* 67, (2): 48–53.

Kaumeyer, Jr., R. A. 1979. *Planning and Using Skills Inventory Systems* New York: Van Nostrand Reinhold Company.

Manning, M. B. and McPherson, J. 1985. The skills audit. *The Cornell Quarterly* 26, (2): 45–49.

END NOTES

1. Kaumeyer, Richard A., *Planning and Using Skills Inventory Systems.* (New York: Van Nostrand Reinhold Company, 1979): 1.

DISCUSSION QUESTIONS

1. Distinguish between job analysis and task identification. Why are each performed?
2. Describe the relationship between job analysis and all other human resources functions.
3. Identify and define the techniques for collecting job-related information.
4. Describe the key elements of a job inventory. What information is obtained?
5. What items are typically contained in a job description.
6. Discuss the importance of, and uses for, a job description.
7. Discuss the idea of redesigning jobs to meet employees abilities. How do you respond to this idea?
8. Define a job specification.
9. What is a skills inventory? How would you use it in a hospitality operation? For hourly employees? For salaried?
10. What is the major difficulty in using a skills inventory? Identify the various uses of skills inventory data.
11. Describe the process of succession planning and its importance to the hospitality enterpise.
12. What possible decisions do you have to make as a human resources manager when the gap shows a surplus? When the gap shows a shortage?

SECTION 2
THE EMPLOYMENT PROCESS

CHAPTER 5

THE LABOR MARKET
AND HOSPITALITY RECRUITMENT

INDUSTRY
ADVISOR

David R. Murphy
Former Director, Corporate College Relations, Marriott Corporation

"Even if you're on the right track, you'll get run over if you just sit there."—WILL ROGERS

KEY WORDS

advertisement
affirmative action
baby boomers
challenged
demographic information
electronic media
employment agencies
ethnicity
Executive Order 11246
executive search firms
external recruitment
I-9 form
immigrants
Immigration Reform and Control Act
internal recruitment
job candidate
Job Service Center

labor shortage
leasing company
Legally Authorized Worker's Program
nontraditional labor
recruitment
referrals
Rehabilitation Act of 1973
rehabilitation agency
Revised Order No. 4
staff requisition form
temp-help
The Education of Handicapped Children Act
Veteran's Readjustment Assistance Act
warm-body syndrome

INTRODUCTION

I n the introductory chapter of this text we stated that one of your greatest challenges as a manager with human resources responsibilities in "the next chapter" will be to find quality people to fill your vacant job positions. As you will soon read, the demographic changes occurring in the United States today are all indicating the greatest labor shortage of this century. From today forward our human resources will become increasingly scarce. Knowing this, you should begin today planning creative approaches for the recruitment efforts of your hospitality organization. You cannot afford to wait until the crisis peaks. With the census data available from the Bureau of Labor Statistics we know exactly how many people will be available in labor pools five years from now, ten years from now and twenty years from today. Competition for the limited human resources available to us will be incredible! For those hospitality managers who wait, labor will not be available to staff their hospitality operations.

Recruitment needs to be innovative, from the sources of available labor to the methods used, to find the people you need. Hospitality operators no longer have the luxury of having a desk drawer full of applications from eager applicants. Young people no longer stop by our operations every day after school to see if there is a possible opening. The next time you are out running errands notice the number of help wanted signs hanging in fast food operations, pizza delivery chains and grocery stores. These employers have always relied on large numbers of people, ages 16–24, to supply the majority of their work force. And in the 1990s they simply can't find those people. Look to what these operators are doing to recruit human resources, and you will find the most innovative approaches today.

At the conclusion of this chapter you will be able to:
1. Relate the demographic changes occurring in the United States to your role as a manager with human resources responsibilities in the hospitality industry.
2. Distinguish between internal and external recruitment methods.
3. Identify several different pools of nontraditional labor supplies.
4. Develop a plan for incorporating the mature worker and challenged worker into your work force with the assistance of state and federal programs.
5. Understand where recruitment fits into the human resources planning process.
6. Describe a variety of recruitment methods that will assist you in locating human resources in a tight labor market.
7. Maintain an awareness of several alternatives to recruitment.
8. Discuss the legal issues surrounding the recruitment of human resources.
9. Have an open mind that will permit you to change the job structure to accommodate the needs of today's work force.

The Labor Market

Whether you are planning on entering the lodging or food service sector of the hospitality industry, labor shortages are rapidly becoming a predominant factor in human resources planning. To understand why these labor shortages exist, we must turn to information about the changing demographic patterns in the United States.

Age Factors

The hospitality industry has historically relied on human resources between the ages of 16–24 to supply the largest percentage of workers. For teenagers, the hospitality industry has offered numerous types of entry-level jobs. Finding these jobs in hospitality in the '60s and mid-70s was not all that easy. Hopeful teens needed to be persistent, filling out job applications at several restaurants and/or motels if they truly wanted to work. And want to work they did. The jobs in hospitality, especially those that received tips as part of their compensation, were considered excellent opportunities to make money for that car or stereo you had your eye on. With the baby boom peaking, hospitality operators had more applicants than jobs to fill. What a comfortable position for a human resources manager to be in! We could afford to be highly selective in the applicants we chose and if they did not work out or "tow the line," we could let them go, knowing another eager applicant would take their place.

This is no longer the case. And because of this fact, we are running our operations differently. Since 1980, the number of teens in the 16- to 19-year-old age group has shrunk, and by the year 2000 will have declined even farther. According to the Bureau of Labor Statistics, this age group will only account for 16 percent of the total work force as compared to the 20 percent in 1986. Our more affluent lifestyle makes hands-on food jobs less desirable. Fewer teens are walking into our hospitality operations looking for jobs. The drawer full of teenage applications is empty (Figure 5-1).

What other changes have occurred in age group patterns? Traditionally, the 20- to 24-year-old age group has been the second largest in the food service industry. By 1986, that group switched places with the 25- to 34-year-old age group. As the baby boomers are growing up, the age patterns change to reflect their position in society. Currently the 35- to 44-year-old group has started to swell. And by the year 2000, this age group is projected to account for 27.8 percent of the total work force (Table 5-1). Add to that figure employees between the ages of 45 and 54 and you have almost 50 percent of your work force in the year 2000. America is graying, and as it ages so does the age of the work force in the hospitality industry. This aging brings with it new human resources management challenges.

The age differential is magnified by the fewer number of teens who will be entering the work force. The baby boomers, unlike their parents, choose to have smaller (and in some cases, no) families. This translates into a smaller group of people available for the entry-level positions that our industry has historically filled with the teenage group. As we enter the new century, we will also need to be prepared for an increasing number of human resources that will be approaching retirement age (60 and over). An additional trend in American society is earlier retirement.

Figure 5-1. The hospitality work place will contain more employees from nontraditional labor pools in the future.
Courtesy of Marriott Corporation

		Table 5-1. Total Workforce Projections		
Age Group	1986	Percent of Total Workforce	Projected for Year 2000	Percent of Total Workforce
16 to 19	7,926,000	6.7	8,880,000	6.4
20 to 24	15,442,000	13.1	13,751,000	9.9
25 to 34	34,592,000	29.3	31,675,000	22.8
35 to 44	27,233,000	23.2	38,571,000	27.8
45 to 54	17,740,000	15.1	30,552,000	22.0
55 to 64	11,894,000	10.1	12,970,000	9.3
65 and older	3,010,000	2.5	2,394,000	1.8
Total	117,837,000	100.0%	138,775,000	100.0%

Source: U.S. Department of Labor, Bureau of Labor Statistics

Ethnicity

The ethnic composition in our work force will become increasingly diverse. As you learned in chapter 3, your ability to manage cultural diversity will be one of the most important factors in your success as a manager with human resources responsibilities in the hospitality industry. The Hispanic, Black and Asian populations will continue to grow between now and the year 2000 (Table 5-2). This is a result of both immigration patterns and higher birth rates among these ethnic groups. The Bureau of Labor Statistics indicates that out of every ten new hires into the work force, six of those will be members of an ethnic minority group. Certain geographic regions of the country will be more heavily affected than others, but ethnic diversity is no longer confined just to the large metropolitan areas.

The Effect of Women

Women will make up a larger proportion of the work force than ever before. In the hospitality industry, this means that we will be hiring women in job positions traditionally held by men. As we will discuss in future chapters, this will have implications for benefit planning which will assist women with childcare, parental leave and flexible working hours. The hospitality industry is well suited to accommodate the needs of more women in our work force, making women a very viable pool of candidates.

Other Demographic Considerations

The United States unemployment rate hit a low of 5.3 percent in 1988, and in New England the rate dropped to an amazing 3.3 percent. Taking into account that a certain percentage of that group is unemployable, those figures are very, very low. And while that may be good news for the economic health of our country it means that the pool of available labor for vacant hospitality jobs is lower than ever before.

The hospitality industry is not the only industry suffering from these changes in demographics. All service industries from health care

Table 5-2. Ethnic Group Expansion in the Workforce

Ethnic Group	Workforce*	
	1986	2000
Asian and other	3.4	5.7
Blacks	12.7	16.3
Hispanic	8.1	14.1
Total	117.8	138.8

*figures in millions

Source: U.S. Department of Labor, Bureau of Labor Statistics

to grocery store chains are feeling the labor shortage in nurses and checkout clerks. The need for human resources in the hospitality industry is also projected to increase. The lodging industry expects that 800,000 employees will be added to their existing work force by the year 2000.[1] According to the American Hotel and Motel Association, this is an increase of between 25 to 39 percent. Similarly, the food service sector will increase its employment by 36 percent.[2]

Competition is not only more intense for customers, but equally intense for human resources to meet our work force requirements. And all service industries will be competing for the same people. The greatest shortages will be felt in the unskilled, lower paying job positions, in particular the evening part-time shifts that traditionally have been held by our teenage workers. They are often the people who have the first contact with our guests.

Turnover has continued to increase in unskilled and semiskilled job positions. Workers filling these jobs no longer have to tolerate the poor working conditions, long hours, autocratic treatment and low pay that has accompanied these positions. Nor do workers have to accept positions with no advancement opportunities, poor management or little training. Why? Because if you don't satisfy their basic needs, the operation down the street will. Curbing turnover is the major answer to solving the staffing needs of the future.

The Labor Shortage: Solutions

Throughout the remainder of this text we will be focusing on how each of the human resources function areas can contribute to either the attraction or retention of your human resources. *Attract* and *retain* are the two words that will repeatedly be seen in these pages, for as a manager with human resources responsibilities in the hospitality industry, your focus must be directed towards these two goals.

To attract more job applicants here are just some of the methods being used in the hospitality industry today:

- raising wages. With an unemployment rate of 3.3 percent employees will not work for minimum wage.
- using nontraditional sources of labor. A smaller number of available teens means we have to look for labor pools to replace them.
- implementing innovative methods of recruitment. An ad in the help-wanted section of the daily newspaper is no longer sufficient.
- bussing employees to your work location. If there is no labor in your geographic area you will need to look beyond and provide transportation to work (and frequently pay the employees for their transportation time as well).

- improving benefit offerings. Part-time employees have not always been entitled to health and other benefit plans that our full-time employees have been receiving. With a trend towards part-time employment this restriction may need to be reconsidered.
- offering flexible scheduling. According to Dave Murphy, Marriott Corporation, this is the **key** issue. It is not only attractive to the teens who are out there, but it is attractive to single parents, and the mature worker.
- making work fun. The best managers we have ever worked for are those who made the work environment enjoyable. Create a place where your human resources want to be, not have to be.
- putting the "human" back into your management philosophy. People want to work in an environment where others care and are concerned about their welfare. Treat them like the valuable assets that they are to your success.
- improving orientation and training programs. We simply can't throw people into the work force and expect them to survive, let alone succeed. Too often employees are considered a high cost of doing business. They should be considered an asset to increasing sales, *human* resources.

All of these solutions are aimed to either attracting or retaining quality human resources. Table 5-3 shows the percentage of food service managers who have already taken some of these steps to attract human resources to their operations. Treating your human resources as an investment is really what human resources management is all about. Just as you protect your physical assets, you should be equally concerned about the protection and care of your human assets.

Table 5-3. Percentage of Foodservice Managers Responding to Labor Shortages

	Have Already Done	Expect to Do	Have not Done/ Do Not Expect To
Improve training	39%	33%	27%
Increase starting wages	31	23	43
Improve benefits package	18	21	58
Expand recruiting efforts	16	23	59
Increase hours worked for hourly employees	16	17	65

Source: Reprinted from The Foodservice and the Labor Shortage manual published by the National Restaurant Association

The demographic information we have shared with you is intended to raise your awareness of a critical situation facing the hospitality industry. A better understanding of the labor market will enable you to maximize your efforts in attracting and retention. We begin with a look at recruitment in "the next chapter."

Hospitality Recruitment

Recruitment can be defined as the process by which the best qualified applicant for a specified job vacancy is found in compliance with all federal, state and local regulations pertaining to employment. We will identify several methods for conducting the recruitment activity that will include both internal and external searches for potential job candidates. The laws regarding employment are strict, particularly those for hiring non-U.S. citizens. The responsibility for the recruitment of job applicants for employment varies depending on the size of the hospitality organization. In some companies you will be responsible for the recruitment of all nonmanagement positions at the unit level. Other organizations use their human resources department for the recruitment of all job applicants. Regardless of the level at which recruitment is conducted, the methods and legal issues remain unchanged. However, before we can discuss how to recruit, let's first identify several different pools of available, yet perhaps nontraditional, labor supplies.

Sources of Non-Traditional Labor Pools

You have just been given the responsibility for recruitment in your hospitality operation. You are aware that most of the operation's human resources are working on overload because of a lack of staff. A dangerous situation that, according to industry advisor Dave Murphy, leads to management turnover. In order for you to become successful given your new responsibility, you need to fill these vacant positions as quickly as you can but, at the same time, with the right people. How can you do this effectively without falling into the "warm body" syndrome. The warm body syndrome strikes a hospitality operation when the manager simply hires the first warm body that walks in the door and can fill out a job application. With fewer bodies walking in the door, this style of hiring should, thankfully, become the exception in hospitality employment practices.

The key word in our previous definition of recruitment is *qualified*. The job applicants we seek in the recruitment process should be qualified if we ever hope to reduce the high turnover rates we experience in this industry. So if job applications aren't walking in the front doors of our operations, where are you and I going to find them?

Sources of labor supplies may be found from either internal or external sources. Internal sources include those found within your own hospitality organization. External sources of labor are those from outside your organization. We will first discuss internal sources collectively and then examine in detail some of the nontraditional labor pools that are found in external recruitment searches.

Internal Methods. Promotion from within your own organization has numerous advantages over bringing in people from external sources. The most significant advantage is that these human resources are completely familiar with the hospitality operation and organizational culture. Corporate culture is a topic we will discuss at length later in this text, but it is an important consideration in the recruitment of qualified job applicants. An understanding of the hospitality operation, its procedures, its layout and design, along with a knowledge of operating policies, is a great advantage for a job applicant to have. If you have conducted a planned process for crosstraining or if you have been specifically grooming an employee for your job vacancy, the decision to promote or transfer from within is quite obvious.

In most situations, however, vacancies do not occur on such a timely, planned basis, and a decision needs to be made on whether to hire someone from within. If your hospitality organization has a succession plan for both management and nonmanagerial positions, you have some direction in which to look. If it does not, then careful consideration needs to be given to each of the human resources already in your employ. The following are examples of the types of questions you should ask:

- Is the individual, or can the individual, become qualified for the job vacancy? A tradeoff for job knowledge vs company experience often results in a positive match. This person does not need all the skills and knowledge base of the new job if he or she can be trained into it. You might not find someone with 100 percent of the qualities that you are looking for. The qualities that are lacking should be weighed against the advantages of knowing what kind of person he or she is, an awareness and understanding on the person's part of the corporate culture and the support of peers in making the job transfer.
- Is the individual available? What is the nature of the job position he or she will be vacating? How critical is it to the success of your hospitality organization? How difficult will that job position be to fill? Much of this depends upon your long-range employment goals. If your hiring is done to maximize flexibility and you offer ongoing training programs to prepare your human resources for job vacancies, then availability should not be a problem with internal recruitment.

- Is the climate of the hospitality operation such that other human resources will not feel threatened or jealous by job transfers or promotions? If you have established an individual development program which fosters the growth of all human resources in your operation, then internal recruitment should not have a negative affect on your work force. In fact, in the right climate, internal recruitment can raise employee moral by indicating to your staff that you are loyal to them. Sometimes bringing in an employee from the outside can send the message that no one in your employ is worth your consideration. The underlying message that could be seen is that the job the person presently holds is a dead-end position with no opportunity for advancement or change.

If there are no viable job candidates within your hospitality organization, then you will have to turn to external labor sources. In some situations, it is necessary to bring in new blood, even if there are qualified human resources within your organization. When this occurs, it is critical that you keep the lines of communication open with your current work force. It will be important that they understand the necessity to look outside the organization for job applicants. If they do not understand your reasons, you are likely to bring a new job candidate into a hostile work environment thereby minimizing his or her chance to succeed. With all of the dollars you have invested into the recruitment process this can be a costly lesson to learn.

The Mature Worker. Just because the pools of labor we are about to discuss are nontraditional sources of job applicants does not mean that they are unqualified or of a lesser quality than the labor markets we have historically tapped. It makes sense to examine the demographic shifts to see where there will be sources of labor for us to draw upon. With the aging of America the employment of the elderly becomes a natural alternative.

According to labor statistics, there are over 65 million people over the age of 50 in the United States, yet fewer than 25 million are found in the labor force.[3] While some of our human resources are seeking early retirement, others are not and would like very much to remain contributing members of the hospitality work force.

What kinds of attitudes and adjustments do we need to make to become attractive work environments for the mature worker? One thing that we can do as managers is to continue to provide opportunities for career development. Just because our human resources are older does not mean that they have lost their incentive, initiative or motivation for advancement. Human resources at the age of 60 still have 10 to 15 years of productivity. And wouldn't you be eager to hire an individual who you knew would remain in your hospitality organization for 10 years? We think you would.

Providing the opportunity to reduce the number of work hours from full-time to part-time can be an incentive to retain our mature human resources. Frequently, the number of hours a mature worker desires is dependent on Social Security restrictions. Currently, workers are entitled to $6,000 of earnings per year without affecting their Social Security benefits. Many job positions in the hospitality industry are highly conducive to part-time employment, providing opportunities for more mature workers to stay or join the hospitality work force.

The mature individual can also be enticed to continue working by proving him or her with health insurance that supplements Medicare. While an expensive benefit to offer, the expense needs to be weighed against the costs of hiring an inexperienced worker that will require training and still not be as productive.

How else can we attract and retain the mature worker as a hiring resource? By providing more flexibility in schedules, permitting weekends off (when you can supplement your staffing needs with school-age workers) and allowing for extended vacations. Part of the advantage to being retired is that you have the free time to participate in the leisure activities that you previously could not work into your schedule. In recruiting mature workers we need to be sensitive to their needs, knowing that in turn we will have a work force of knowledgeable, loyal human resources. They can be a tremendous networking source to recruit other older workers.

What then are the advantages to recruiting the mature employee? A study of food service managers reported in 1988 found mature workers to be rated highly in the areas of attitude, dependability, emotional maturity, guest relations and quality of work produced. The same managers indicated that the mature worker was not very adaptable or creative.[4] This study certainly dispels some of the myths about recruiting a mature worker. Advantages include:

- an employee who is more likely to take his or her job seriously. These human resources are not using their job as a stepping stone to bigger and better positions. Rather, they are quite content to do a good job within the scope of their job description.
- an employee who is less likely to have behavior problems that might interfere with the quality of work performed. Recreational drugs, young children and night life are not likely to be part of the mature employee's lifestyle.
- an employee whose pattern of sick leave and unexplained absences has already been determined. Sick leave is not more common among the mature workers, but is rather dependent upon the lifetime health of an individual. Thus, while benefit needs may differ from those of the younger human resources, they are no more expense to retain.

- an employee with higher productivity rates. Remember these are an experienced pool of human resources. Their life experiences give them an advantage over younger workers.

The next time you question the quality of a mature work force, remember our industry's success story. Colonel Harlan Sanders, penniless at retirement at age 65, went on to found Kentucky Fried Chicken with his first Social Security check of $105 dollars. At age 73 he became a millionaire by selling his rights for the recipe!

The Disabled. There are many job positions in the hospitality industry that have been satisfactorily filled with disabled, or challenged persons. While similar to hiring the elderly, these potential employees have special needs. The results of hiring the disabled have generally been favorable. Table 5-4 provides you with an explanation of the Marriott

---

Table 5-4. Marriott Corporation Program for Employment of Disabled Persons

Marriott Corporation employs over 6,000 disabled persons. Marriott Corporation's employment program for the disabled is based on the philosophy that an individual identified and properly matched with a job, followed by proper training and support, can significantly benefit both the Company and the employee.

The Program for Employment of Disabled Persons consists of seven specific components at three distinct geographical levels—national, regional and local.

Liaison with Organizations

On the national level, the Company's Corporate Equal Opportunity staff works with a national network of organizations which represent the disabled to learn about the specific nature of disabilities, identify barriers to employment, and learn about new technology which can be used to adapt the work environment to enable the disabled to effectively function. By working with public and private organizations who provide rehabilitation, education, medical care, job training, etc., Marriott representatives communicate the needs of employers. Particular emphasis is given to job seeking skills, career education, curriculum development, and on-the-job training programs. Organizations are selected which represent a total spectrum of the employment life cycle, beginning at the transition from school to work, the middle years including job changing, to that of the older worker.

Job Referral Network

At the regional level, the Company's Human Resource Representatives and Operations Managers seek out referral sources. These representatives work first with the organizations to communicate the Company's business objectives, types of jobs available and skills necessary. Often, on-site visits are arranged so that individuals, such as rehabilitation counselors who refer the disabled job candidates, understand the job site and the job requirements. The regional company representatives,

(continues. . .)

in turn, refer the organizations to specific units where jobs are available. The Company encourages local unit managers to seek out specific referral sources within their communities.

Job Match

Critical to the success of the employment relationship is the proper job match— matching the individual job seeker's skills and abilities with the actual job require- ments. In the case of the disabled worker, a trained specialist who understands both the charactertistics of the disabled person and the job requirements can serve as the translator and consultant to identify job accommodations, training and support, and supervisory requirements.

101

Management Training

The Marriott Corporate EEO department designs and delivers management train- ing programs which outline laws and regulations which apply to the disabled. These training programs address techniques in identifying, hiring, and supervising the disabled. Most importantly, these programs seek to change attitudinal barriers which impede the employment of the disabled. Often accurate information to managers about disabilities and identification of networks to the disabled are the best weapons to counteract stereotypes and remove barriers.

Employment Training

Once successful job matches are made at the local level, the Marriott managers implement the standardized company training programs. However, in conjunction with the referral sources, managers learn to modify and/or augment the training programs to maximize successful job training.

Communications/Recognition Programs

The Company uses its in-house communications vehicles, such as *Marriott World*, which is distributed to each of the 200,000 employees, to praise and recognize managers who have hired the disabled, many of whom have won local, state, or national awards. These publications feature articles highlighting success stories which describe how referral sources, Marriott managers, and disabled employees have worked together to make job matches work and succeed. It is the belief of the Company that such articles inform and inspire other Marriott managers in other locations to undertake similar activities.

Corporate Giving

The Corporate Giving Program selects organizations, whose needs meets the corporate giving criteria, to receive monetary and inkind support. In organizations which serve the disabled, the Corporation supports those education and employ- ment related programs corresponding to the basic theme of helping others prepare, gain, and retain employment. The Corporation participates in the United Way of America Giving Program which also helps organizations directly serving disabled individuals as well as organizations which conduct research and reha- bilitation of disabled individuals.

It is through this multifaceted, geographically dispersed program that Marriott Corporation seeks to identify, recruit, hire, and train the disabled worker.

Courtesy of Marriott Corporation

Corporation Program for Disabled Persons. Many other companies such as Friendly's, Burger King and Radisson Hotel Corporation have similar programs. These hospitality organizations have recognized the benefit to recruiting this nontraditional source of labor.

What should you keep in mind when developing and implementing such a program in the hospitality organization you work for? Disabilities may be of either a mental or physical nature. In most areas, there will be a government or nonprofit rehabilitation agency that can assist you in planning a specific program for the needs of your operation in conjunction with the needs of the disabled in your area. You will need to prepare a very detailed list of the job tasks that you need the employee to perform. This assists the agency in matching your organization with a suitable employee. Your state's unemployment office can refer you to an appropriate agency. A list of state rehabilitation offices has been provided (Table 5-5). The National Restaurant Association will also assist its members in locating agencies that will help you in the recruitment and placement of the disabled.

In addition to recruitment assistance, the federal government provides reimbursement dollars to employers who establish on-the-job training programs for disabled employees. This is to assist employers with the extra expenses incurred in training employees with special needs. Different states have set aside special funds in addition to that provided by the federal government. It pays to investigate what reimbursements you might be entitled to when implementing recruitment programs for the challenged.

One of the improvements you might need to make in your hospitality operation is to increase accessibility. This can have additional benefits that include making the operation barrier free for both your mature workers and your disabled patrons. Legal requirements such as the Rehabilitation Act of 1973 mandated equal rights for all disabled individuals. The veterans from the Vietnam War have been protected by the Veterans Readjustment Assistance Act, 1974. The Education of All Handicapped Children Act guarantees education for every disabled child,

Table 5-5. State Vocational Rehabilitation Offices

ALABAMA: Div. of Rehab. (205) 281-8780
ALASKA: Div. of Voc. Rehab. (907) 465-2814
ARIZONA: Rehab. Services Admin., Depart. of Economic Security (602) 255-3332
ARKANSAS: Rehab. Services Div., Dept. of Human Service (501) 371-2571
CALIFORNIA: Dept. of Rehab. (916) 445-3971
COLORADO: Div. of Rehab., Dept. of Social Services (303) 294-2804
CONNECTICUT: Div. of Voc. Rehab., Dept. of Educ. (203) 566-4440
DELAWARE: Div. of Voc. Rehab. (302) 571-2850
DISTRICT OF COLUMBIA: Rehab. Services Admin., Dept. of Human Services (202) 727-3227

(continues...)

FLORIDA: Office of Voc. Rehab., Dept. of Health & Rehab. Services (904) 488-6210

GEORGIA: Div. of Rehab. Services, Dept. of Human Services (404) 894-6670

HAWAII: Div. of Voc. Rehab. (808) 548-4769

IDAHO: Div. of Voc. Rehab (208) 334-3390

ILLINOIS: Dept. of Rehab. Services (217) 782-2093

INDIANA: Ind. Rehab. Services (317) 232-1139

IOWA: Rehab. Educ. Services Branch, Dept. of Public Instruction (515) 281-4311

KANSAS: Dept. of Social Services & Rehab. (913) 296-3911

KENTUCKY: Dept. of Educ., Bureau of Rehab. Services (502) 564-4440

LOUISIANA: Div. of Voc. Rehab., Dept of Health & Human Resources (504) 342-2285

MAINE: Bureau of Rehab. Services, Dept. of Human Services (207) 289-2266

MARYLAND: Div. of Voc. Rehab., Dept. of Educ. (301) 659-2294

MASSACHUSETTS: Rehab. Commission (617) 727-2172

MICHIGAN: Bureau of Voc. Rehab., Dept. of Educ. (517) 373-0683

MINNESOTA: Div. of Voc. Rehab., Dept. of Jobs & Training (612) 296-1822

MISSISSIPPI: Voc. Rehab. Div. (601) 354-6825

MISSOURI: Div. of Voc. Rehab., Dept. of Educ. (314) 751-3251

MONTANA: Rehab. Services Div., Dept. of Social & Rehab. Services (406) 444-3434

NEBRASKA: Div. of Rehab. Services, Dept. of Educ. (402) 471-2961

NEVADA: Rehab. Div., Dept. of Human Resources (702) 885-4440

NEW HAMPSHIRE: Div. of Voc. Rehab., Dept. of Educ. (603) 271-3121

NEW JERSEY: Div. of Voc. Rehab. Services (609) 292-5987

NEW YORK: Office of Voc. Rehab., Educ. Dept. (518) 474-2714

NEW MEXICO: Div. of Voc. Rehab., Dept. of Educ. (505) 827-3500

NORTH CAROLINA: Div. of Voc. Rehab. Services, Dept. of Human Resources (919) 733-3364

NORTH DAKOTA: Div. of Voc. Rehab. (701) 224-2907

OHIO: Rehab. Services Commission (614) 438-1210

OKLAHOMA: Div. of Rehab., Dept. of Human Services (405) 424-4311 ext. 2840

OREGON: Div. of Voc. Rehab., Dept. of Human Resources (503) 378-3850

PENNSYLVANIA: Office of Voc. Rehab. (717) 787-5244

RHODE ISLAND: Voc. Rehab. Services, Dept. of Human Services (401) 421-7005

SOUTH CAROLINA: Voc. Rehab. Dept. (803) 758-3237

SOUTH DAKOTA: Dept. of Voc. Rehab. (605) 773-3125

TENNESSEE: Div. of Rehab. Services, Dept. of Human Services (615) 741-2030

TEXAS: Rehab. Commission (512) 445-8108

UTAH: Div. of Rehab. Services, Office of Educ. (801) 533-5991

VERMONT: Voc. Rehab. Div. (802) 241-2189

VIRGINA: Dept. of Rehab. Services (804) 257-0316

WASHINGTON: Div. of Voc. Rehab., Dept. of Social & Health Services (206) 753-0293

WEST VIRGINIA: Div. of Voc. Rehab., Board of Voc. Educ. (304) 766-4601

WISCONSIN: Div. of Voc. Rehab., Div. of Health & Social Services (608) 266-2168

WYOMING: Div. of Voc. Rehab., Dept. of Health & Social Services (307) 777-7385

Courtesy of Lodging Magazine, January 1989

103

meaning that the challenged population in "the next chapter" will be better educated than ever before. All of this translates to a larger proportion of challenged employees in the labor force. And with the predicted labor shortages, this potential labor pool is being used in hospitality organizations throughout the United States. Even with all the efforts over half of the challenged people capable of working still remain jobless.[5]

104

The Immigrant Populace. Even though we have already discussed the importance of managing cultural, ethnic and racial diversity, it is essential that we don't loose sight of this growing segment of potential labor. This is especially true for hospitality organizations that make Multicultural Management part of their company wide philosophies. Ethnic groups will not just be found in border states or metropolitan areas. Throughout the country, rural and urban regions will experience a diversity of cultures and ethnic composition.

The Immigration and Naturalization Service will assist you in locating legal immigrants through its Legally Authorized Worker's (LAW) program. This program was in response to the Immigration Reform and Control Act that was signed into law in 1986.

As with other nontraditional sources of labor, the immigrants you recruit may require special assistance. One of the most obvious concerns is the ability to speak English. There are several alternatives to this problem. One is to place non-English speaking human resources in work groups with others who are bilingual. We feel that this should be a short-term solution to a long term problem. Many hospitality organizations are finding that the best solution is to provide instructional classes in the English language for these valuable human resources. The structure to these programs varies. Some companies provide the instruction at no cost, others pay employee wages while they attend class. Some companies make the instruction part of their shift hours, others require the employees to take the classes at times that do not interfere with the work schedule.

Speaking English is a skill, one that native Americans take for granted. If any of you have visited abroad in a country where you did not speak the language, you know firsthand how frustrating the experience can be. No matter how intelligent, capable or skilled you are, without the ability to communicate, you feel like the most ignorant person in the world. If we can teach human resources to perform job tasks that they are not skilled at, then why can we not also educate our human resources to effectively communicate?

Other Alternative Sources. Women have become an increasingly important component of the hospitality work force. In the early 1970s, rarely did you see a female working in the back of the house; that environment consisted solely of men. Today, there are more women working in both the front and the back of the house in hospitality operations than ever before.

The demographic data supports the increase of women in the work force. As more and more families depend on two-paycheck incomes, as women become better educated and trained and as the childcare service in the country improves, it is easier to attract women to your labor force. These women make up the greatest percent of part-time employees in the hospitality industry. Accommodating part-time schedules for young mothers that want to spend time with both work and family is relatively easy due to the natural peaks and valleys of our business day. Oftentimes, our operations become more labor efficient when work schedules are supplemented with part-time human resources.

Part-time employees include more than just women. Flextime and job sharing (where two employees share the same full-time job position) serve to attract moonlighters, single parents, individuals seeking supplemental income and students in both high schools and colleges.

Other viable alternative sources of labor include:

- Employees in transition:
    - retirees
    - retired military (veterans)
    - ex-offenders
- on-call human resources
- relatives of present human resources

Table 5-6 shows the use of nontraditional sources of labor in the hospitality industry.

Table 5-6. The Utilization of Non-Traditional Labor Sources

	Successful	Unsuccessful	Never Tried
older workers	34	4	17
housewives	30	4	21
displaced housewives	28	4	23
physically handicapped	26	5	24
mentally handicapped	26	8	21
retired military	23	7	25
immigrants	20	3	32
former industrial workers	9	9	37
adopt-a-school	9	4	42
prisoners	5	13	37

Courtesy of Council on Hotel, Restaurant, and Institutional Education

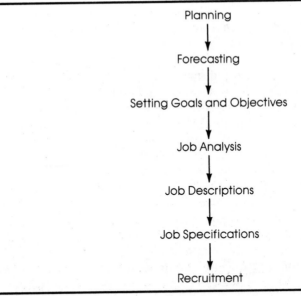

Figure 5-2. Recruitment's Role in the Planning Process

The Role of Recruitment in the Planning Process

If we are to attract the individuals who possess the education, skills and experience to perform the job tasks that our vacant job positions require, we must rely on our job descriptions and job specifications. Figure 5-2 shows you where recruitment falls in the human resources planning process that we initiated in Chapter 2.

All too frequently, managers with human resources responsibilities view recruitment merely as the process of obtaining job candidates without considering that these activities also need to be carefully planned. When developing a recruitment program for your hospitality organization you must consider your needs. As you recall, this is determined in the skill inventories. The gap between the human resources needed to fill your job positions and the number you currently have in your inventory is the total number that you must recruit.

The specific procedures for recruitment should be developed into a written policy. A written policy can often save you when it comes to employee-filed discrimination suits. Your selection is largely dependent upon the size of the hospitality operation. Usually, the department that has a job vacancy issues a hiring requisition to the human resources department (Table 5-7) indicating that position needs to be filled. The job descriptions and specifications for that job position are reviewed with the human resources manager to ensure accuracy. After gaining a full knowledge and understanding of what the job position entails, recruitment takes place.

If internal sources of recruitment are to be used, the job is posted within the hospitality organization. There needs to be a limit on the number of days the job vacancy will be posted. Methods of external recruitment will be discussed next.

Table 5-7 Crystal Gateway Marriott Hotel Job Requisition

DEPT. _____   POSITION _____
MANAGER _____   HOURS _____
DATE OF REQUEST _____   WAGE RANGE _____
DATE NEEDED _____   NUMBER REQUIRED _____
_____ REPLACEMENT _____   _____ ADDITION TO STAFF
        (NAME OF TERM. EMPLOYEE)
INTERVIEW AVAILABILITY:

_____
_____

AUTHORIZATION OF EXECUTIVE COMMITTEE MEMBER: _____

SPECIFIC
REQUIREMENTS: _____
_____
_____

APPLICANT REFERRED: DATE: HIRED OR REJECTED:

1. _____   _____   _____
2. _____   _____   _____
3. _____   _____   _____
4. _____   _____   _____
5. _____   _____   _____
6. _____   _____   _____

SOURCES CONTACTED:

1. _____
2. _____
3. _____
4. _____
5. _____

ADS PLACED:

1. _____
2. _____
3. _____
4. _____   _____

Courtesy of Marriott Corporation

External Recruitment Methods

So far in the recruitment process we have verified the accuracy of our job descriptions and specifications and discovered that none of our human resources is qualified or interested in the job vacancy. We now turn to the variety of external sources we need to examine. One of the things we will be looking for is the relevancy of the method we select to the type of job position that is vacant. Geographically, academically, from the standpoint of experience level and pay structure, we need to determine the best approach for attracting candidates with the job specifications our vacant job requires.

Advertisement. The oldest, but not necessarily the most effective recruitment method, is advertising. The key to advertising is knowing when and where to run an ad that will be viewed by the greatest number of qualified readers. This is not an easy task. Most hospitality organizations rely on experts in the field of advertising to help them design an ad that will appeal to the ideal job candidate. Recruitment advertising agencies are not a cost to the employer. They receive their commission from the newspaper. Most hospitality managers do not have the expertise required to target an ad to the intended audience.

Effective advertising requires creativity and market research. The goal for recruitment advertising is to provide your hospitality organization with a competitive edge over other hospitality organizations in attracting the right calibre of human resources, whether the job vacancy is for a dishwasher or unit manager. Advertising objectives might include capturing the image your company wants to portray, establishing an identity with the products and services you offer within a geographic region, letting people know what kind of an employer you are with respect to benefits, promoting career opportunities or attempting to overcome a negative public image of the hospitality industry. Advertising also must conform to government regulations regarding discrimination.

In developing recruitment advertising always keep in mind what the ideal job candidate would look like and write all copy to attract that person. Position your copy in sources that the ideal candidate is likely to read. Be creative with your advertising strategy and experiment with brochures, posters, radio and events, as well as newspapers. Examples of advertising used by Marriott Corporation to attract hourly employees to work for the company are seen in Figure 5-3. Notice how the company uses its benefit package to attract reservationists. Figure 5-4 was used in a direct mail campaign to attract "mommy" to the work place.

While newspapers are still the most popular vehicle for recruitment advertising, in "the next chapter" look for electronic media to change traditional advertising methods. And when hiring an advertising agency, look for those that provide a maximum number of services such as market research, art design and employee referral, and has a good track record attracting the type of candidates you need for your hospitality organization.

Figure 5-3. Advertisement, Marriott Corporation
Courtesy of Marriott Corporation; produced by AdVantage Advertising, Inc.

Figure 5-4. Direct Mail Campaign, Marriott Corporation
Courtesy of Marriott Corporation; produced by AdVantage Advertising, Inc.

Referrals.   Referrals are oftentimes the best source for locating potential job applicants. Referrals come from a number of sources. Employee referrals are individuals recommended to you by an employee. In most cases, employees will only recommend a person if they feel he or she would like to work with them. Some hospitality organizations have instituted an employee referral system that rewards employees with cash bonuses for recommending a person that is hired and stays with the organization for a specified period of time (generally 90 days). Some companies offer cash incentives, others offer gifts and prizes. For these systems to be most effective they need to be publicized by posters and flyers enclosed in paycheck envelopes. Some companies present the awards at a luncheon, again communicating the advantages of the referral system to all employees.

Referrals may also stem from personal friends, suppliers or other industry professionals. If you work in a large hospitality organization, check with other local managers to see if they have some good applications on file. Your suppliers visit numerous accounts and may know of individuals who are looking for a position like the one you have vacant. Think about other organizations in your location that might be able to refer people to you such as the Boy's or Girl's Clubs, YMCA or YWCA, clergy or youth organizations such as 4-H clubs. While it takes time and effort to create effective working relationships with community organizations, they can be of enormous assistance when they understand the type of individuals your hospitality organization is looking for.

Schools.   Schools include more than universities and high schools. Vocational and two-year programs should also be considered. Many high schools hold job fairs that are excellent opportunities not only to attract the workers you need to fulfill your immediate needs, but also to promote the hospitality industry as a viable career choice. Many colleges and universities will provide you with an opportunity to recruit on their campuses. Mailings could also be sent to these programs in an effort to attract their students. Contact should be maintained with program heads and faculty members. Opportunities to speak in class might also be available. If you have employees who attend these schools, make sure the other students you talk to know who they are. They can serve as excellent representatives of your company.

| INDUSTRY EXPERTS SPEAK | Dave Murphy relates one of his favorite recruiting stories: "While interviewing at a major HRI school, my schedule was late by ten minutes. When approaching the next interviewee, I was told "We had better get started," as I had detained him ten minutes! Once we were inside the interview room, I was about to apologize for the late start and indicate that he would be assured of his allotted thirty minutes, when he replied, "We |

only have fifteen minutes left and I should ask some meaningful questions." At that point, I replied that we had a long list of students who really want to work for our company and that his behavior indicated that he was not seriously interested. I suggested that he leave to make room for someone who appreciated the opportunity, and he left in a huff to "report" me to the school.

Five years later, after giving a presentation to hundreds of people at the National Restaurant Show, I was answering questions for those who lingered afterward. As people began to leave, I noticed a man pacing back and forth at the rear of the room. Finally, when all others had left, he approached me and introduced himself as a professor of hotel management who had an apology for me! I had no idea what he was talking about. He then identified himself as the student who, five years earlier, had been so out of line in the interview. It had been on his mind ever since, and when he saw my name on the program, this was his chance to ease his mind"!

Employment Agencies. The U.S. Department of Employment Security supervises a national computer network of job openings. Its major goal is to assist individuals drawing unemployment compensation in finding jobs. The federal government also sponsors training programs for youths, veterans and women. The Job Service Center is the state agency that assists unemployed individuals in locating job openings. Job vacancies that you have may be listed with these agencies. Some offer assistance in screening potential job candidates. You should also investigate the services provided by local government agencies. A phone call to the county court house and/or city hall will direct you to the appropriate departments.

In addition to government agencies, there are professional employment agencies who will locate potential job applicants for a fee. Individuals seeking employment list their names with these services. You, as an employer, pay a fee to obtain names of qualified candidates. All of these agencies operate a little differently. Some only charge a fee if you actually hire someone they have referred to you. Frequently, these agencies act as middlemen and conduct the interview. Sometimes even wage negotiations between you and the potential job candidate are handled. Others simply refer individuals to you that meet job specification qualifications and charge a fee for the potential candidates they refer to you. Many of these firms sponsor career nights that attract many job candidates.

You must be sure to do a careful screening of the agency under consideration to make sure that it can provide you with the type of individuals you will need. Don't hesitate to conduct reference checks on the agency and make sure that it fully understands the nature of your specific operation. Some hospitality organizations have specific policies pertaining to the use of private employment firms. Make sure that your actions conform to your organization's policy.

Executive search firms specialize in locating professional and management job candidates. These firms typically have a minimum salary base that they will recruit for. The services they provide are extensive, leaving you only with the tasks of final interview and the hiring decision. Often a financial commitment is made up front. Since their job is to fill an executive position, it is critical that the search firm you select thoroughly understands your hospitality operation as well as the job qualifications.

Alternatives to Recruitment

There are many considerations which you need to take into account before the decision can be made to hire human resources for your hospitality organization. The growth and career advancement of your human resources is one of the most important influences on recruiting. If you have established a good program for individual development, then you expect your human resources to progress through the career ladder. This means that the entry level positions are the ones that need to be filled most frequently. When recruiting you are looking for people who have the capability to be promoted, and must take that into consideration when planning your recruitment efforts. You must not, however, expect all your human resources to want to move up the corporate ladder. Some individuals might be perfectly content simply being the best dishwasher they can be. As the manager with human resources responsibilities, you must be aware of the potential advancement capabilities and desires of your work force.

Employee turnover also affects recruitment planning. As you have already learned, forecasting assists you in estimating the number of job vacancies you will have so that you can be better prepared.

The projected growth of your hospitality organization will also affect the need for recruitment. Acquisitions, mergers, expansions and new product and service offerings all equate to a need for more employees. Plans for recruitment must take organizational growth into consideration.

Recruiting individuals either externally or internally is not your only alternative for filling vacant job positions. Some hospitality organizations are relying on companies which provide temp-help. Temporary help is advantageous to companies that have short-term staffing needs. Caterers and seasonal operations are two examples of organizations that can maximize the advantages of temp-help services.

These companies will lease trained human resources for a day, week or even for several months. The advantage for you is that you can keep your permanent staff down to a minimum, while filling positions that you cannot afford to staff on a continual basis. Bookkeeping advantages abound. The temporary-help company writes all the paychecks. You write one check in place of several. Leasing companies can frequently afford to offer better benefit packages than can small hospitality operations. Benefit plans such as medical are proportionally cheaper per person and decrease in cost when you have a large number of employees. The more individuals who ascribe to the plan the least the cost per individual.

When you consider a leasing company, you must carefully check its financial stability, as well as the quality of human resources it will be leasing to you. The training that it provides must match the standards of your hospitality organization, as your reputation, not the leasing company's is at stake. There are professional organizations that monitor their members for financial stability and accountability. It is a good idea to make sure that the leasing company you deal with belongs to such a certifying organization.

Recruitment and the Law

We have already mentioned two pieces of federal legislation: The Veterans Readjustment Act, 1974 requires government contractors (such as Marriott Corporation) to take affirmative action in the hiring and promotion of the disabled and Vietnam-era veterans. The Rehabilitation Act of 1973 requires government contractors to take affirmative action to prevent discrimination in the employment of mentally and physically disabled persons. Just what exactly is meant by the words "affirmative action"?

Affirmative action programs and requirements are a result of past difficulties in enforcing the civil rights policies. Executive Order 11246 (1965, amended in 1968 to include sex) states that any employer signing a government contract agrees it will not discriminate on the basis of race, creed, national origin or sex. Revised Order No. 4 (1971) requires employers receiving government contracts of $50,000 or more with a work force of at least 50 employees to develop and maintain a written affirmative action program to ensure minorities and women are hired at a rate that their availability in the work force would suggest.

Thus, Executive Order 11246 encompasses two concepts, nondiscrimination and affirmative action. Nondiscrimination requires the elimination of all existing discriminatory conditions. Affirmative action requires that you as the employer move to ensure employment neutrality with regard to race, color, religion, sex and national origin. Affirmative action requires that you make additional efforts to recruit, employ and promote qualified members of groups covered under the order that you have formerly excluded, even if that exclusion was not due to discriminatory action on your part.

Revised Order No.4 requires you to determine if minorities and women are being underutilized in your hospitality organization and, if that is the case, that you develop specific goals and timetables designed to overcome the underutilization. This then becomes part of your affirmative action program. These goals and timetables are at the heart of the effort to monitor the affirmative action procedures. Critics have argued that goals are simply another name for quotas. Supporters argue that goals and timetables are merely management tools to monitor the progress of affirmative action.

The Carnegie Report issued in 1975 identified several features of a formal recruitment effort. Included in these recommendations was the idea that all recruitment announcements should state that the company is an equal opportunity or affirmative action employer. It also suggested that interviewers include women and minority group members whenever possible, and that there should be a specific waiting period between the announcement of a vacancy and the selection of the job candidate.

The Immigration Reform and Control Act of 1986 makes the hiring of undocumented employees illegal. The act further specifies that it is the employer's responsibility to verify the legal immigration status of all employees hired since November 7, 1986. You are not required, however, to verify the authenticity of the documents. We suggest that you retain copies of all documents that you check as part of the employee's personnel file. This will serve as proof that you have inspected all immigration documents. The now famous I-9 form (Figure 5-5) that you must sign states that these hiring documents have been seen by you. Documents that serve to verify citizenship include a U.S. passport, certificate of U.S. citizenship, green card, foreign passport with Immigration and Naturalization Service (INS) stamp authorizing the individual to work, certificate of naturalization, U.S. birth certificate with picture ID or social security number with picture ID.

Conclusion

The National Restaurant Association states that the food service sector of the hospitality industry could be short 1.1 million workers by the year 1995. While hospitality organizations were once accustomed to selecting their human resources from piles of applications, the baby boomers have forced us to become more aggressive and innovative in our recruitment methods. Recruiting the labor we need has become very competitive, not only among other hospitality organizations, but among all service industries. That means that we need to become more flexible in our recruitment practices.

Recruitment is a necessary function in every hospitality organization. If you can't staff your operations, you can't open your doors for business. The human resources hiring process begins with recruiting. As a manager with human resources responsibilities it will be necessary for

EMPLOYMENT ELIGIBILITY VERIFICATION (Form I-9)

1 **EMPLOYEE INFORMATION AND VERIFICATION:** (To be completed and signed by employee.)

Name: (Print or Type) Last	First	Middle	Birth Name

Address: Street Name and Number	City	State	ZIP Code

Date of Birth (Month/Day/Year)	Social Security Number

I attest, under penalty of perjury, that I am (check a box):

☐ 1. A citizen or national of the United States.
☐ 2. An alien lawfully admitted for permanent residence (Alien Number A _____) .
☐ 3. An alien authorized by the Immigration and Naturalization Service to work in the United States (Alien Number A _____ ,
or Admission Number _____ , expiration of employment authorization, if any _____) .

I attest, under penalty of perjury, the documents that I have presented as evidence of identity and employment eligibility are genuine and relate to me. I am aware that federal law provides for imprisonment and/or fine for any false statements or use of false documents in connection with this certificate.

Signature	Date (Month/Day/Year)

PREPARER/TRANSLATOR CERTIFICATION (To be completed if prepared by person other than the employee). I attest, under penalty of perjury, that the above was prepared by me at the request of the named individual and is based on all information of which I have any knowledge.

Signature	Name (Print or Type)
Address (Street Name and Number)	City	State	Zip Code

2 **EMPLOYER REVIEW AND VERIFICATION:** (To be completed and signed by employer.)

Instructions:
Examine one document from List A and check the appropriate box, **OR** examine one document from List B **and** one from List C and check the appropriate boxes. Provide the **Document Identification Number** and **Expiration Date** for the document checked.

List A Documents that Establish Identity and Employment Eligibility	List B Documents that Establish Identity	and	List C Documents that Establish Employment Eligibility
☐ 1. United States Passport ☐ 2. Certificate of United States Citizenship ☐ 3. Certificate of Naturalization ☐ 4. Unexpired foreign passport with attached Employment Authorization ☐ 5. Alien Registration Card with photograph	☐ 1. A State-issued driver's license or a State-issued I.D. card with a photograph, or information, including name, sex, date of birth, height, weight, and color of eyes. (Specify State)_____ ☐ 2. U.S. Military Card ☐ 3. Other (Specify document and issuing authority) _____		☐ 1. Original Social Security Number Card (other than a card stating it is not valid for employment) ☐ 2. A birth certificate issued by State, county, or municipal authority bearing a seal or other certification ☐ 3. Unexpired INS Employment Authorization Specify form # _____
Document Identification # _____	*Document Identification* # _____		*Document Identification* # _____
Expiration Date (if any) _____	*Expiration Date (if any)* _____		*Expiration Date (if any)* _____

CERTIFICATION: I attest, under penalty of perjury, that I have examined the documents presented by the above individual, that they appear to be genuine and to relate to the individual named, and that the individual, to the best of my knowledge, is eligible to work in the United States.

Signature	Name (Print or Type)	Title
Employer Name	Address	Date

Form I-9 (05/07/87)
OMB No. 1115-0136

U.S. Department of Justice
Immigration and Naturalization Service

Figure 5-5. Example of I-9 form
Courtesy of U.S. Department of Justice, Immigration and Naturalization Service

116

you to develop a plan for your recruitment strategy. While there is no one best strategy for all hospitality operations, with proper identification of viable labor pools and effective utilization of recruitment methods, we can accomplish our goal of locating qualified job applicants when we need them.

The employment process for your hospitality organization begins with recruitment. We now turn to a discussion on selection, hiring and placement to complete the employment function of human resources management.

CASE PROBLEM 5

Case Problem 5-1

118

You are the manager of a fast-food operation in the suburbs of a town in the Midwest and have been finding it increasingly difficult to attract the human resources necessary to run your operation. In the past several years you have been able to rely upon the high school students to fill your shifts from 3:00 to closing and on the weekends.

You feel there are two predominant reasons for no longer being able to rely on the teenage work force. The first is that due to increasing competition for teenage labor, such as grocery and retail stores in the area, fast food doesn't seem to be an exciting job anymore. Your first challenge is how to make jobs in the fast food industry seem more exciting and appealing to the teenage labor market. What are some of the things you might do to stimulate their interest, not only in a part-time job in your operation while they are going to school, but as a potential career opportunity?

The second reason you feel that you can no longer depend on the teenage labor force is that the size of this labor market is decreasing in size, not only in your geographical area, but all over the United States. Realizing this you need to develop an action plan of alternative sources of labor that you could seek through your recruitment efforts. Based upon your knowledge of the geographic location of this fast-food operation, develop a list of alternative sources of labor that might be available to you.

In addition, you will want to identify what *you* feel are the advantages and disadvantages of each of these labor sources. What labor pools do you feel will work out best for your particular operation?

Case Problem 5-2

You are the general manager of an economy lodging property located in the South at an interstate exchange outside a major city. You have been with this company for four years and the general manager at this particular property for six months. The property has 120 rooms with no foodservice facilities. Since this property is part of a national chain there is some name recognition. The management personnel are recruited by the corporate office while the recruitment of human resources for hourly positions is conducted at the property. This means that it is up to you, the general manager, to develop a recruitment campaign for your property.

What do you feel would be the best method of reaching your target populations? The positions you need to recruit for include housekeepers, front-office staff, and laundry room attendants (You have an in-house laundry system.). You have a head housekeeper who has been at the property since its opening, and you do not foresee a replacement being needed. Nor are you concerned at the present time about the one position your property has for a maintenance person, as that individual has also been on board since prior to opening.

Since your property is located on a major interchange, which is a major travel route, the business is somewhat seasonal with a heavier traffic flow during the winter months as opposed to the summer months. Your occupancy rate in winter is 97% and 85% in summer. In winter you supplement your full-time staff with part-time human resources.

As part of your overall human resources plan, you need to formulate a strategy for recruitment. What methods would you use to recruit the human resources you need? Would it be more appropriate to use internal or external recruitment? Or, would the utilization of both methods be necessary? What might be some possible alternatives to recruitment that might be used for your property? Give specific examples of the types of external or internal methods you would use along with the reasons you selected them.

119

RECOMMENDED READING

Doering, M., Rhodes, S. and Schuster, M. 1983. *The Aging Worker Research and Recommendations* Beverly Hills: Sage Publications.

Driskell, P. C. 1986. Recruitment a manager's checklist for labor leasing. *Personnel Journal* 65, (10): 108–112.

Fleisher, G. M. 1988. Temporaries: a sure bet in uncertain times. *The Office* 108, (2): 44, 46.

LoPresto, R. 1986. Ethical recruiting. *Personnel Administrator* 31, (11): 90–91.

Madison, R. and Knudson-Fields, B. 1987. The law and employee-employer relationships: the hiring process. *Management Solutions* 32 (2): 12–20.

McCool, A. C. 1988. Older workers: understanding, reaching and using this important labor resource effectively in the hospitality industry. *Hospitality Education and Research Journal* 12, (2): 365–376.

National Restaurant Association. 1988. *A 1988 Update: Foodservice and the Labor Shortages* Washington, D.C.: The National Restaurant Association.

Personnel Journal. 1986. Don't follow the leader. *Personnel Journal* 65, (8): 70–72.

Peters, J. 1987. Alternative labor pools. *Restaurant Business* 86, (13): 183–184.

Taylor A. R. 1984. *How to Select and Use An Executive Search Firm* New York; McGraw-Hill Book Company.

Winfield, F. E. 1988. *The Work and Family Sourcebook* New York: Panel Publishers, Inc.

120

END NOTES

1. Martin, Frances, "Staed Speaks Out on Labor Shortages, Mergers," *Hotels and Restaurants International,* 23, (1989, 1): 13–14.
2. Greenberg, Laurence, "Foodservice Employment to Top 11 million by 2000," *Restaurants USA,* 8, (1988, 4): 42–44.
3. Peters, Jim, "Alternative Labor Pools," *Restaurant Business* 86, (1987, 13): 183–187.
4. De Micco, Frederick J., and Reid, Robert, "Older Workers: A Hiring Resource for the Hospitality Industry," *Cornell Quarterly,* 29, (1988, 1): 56–61.
5. Peters, Jim, "Alternative Labor Pools," *Restaurant Business,* 86, (1987, 13): 183–187.

DISCUSSION QUESTIONS

1. What is recruitment? Explain recruitment's relationship to human resources planning and analysis functions.
2. Describe the effect of demographic changes in American society on the recruitment of human resources for the hospitality industry. What actions can you take in a tight labor market?
3. Identify four viable labor pools that might be tapped for recruitment purposes. Discuss the advantages and the disadvantages of recruiting each of the four groups you identified.
4. List several advantages of recruiting internal sources. List several advantages from recruiting from external labor sources. Which do you prefer? Why?
5. Identify and describe at least six methods of recruiting.
6. Explain affirmative action and how it affects your job of recruiting qualified candidates for job vacancies.
7. Describe the use of temporary help agencies. When might you use their services as a manager with human resources responsibilities in the hospitality industry?
8. How do you feel about recruiting former employees and job applicants? Defend your position.

CHAPTER 6

SELECTION, HIRING, AND PLACEMENT

INDUSTRY
ADVISOR

Cathy Conner
Manager/Recruiting, Gilbert/Robinson, Inc.

"The closest to perfection a person ever comes is when he fills out a job application form."—STANLEY J. RANDALL

KEY WORDS

Age Discrimination in
   Employment Act of 1967
applicant flow log
Bona Fide Occupational
   Qualification (BFOQ)
employment application
Equal Employment Opportunity
   (EEO)
harassment
hiring
integrity tests
intelligence tests
interview
job applicant
job candidate
job offer
job vacancy
negligent hiring

personality test
placement
preemployment testing
Pregnancy Discrimination Act of
   1978
probationary period
reference check
Rehabilitation Act of 1973
screening
secondary interviews
selection
semistructured interview
skill tests
structured interview
Title VII; Civil Rights Acts, 1964
unstructured interview
Veterans Readjustment
   Assistance Act of 1974

INTRODUCTION

Employment policies are designed to meet the needs of the hospitality organization and the people who are affected by them. The organization's policies provide answers to employment questions, so it is important that the content be communicated to all members of the hospitality organization to whom they apply. Policies must be developed that pertain to proper selection, hiring and placement, and individuals in your organization need to be identified that will take part in the employment process.

The employment process varies from hospitality organization to hospitality organization. Each establishment must decide the policies and procedures that best serve the mission statement of the enterprise. Due to the very high turnover ratios in the hospitality industry (fast food operations have reported ratios as high as 400 percent), the proper screening of job applicants has taken on a new importance. Oftentimes, the individuals who leave our operations should never have been hired in the first place. Choosing the wrong individual for a job vacancy can be both time consuming and a waste of money. In this chapter we will provide you with insight on selecting, hiring and placing the right job applicant.

At the conclusion of this chapter you will be able to:
1. Understand the implications of Equal Employment Opportunity (EEO) and other legal restrictions regarding the discrimination of job applicants.
2. Identify the items that should be included on an employment application.
3. Describe what you should do to prepare for conducting a job interview.
4. Develop interview questions pertinent to the job vacancy.
5. Identify questions that are illegal to ask during a job interview.
6. Prepare the necessary forms used for documentation during the employment process.
7. Conduct a reference check for a job applicant.
8. Maintain a knowledge of preemployment tests that you might want to use as a screening tool.
9. Understand the objectives involved in making a hiring decision.
10. Identify the benefits of instituting a probationary hiring period.

Selection

The selection process involves several different screening methods. **Screening** can be defined as a method that allows you to make the best selection from the pool of available job applicants that is in compliance with the legal restrictions and requirements at federal, state and local levels. The organizational level at which the screening of hourly employees occurs varies among hospitality organizations, depending upon their departmental structure. Regardless of the level the screening occurs, the objective is the same: to identify the job applicant who will develop into a valuable human resource and a good representative of your hospitality organization. A human resource is only an asset when he or she performs his or her job efficiently and in accordance with job standards.

It is evident in the hospitality industry that poor selection methods are a major factor in high employee turnover. The selection methods used for your hospitality organization should be developed with great care. Proper tools for selection need to be in place. These include employment application forms, interviewing procedures, reference checks and even preemployment testing. Each tool must be designed so that only information pertinent to that particular job is obtained. Otherwise you may violate legal requirements. The type of information you are looking for is that which will predict the behavior and performance of each job applicant. Sound easy?

The administration of these selection tools requires qualified, experienced and trained individuals. Interviewers and other selection personnel must understand the job position, the hospitality organization and how to draw as much information as possible from the job applicant. If selection is the responsibility of the human resources division then open channels of communication must be maintained with the operations division. Both divisions should play a major role in the selection process.

Before we look at the tools you will need to ensure that your selection decision is the best one for your hospitality organization, we need to discuss the legalities of the employment process. These restrictions will need to be kept in mind in our future discussions of employment methods and techniques.

Legal Guidelines

Equal Employment Opportunity (EEO) is the legal right of all individuals to be considered for employment and promotion solely on the basis of their ability, merit and potential. EEO is mandated by law and prohibits the intentional or unintentional discrimination of employees because of race, color, sex, religion, age, non-job related mental or physical disability, national origin or veteran status. To discriminate means that you have treated an employee unfairly because of one or more of these conditions. When selection and advancement decisions are made they must be done solely on the basis of ability, merit and potential.

To provide Equal Employment Opportunity in your hospitality organization management and nonmanagement human resources must act fairly and without bias in all employment matters. This is true for the handling of applications, the conduct of the job interview, the questions that are asked of job candidates, the manner in which references are checked and the administration of any preemployment tests. Employment decisions must be based on job-related elements, or they may be considered to be discriminatory. Title VII of the Civil Rights Act, 1964 is the federal legislation prohibiting discrimination.

Your position regarding EEO must be proactive, as good intentions are not enough. Any one of your employees or job applicants may go to the Equal Employment Opportunity Commission (EEOC) and file charges of discrimination against your hospitality organization. If that occurs and the EEOC finds that they have jurisdiction in the charges filed against you, the burden of proof is on you to prove that your actions were not discriminatory. Again, it does not matter if you did not intend to discriminate, the EEO law holds you accountable for compliance. If EEOC finds that you did take discriminatory actions in the employment process, then you will have to eliminate the cause of this discrimination and pay monetary compensation to the victims. Violation of EEO law can be very costly to your hospitality organization.

Most hospitality organizations have developed an Equal Employment Opportunity policy which specifies the intent of the organization with respect to discrimination. Procedures are developed for communicating this policy both externally and internally. Responsibilities for implementation of EEO policy are clearly defined. Periodic surveys are conducted to measure the effectiveness of the hospitality organization's EEO program. These surveys include monitoring the employment practices with respect to the racial-gender mix of the work force, the number of disabled in the work force, the place of residence of the work force, and promotion and termination activity.

The key to avoiding EEO complaints is to ensure that all procedures in the employment process are job related, applied uniformly to every job applicant and objective. Promotions, transfers and terminations also should be viewed from this perspective. Ask yourself these questions about the procedures you use:

- Is it related to job performance?
- Do you apply it in the same way to all job candidates?
- Will it have the same effect on all job candidates?
- Is it stated in objective terms that do not require subjective judgement?

Harassment

EEO is not the only legal concern in the employment process. Employers are also responsible for maintaining a work environment that is free from all forms of unlawful harassment. This includes the harassment of one employee by another on the basis of sex, race, religious preference, ethnicity and/or age. While harassment is difficult to define it does include unwelcome sexual advances, requests for sexual favors, unsolicited comments regarding one or more of the previously mentioned protected categories, deliberate and repeated name calling or physical actions of a sexual nature. It is management's responsibility to keep the work place free of discriminatory conduct or statements.

Other laws which you need to be aware of are The Age Discrimination in Employment Act of 1967 (amended 1978) that prohibits discrimination against individuals between the ages of 40 and 70. The Pregnancy Discrimination Act of 1978 requires employers to treat pregnancy the same as they would any other medical condition. The Rehabilitation Act of 1973 prohibits discrimination against the disabled and the Veterans

Readjustment Assistance Act of 1974 requires the affirmative hiring practices of Vietnam and disabled veterans.

Confidentiality

Every employee and job applicant has the right to privacy in their employment file. These files contain personal information and can only be viewed by those individuals who have a bona fide right to see their contents. It is typically policy in hospitality organizations to permit the employee to view his or her own file at any time, however, no contents of this file can be removed.

The Employment Application

Applications for employment are generally filled out by all individuals who express an interest in working for your hospitality organization. On this form the applicant lists skills, work experience and educational background along with job relevant personal information.

The employment application is one of the most common screening tools used today. It can screen out individuals who do not meet the basic job requirements as identified in the job specification. This prevents taking time to interview job applicants who are unsuitable for a particular job vacancy. As such, the application provides a quick and systematic approach to obtaining information about the applicant.

Employment applications (Figure 6-1) should be carefully designed to obtain enough information so that job applicants can be screened for a possible match with a job vacancy. At the same time, they should not invade the privacy of the applicant. Again, we repeat, if the information is not job related, then it probably should not be included on the application form. Many hospitality organizations have had to modify their employment applications in order to comply with constantly changing legislation. EEOC will act on complaints by job applicants who feel that the information asked on the employment application discriminates against them.

Questions cannot be asked pertaining to race, marital status, height or weight unless they can be proven to be a Bona Fide Occupational Qualification (BFOQ). BFOQ permits hiring practices normally prohibited by the EEOC, if the employer can prove that the violation is necessary to meet the duties and responsibilities of the job position. For example, you would be permitted to recruit and interview only males if the job opening was for a male locker room attendant. Historically, guest preference has not been accepted as a BFOQ defense, while sex and age have in some specific instances. The law basically believes that an applicant has a right to prove his or her ability to perform the job tasks.

It is well worth the time to design an employment application that will allow you to glean as much information as possible. Interviews are time consuming and a waste of time when the applicant is clearly not

126

NAME (Print)		Telephone	Date
ADDRESS		Zip Code	Position Desired
How Long Have You Lived In City?	Do You Have Transportation?	Soc. Sec. No.	Date You Can Start
Ever Worked For Gilbert/Robinson Before?	Date(s)	Location(s) / Supervisor's Name	Pay Desired

Are You Over Age of Twenty-one? Yes ☐ No ☐
If no, give birth date ___
If no, hire is subject to age verification.

Birthday Month Day

Part-Time ☐ Day Work ☐
Full-Time ☐ Night Work ☐

EDUCATION

What Days Are You NOT Available To Work?

	Name of School	Location	Dates
High School			
College			

Sun ☐ Th ☐
M ☐ F ☐
T ☐ Sat ☐
W ☐ Holidays ☐

PREVIOUS EXPERIENCE—LAST POSITION FIRST

FROM	TO	FIRM NAME, ADDRESS & PHONE NO.	POSITION	SALARY	REASON FOR LEAVING	SUPERVISOR'S NAME

COMPLETE BACK OF APPLICATION

Do you have any physical condition which may limit your ability to perform the job applied for? ☐ Yes ☐ No

In Case of an Emergency-who may we contact?

Name___ Relationship___
Address___ Phone___
Referred By:___

"If employed, I hereby agree to abide by all policies and rules of the company as stated in the Personnel Manual, including those which govern job related appearance requirements. I understand that any provision of the Manual may be amended or revised by the Company at any time and that nothing in the Manual or this application creates an express or implied contract of employment between the Company and me. I further agree that if at any time my employer shall desire to search my person, trunks, clothing and effects for property lost, I will submit to such examination without objection and hereby waive all claims for damages on such search. In addition, I hereby acknowledge that all statements contained within this application are complete and true to the best of my knowledge."

DO NOT WRITE BELOW THIS LINE Signature of Applicant ___

Hired By	Date	Rate	Position	MII Contacted? ☐ Yes ☐ No
Check Forms Completed: W4 Federal ☐ W4 State ☐ Group Ins. ☐		Liquor/Health Permit No. & Expiration Date		Birth Date
Starting Date:	Shift	Full Time	Part Time	

G/R Form 3 Rev 6/83

An Equal Opportunity Employer

Applicants will only be considered for employment for a period of 30 days from the date of application.

Figure 6-1. Application for Employment, Gilbert/Robinson
Courtesy of Gilbert/Robinson, Inc.

qualified or suitable. The information you ask is based upon the qualities that are important to you and your hospitality organization. For example, short lengths of residence might indicate the applicant is a drifter. Is the distance from work so great that it might affect punctuality. Gaps in employment history might indicate a behavior problem or a period of incarceration.

Some hospitality organizations establish a point system for various job positions. Each item on the employment application such as education, work experience and number of jobs held is assigned a specific number of points. For recruiting campaigns that stimulate many employment applications each application is scored to determine how many points the applicant has. Then only those applicants with the most number of points are called in for interviews.

The Preinterview Process

After reviewing the completed application forms we hopefully have some viable job candidates that we now would like to interview. **Interviewing** can be defined as a two-way communication process that is designed to predict both a job candidate's ability to perform the job tasks required and the ability to adapt to the hospitality organizations social environment.

If you have held a job, chances are you have experienced the interview first hand. There is no one right way to interview a job candidate. As a manager with human resources responsibilities you will have to select an approach that is the most comfortable for you. However, to keep the job interview on track so that you accomplish your purpose in a minimum amount of time, a plan must be developed before you call in the job candidate.

Preparing for the Selection Interview

The interview, above everything else, must be relevant. What do we mean by relevant? Remember that you are conducting an interview to select a candidate for a specific job position. And, because you have already conducted an analysis of the hospitality work place, that job position has a job description and a job specification. Preparation for the interview means that you have carefully reviewed the job profile for this position so that you know what the job requirements are. By knowing what the job requirements are questions can be prepared that focus on specific content which is relevant to the job vacancy (see Figure 6-2).

The structure of the selection interview must now be determined. The **structured interview** consists of a series of carefully designed questions that are asked by the interviewer of each job candidate. The interviewer asks only what is on the prepared list of questions and does

Figure 6-2. The interview process can be a positive experience when the interviewer is well prepared.
Photo by Michael Upright

not deviate from this list. This interview structure has two advantages. First, when the same list of questions is asked of every job candidate you have optimized your ability to make comparisons among the candidates. The second advantage relates to Equal Employment Opportunity. The structured interview maximizes the amount of consistent documentation that you acquire for each candidate. When you ask the same questions of all job applicants it is more difficult for rejected job applicants to claim that the questions they were asked discriminated against them. The disadvantage is that it does not permit you to react to the interviewee's responses.

Another type of interview is the **unstructured interview.** This requires the least amount of preparation on the part of interviewer. While it is essential that the interviewer have a complete understanding of the job requirements and skill levels, only general questions are formulated prior to the actual interview. The advantage is that the interviewer can respond to the job candidates responses to formulate additional questions. For example, if you ask "What has been your success?" The interviewee responds that he or she had received a promotion at their most recent position. You, as interviewer, could follow up with "What qualities do you possess that made you the best choice for this promotion?"

The disadvantage here is the amount of time this interview takes. If you are fortunate to have a large pool of applicants to interview, then you will probably not have time for the unstructured interview. Caution must also be exercised that you, as the interviewer, do not lose sight of the job position for which you are interviewing. It takes a lot of skill in the interview situation to conduct an unstructured interview that also provides you with the necessary information to make your selection decision.

A mixture of these two interview types can be developed into what is known as the **semistructured interview**. Here a preplanned list of interview questions is developed and asked of all job candidates. You can think of this list as the minimal amount of information which you will be looking for during the interview. You can then ask additional questions stemming from the job candidate's responses during the interview session.

Question Development

The questions that you develop must address the types of information you will need to elicit from the job candidate. In order to find the most qualified candidate from your applicant pool the questions must assist you in learning about each applicant. Some information will already be available from the employment application. It is during the interview, however, that you will have the opportunity to obtain additional information to assist you with your selection decision.

It is generally agreed that open-ended questions, those that can't be answered with a simple "yes" or "no" response, yield the greatest amount of information from the job applicant. While open-ended questions represent information gathering, close-ended questions tend to give the job applicant information that might alter or affect his or her response. In other words, applicants will pick up cues from the question and answer the way they think they should as opposed to how or what they really feel.

What information should the questions you developed attempt to obtain? Your questions should elicit information about what the job applicant has done in the past. The employment application will provide you with the direction for this line of questions. What information does the job applicant know? This would include questions about skills, education, and any special training the applicant has. What are the applicant's potential capabilities? A job applicant's past performance is generally a good indication of future success in your organization. Hospitality companies generally prefer to promote from within. If this is part of your organization's mission statement then you need to consider the future opportunities for this applicant.

In the hospitality industry it is essential that we also determine the job applicant's attitudes and interpersonal skills. Over 75 percent of the employees in a typical hospitality operation come into direct contact with our guests. Our human resources represent our company to those guests so it is important that the individuals we select have the ability to relate positively to other people. If they don't make a positive impression on you in the interview situation, when people are generally at their best, then you will not want them representing you and your hospitality organization to your guests. Table 6-1 presents some sample interview questions that are designed to obtain specific information from the job applicant.

Let's recap the steps that we have taken so far in the development of interview questions:

1-based upon the job description and the job specification we have analyzed the skills, attributes and characteristics that an individual must have in order to successfully fill our job vacancy.

2-based upon our job analysis we list the qualities that our job applicant must have. Some interviewers like to group the qualities they are looking for into three categories; "must have," "desirables" and "undesirables."

3-based upon the qualities we have identified we then develop questions that will elicit information about the job applicant in each of those areas.

Table 6-1. Sample Interview Questions

Work Experience

Tell me about your current responsibilities at work.

Tell me about problems you have had on the job and how they were handled.

What did you dislike about your last job position?

What would your last two employers say about your job performance?

Education:

Tell me about your major accomplishments in high school.

What subjects did you enjoy the most? Why?

Job Perspective

Why did you choose to apply for this job with our hospitality company?

How long do you plan to work for us if hired?

What other job opportunities have you sought?

Motivation

What benefits do you see in this job position?

Where do you see yourself one year from now?

Personal

Are you bilingual?

What kinds of hobbies or interests do you have?

How would you describe yourself?

In Closing

Why should we consider you for this job position?

What else should I know about you in making the selection decision?

130

Conducting the Interview

Before we actually call in our first job applicant we must:

- review the job requirements so that we are familiar with the job position
- review the employment application so that we are familiar with the applicant
- decide on the structure of the interview
- decide on the questions we will ask
- decide on the right answers to these questions
- understand the hospitality organization's mission statement, goals, objectives and corporate culture
- find a comfortable, distraction-free environment in which to conduct the interview

Interview Structure

The interview contains primarily four different phases. The first is the **opening** where you attempt to establish rapport with the job applicant. A nervous applicant is not going to interview well and you are going to have great difficulty in judging his or her true capabilities. A relaxed applicant is much more likely to provide you with the information you will need to make a selection decision. Icebreakers, such as those non-threatening questions listed in Table 6-2, will often assist you in calming the applicant. You also want to ask some basic questions that need to be asked to avoid wasting time. For example: the hours the interviewee is available for work and the wage he or she requires.

You now shift into the **information gathering** phase of the interview. This is *not* the time to discuss either the job, the hospitality organization or what a great company this is to work for. Interviewers who are great at gathering information know that 95 percent of their time is spent listening in this phase of the interview. The focus should be on the job applicant's experiences, skills and personal qualities. You should also be noting the applicant's behavior and mannerisms while you are listening to his or her responses. Body language and speech patterns can be indicators of personality traits that may or may not be desirable for the

---

Table 6-2. Icebreakers

I see you're from NY. How do you like living in Florida instead?

Did you have any trouble getting here today?

What is your greatest accomplishment?

Are you familiar with our company? Or this property?

---

position or company for which you are interviewing. Remember that the way a person looks in the interview is the best they are going to look!

If the information the job applicant provides to you raises other questions be sure to follow up on them. At the conclusion of the interview you should not have any unanswered questions. An interview is a chance for the job applicant to sell himself or herself and you are giving him or her the opportunity.

The third phase of the interview is where you **provide information** about both the job and the hospitality organization to the job applicant.

INDUSTRY EXPERTS SPEAK

Cathy Conner helps us listen in to a part of a well conducted, productive interview for an evening waitstaff position in your 200 seat, family dining operation. After each question and response an explanation will be presented of why the question was asked:

Question: Why do you want to be a server?
Poor response: I like people.
Good response: I like serving people and helping them have a good time.
Intent: To discover the real motivation behind the person's desire for the position. Why they like the job.

Question: Why did you leave your prior job as a server at XYZ restaurant?
Poor response: I disliked doing so much sidework.
Good response: I didn't get enough hours or it's too far from where I live.
Intent: To make sure the applicant won't have the same problem at your restaurant.

Question: What would you look for if you were the manager here and you were hiring a new server?
Poor response: I don't know; I never hired someone before.
Good response: Good communication skills, stamina, outgoing, etc.
Intent: To see if they identify the same characteristics that you have determined to be essential to a good performer in this position.

As you can see, each of the open-ended questions was asked to elicit specific information that will be useful to you when making your final selection decision.

Information that you should provide would include the specific job duties and responsibilities, working hours and conditions, opportunities for advancement and departmental organization. Both the positive and negative aspects of the job should be presented. It serves no purpose to hire a job applicant only to discover that there is some element of the job that he or she is uncomfortable with that will eventually force him or her to resign.

133

Remember that the applicant's only perception of the company is the impression that you are making. An interview's purpose is not only to elicit information from the applicant, but also to provide an excellent opportunity for you to sell both the job and the hospitality organization you represent. It's up to you to create a positive picture of both in the applicant's mind.

The final phase is **closing** the interview. Indicate to the applicant that the interview is coming to a close so that he or she has an opportunity to provide you with any additional information that may be useful. Putting down your pen is a good way to signal that you're finished. Always end the interview positively. While this applicant might not be suitable for the job position his or her best friend might be, and you don't want to offend him or her. And even if this applicant will not become one of your valued human resources, he or she might become one of your valued guests.

You should also let the applicant know when he or she can expect to learn the outcome of the interview. And please don't forget to follow-up within the time frame you have given. For many people, the job interview is a critical part of their life. They are likely to be anxiously waiting to learn of your decision. If you are not interested in the job applicant you should tell him or her the reasons why. Most interviewers, when interviewing hourly job candidates, will let the person know at the end of the interview. If you are interested in hiring the applicant be careful not to make any commitments to him or her until you have checked his or her references. Always make sure that you contact all job applicants you have interviewed about your decision.

The use of an interview guide such as the one used at Gilbert/Robinson (Figure 6-3) can assist you in keeping the job interview on track. The guide allows you to vary the questions depending upon the job position while at the same time maintaining a degree of consistency in the format of each interview.

Questions You Can't Ask

Even though we discussed the implications of EEO earlier in this chapter, we now want to take this opportunity to provide you with specific information regarding the types of questions that you cannot ask during the interview. As you begin the interview it is essential that you are thoroughly familiar with both EEO and affirmative action's implications

G/R INTERVIEW FORMAT

> AN INTERVIEW ON A GOOD CANDIDATE SHOULD
> LAST 10-15 MINUTES, ON A POOR CANDIDATE
> ONLY 3-5 MINUTES

I. **Review the Application** (30 seconds)

II. **Establish a Rapport** (1 minute)
1. Make person physically and mentally comfortable and make them feel important.
2. Use "useful small talk" as opposed to trivial talk about the weather (i.e. I see you went to Michigan State - so did II).

III. **Knock-Out Questions** (2 minutes)
1. What job are you applying for?
2. What hours are you available to work?
3. What salary do you expect to receive?
4. Do you have adequate transportation? (If responses do not meet the requirements/criteria of the position, proceed to Step VII)

IV. **Gather Information/Assess Personality** (5 minutes)
1. Review Background
   a. Why do you want to be a server (or bartender, cook, etc.)?
   b. Why did you leave your job at _____?
   c. What would your former boss tell me about your work performance?
   d. What did you like/dislike about working at _____?
   e. What qualities would you look for in a server (or bartender, cook, etc)?
   f. Who was your favorite boss? Why?
2. What has been your success?
3. What's been the best time of your life?
4. Do you try to be the best at what you do? If so, when?
5. How do you react under pressure?
6. How would your friends describe you?
7. Why would you be an asset to our restaurant?

V. **Give Info/Sell Position** (2-3 minutes)
(Only if interested in the candidate. If not, go to step VII)

VI. **Complete Testing** (if necessary)
1. Administer Reid Report to bartenders, bookkeepers, receiving clerks and cashier applicants by saying "Please take time to complete this survey." (It is not necessary to elaborate further.)
2. Provide a quiet place for testing.

VII. **Close the Interview** (1 minute)
1. Make the person feel good about the interview.
2. Set time for second interview within 24 hours.
3. "If you haven't heard from me within 24 hours, I have selected another candidate."

VIII. **Follow-Up**
1. Check references.
2. Conduct second interview if possible.
3. Call the candidate as soon as possible to offer the position.

Figure 6-3. G/R Interview Format
Courtesy of Gilbert/Robinson, Inc.

for the selection process. And, in addition to the federal regulations, state and local discrimination and employment laws also may regulate the employment process.

Questions should never be asked in the areas of age, race, marital status, national origin, religion, physical or mental disabilities, sex, transportation, children, height or weight, type of discharge from the military, credit history or references, or arrest record. You may ask if the interviewee has any handicaps that would prevent them from doing the job he or she applied for. Questions may not be asked of citizenship as they may be discriminatory on the basis of national origin. *After* you have decided to hire the interviewee, the Immigration Reform and Control Act requires that you inquire about authorization to work in the United States and fill out a Form I-9, and if the job candidate is an alien, you may request an Alien Registration Number.

Hospitality recruiters recommed that you not ask a question unless you can prove that it is job related. Some applicants upon not receiving a job offer will allege that the reason they were denied employment was due to a discriminatory cause. The number of discrimination lawsuits has risen in recent years. Even if you win, these cases can be quite costly both in real dollars and in public goodwill. Let's see how well you can identify interview questions that are discriminatory in nature.

Indicate if each of the questions listed below is legal or illegal to ask during a job interview. You will find the answers along with a brief explanation following the discussion questions at the end of this chapter.

1. Where were you born?
2. What clubs, organizations, societies or lodges do you belong to?
3. How would you describe yourself?
4. What is more important, the wage we can pay you or the type of job position we can offer you?
5. How many children do you have?
6. Could you provide me with the name of a pastor or priest who would provide me with a recommendation?
7. Why should I hire you for this job?
8. How much time have you lost from work or school in the past year due to illness?
9. Will you include a photograph with employment application?
10. Will you provide names of relatives?

Winners vs. Losers

How will you interpret the answers to the questions that you ask in the interview so that you know you will make the correct selection decision? How do you know if the job applicant is a winner, meaning that the individual will succeed once on the job? The question that you need to constantly ask yourself during the interview is "Can the person do the job?"

To be able to honestly answer that question for yourself you will have to learn how to get beyond the person's neat, clean appearance—their "glare"—and further get beyond the person's friendly, nice attitude—

"their woo." Glare and woo can cloud an interviewer's judgment pertaining to the job applicant's ability to perform the job. And that ability is what you hope to be hiring them to do. You can't simply like them or want to date them.

The best way to select winners over losers is to stick to the interview plan you have established. Determine what the skills and abilities necessary to do the job are, develop questions and answers that will indicate to you whether they have these skills and abilities and evaluate their performance in the interview based upon the extent of their skills and abilities. In order to keep track of where a job applicant stands in the interview, we recommend use of an interview evaluation worksheet similar to the one shown in Table 6-3. This form will permit you to summarize the applicant on each characteristic required by the vacant job position.

Common Interviewing Mistakes

Interviews are a subjective selection tool. To keep them as objective as possible we suggest that you take notes during the actual interview.

Table 6-3. Interview Evaluation Worksheet				
	Weak	Marginal	Meets Minimum Standards	Strong
Appearance/grooming				
Self-expression/ communication skills				
Personality				
Relevant job experience				
Job stability				
Enthusiasm				
Maturity				
Level of interest in position				
Flexibility in schedule				
Working hours				
Willingness to learn				
Maturity				
Attitude				
Public Impression				

While some people argue that this makes the job applicant nervous, we believe that if you give them an explanation of why you are writing items down the job applicant anxiety can be reduced. Furthermore, the importance of having written comments can be invaluable when interviewing a number of job applicants. We also recommend that after the interview is over, and the job applicant has left the interview area, that you take time to make a written evaluation of the job applicant. This should be done before beginning another interview session. Care must be taken to keep all written comments job related.

As an interviewer you are representing the hospitality organization to the job applicant. Interviews should be kept professonal with a business atmosphere. During the interview you must remain open minded and objective about the applicant sitting across from you. Do not make comparisons during the interview with other job applicants, former or present employees.

Let the interviewee do the talking, avoid interrupting and agreeing or disagreeing with what they are telling you. Use active listening techniques that would include nodding your head, saying "uh huh" or using the "echo back." An example of an echo back is when the interviewee responds "I did several creative projects while I was at my last job." You, as interviewer, respond "Creative projects?" It forces the interviewee to expand upon his or her background providing you with more information. This is an information gathering-and-giving session, not a debate. At the same time, do not let the interviewee wander into topics that have no relevancy to the job position. Stick to your interview plan and avoid asking irrelevant questions.

Be sensitive to the educational level of the interviewee. Do not use terminology that they might not be familiar with unless it relates to a skill or knowledge required by the job. Avoid talking down to the interviewee. No matter what the individual's job history or experience level he or she is still a human being that deserves to be treated with respect and dignity. The nicer you are the more the individual will want to tell you. Avoid any indication of being judgmental. If you seem to have heard it all and nothing fazes you, chances are they'll "come clean."

Whatever particular interviewing style you select, it has to be one that is comfortable to you. Don't attempt to duplicate the style or questions that might have been used on you during an interview!

Secondary Interviews

Depending upon the job position that you are interviewing for and the policies of the hospitality organization for which you are hiring, more than one interview might be required of the job applicant. Some companies use the initial interview as a prescreening tool. Job candidates that do not meet the basic job requirements or skill levels are eliminated from the selection process. Initial interviews can also be used to

MANAGEMENT INTERVIEW FORM

INTERVIEWER #1 _____ INTERVIEWER #2 _____

DATE: _____ INTERVIEWED AT: _____ DATE: _____ INTERVIEWED AT: _____

138

PERSONAL DATA

NAME: MR. MS _____

LOCATION PREFERENCES: _____ GRADUATION DATE (IA): _____

SALARY - CURRENT: _____ DATE AVAILABLE: _____

SALARY - REQUIRED: _____ POSITION APPLYING FOR: _____

ACTIONS - CHECK ALL THAT APPLY

1. VERBAL "NO POSITION" GIVEN ☐

2. A) SEND A "NO POSITION LETTER" (NO FUTURE INTEREST) ☐
    B) SEND A "NO POSITION LETTER" AND FILE FOR BRING UP IN 6 OR 12 MONTHS (CIRCLE ONE) FOR RECONSIDERATION, AS CANDIDATE IS NOT SUITABLE AT THIS TIME. ☐

3. REID REPORT WAS GIVEN AND IS ATTACHED ☐

4. REID REPORT TO BE MAILED TO KC BY CANDIDATE ☐

5. REID REPORT TO BE SENT FROM G/R TO CANDIDATE ☐

6. SECOND INTERVIEW REQUIRED ☐   REFER TO _____

7. REID REPORT SCORE ☐   R   Q   NR

8. REFERENCES CHECKED ☐   COMMENTS _____

OFFER (FOR OFFICE USE ONLY)

SALARY: _____ TRAINING LOCATION: _____ REVIEW SCHEDULE: _____

POSITION: _____ 1ST LOCATION: _____ START DATE: _____

RELOCATION: $ _____ BONUS PROGRAM: _____

WEEKS OF TRAINING: _____ CLASS DATE & NUMBER: _____

SOURCE OF HIRE (CIRCLE ONE):   CC   NRN   ADV   REC   REF   HH   OSH   PFW

TYPE OF LETTER (CIRCLE ONE):   FO   RNP   HNP   OFR   ACPT

COMMENTS/OTHER COMMITMENTS: _____

_____

_____

Figure 6-4. Management Interview Form, Gilbert/Robinson
Courtesy of Gilbert/Robinson, Inc.

determine the applicant's interests or as a method of disseminating information about your hospitality company.

Secondary interviews are used to gain more specific information about the job applicant's suitability to the job position opening. Company philosophies also vary as to whom should conduct the second interview. In most hospitality companies the manager or supervisor of the vacant job position will conduct this interview. An applicant flow log similar to the one used for management by Gilbert/Robinson shown in Figure 6-4 should be maintained so that you can track each of the job applicants through the selection process.

Conducting an interview can be a very awkward and uncomfortable activity unless you have developed a good interview plan. Your objective in the interview process is to gather as much information as possible about the job candidate so that an intelligent hiring decision can be made. You must constantly be aware of the legal restrictions imposed upon the employment process by federal, state and local laws, yet develop questions that will entice the applicant to tell all. Remember that while in the course of your day an interview might be viewed as an interruption, it is likely to be one of the most important events that day for the job candidate. And when you think about the costs and headaches of a poor hiring decision it just might be the most important human resources activity that you perform that day.

Reference Checking

If a job applicant appears to be qualified for the job vacancy a reference check should be made before a job offer is extended. A reference check can be conducted by phone or mail. Due to recent litigation involving slander and defamation of character many businesses are careful not to release any information other than dates of employment and salary. In many cases, written permission by the job candidate is required.

While reference checks may not be good predictors of job performance they do provide you with an evaluation of the applicant's attributes and qualifications. If valuative comments can be obtained during a reference check the referees are likely to give more favorable information than negative. In the hospitality industry, however, information that gives us an indication of the applicant's personality can be useful in the screening process. Certain personality traits are critical if the applicant is to be successful in many hospitality jobs. You might use a telephone checklist like the one seen in Figure 6-5.

At a minimum a reference check should seek to obtain prior dates of employment, positions, duties and performance quality (Figure 6-6). Questions such as "Why did the employee leave?", "Is he eligible for rehire?", and "Did he have a high absenteeism?" are useful for verifying information on the employment application. Remember that it is not

140

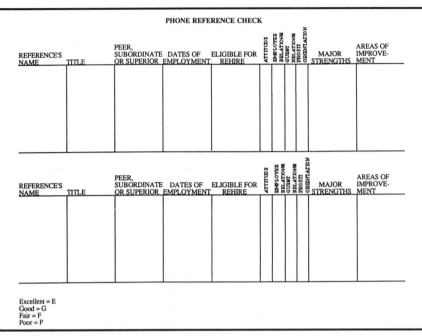

Figure 6-5. Phone Reference Checklist Gilbert/Robinson
Courtesy Gilbert/Robinson, Inc.

Figure 6-6. Reference checks are an important part of the selection process.
Courtesy of Gilbert/Robinson, Inc.

illegal to ask anything of a reference, it is up to them to tell you or refuse you the information. If you get a negative reference, protect your source. Do not tell the applicant the reference was the reason for not hiring them.

INDUSTRY EXPERTS SPEAK

Cathy Conner relates the following story, "A woman employed in the accounting department of a hospitality company's corporate office developed asthma problems. As a result, her absenteeism began to increase and her attitude began to decline. She discovered a job opening as a bookkeeper in one of the company's properties, located in the same city, and she applied. The general manager hired her without checking a reference from her supervisor at corporate office, which would have been a simple action to take.

A few weeks after she had started her new position, the property was sprayed with a pesticide to exterminate insects. Because she had asthma, she suffered a severe reaction to the chemicals used by the exterminators. Since this event, she has been absent over a year and has cost the company $78,000 in Workers' Compensation. She is also suing the company for permanent disability, the amount yet to be determined. The company is continuing to pay all her medical bills and two-thirds of her salary.

This costly situation could have been avoided in the first place had the general manager checked a reference. Her excessive absenteeism and poor attitude would have been reason enough not to hire her."

Preemployment Testing

There is strong evidence that suggests that the use of standardized tests, which assess abilities, personality and integrity, are a valuable screening tool. While initially many companies and selection experts were hesitant about the use of these tools, many hospitality organizations now use testing as a regular component in the selection process. We predict in "the next chapter" that testing will become both more sophisticated and widely used in our industry.

The following list represents just some of the types of tests that you might select from:

Skill tests. These may be conducted to determine if the job candidate meets the qualifications directly related to the job requirements. For example, if a bartender needs to be able to mix drinks with a certain speed, then you could place him or her behind the bar and time his or her performance.

Intelligence tests. These tests will measure the job candidate's mental capacity, memory (which might be of importance in hiring a short order cook), ability to see relationships and speed of thought.

Personality tests. These tests assist in matching the job candidate with the job position in which he or she is most likely to succeed. This is based upon a measure of that individual's personality characteristics, not his or her experiences and abilities.

Integrity tests. These tests measure a person's honesty. Most of the internal theft that occurs in hospitality operations can be solved by hiring better people. Legislation passed in 1988 severely restricted the use of polygraph tests given by employers for preemployment. Since then employers have come to rely more heavily upon written tests that measure an applicant's honesty.

Preemployment testing is not meant as a replacement for other selection tools, but merely as one additional source of information that can help you in making the best hiring decision. It is objective information that is consistent from applicant to applicant. While administering these tests to job candidates is not illegal, it must be shown that the test is job related. Care must be taken in selecting the most appropriate test for your particular needs.

Record Retention

It is legally necessary to retain all pertinent records on job applicants for employment. As we discussed, an applicant flow record should be maintained on all candidates. A "hold" file is generally maintained for applicants that were qualified for jobs but were not hired. A "reject" file is maintained for all applicants who did not qualify for any job positions. These applications must be held for a period of at least thirteen months. In the case of an EEOC charge, they may not be destroyed until approval is given by the investigating agency.

Care should be taken that employment applications and other selection data are not left out to be viewed by unauthorized individuals. The confidentiality of employee records must be maintained at all times.

Effective employee selection is a process by which you, the manager with human resources responsibilities, seek the best candidate for a specific job vacancy. Your search is aided with a variety of selection tools that you have at your disposal. The particular tools you choose to use in your hospitality organization will depend upon your comfort level with each of them, along with the goals and objectives of the operation for which you are making the selection.

The direct result of a poor selection decision is seen in high turnover that translates into higher costs for recruitment, selection and training. To calculate the costs, you must add in recruitment where you have the expense of advertising, and then you must add the selection expenses of interviewing and testing, to which you must add the training expenses of management time, effort and reduced productivity levels plus the salary and benefits that you have compensated the poorly selected human resource.

143

The process of selection has dramatically improved in the past decade. Hospitality managers who once hired just to fill a job vacancy have come to realize the importance of developing a comprehensive selection plan for their hospitality organization. A successful selection plan, conducted by trained, skilled professionals can improve the quality and productivity of the hospitality organization.

Now that we have examined the selection process we are ready to make our hire decision.

Hiring and Placement

Through our sophisticated selection plan we now have a number of individuals who after screening, reference checks and preemployment testing are still viable candidates for the job vacancy. It is now time to make the hire decision! Again, where and by whom this decision is made will depend upon the structure of your hospitality organization. In some cases it will be made by the human resources department and in other organizations by the departmental manager/supervisor where the job vacancy exists.

If the job analysis, recruitment and selection processes have been dutifully carried out, the last task of actually making the hire decision becomes a mere formality. If done thoroughly, the first three components of the employment process can lead you to an easy decision. But what happens when you complete these steps and still have a pool of job candidates? Other than considering yourself very lucky that you still have a decision to make, what considerations go into making that final determination?

Making the Decision

What are some of the criteria you should keep in mind in making this decision? We suggest the following guidelines:

- you can only hire what you can afford. The candidate's experience and qualifications should equate to the compensation received. If the job vacancy you have pays less then he or she is worth, and if you do not have immediate opportunities for this individual to advance into, the candidate will be looking for a better paying job elsewhere.

- don't play it safe all the time. Every hospitality organization needs its "stars," regardless of job level. Stars are also those job candidates that come in at high risk. You like everything about them, but there is something in their background or behavior that is unconventional. High-risk hires will either be very successful or very unsuccessful.

- what is the hire objective? In the particular hire are you looking for someone to improve the current situation in the department in which he or she will be working? Or are you content with an individual who will maintain the current situation?

- look at the job candidate's temperament. How well is this individual suited for the work that the job vacancy requires? If the job candidate is a very vivacious, gregarious type person, and the job vacancy requires work that is repetitious and done in an area with very little social interaction, this person will not be very happy in the work environment.

- what you see is what you get. Remember the quote at the beginning of this chapter. These job candidates will never look or behave any better than they have throughout the screening process. If you encounter a red flag or negative feeling about the candidate then carefully consider if you and your hospitality organization can live with this appearance or behavior. "You can't teach a pig to sing. You'll only annoy the pig and frustrate yourself."

- does the candidate like being around people? Hospitality is a people business. Examine his or her hobbies and interests to determine if this person enjoys being with people in his or her leisure time. If all of the individual's interests center on reading, needlework or stamp collecting, this might be a job candidate who prefers not to be around people.

- have a belief in talent. Don't be afraid of talented people or those more attractive or brighter than yourself (Figure 6-7).

- what is the candidate's energy level? We work in an environment that is full of peaks and valleys. When our hospitality operation is at its maximum productivity level, all of your human resources need to maximize their own energy levels. We must look for job candidates whom we believe to be hard workers.

In making the final hire decision, we suggest that you use a candidate evaluation form similar to the one we discussed previously. This will permit you to objectively evaluate each of the final candidates by conducting a comparative analysis. Remember that the only comments that are written on this evaluation sheet or on the interviewer's

144

Figure 6-7. Following proper selection procedures can lead to successful hiring! Courtesy Gilbert/Robinson, Inc.

comment sheet are job related. You must take great care not to write down subjective personal impressions about the job candidate. In the event of a discrimination charge, these selection documents will become part of the evidence used in determining if such a charge is valid.

Negligent Hiring

Negligent hiring practices are being used increasingly by third parties that have been injured as a result of one of your employees' negligence. Historically, you, as an employer, have always been responsible for the actions of your employees while they were in your employ. Hence, if one of your valet parkers, while parking a guest's car hits a pedestrian, you could be held liable for his or her actions.

Negligent hiring expands the duty an employer has to its guests, and states that your duty is to hire only individuals who can be trusted and are qualified to do the job in which you placed them. Hence, if a bellman whose job is to take guests to their rooms and carry in their baggage, assaults one of those guests, you are liable. Particularly, if it is found that the bellman you hired had been imprisoned for assault. The negligent hiring actions state that you breached the duty to your guests in your initial hire decision by not conducting a proper screening review. In other words, you acted unreasonably in your hire decision.

146

Hire decisions must be carefully made on an individual basis. While we have presented general guidelines for you to follow, common sense must be integrated in the process. Some job positions require more careful screening, in that the foreseeable risk to your guests is increased. Unfortunately, the legislation pertaining to discrimination prevents you from directly asking many questions that could assist you in screening out job candidates that are high security risks. This is where your judgment is invaluable. Keep in mind where these job candidates will be working if you hire them. Do you have enough information about them to guarantee the safety of your guests. If not, then you should think twice about making them a job offer.

The Job Offer

At the time of the job offer you should provide the job candidate with the following information:

- starting date
- orientation and training schedule
- wages and benefits
- nature of the job
- work schedule

The job candidate now has a decision to make. Make sure that he or she understand the negatives as well as the positives of this particular job position. The candidate should understand your expectations in the performance of the job duties and responsibilities. The candidate's decision to accept or reject your offer will be based upon the information that you provide the job candidate with at this stage of the employment process. Make sure that there are no misunderstandings, because if there are you will end up with the same job vacancy to refill.

We recommend that you follow an established procedure for hiring or rejecting the job candidates. The offer, while initially made orally, should be placed in writing, again in an attempt to eliminate any misunderstandings. If the candidate is to be rejected he or she should be notified as soon as possible. If the candidate requests a reason for the rejection you must be very careful in how you state it. Remember the legal consequences of discriminating against a job candidate.

An alternative to making a firm job offer is to offer the job candidate a probationary period of employment. This enables both you and the candidate to better determine if the job vacancy is a good match with the candidate. Probationary periods usually last from one to three months. At the end of this time neither party has an obligation to the other. If you elect to use a probationary period, we recommend that you have the employee sign a statement that indicates that the employment period is for a specified period of time, and that no further obligation is extended past that period on the part of either party.

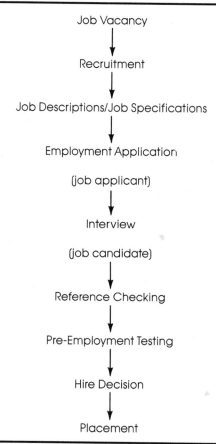

Figure 6-8. Planning the Employment Process

Placement

Once a job candidate is hired there is additional information that you must obtain. Much of this information such as marital status, age, number of children and ability to work legally in the U.S., if of another national origin, could not legally be asked before the hire decision was made. It is now necessary to complete the I-9 (Employment Eligibility Verification Form, previously discussed in chapter 5) for immigration purposes. This information is now necessary so that your payroll and benefits divisions can effectively do their job. Since this information may not be used for future promotion decisions you should keep this data separate from the employee's personnel file. Figure 6-8 represents a complete picture of the employment process.

148

Conclusion

Proper implementation of the selection, hiring and placement process is crucial to the success of a hospitality organization. These processes require a well thought out and executed plan, which will require time for effective implementation. The employment process cannot be rushed. Throughout the hospitality industry professionals are recognizing the great amount of attention that is needed in this human resources functional activity and are taking steps to develop programs or improve upon those already in place. Managers are now being taught to treat the employment process with the same care and respect as in making a capital acquisition.

The selection of your human resources is the starting point for building quality into your hospitality organization. In order to become a first class operation, you must begin by selecting high quality job candidates to become members of your organization. Each job applicant comes to you with his or her own special skills, talents and abilities. It is your job to match these individuals to the job positions in your operation.

Over the years, the employment process has become complicated with legal restrictions and requirements. Lawsuits alleging discrimination are commonplace. The damages, both in monetary loses and in public goodwill, have prompted hospitality managers with human resources responsibilities to become cautious in their screening procedures. We must always be well informed of the legal issues surrounding the employment process.

Today, we are beginning to view our work force in a different light. We see our employees as valuable resources in the success of our hospitality operations. Personnel is not just a bunch of numbers waiting for their paychecks each week for a job that holds no opportunity for growth or advancement. Hiring employees is a critical function. Poor human resources are the result of poor selection. Only through the development of an outstanding selection process can outstanding human resources become a part of your hospitality organization.

We now turn our focus to the orientation, training and development of the human resources we have so carefully selected, hired and placed in our hospitality organization.

Case Problem 6-1

Congratulations! Your recruitment campaign for part-time waitstaff positions was a great success! As the manager with human resources responsibilities for a theme restaurant with 200 seats located in southern California you have fifteen applications in front of you for three part-time waitstaff job vacancies. Only limited screening has been done. You know that they can work the hours required and that they are old enough to serve alcoholic beverages. Your task is to determine which three (if any) you should hire. Where should you begin? What critical information should you be looking for as you review the applications? (Hint: before you can answer any of these questions job specifications will need to be developed.)

Based upon the job specifications what are the minimum qualifications you will be looking for on the job applications before setting up any interviews? What qualifications would it be nice for the job applicants to have? And finally what would the qualifications look like for the "ideal" waitstaff person for your operation? Identify each of these qualifications by placing an asterisk (*) by minimum qualifications, two asterisks (**) by those qualifications that would be nice to have and three (***) next to those qualifications that identify the ideal job qualifications.

Case Problem 6-2

Attached, you see a completed job application for one of the job candidates that you have decided to interview for the position described in Case Problem 6-1. Based upon the information presented, prepare a set of interview questions for this job candidate. For each question that you ask, you should identify what an acceptable answer would be. Next to the set of questions you will ask, draw horizontal lines to form three columns. In the left-hand column place answers to the interview questions that you find acceptable, in the middle column place the answers that you prefer and in the right-hand column place answers that you find unacceptable. For example, if one of your interview questions relates to the candidate's amount of experience, you might prefer that they have waitstaff experience serving food and beverages in a similar type of operation but you might find cocktail service acceptable. In this example on work experience you might feel that no experience or merely counter service in a fast-food operation is *not* acceptable.

Be sure to include, with your list of interview questions, two icebreakers.

You interviewed the job candidate described above and they passed the interview with flying colors. At this point in the selection process you

APPLICATION FOR EMPLOYMENT

150

NAME (Print) GREGG   JOSEPH   B

Telephone (305) 555-

Date 10-20-8?

ADDRESS 11 S.W. Place DAVIE, FL.

Zip Code 33324

Position Desired

How Long Have You Lived In City? 3 years

Do You Have Transportation? Yes

Soc. Sec. No. 080-00-1814

Date You Can Start 15 Nov.

Ever Worked For Gilbert/Robinson Before? No

Date(s)

Location(s)

Supervisor's Name

Pay Desired

Are You Over Age of Twenty-one? Yes X No
If no, give birth date
If no, hire is subject to age verification.

Birthday

Month   Day

Part-Time ☑ Day Work ☑
Full-Time ☐ Night Work ☑

EDUCATION

What Days Are You NOT Available To Work?

	Name of School	Location	Dates
High School	M. Coyle	TAUNTON, MA.	1977
College	Bridgewater State NOVA U.	Middleboro, MA Ft. Laud., Fl	1981 1987

Sun ☐ Th ☐
M ☑ F ☐
T ☐ Sat ☐
W ☐ Holidays ☐

PREVIOUS EXPERIENCE—LAST POSITION FIRST

FROM	TO	FIRM NAME, ADDRESS & PHONE NO.	POSITION	SALARY	REASON FOR LEAVING	SUPERVISOR'S NAME
1987	1988	Rocco's Place	ASS'T MGR.	$17M	Closed for Summer	R. Angelo
1988	Present	ABC Motel	Res't Asst Mgr.	$18,500	—	M. Jones

Do you have any physical condition which may limit your ability to perform the job applied for? ☐ Yes ☑ No

In Case of an Emergency who may we contact?
Name RUTH E. GREGG   Relationship WIFE
Address above   Phone same

Referred By: Michael Kobasky

"If employed, I hereby agree to abide by all policies and rules of the company as stated in the Personnel Manual, including those which govern job related appearance requirements. I understand that any provision of the Manual may be amended or revised by the Company at any time and that nothing in the Manual or this application creates or will create an express or implied contract of employment between the Company and me. I further agree that if at any time my employer shall desire to search my person, trunks, clothing and effects for property lost, I will submit to such examination without objection and hereby waive all claims for damages on account of such search.

In addition, I hereby acknowledge that all statements contained within this application are complete and true to the best of my knowledge."

DO NOT WRITE BELOW THIS LINE

Signature of Applicant Joseph B Gregg

Hired By		Date	Rate	Position	MII Contacted? ☐ Yes ☐ No
Check Forms Completed: W4 Federal ☐ W4 State ☐ Group Ins. ☐			Liquor/Health Permit No. & Expiration Date		Birth Date
Starting Date:	Shift		Full Time	Part Time	

G/R Form 3-Rev 8/83

An Equal Opportunity Employer

Applicants will only be considered for employment for a period of 30 days from the date of application.

Courtesy of Gilbert/Robinson, Inc.

feel that you would like to make this job candidate a job offer. Before doing so, however, you need to conduct a reference check. Based upon the information presented in the job application (and making the assumption that the job applicant's last employer is willing to provide a job reference for you), what questions would you like to ask the past employer?

151

RECOMMENDED READING

Brown, P. B. 1987. Every picture tells a story *Inc.* 9, (9): 18, 20–21.

Collinson, D. 1987. Who controls selection? *Personnel Management* 19, (5): 32–35.

Frumkin, P. 1989. Smart hiring. *Restaurant Business* 88, (2): 80, 82, 86, 88.

Kennedy, J. 1987. *Getting Behind the Resume Interviewing Today's Candidates* Paramus, N.J.: Prentice Hall Information Services.

Kolton, E. 1985. The educated hunch. *Inc.* 7, (1): 93–94, 96.

Melohn, T. 1987. Screening for the best employees. *Inc.* 9, (1): 104–106.

National Restaurant Association. 1987. *How to Recruit, Hire and Retain Employees* Washington, D.C.: National Restaurant Association.

Odiorne, G. S. 1987. Nine rules for hiring. *Working Women* 12, (11): 40, 43.

Panken, P. M. 1985. The road to court is paved with good intentions. *Nation's Business* 73, (6): 45–46.

Potter, E. E. 1986. *Employee Selection: Legal and Practical Alternatives to Compliance and Litigation* Washington, D.C.: National Foundation for the Study of Equal Employment Policy.

Wermiel, S. 1988. Subjective bias in hiring may be illegal even without proof of intent, court says. *Wall Street Journal* CCXI, (127): 2.

DISCUSSION QUESTIONS

1. What is the objective of the screening process? How can you, as human resources manager, ensure that this objective is met in your hospitality organization?
2. What information do those involved in the selection process need to know before they can begin screening job applicants?
3. Discuss EEO legislation. What does it require? Who does it cover? What is the role of the EEOC? Who may file a complaint? How can you monitor compliance? How can complaints be avoided?

4. Explain your responsibilities as human resources manager, if harassment is occuring in your hospitality operation. How would you recognize it? What actions would you take?
5. What are the advantages and disadvantages of using the employment application as a screening test?
6. Describe the advantages and disadvantages of the structured, unstructured and semistructured interview. Which do you prefer? Why?
7. What must you do before interviewing a job applicant so that the interview is relevant?
8. Describe the three phases of the interview and identify the objective or purpose of each phase.
9. What kind of information is useful to obtain during a reference check?
10. Describe the difference between personality tests and integrity tests. Would you use preemployment testing in a hospitality operation? Why or why not?
11. What is negligent hiring? How can it be avoided?
12. What information should you provide the job candidate at the time of job offer?

ANSWERS TO LEGALITY OF INTERVIEW QUESTIONS

1. Illegal. Questions may not be asked about an applicant's birthplace, that of his or her parents, nor may you ask to see a birth certificate, naturalization or baptismal certificate. You may ask about an applicant's place and length of residence or where his or her current employer is located.
2. Illegal. You may not inquire about clubs, societies, fraternities or other social organizations to which the applicant might belong. These might be of ethnic or religious origin. You may ask about membership in professional or service organizations.
3. Legal.
4. Legal.
5. Illegal. You may not ask questions about the composition of the family, marital status or sex of the applicant.
6. Illegal. This relates to religious preference. You may ask names of character or professional references. If the applicant supplies the name of a religious leader you have not violated the law.
7. Legal.
8. Illegal. You cannot discriminate against mental or physical disabilities unless directly job related.
9. Illegal. The reasons are obvious!
10. Illegal. You may ask names of relatives you already employ or the name of a relative to notify in case of an emergency.

SECTION 3

HUMAN RESOURCES TRAINING, DEVELOPMENT AND EVALUATION

CHAPTER 7

HOSPITALITY ORIENTATION

AND TRAINING PROGRAMS

INDUSTRY ADVISOR *Nicholas F. Horney, Director Training and Development*
Stouffer Hotels & Resorts

> **"Training is everything. The peach was once a bitter almond; cauliflower is nothing but cabbage with a college education."**
> **—MARK TWAIN**

KEY WORDS

computer-based training programs
job instruction training
in-house training methods
learning
lecture method
needs assessment
on-the-job training (OJT)

orientation program
retraining
survival information
role playing
training plan
training program
vestibule training

INTRODUCTION

Orientation and training; familiar words to most students in hospitality administration. Your hospitality employees have been successfully recruited, selected, hired and placed into vacant job positions. The next step in the human resources process is to properly orient and train your new employees. Unfortunately, too many hospitality organizations underestimate the overall value of having a well planned orientation and training program. Both programs relate directly to the success of the new employees as well as the success of your hospitality organization.

As managers assuming human resources responsibilities, it will be your job to prepare your employees to perform their jobs. You've both made a commitment to work together. The orientation program will be the new employees' first taste of your role as team leader. It is here that they will begin to develop the sense of teamwork, enthusiasm and drive that makes your hospitality organization a special place to work. The training program will give you an opportunity to capitalize upon the natural attributes of the new employees, which are, after all, the reason you hired them in the first place!

At the conclusion of the chapter you will be able to:
1. Describe why a good orientation program is a necessity in a hospitality operation.
2. Identify the characteristics of a beneficial orientation program.
3. Explain the importance and goals of a training program.
4. Identify when and what types of training are needed in your hospitality operation.
5. Develop a training plan.
6. Distinguish among several types of training methods.
7. Identify the elements of a successful training program.

Orientation

All new employees should be given a well planned orientation that will help them in getting off to a positive start in their new job. A thorough orientation program will acquaint the new employee to the hospitality organization, his or her specific work unit and job position. In its broadest sense, the orientation process can be thought of as an extension of the recruitment and selection processes.

Just because a person is now an employee it doesn't mean that they know what they are supposed to do, how they are supposed to behave, or even where they are supposed to be at any given time. Although an orientation should take place every time an employee begins a new position or takes on new responsibilities, we will be discussing new hire orientation in this chapter.

What Do You Do With A New Employee?

What is orientation? A good way to think of orientation is as a way of introducing new employees to the hospitality organization. Can you recall your first day on the job you have now? Even if that job was one you had performed for another hospitality company, such as bartender or room service waitstaff, didn't you feel at least a slight apprehension when going to work on that first day? We can relate to those feelings of anxiety with each of you; the "first day" means that you are entering into the unexpected.

So what can you, as a manager with human resources responsibilities, do to make the "first day" experience a pleasant one for your newly hired human resources? You can begin by making the employees feel at home with each other and their new hospitality work environment.

The social contact that is established between you, the employer and the new hire is very important.

We will define **orientation programs** as a method of socializing new employees to the hospitality organization, their work unit or department and to their job positions, in an effort to minimize problems so that they can make a maximum contribution to the work of the hospitality operation while at the same time realizing personal satisfaction. The word socialize indicates that we want our new employees to fit in with the proper ways of doing business. Those "proper" ways depend upon your hospitality organization's goals, policies and standard operating procedures.

By defining orientation in this way we begin to see the importance and value of planned programs. In too many situations hospitality managers are content in turning over the responsibility of orientation to the new employee's co-workers. This unstructured orientation process can, in the long term, be very destructive to the success of the hospitality organization. Not only is this type of orientation unplanned, but it can also be misleading.

Goals of Hospitality Orientation Programs

The purpose of a new hire orientation program is to give new employees an idea of the culture, behavior, facilities, people and survival skills necessary to make it through their first few months of employment. Orientation programs vary in both length and content based upon the job position for which the employee was hired, but need to be thorough enough to enable the employee to function fully and effectively as a member of the hospitality work team.

Communicating expectations and eliminating preconceptions are perhaps the most important goals of an orientation program. Getting employees to understand what is expected of them is the most valuable message you can communicate. Never assume that people know about your hospitality organization or the job for which they have been hired. These assumptions can seriously hinder employee performance once on the job. Not making any assumptions about what the employees know or don't know can help ensure that their initial progress is successful. This can prevent problems initially and in the future.

An additional goal of orientation programs is to attempt to provide successful experiences. As you will learn in the following chapter, coaching and team building will be part of your job when assuming human resources responsibilities. During the orientation it is important that your new recruits begin to feel like they will be making an important contribution to the team. Not only will your new human resources become contributing members of the team more quickly, many of their anxieties will be relieved when they are guided towards achieving initial successes. Confidence levels will be boosted along with future productivity. By designing positive experiences into the orientation program motivation will be fostered that will promote early success.

Studies have been conducted by organizations that show that orientation programs are beneficial.[1] These studies conclude that the more complete the orientation program, the more quickly the human resources become productive, contributing members to the organization. In addition, reduction in tardiness and absenteeism have also been found. This is felt to occur due to a decrease in job entry anxiety that leads to a more positive working attitude.

Commitment. Accomplishing this will not only require a commitment by unit level managers, but also a *real* commitment by senior management to make the new human resources feel like they are part of your hospitality organization.

Participation in the orientation program by all levels of management is one way to show the new hires that they are important members of the team. It is also an excellent way for them to meet key people in your hospitality organization, so they can place the names they will be seeing on memorandums with actual faces. Having all levels of management participating in the orientation allows them to become role models for all those entering your organization. If top management is actively involved in operational functions, the hourly human resources will tend to support them with greater enthusiasm.

What to Cover . . .

INDUSTRY EXPERTS SPEAK	Hospitality orientation programs are methods of giving employees information and answering their questions about the organization, their departmental unit, the job itself and how they will fit into the overall structure of the hospitality operation. According to Nick Horney, Director of Training and Development for Stouffer Hotels and Resorts, this should be a formalized process to socialize new employees to the hospitality organization's culture (if part of a chain), the specific operation and the new employee's department and job. It should reinforce in the mind of the new employee why he or she selected the company and why the company selected him or her.

What are the mission statement, goals and objectives of the organization? What does it expect of you as an employee? What can you expect the hospitality organization to provide for you? These are all some examples of the types of questions that human resources entering your organization or operation for the first time might have, and these questions should be covered in an effective orientation program.

For Whom and By Whom

Orientation programs can be effectively developed and implemented for hourly human resources as well as for management trainees. Upon graduation, many of you will personally experience a management trainee orientation. This chapter focuses primarily on the orientation programs you will be conducting for the hourly employees in your hospitality operation. While many of the elements will be similar to what you will experience, the program for management trainees is likely to be more intensified, therefore taking a greater length of time.

For example, Stouffer Hotels and Resorts offers what they call their Generalist Management Training Program. If you are a trainee and wish to become an entry level manager, you are rotated through each of the hourly job positions. You learn how the hotel is run, how each department operates and pick up on a variety of management styles. This program is an extensive orientation *and* training program.

Orientation programs are not always just for the new employee, although that is their primary function. Orientation programs are important in hospitality organizations that undergo changes in structure or policies, which is frequently the case in today's world of corporate takeovers. Acquisitions require a special orientation so that the employees of the acquired company feel a part of your hospitality organization.

Orientation programs can be conducted by either the human resources department or by the individual department manager or supervisor. To maximize effectiveness there needs to be a great deal of cooperation from both areas. Typically, the orientation in large, more complex hospitality organizations would be implemented so that the human resources department would describe company-wide policies. The departmental manager or supervisor would then orient the employee to the department he or she will be working in.

The orientation process is so important that care must be taken to make the new employee comfortable and relaxed so that the maximum amount of information can be relayed to him or her. While first impressions are important, the goal here and in training is to learn and become informed. The new employee must not be afraid to ask questions for fear they will seem not knowledgeable. Icebreaker tools work well in relaxing a group of employees and making them feel more comfortable. Your friendly, open attitude when conducting the orientation will also help abate fears.

Great care must be taken not to load the new employee with too much information at one time or information overload will occur. Taking the time to develop a formalized orientation program specifically for your hospitality organization will prevent this from occurring. It will also assure that all of the necessary information is contained in the program.

Characteristics of Well-Designed Orientation Programs

160

In the hospitality business, it is important that our human resources have a global view of our hospitality organization. Emphasis should be placed on the culture of the organization, and why it's important. The Disney experience is probably the best example of a company that makes sure that each of its employees knows and understands the Disney organization. The employees must be able to see how their specific job relates to other jobs and departments within the hospitality operation. Let's look, for example, at the importance of the relationship between the front office job position and the position of housekeeper. For the new employee who is going to work in housekeeping, an orientation of the front desk should be provided. Showing the human resources working in housekeeping how the front desk operates will give them a better understanding of where their work fits into the total goals of the hotel. It will demonstrate more clearly the awkward position the rooms clerks are in when they have guests waiting to check in, but do not have enough clean rooms ready. Likewise, showing the room clerks what it takes to clean a room will give them a better appreciation of why all the rooms are not ready for check-in by 10:00 a.m.!

Even though each of the human resources working in a hospitality operation has a specific job position, the nature of our business finds these employees walking around the operation. This means that our

---

Table 7-1. Positive Characteristics of Hospitality Orientation Programs

- presents a complete overview of the hospitality operation/property
- recognizes the specific problems and needs the new human resources might face and addresses those problems and needs
- orientation procedures are planned, well organized and effectively administered
- orientation plans are adapted to the particular department and job position of the new human resource
- keeps the focus on the welfare of the new human resource
- provides a honest outlook of the hospitality organization, negatives as well as positives
- is continually evaluated and improved
- provides an explanation of the hospitality organization's culture
- presents a historical perspective
- presents a vision of where the hospitality organization and specific operation is headed

---

employees frequently come into direct contact with our guests in areas outside of their immediate work area. As a service to our guests, our human resources need to be informed about many of the operation's functions and activities so that they can correctly answer questions and inquiries made to them by our guests. Table 7-1 identifies some of the characteristics that a well designed hospitality orientation program should contain.

161

The Specifics

"Hi, I'm. . . ." The new employee who is made to feel welcome and immediately a part of the work team is sure to make the guests in your hospitality operation also feel welcome. Hospitality is a service industry, and if we are to excel in service to our guests, then our operations must have employees with a service orientation. Don't tell them what hospitality is; show them! One way might be to give all new hires a certificate for a dinner for two before their first day on the job. Not only is this a warm welcome to your company, it also gives them a familiarity with your operation from the guest's perspective. You can use this during the orientation to describe how you expect them to treat the guests they will be encountering.

Throughout the orientation, then, the importance of good service and your guests is the theme of all discussions. A well-thought out orientation will make employees feel welcome and help reduce those first day anxieties. While orientations will vary somewhat depending upon the specific job position, they should at a minimum include the following:

The company.   At this point it is appropriate to discuss the operation's history and development. This can lead into a discussion of the hospitality organization's structure and chain of command. A thorough description of the organizational goals and operational objectives should be presented, including the mission statement of the hospitality enterprise. The importance of the contribution the new human resources is expected to make to those goals and objectives should be made clear.

Survival information.   While not the most exciting information you share with the new employee, this certainly is some of the most important information you can share. Care must be taken so that no specifics are overlooked. What may be routine and obvious for present employees can become a major problem area for the new employee who lacks information.

Some of the necessary survival information includes:

- check-in procedures; the use of time cards.
- issuance of keys, uniforms and necessary supplies.
- medical insurance and other benefit forms. Assistance should be

provided in filling out these forms, which can be confusing to even the most knowledgeable employee. As you will learn in a future chapter on benefits, this area is rapidly changing and becoming more complex. Table 7-2 identifies some of the employment papers that need to be filled out by new employees.

- explanation of how to read the paycheck stub. This includes information on your compensation policy, such as when the employee will be paid and what deductions are taken.
- locations of restrooms, lockers, employee eating facilities/break room, vending machines, parking space, employee entrance and timeclock.
- work hours and scheduling procedures. Overtime, flextime and comp-time policies.

This is a good time to distribute the organization's employee handbook, which should contain much of this information.

- **Organizational policies.** Time-off policy, vacation time and scheduling, paid holidays, call-in policy for illness, accrual of sickleave, substitute policy, meal and break policies.
- **Operational policies.** If you have done a good job explaining the hospitality company to the new employee, he or she will already have a good appreciation for why "the way we do things here" is so important. We always refer to our customers as "guests," or we always greet our guests with a smile are two examples of operational policies that might be part of your hospitality organization's corporate culture. Every operation has values and traditions of which every new employee must be made aware.
- Here you would also want to include information on your organization's policies relating to promotion, performance appraisals and career development opportunities.
- **A tour.** Familiarizing the new employee with the hospitality premises is important not only for his or her own knowledge, but

---

Table 7-2. Information Needed for New Hires

- Medical insurance forms
- Life insurance forms
- Federal Withholding form (Form W-4)
- Signatures acknowledging:
    - receipt of keys
    - receipt of company's rules of conduct
    - receipt of policies and procedures manual
- Medical examiners report (if required)
- Health certificate

---

just in case a guest asks for directions. The tour should include all areas that will help the new employee to perform his or her job more effectively. The locations of departments that interact with the new hire's department should be given special attention.

- **Departmental responsibilities.** Every human resource needs to understand the contribution of his or her work unit to the hospitality operation as well as his or her department's relationship to other departments. Introductions to other people the new employee will be working with should be made.

- **Job responsibilities.** This is an introduction to what the individual's job will consist of, including how it relates to other jobs in the department. The new employee is shown his or her work area along with any equipment the individual might be working with in his or her job position. An introduction to the employee's immediate supervisor should occur, if it has not been made already.

- **Sanitation and safety procedures.** Many hospitality organizations, especially those involved in the preparation and service of food, incorporate a session on sanitation procedures to all food service workers. Many others routinely include information on safety, as many departments in hospitality organizations contain equipment and chemicals that if not handled correctly and with great care could be dangerous to our human resources, and in some cases to our guests. OSHA federal guidelines require all operations to maintain a hazard communication program.

Some hospitality organizations prepare a welcome kit that contains information useful to the new employee trying to become familiar with his or her new work environment. This can be read over by the employee at his or her leisure and can serve as a future reference guide when questions arise. The specific listing you develop for your hospitality organization will depend on its size, mission and what management considers to be important information for new hires. In unionized operations, for example, it would be important to cover the significant provisions in the labor contract. In nonunionized operations statements about *remaining* non-unionized might be included. A well-thought-out orientation will help new employees feel comfortable and at ease in their new job position (see Table 7-3).

Follow-up and Evaluation

Once the hospitality organization has formally established a good orientation program and checklist, the responsibility does not end for

Table 7-3. New Employee Orientation Checklist

- review of job descriptions, hours and days to work, job duties and responsibilities
- rate of pay, pay policies and periods
- special uniform requirements
- break periods and meal hours
- review of rules of conduct and employee handbook
- unforeseen absences and tardiness
- review of Equal Employment Opportunity Policy
- fill out and sign W-4
- tour of operation and work unit
- introduction to co-workers
- to whom to report, when and where
- list of frequently called phone numbers
- sanitation and safety procedures

assuring a successful orientation. It is extremely critical that during the first few weeks of employment some follow-up takes place. This is to ensure that the employee is adjusting to his or her new work environment with the least amount of job anxiety and problems possible.

A follow-up will also clarify any questions that might have arisen as a result of the orientation program. Once your new hire has been on the job for a few days, clarification might be needed on departmental rules or regulations; after he or she receives the first paycheck, another explanation of how to read the paycheck might be needed; another tour might be in order especially if your property is very large and complex. All these measures are taken to assist your human resources in assimilating into the hospitality work place with as much ease as possible.

Orientation programs, while separate from training, do compose an important part of the human resources planning and employment processes. The more quickly you can reduce the anxieties of your new hire, the more quickly that employee will become a productive member of the overall hospitality team. Orientation programs are about more than just the benefits, rules and regulations; it is your opportunity to socialize the newest human resources in your hospitality organization and make them team members!

Why Train?

Training programs need to be distinguished from orientation programs. While orientation programs provide information, training goes farther in that it seeks to teach or improve skills and concepts. One of the main objectives of training is to sustain performance at or improve performance to acceptable levels. Orientation aids us in meeting this training objective, for without information about the organization, department and job, we can hardly expect performance levels to be satisfactory.

In recent years service—or the seeming lack of it—in American society has been making headlines. The hospitality industry has, along with other industries that provide service, had its share of negative publicity. When you think about it, it is really amazing that individuals that are willing to spend thousands and even millions of dollars building a new restaurant or renovating an old landmark hotel fail to allocate enough dollars for training. According to Nick Horney, other industries have more readily invested in training than has hospitality.

How much do you think should be allocated per human resource for training each year? A hundred dollars? A thousand dollars? Two thousand? Three thousand? Or less? Maybe twenty dollars for a self-study training manual. And how much would you allocate for a redesigned menu for your restaurant, new bed linens for the rooms or updated software to handle your daily receipts. The last three items are all considered investments: items that improve the quality of the service you offer your guests. Similarly, you cannot afford to consider training any less of an investment.

What It Is

With the growing emphasis on guest service in the hospitality industry, we must understand how to develop, implement and maintain effective training programs. We will define **training** as a systematic process through which the human resources in the hospitality industry gain knowledge and develop skills by instruction and practical activities that result in improved performance.

Training can be conducted at a number of different levels making training an on-going activity in your hospitality operation. Upon graduation many of you will be experiencing the management candidate training program, such as the one we discussed earlier that is offered by Stouffer Hotels and Resorts and outlined in Table 7-4. At this level, training provides the management candidate with an overview of every department along with supervisory training experiences.

Training can also be conducted for supervisory human resources. These are individuals such as shift managers and floor supervisors, similar to foremen in other industries. Frequently, these people have been hourly employees that have exhibited some of the leadership qualities you look for in your supervisors. The skills they need to develop relate more to a people orientation than the skills orientation they have had in their hourly job positions.

Training programs also need to be established for promotable human resources. These are the individuals who excel in their performance levels and are ready to accept more responsibility. Failing to

Table 7-4. Generalist Management Training Program Departmental Breakdown, Stouffer Hotels and Resorts—An Approximate Timetable

3	Days	1)	General Orientation

1	Day	1)	Rooms Department General Orientation
20	Days	2)	Housekeeping
10	Days	3)	Bellstand, Concierge and PBX
30	Days	4)	Reservations
140	Days	5)	Front Desk

201 Total Days—Rooms

1	Day	1)	F & B General Orientation
8	Days	2)	Stewarding
3	Days	3)	Purchasing/Receiving
6	Days	4)	Culinary
15	Days	4)	Restaurant Service (All-Day Dining)
4	Days	6)	Restaurant Service (Fine Dining)
6	Days	7)	Beverage
9	Days	8)	Banquets
6	Days	9)	Catering
2	Days	10)	Room Service

60 Total Days—Food and Beverage

15	Days	1)	Sales and Marketing
12	Days	2)	Personnel
17	Days	3)	Accounting
2	Days	4)	Engineering
2	Days	5)	Loss Prevention

312 Total Days

Source: Stouffer Hotels & Resorts

provide this opportunity may result in the loss of some of your best people. As you will see in future chapters, these training programs will become part of the development opportunities you provide for all of your human resources.

Retraining needs might also occur with current employees who display a deficiency or need to be trained in a particular area or areas. This could be due to a skill deficiency causing substandard performance, the need for new skills due to a change in job positions or merely a refresher on skills that the employee has mastered but has not had cause to use. It is your responsibility, in human resources management, to pick up on signals that indicate a training need. What are some of those signals? Can you think of any? The following is a list of our ideas:

- **Low Productivity.** All hospitality organizations operate according to standards and policies. When you find that an employee is not keeping up with standards, such as a housekeeper who cannot consistently clean his or her assigned number of rooms each day, then you need to look into the reasons why productivity levels are not being maintained.

- **High Waste.** Whether it is too many onions being used in your restaurant, too many mixers in your bar or too much window cleaner in your housekeeping department, high usages can indicate waste. Maybe your cooks don't know the proper way to peel onions, the bartender is using the wrong size glasses or the housekeepers are using window cleaner to clean everything. Each of these situations could mean that a training need exists.

- **Grievances and High Turnover of Employees.** What is the cause of these grievances and high turnover? While not always related to a lack of training, it could be a plausible reason. If you have ever worked in a job where you were not told what to do or how to do it, you know how frustrated and inadequate you can feel. No one wants to go to work and perform a job he or she really doesn't understand and is uncomfortable with doing for fear of making a mistake. People generally want to be successful and it is our job to provide them with the proper tools to achieve that success.

- **Guest Complaints.** Listen to your guests and find out the reasons when they indicate that they are not satisfied. These reasons could spell T-R-A-I-N-I-N-G.

All of these situations could indicate a need for training or retraining your present staff. Training should always strive to be responsive to the needs of the hospitality operation. This goes back to the human resources planning that we discussed earlier in this text. For the remainder of this chapter we are going to examine training from the perspective of our new hires. Those human resources have successfully completed our well thought out orientation program, but have yet to start their job tasks, duties and responsibilities. These individuals will work more effectively if we provide them with the proper training *before* placing them into their new job position.

A Historical Perspective

Once upon a time in the hospitality industry, you could tell an employee to do a task, furthermore you could tell that employee to do it in a specific manner and he or she would. In the 1990s, our human resources don't want to perform a task simply because you have told them to, but rather they want to understand the reason why they are doing that task.

The notion of training can be traced back to very early civilizations when apprenticeships were developed to pass down the skills to perform

167

various crafts. A young person would actually be bound to his or her employer by a legal agreement, and in exchange for work the apprentice would learn the craft from the skilled worker. The idea of apprenticeships is still prevalent in the hospitality industry in Europe today, and exists to a lesser degree in the United States, particularly in the area of culinary training.

The beginnings of vocational education have been traced to the 1700s. Many of you probably attended "voc ed" classes when you were in high school. In the 1980s these high school programs changed dramatically, and now serve as places where students can be exposed to a partial view of the hospitality industry. Historically, though, these programs were developed merely for the purpose of craft training.

Numerous training programs resulted from World War II efforts to rapidly train individuals to assist in our nation's defense. Among them are the job instructor training program, and the job safety training program. At the same time, the need for management training occurred and was met through the Engineering, Science, and Management War Training program (ESMWT).

In the 1990s training can no longer be thought of as a stop-gap activity. We can trace this increasing importance and value of training to the hospitality industry by examining training departments throughout the past several years. An example of the commitment being made to training and development by hospitality companies, such as Stouffer Hotels and Resorts, is exhibited in Figure 7-1.

Objectives of Training in "the Next Chapter"

The human resources who work for us, like, we, ourselves, have choices. The more frequently they make the right choices, the better off you, the manager, are. The better trained your human resources are, the more likely it is that they will make the right choices. The less training you provide, the more likely your human resources will make the wrong choices. Poorly trained human resources with low morale translates into poor quality service. The more you can maximize the abilities of your staff, the more successful they, and you, will be. We guarantee that you will have a lot more fun. Well trained employees can assume more responsibility and that makes your job easier.

In the hospitality industry, regardless of the job position they hold, what is the predominant job responsibility for each of your human resources? We want you to think very carefully about this question, because its answer becomes the focus of all training activities that take place. Maximizing guest satisfaction is the predominant job responsibility for each human resource you employ, even the dishwashers who might never come into direct contact with the guests.

Figure 7-1. Stouffer Hospitality Academy for Professional Education (S.H.A.P.E.)
Courtesy of Stouffer Hotels and Resorts

Before training actually takes place, the first thing you must tell your hourly employees is their job responsibilities. The job tasks that you are about to train them to perform are merely the means of achieving maximum guest satisfaction.

The following is a listing of specific training objectives that are commonly found in the hospitality industry. Please note that all can be related directly back to maximizing guest satisfaction:

- to make the hospitality operation a safe place for both employees and guests.
  - accident prevention
  - security measures
- to increase worker satisfaction.
  - reduce turnover costs
- to provide the knowledge and skills levels necessary to perform assigned job position.
- to improve skill levels and performance abilities of our human resources.
  - increased productivity
  - improved labor efficiency
  - improved development and promotional opportunities

Training is important. Both the guest and the employee benefit from an effective training program. Table 7-5 identifies several of the

**Table 7-5. Benefits to Be Gained
from the Implementation of a Training Program**

- improves quality of guest services
- increases comradely and sense of teamwork
- improved quality
- reduces work conflicts
- relieves stress and tension
- reduces high turnover and absenteeism
- improves performance resulting in cost savings
- prepares employee for promotion
- improves self esteem of our human resources
- instills sense of professionalism
- improves relationships between management and staff
- reduction in accidents
- increased productivity
- improved sanitation and cleanliness
- decreases fatigue
- improved sense of job security
- reduction in amount of supervision required
- happier work environment

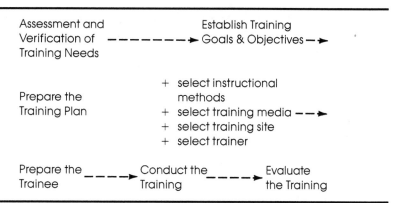

Figure 7-2. Development of a Training Program

advantages gained from training human resources in the hospitality industry.

A Guide to Developing Your Hospitality Training Program

As we have seen, there are numerous benefits that can be gained from an effective training program in the hospitality industry. But just what do we mean by "effective"? How do we get our training program to pay off with results? Planning and dedication to the training effort are required. Before you can start training, you must first assess the needs of your hospitality operation and then outline the training program so that it meets current and future needs. Figure 7-2 displays the development process of a training program.

Knowing When Training Is Needed

To initiate a training program you will need an outline of the topics to be covered. The training topics that will be taught are based upon the needs of your human resources. So the question that you must first answer is "What are the needs of my trainees?". Once the needs are identified, the training program can then be designed to specifically address those needs.

There are three areas that require analysis for your needs assessment; the hospitality organization, the job position and the knowledge and skill level of the trainee. If your training program is going to be effective it must meet the goals of the hospitality organization, it must be relevant to the particular job duties and tasks required of the job position and it must satisfy a deficiency in the knowledge or skill level of the trainee.

- **Organizational assessment.** The assessment of your hospitality organization was discussed in chapter 2. It was during the planning phase that we developed the mission statement for our hospitality enterprise, and from it prepared our organizational goals and operational objectives.

172

INDUSTRY EXPERTS SPEAK	Nick Horney emphasizes that if the human resources planning process isn't used as a beginning point, the situation is analogous to seeing only individual trees and not the forest. He continues: just like a financial plan, operating plan, and marketing plan, human resources planning and the resulting training plan are used to monitor progress towards the organization's goal. Taking into account the needs of our hospitality organization in the development of our training program is important if we are to keep the owners or, in many cases, the stockholders of our company happy. It is this assessment that will provide you with your hospitality company's training philosophy. While, as we have seen, the role of training is increasing in importance in many hospitality organizations, unfortunately this is not always the case.

- **Job analysis.** Job analysis provides valuable information for a variety of human resources functions. We have already seen the value of job analysis in the recruitment, selection, hiring and placement functions. Now it serves us again as we attempt to determine the training needs.

You will recall from chapter 4, Analysis of the Work Place, that job information was collected by a variety of methods, for each job position in the hospitality work place. A job listing was compiled that contained the specific tasks required in the performance of each job position. A sample task listing for a housekeeper is found in Table 7-6. From this information job descriptions and specifications were written.

The information from the task analysis will give us an indication of the difficulty of learning the task. This will be useful to us in selecting the instructional methods and training media. Information is also obtained relating to the importance of the task in the performance of the job that will help us prioritize our training needs.

Table 7-6. Task Listing for a Housekeeper

---

1. Locate the cart with the same section number written on it as the one to which you are assigned.

2. Place the bucket and basket on top of your cart and quietly push it out into the hallway outside the linen closet.

3. Go into the linen closet, collect a small group of linens and put them on top of your cart.

4. Fold and neatly stack linens for 5 rooms on your cart.
   a. Fold the bath towels, hand towels and wash cloths and stack them on the top shelf inside the cart.
   b. Fold the sheets, pillow cases and bath mats and stack them on the top shelf inside the cart.

5. Prepare the top of your cart.
   a. Place a pillow case in the space on top of your cart under the bucket and basket.
   b. Organize toilet paper, facial tissue, glasses and current magazines on top of the cart.
   c. Hook five hangers of each type to the back rim of the top of the cart.
   d. Place a broom and a toilet brush up-side down between the garbage bag and the cart.

- **Assessment of our human resources.** Our recruitment and selection efforts have provided us with the most qualified individuals for the vacant job positions. Ideally they would walk into the work place after orientation and have all the knowledge, skills and abilities to perform the job at a level equal to or higher than our stated performance standards. Neither one of us, however, can think of one case in our operational experience where this situation has occurred. So don't blame those recruiters or that placement department with bringing you inferior new hires. Your job is now to take those human resources and assess their knowledge, skills and abilities.

For those of you who work for a hospitality organization that requires preemployment testing some of this work has already been done by the placement department. From the job analysis you know the knowledge, skills and abilities needed to perform the job. Whether through preemployment or diagnostic testing you must now determine the performance levels of your trainees. Training needs are indicated by

174

performance levels that are substandard to those required to successfully perform the duties and responsibilities of the job position.

Another indication of a training need is evidence of a conflict between the needs of the hospitality organization and the needs of the employees. Training is not only necessary when there is a deficiency in skills, it is also necessary to change or improve employee attitudes and behaviors.

This relates directly to our earlier discussion of maximizing guest satisfaction. Our human resources have to be trained to maximize satisfaction for every guest that enters our hospitality operation. We can do this by reinforcing that message throughout the entire training program by relating everything we teach to the objective of maximum guest satisfaction. That is *why* the dishwashers must be sure to drain the dishmachine on a regular basis, that is *why* the housekeepers must recheck the room they just cleaned before leaving and that is *why* the bartenders must follow drink recipes.

It is clear that completing a needs assessment is a logical first step in the development of a training program. But if it is so logical, then why don't more hospitality organizations complete this critical step?

Completing needs assessments is a time consuming process. Unfortunately, in the hospitality industry we need our new hires trained yesterday, and many managers feel that they simply cannot wait for a needs assessment to occur for every new hire. So instead—at best—everyone goes through a general orientation and generic training program with assurances that his or her supervisor will follow-up with training in any deficiencies that they see while the employee is on the job. In the worst scenario, no training occurs and the new hire is simply shown his or her work station and told to feel free to ask any questions. Not wanting to appear stupid, the new hire will either attempt to figure out procedures independently, or will become so frustrated that the first day at work is also the last. Then management is left wondering what happened. But worst of all, you have neglected your number one objective of maximizing guest satisfaction.

Another reason that needs assessments aren't performed more often is that many people don't have your understanding of what need assessments are and the results that they generate. Hospitality is an action-oriented industry and if management does not see immediate results, they are likely to question how you are spending your time.

One cautionary note: when making observations for your needs analysis, care must to taken to differentiate between problems and needs that are the result of inadequate training and those that result from inadequate equipment, poor procedures, lack of feedback or poor supervision. Training needs include only those problems that can be solved through training. Not all problems are training problems nor are all needs training needs!

Training Goals and Objectives

Your analysis of the organization, the job and the human resources has provided you with a list of training needs matched with trainees. If your training needs are numerous you might want to consider prioritizing them into "A," "B" and "C" categories. Your "A" category would be those needs of primary importance for the day-to-day operations of your establishment. For the waitstaff this might consist of learning the proper serving procedures. "B" training needs would be secondary to the functioning of the operation, but critical in maximizing guest satisfaction. For the waitstaff this might include learning how each dish they will be serving is prepared. "C" needs have even a lower immediate priority, but again are necessary to set your hospitality operation above the competition. An example for the waitstaff could include knowing the characteristics of the most recently released wines available on the market.

175

It is important that your prioritized training needs and broad training goals such as maximizing guest satisfaction, providing basic job knowledge and skills and providing a means to achieve job satisfaction are translated, in writing, to specific training objectives. Table 7-7 provides you with an example of a training objective for the housekeeper's position we identified when we conducted our needs analysis.

You should always specify the behavior or performance desired at the end of the training program. Training objectives must be realistic and should provide for some form of evaluation to determine whether or not they have been obtained. Training objectives must be developed from the perspective of your own hospitality operation; you can't open a book to find a list of training objectives that will be suitable to your situation. The work you have accomplished so far will make the preparation of your training plan much easier.

The Training Plan

The training plan could be considered the heart of the training program. It is an outline that takes the training needs, goals, and objectives—or what your operation must do with respect to training—and identifies when, where, by whom and how the training will be accomplished. Where the training takes place is answered by selection of

Table 7-7. Sample Training Objective

Objective: To be able to clean 15 guest rooms satisfactorily and in accordance with _____ standards of cleanliness, during one shift.

the training site. By whom, is answered by the selection of the trainer. How the training will be accomplished is answered by selecting the instructional methods and the training media. When the training should occur is determined by the priority of the training need.

Many job positions in the hospitality industry require a great deal of decision making on the part of our human resources. They just simply cannot be trained for every possible situation that they will experience in the course of performing their job tasks. Part of the assessment of the individual trainee must take into account his or her decision-making abilities and, if deficient, the training plan must meet this critical need.

We are going to initiate our preparation of a training plan by first selecting the training site, then looking at the selection of the trainer and finally discussing the variety of training methods and media available to assist you in meeting your hospitality organization's training needs.

The Training Location

Selecting the training location will be partially determined by the type of training method that you select, whether it is classroom or on-the-job training that you want to provide. The environment is a critical factor in determining the success of your training program. The area should be pleasant with a minimum of distractions.

Think about the type of environment that you learned best in while you were at school. What do you consider distractions to learning? The environment temperature, humidity, lighting, your comfort at your desk or chair, the list could go on and on. If something in the environment causes the training experience to be less than it could be, than we bet that those same factors will affect the amount of learning your trainees will do. Without the proper environment and facilities training will be harder and less effective.

The appropriate training aids also need to be available. Can you imagine your accounting professor giving a lecture without chalk and a blackboard or an overhead marking pen and transparencies? Can you imagine training your housekeeper in making a bed without sheets, blankets, pillows and a bed? Of course not! Almost every training session will require tools, equipment, supplies or materials of some type. These should be identified and gathered ahead of time so that they are ready for the training session. This would include any audiovisual equipment or materials which you might need.

Training the Trainer

Many of you who will be assuming human resources responsibilities will also find yourself in the role of trainer. And we also know that for some of you that will be a very uncomfortable position. Getting up in front of a group of people and giving a presentation is not an easy thing for many of us! Those of you who get nervous giving classroom speeches as part of your course work understand exactly what we mean.

Some of you might be planning on having your best employees train your new hires by using the "buddy system." It is generally felt that this is not the best training method. You, as manager, lose control over what learning takes place by the trainee. Shortcuts or other procedures that are not up to your performance standards may be taught instead of the correct way to perform a task.

If your hospitality organization is large enough, you might have a staff of trainers employed on your payroll, but in most cases the training will fall on your shoulders, and you should be prepared to assume these human resources responsibilities. The following characteristics are needed in a trainer:

- knowledge of job skills
- knowledge of trainee abilities and skill levels
- knowledge of learning principles
- ability to communicate effectively
- ability to motivate
- patience
- enthusiasm
- understanding

Dr. Nick Horney points out that your role as trainer will depend on the philosophy of the hospitality organization. The philosophy of Stouffer Hotels, for example, is not to hire training managers, but to ensure that the accountability for training properly rests with the management team. You can't expect people to train themselves, at least not in accordance with the standards and operating policies that you want to maintain in your hospitality organization. But if you don't train your new hires they will still learn, and unfortunately, they won't learn what you want them to learn.

Selecting the Training Method

The next decision that you have to make is to determine which method to use in your training program to maximize the amount of learning that occurs for each of your trainees. The training of your human resources can take place in many ways in the hospitality industry. Some of these methods are formal and some are informal. Frequently, multiple methods are used to assist the trainees in developing their skills. Selection of a particular method depends on the training objective (what is to be learned), the number of trainees involved, the skill and ability levels of the trainees and the training budget.

While this chapter will deal primarily with in-house training methods, the following vehicles can be used when in-house methods are not suitable for your particular situation. They include:

- **College/University courses.** These frequently extend beyond the management development program that you are enrolled in. Many of the same courses that you take would serve as training vehicles for some job positions.
- **Correspondence courses.** The educational arms of both the American Hotel and Motel Association and the National Restaurant Association offer correspondence courses to which your hospitality operation could subscribe. There are several other organizations, frequently associated with universities, that also supply correspondence courses.
- **Educational seminars.** There are numerous hospitality groups that sponsor seminars throughout the year. Frequently you will find topics that are relevant to the training needs of your hospitality organization.

Each trainee will respond differently to training, so as managers with human resources responsibilities, it is up to us to use the right method of training, at the right time for each of our human resources. Let's examine some of the various methods you can choose from when conducting an in-house training program.

The Lecture method.   We know that this is the method that each of you know best! Its greatest advantage? The lecture method is very cost effective when training large numbers of trainees. Its greatest disadvantage? Unless you're a very clever and witty speaker, it can be very boring and cause you to lose the attention of your audience. Trainee retention is also less than with other methods.

What can you do then to overcome the disadvantages of using the lecture method? Think about experiences you have had while in school. Audiovisual materials can be used to supplement the lecturer. Everything from films, slides, videotapes, flipcharts, overheads to interactions with computer monitors can be incorporated to make the lecture method seem less tedious to the trainees. Another way you can pep up lectures is to encourage questions and feedback from the trainees to get them involved in the training session. This also helps you measure how well your message is coming across.

On-the-Job training.   On-the-job training (OJT) is designed so that learning occurs while the trainee is actually performing the tasks required of his or her job position (Figure 7-3). Those who advocate OJT believe that trainees will learn best when faced with the actual job situation. Those who don't use OJT state as some of their reasons:

179

Figure 7-3. On-the-job training permits learning to occur while the trainee is actually in his or her job position.
Courtesy of Stouffer Hotels and Resorts

- a good way to pass along bad work habits
- can interfere with your objective of maximizing guest satisfaction if OJT takes precedence over, let's say, getting the food to the guest
- can cause an increase in waste and lost productivity
- training can take second place to the job being done and result in a less than satisfactory learning experience.

A good OJT design that is well implemented can overcome these potential problems.

Job instruction training. Even though job instruction training is really a form of on-the-job training, we want to discuss it in more detail, since it is the most typical technique used in the training of a new hire.

If any of you have taken a speech class you know that the way to present new material to an audience is to tell them what you're going to tell them; tell them; and then tell them what you told them. Job instruction training is where the trainer *tells* the trainee how to do the task; *shows* the trainee how to do the task; *observes* the trainee doing the task; and then provides *feedback* to the trainee on how well he or she did the task.

We would like to incorporate our basic objective of maximizing guest satisfaction into the technique of job instruction training. When the trainee truly understands, without question, the reason *why* he or she is performing a task the trainee will work with greater efficiency, increasing your chances of achieving maximum guest satisfaction. Furthermore, you should explain *how* the performance of that task affects your operation in relationship to guest satisfaction. For example, if the salad prep person does not rinse the fresh spinach three times using fresh warm water for each rinse, the guest is likely to be chewing sand in his or her fresh spinach salad: a very unpleasant guest experience!

At this point, you should explain to the trainee how his or her job performance can affect the jobs of other employees in your operation. It will probably be the waitstaff person who will incur the effects of the guest having a spinach salad with sand. As a final step in job instruction training it never hurts to ask the trainee "Do you understand?", which is your confirmation that the trainee knows what you are talking about. Remember that practice makes perfect. The training cycle is really quite simple: the trainer observes and provides feedback while the trainee practices. Observe—Feedback—Practice—Observe—Feedback—Practice—Observe—Feedback—Practice—"perfect practice makes perfect"—Vince Lombardi.

Vestibule. Vestibule or simulation training methods are those in which the real work environment is duplicated for the purpose of training. This has the advantages of on-the-job training without the potential of interfering, or negatively affecting, the day-to-day operations of your establishment. The simulated approach works best with small groups. Its biggest disadvantage is the high cost of duplicating a work environment that is essentially nonrevenue producing. The long term training effect should be evaluated to see if it results in a better return on investment (ROI) than other techniques.

Role Playing. Role playing is a training technique that stimulates learning by having the trainees act out real life situations that they might incur in the performance of their jobs. The advantage is that learning results from doing, which usually generates a higher retention than learning from merely observing. Role playing can be used to show trainees how to deal with difficult people, be they guests or other employees, as well as proper serving methods. Skills and behaviors both can be learned through role playing.

Choosing the Training Media

We have already discussed some of the more common training media available to you when we explained the lecture method of training. In "the next chapter" you will have available to you many innovative training aids. Videotapes have almost replaced the use of filmstrips and slides in training presentations. As the cost of video equipment decreases, more and more hospitality operations are finding videotapes to be an effective training median.[2] Many hospitality companies are building in-house audiovisual libraries to use as a supplement with their on-the-job training programs.

More recently, some hotel companies have implemented a program called teletraining. In teletraining the trainer is located in a central location and remotes at any site in the country (or world) can tap in and participate in the training session. This is a very cost effective training median.

Computer-based training programs allow the trainee to advance through the training at his or her own pace. It works similar to the simulation method, only the computer serves as the simulator duplicating real life industry experiences. Because the trainee can control the pace of the program, the individual can also go back and repeat segments that he or she feel need clarification. The disadvantage is the lack of human interaction. Interactive video programs can be used to overcome this disadvantage.

All these methods of training are worthless unless management is behind the programs one hundred percent. You can tell if you have management's commitment by their participation in the programs, their role as a trainer of the program, and the focus they give to each manager's performance objectives regarding people development.

Preparing the Trainee

Remember that for many of our hourly employees training is likely to be a new experience. They probably don't know what to expect so it will be up to you, as trainer, to make them feel comfortable and at ease. It will help if they understand directly how this training will benefit them. Assure them that your job is to help and support them through the training program and that they will not be punished for their mistakes. They need to have confidence in you, so it is important that you have your act together and come to the training session well organized and prepared.

You might want to begin by giving them a brief overview of their new job position. As they begin to relax with you they can turn their thoughts towards learning. Although they saw their work station during orientation, now is the time to take them back to the work area and explain briefly the equipment that is found there. It is important that the trainee understands how each task fits into his or her total job.

During this overview you will also gain a more personal perspective on what the trainee knows, what equipment the trainee may have worked with before, and what kinds of skills he or she has used in previous jobs. All of this will serve to help generate employee interest in the training program.

Conduct the Training Session

In your role as trainer you will be facilitating the training of the new hire so that the trainee is able to learn the skills, duties and responsibilities of his or her new job position as thoroughly and quickly as possible. As we have stated throughout this section, training should always be responsive to the needs of the hospitality organization. While you are aware of the importance of guest satisfaction, you cannot expect the trainee to have this awareness unless you incorporate it into the implementation of your training program.

Conducting the training program requires the implementation of all elements of the training plan. After you present the job to the employee using the job task listings you developed, have the employee try out each of the tasks while you watch. While we know that operational pressures and responsibilities can be enormous, you must keep in mind the importance of a well conducted training session. It is up to you to instill in the trainee the commitment to persist when left on his or her own in the job.

Evaluate the Training

This step is perhaps the most critical in the training program. Once the transition has been made from training to job, follow-up and evaluation play an important part in maintaining acceptable job performance. Ideally, follow-up never really ends. Even under regular supervision and day-to-day activities, our human resources deserve feedback on how well they are doing in their jobs.

Before leaving trainees on their own, they should be told who they can go to if they have questions. You should make sure that they completely understand the standards of performance for all job tasks that they will be performing. After training is completed, try to be available and encourage questions. Performance should be checked frequently at first, with a gradual tapering off. Evaluating the trainees at the completion of the training program involves measuring the quality of their work based upon the specific performance standards of their job. Let the employees know how they are doing and where they need improvement.

The purpose of evaluating the training program is to determine whether the training has achieved its goals and objectives. Both the training method and the results of the training program should be evaluated. Methods need to be implemented to determine if the training objectives were met. Does trainee performance match organizational performance standards? This in turn measures the success of the training plan.

Maximizing Your Training Investment

You have spent a lot of time and effort in the development and implementation of your hospitality training program (Figure 7-4). What are some of the things that you can do to make sure that you are getting the best return on your investment? One way of answering that question is to look at some of the errors made in training:

STOUFFER
HOTELS & RESORTS

est. **EMPLOYEE SERVICE TRAINING**
BELL STAND PERSONNEL
Participant's Guide

© 1989 Stouffer Hotels and Resorts

BELL STAND PERSONNEL
10 (continued)

ACTIVITY	PRACTICE 1st	2nd
Run Errands		
10. Tell Bell Captain/supervisor where and why you are going.	☐	☐
11. Write details about errand.	☐	☐
12. Complete errand pleasantly and efficiently.	☐	☐
13. Cooperate with other hotel employees as necessary.	☐	☐
14. Follow procedures of Transportation Personnel whenever using hotel vehicle. Refer to "EST Transportation Personnel Participant's Guide."	☐	☐
Show Rooms		
15. Escort prospective guest to assigned viewing room.	☐	☐
16. Point out and describe as many facilities and services of hotel as possible.	☐	☐
17. Stay with prospective guest until guest returns to lobby.	☐	☐
18. Escort prospective guest to Sales Office if you feel person should see salesperson.	☐	☐

2/89   25   DO Section

183

BELL STAND PERSONNEL
Table of Contents

2/89   53   REFERENCE Section

BELL STAND PERSONNEL
12 Providing Guest Services

1. Know where to find information.

3. Know location of meeting rooms and daily events.

2/89   83   REFERENCE Section

Figure 7-4. A page from Stouffer Hotels and Resorts new EST training manual. Courtesy of Stouffer Hotels and Resorts

- Giving too much information at one time. While the information presented might be common sense to you, none of the tasks is mere routine for the trainee. The trainee is digesting new concepts and digestion takes time.
- Not tailoring the training to the specific needs of the job. Training cannot be packaged in a generic black-and-white box, put on a shelf and dusted off when needed.
- Treating the training of hourly employees as less important than management training programs. Hourly employees are the eyes and ears of any hospitality operation. Their importance to our success cannot be overstated, hence training should be treated with great importance. Every employee should be treated as a career employee, which could result in a stronger development program.
- Trainers who are not qualified to conduct the training sessions. We've already stated the characteristics necessary to be a good trainer. Trainers who do not know the job position or do not have the skills necessary to perform the job tasks can damage your credibility with the new hires.
- Explanations that are too technical or use of terminology that is unfamiliar to the trainees. Always try to explain things in everyday language and define all hospitality terms and slang when used. Never tell when you can show.
- Lack of patience. As a trainer you must recognize that learning is a slow process. This does not mean that your trainees are slow, but that we all learn at different rates of speed. Take care not to lose half of your training class.
- Failure to build in feedback mechanisms. Always make it possible for the trainees to ask questions whenever they feel the need. Without some type of trainee feedback you don't know whether they have truly learned. Another benefit of feedback mechanisms is that they also help to reduce tension.

Basic Principles of Adult Learning

When we examine learning from a training perspective we need to focus our attention specifically on adult learning. The reasons why adult men and women want to learn is a good place to start, as it is hard to improve the learning situation without understanding the motivations for adult learning. Adults want to learn when:

- they find that their work is interesting
- they can feel important in what they are doing
- they are challenged
- they know that their work is recognized and appreciated
- when they see that the satisfaction of their personal ambition is one of the benefits
- they want to learn
- their focus is on realistic problems

Adults learn what they feel is important and contributes to results that they value. This reinforces the need to relate the "whys" of training throughout the implementation of the training plan. Adults need to feel that they are productive contributors to the hospitality organization and its goals.

Barriers to Learning

There are many conditions that can keep our trainees from learning. When we train under these conditions effectiveness is reduced:

- Fatigue. It can reduce both our physical and mental effectiveness. The more fatigued our trainees are, the longer it takes to learn. This is why training sessions should not be conducted at the end of the workshift. The most beneficial sessions are kept short.
- Monotony. If you as the trainer find the session boring, it is highly likely that the trainees will also find it boring. What you are teaching may be routine to you, but it is not to your trainees. Keep the sessions lively and stimulating so that maximum learning can occur.
- Distractions. Any distractions will inhibit the learning process. This can be a problem in on-the-job training when the daily activities of your operation are going on around you.
- Anxiety. People are usually tense when they enter into new situations and are with unfamiliar individuals. It will be up to you to break the ice and get the trainee to relax, or learning will be inhibited.

There is much information that can be gained from a study of learning theory and methods. Many can be directly applied to training programs in the hospitality industry.

Conclusion

Orientation and training programs are two of the most valuable tools you have available to you as the human resources manager of a hospitality operation. As competition increases we have to look for ways to attract guests to *our* operation as opposed to all the others. Having a staff trained in maximizing guest satisfaction can be the deciding factor for many of our guests. People return to places where they feel at home, and where the staff takes care of their every request.

Successful training does not occur in a vacuum. Many other elements of the system are affected such as performance appraisals, merit increases, pay-for-performance, etc. Training impacts the total human resources management system.

Training is management's responsibility. In too many cases we blame the problems on the poor quality of employees we have when, instead, we should be blaming the lack of training. When planning the training program the manager that assumes human resources responsibilities needs to keep in mind the goals of the organization, the theory of learning, the needs of the job and the trainee, the variety of training methods and media available to them and a method of follow-up and evaluation.

Our human resources desire to be involved in only high-quality training experiences. The quality of the service we provide cannot improve until the quality of our training programs improves. We encourage you to become the most competent trainer you can be. More than just the reputation of your business is at stake. Training is a tool used by management to increase the productivity of all human resources as well as teaching them to learn how to react in whatever situation they may find themselves. Good service training can be achieved using the guidelines we've provided for you in this chapter.

CASE PROBLEM 7

Case Problem 7-1

You are the manager with human resources responsibilities for a national lodging chain composed of both hotel and resort properties. This chain has high name recognition in the United States, but low name recognition internationally. Your property is located downtown in a major Northeastern city and has 500 rooms supporting two lounges and two full-service dining facilities along with a gift shop, fitness center, and pool.

One of your major human resources responsibilities at this property is to conduct the orientation sessions for bellpersons. The bellperson position is a very important one in your organization. After guests are checked into their room at the front desk this is the individual with whom your guests have the most amount of personal contact. When escorting the guests to their hotel room, your property expects the bellperson to describe the facilities that you offer on-site. The guests expect the bellperson to have a lot of information, not only about the property but about the city itself.

You have been asked by the general manager to prepare an orientation session for five newly hired bellpersons next week. These individuals are to go through your orientation program before they will be trained and placed in their positions. Each of these new hires have had prior experience as bellpersons in other lodging operations.

Put together an outline of the items you wish to cover in the orientation session, along with a projected timetable for their completion. The bellpersons will be meeting collectively for the orientation session. Indicate which of these items need to be covered before training begins and which might be conducted simultaneously with training.

Case Problem 7-2

You have been hired by a major lodging chain as an assistant manager and assigned to a property located in the heart of a major city in the Northwest. During your training you are rotated among the various departments within the property. After your training period you will be relocated to another hotel property.

Shortly after beginning your training rotation in the housekeeping department you become aware of irregularities and inconsistencies in the procedures used by the housekeeping staff. When working with Sally you clean the bathroom and then make the beds. When working with Susie you make the beds and then clean the bathrooms. While this did not bother you too much, you also noticed that standards were being ignored regarding the amount of cleaning solutions used, the time required to clean a room, and the amount of linens being left in each guest room.

Since this is your first job after graduation you are not anxious to make a number of enemies. While you will not be assigned to this property after training, the job evaluations you receive *will* weigh heavily in determining the property to which you will be assigned. You decide, therefore, that the best approach would be to discuss the inconsistencies you have witnessed with the executive housekeeper. Upon doing so you are informed that there have been no guest complaints regarding the condition of the rooms nor has the general manager complained about the amount of supplies being consumed or the overtime. "While I am sure you mean well, the housekeeping department of this hotel has an *excellent* reputation! You must be mistaken." You are shown all the in-house awards the department has received throughout the years. "The rooms are spot-checked by a supervisor on a daily basis. Time cards have not reflected unnecessary overtime, nor has an excessive amount of cleaning solutions been consumed. As a matter of fact the housekeeping department is ahead of budget."

As you continue to work within the housekeeping department and get to know the staff a little better you begin to suspect that the violations and inconsistencies in procedures are due, not to a lack of interest or concern, but rather due to a lack of training. The housekeeping staff simply does not know the correct standards and procedures. Could any of your observations be caused by a lack of training? If so what are some of the indicators? Why have there been no guest complaints? Why is the housekeeping staff ahead of budget?

Select one job done by the housekeeping department and prepare a training objective for that training need. Since you suspect that a training need exists, what should you do? How will you "sell" your ideas to the executive housekeeper who doesn't think that a problem exists? Which training method would you select to implement this training? What are your reasons for selecting this particular training method? What might you do to insure the success of your training program, if and when it is approved?

RECOMMENDED READING

Carlisle, K. A.; Murphy, S.; and Tripodi, C. 1986. How to fold a napkin the same way everywhere. *Training and Development Journal* 4, (1): 65–67, 70–71.

Cichy, R. F. 1988. Staff training: 10 critical steps. *Hotel & Resort Industry* 11, (10): 68–74.

Desatnick, R. L. 1987. Building the customer-oriented work force. *Training and Development Journal* 41 (3): 72–74.

Goldstein, I. L. 1986. *Training in Organizations: Needs Assessment, Development, and Evaluation* Monterey: Brooks/Cole Publishing Co.

Gordon, J. 1988. The woo woo factor. *Training* 25, (7): 73–77.

Klubnik, J. P. 1987. Orienting new employees. *Training and Development Journal* 41, (4): 46–49.

Lagreca, G. 1988. Improving hospitality. *Restaurant Business* 87, (2): 80.

Munson, L. S. 1984. *How to Conduct Training Seminars* New York: McGraw-Hill Book Co.

Whitney, D. L. 1988. High performance concentration: applying principles of sports psychology to the hospitality industry. *Hospitality Education and Research Journal* 12, (2): 233–239.

189

END NOTES
1. Reinhardt, Claudia, "Training Supervisors in First-Day Orientation Techniques," *Personnel,* 65, (1988, 6): 24, 26, 28.
2. Rickles, Robert, "Firms Turn to Videos to Teach Workers," *Wall Street Journal,* CCXXII, (1988, 110): B2.

DISCUSSION QUESTIONS
1. What is orientation? What is training?
2. Compare and contrast company orientation, department orientation and job orientation.
3. List topics that you feel should be covered during a company orientation program for dishwashers in a 200-room lodging property with family dining area.
4. What are some of the problems that can occur when we fail to properly orient new employees? What problems occur when training needs are ignored?
5. Discuss how training has changed since the days of apprenticeships.
6. Discuss how the employee, the supervisor and the hospitality organization each benefit from training.
7. Why is it necessary to conduct an assessment of training needs? Describe in detail each of the three levels at which assessment must occur.
8. Identify and describe each of the components of a training plan.
9. Why do most hospitality organizations fail to evaluate their training programs?
10. What factors need to be taken into consideration when applying on-the-job training methods?
11. Why is training more important in "the next chapter" than it was in the 1970s or 1980s?

CHAPTER **8**

DEVELOPMENT PROGRAMS, COACHING AND TEAM BUILDING

INDUSTRY
ADVISOR

Hugh Murphy, Former Vice President Human Resources
Chili's, Inc.

"The highest reward for a person's toil is not what they get for it, but what they become by it."—JOHN RUSKIN

KEY WORDS

career counseling
career development
career pathing
career planning
coaching
development programs
development review
Expectancy Theory
hierarchy of needs
job enrichment

mentor programs
motivation
performance development
   counseling
Pygmalion Effect
self-fulfilling prophecy
team building
Theory X–Theory Y
Two-Factor Theory

INTRODUCTION

How do you get an employee to be the best he or she can be? Each human resource working in your hospitality organization is an individual, different and unique from every other human resource. Now that they have been oriented and trained (at least for their current job position), it is time to ensure that we nurture and care for our human resources as individuals.

Development programs are tailored for the individual needs of your human resources. These programs are designed to assist you, the manager with human resources responsibilities, in identifying these needs in an effort to develop improved performance. These programs are designed to assist our human resources in identifying and then meeting their career expectations and aspirations.

Using individual development programs to assist our human resources in becoming the best they can be requires an understanding of

191

motivation. By understanding what motivates people collectively, we will further our understanding of how to meet the needs of individuals. Our goal is to do what is best for the employee and at the same time to do what is best for the hospitality organization. The achievement of this goal will require us to have a knowledge of the techniques of coaching and team building.

At the conclusion of this chapter you will be able to:
1. Describe the relationship between career development/counseling and performance development/counseling; between career development and succession planning; between development reviews and performance appraisals.
2. Explain how a career development program operates in a hospitality organization.
3. Prepare for conducting a career development review for each of your employees.
4. Distinguish between the different types of career development programs.
5. Identify the basic theories of motivation.
6. Use motivation theory to assist in the planning of an individual development program.
7. Understand your role as a coach and counselor when assisting your human resources in planning their career development.
8. Explain how career development programs, coaching and team building assist you with the retention of your human resources.

Development's Function in Human Resources Management

The goal of a development program is to help our human resources become better each day. "Better" is a personal desire or aspiration that is defined by the individual employee. When we assist the individual employee in achieving his or her career aspirations, the hospitality work place becomes not only a more productive organization, but a more desirable environment to work in.

The development of our employees serves to tie together a number of human resources functions. Not only are these programs designed to improve performance and encourage retention, they also impact upon manpower planning at both the organizational and employee level. To accomplish this, development programs are linked together with performance development, succession planning and performance appraisal systems.

As we discussed in chapter 2, succession planning can be implemented at the hourly as well as at the management level. Succession planning assists you in preparing for the continued growth of your hospitality organization. Career development programs assist succession planning by encouraging the continued growth of talent within that organization. Used in this fashion, succession planning links development to the long-range manpower objectives. This helps to ensure that you will have the talent required to meet your current and future human resources needs. In this way, development programs link human resources needs to the business plans of the hospitality enterprise.

Through career development, opportunities for promotion from within the hospitality organization are increased. Career development reviews provide an opportunity for the employee to let management know where the employee would like to go in his or her career. These reviews also give management the opportunity to provide feedback to the employee regarding the individual's progress towards personal career goals. This is quite different from performance appraisals, which we will discuss in chapter 9, where the employee is evaluated on the degree to which his or her performance meets the organization's expectations and standards.

Both development reviews and performance appraisals provide you, the manager with human resources responsibilities, with information on the promotability each employee. The development reviews are a non-evaluative activity in which management lends support and guidance to each employee's own future job interests and career aspirations. The performance appraisal is an activity in which management evaluates the employee's performance with the results becoming the basis for compensation decisions. Table 8-1 shows you a comparison between performance appraisals and career development.

Performance development counseling occurs when there is a deficiency in performance standards. Problem-solving techniques are instituted that provide an opportunity for the employee to get his or her

Table 8-1. Comparison between Performance Appraisals and Career Development—Traditional Views

Performance Appraisal (Realism without Hope) Managers Ask:	Career Development (Hope without Realism) Employees Ask:
What is the employee contributing?	What are my career goals?
How is the employee measuring up to expectations?	What are my options for career movement?
What do I need to tell the employee about current performance?	What skills and abilities do I need to acquire?
How does current performance reflect on compensation?	What plans do I need to make to move toward my goals?
How does the employee rank against other employees?	What will be my implementation steps and timetable?

Reprinted, by permission of publisher, from *Personnel*, January, 1986, © 1986. American Management Association, New York. All rights reserved.

performance on the right track. These counseling activities are part of disciplinary actions geared at saving an employee from termination procedures. Performance development counseling involves coaching and team building techniques that assist the employee in achieving his or her own personal career aspirations.

The terms *development* and *training* have historically been used interchangeably in the work place. In "the next chapter" these words have very different roles in the hospitality organization. As we saw in the previous chapter, training is a process that teaches our human resources the skills necessary to perform the tasks required of their job position. Development activities assume that the basic skill levels already exist and seek to provide a process through which the employees can grow in their personal development within the company.

As you can see, development programs serve to link together a number of human resources functions. In doing so, they can increase the effectiveness of human resources management in your hospitality organization. By improving the promotability of your human resources you increase your options in the employment process. Your training programs then become tools in developing the talent and potential that already exists.

Career Development Programs for Hospitality Management

Career development, performance development, career management, career guidance and individual development are analogous terms for programs that seek to assist our human resources in becoming the best that they can be. We will define **career development** as a program that seeks to assist employees in their own personal growth and maturity in the hospitality work place. These programs seek a gradual improvement in the employee's working life by functioning in harmony with the employee's needs so that personal working values are satisfied. Both parties benefit by determining what is good for the employee and at the same time good for the organization.

Development programs are ongoing within the hospitality organization. The idea is that a constant upgrading is occurring among both your hourly and salaried staffs. Development programs can lead to career advancement, both horizontally and laterally, an idea that is relatively new in hospitality management. Let's look at an example of a lateral advancement for an hourly employee, a dishwasher. Now, while you might think that no one wants to wash dishes as a career, your thinking might be wrong. What you are really thinking is that *you* certainly would not want to wash dishes for a career! Development programs examine what the employee wants, and in the case of our dishwasher, he or she just wants to be a good dishwasher. This individual doesn't want the unfamiliarity of busing tables (a logical career move to get out of the dishroom) nor do they want the supervisory headaches of being head dishwasher (a typical management ploy that attempts to recognize outstanding performance).

A development program would permit our great dishwasher to remain a great dishwasher. First, through development reviews you, as the human resources manager, would be made aware of the fact that washing dishes is what this person likes and wants to do. Knowing this, you would not make the erroneous assumption that this person wants to be promoted out of the dishroom. Second, a development program would provide a means for lateral advancement and recognition of a job well done. Perhaps the lateral advancement would be to a day shift as opposed to the night shift. Recognition could be awarded in the form of either monetary or nonmonetary incentives.

195

INDUSTRY EXPERTS SPEAK

Hugh Murphy, Former Vice President of Human Resources explains Chili's career enhancement program: "In Chili's, management truly means achieving results through the employees. A company such as Chili's, growing at a rate of 20 + new restaurants per year, must look *inside* for the talent to grow the company. Career development and enhancement begins with tuition reimbursement assistance at both the undergraduate *and* graduate school level. Employees receiving educational assistance are tracked by the recruiting department for possible direct entry into the Chili's Management Training Program. Employees who demonstrate that they have that certain coach's eye can be selected for certification as a restaurant trainer to teach new employees Chili's methods. From the ranks of restaurant trainers come the training teams. The training teams travel the country helping train the "Chiliheads" at new openings. Completing the development opportunity is an employee's selection as a captain for a new opening. A Chili's Captain coordinates all aspects of employee training at the new restaurant, and acts as a liaison between the local management and the corporate team. Chili's, of course, offers opportunities to enter the management team. But Chili's career enhancement program also allows the employees to grow doing what they do best. A Chilihead does not *have* to go into mangement to grow in his or her profession."

What your development program must provide is a means by which your dishwashers can continue to do what they feel is in their best interest, while at the same time serving the hospitality operation's need for reliable dishroom personnel. Your challenge in the implementation of development programs is to keep your human resources challenged, or motivated, to seek continual improvement. This goes beyond merely seeing that the job tasks are performed, and that performance standards are maintained. The development programs you establish can be what makes your hospitality organization different from all the others because people want to work in an environment where management cares about their needs and desires. People want to work in an environment that is in harmony with their work values.

The Purpose of a Development Program

Career development is not something that occurs once or even occasionally, but is a continuous ongoing process that is constantly evolving based upon the needs of the participating individuals. Hospitality organizations that provide development programs offer their human resources the opportunity for maximum job satisfaction.

Maintaining productivity and job satisfaction are two outcomes of a successful development program. Even our dishwashers can find meaning in their work when we provide opportunities for lateral promotions, job enrichment and skill acquisition. Development programs translate into a "we care" and "you are important" attitude in the hospitality work place. By providing career counseling, we can make sure that our employee's expectations are both realistic and in harmony with the goals of the hospitality organization.

People, for the most part, want to do well in their work lives. Meaningful work is a goal for most everyone. By linking the growth needs of our human resources with the performance needs of the organization, job satisfaction occurs for both parties. Career development programs are the planned effort that cause this linkage to occur. Numerous advantages can be identified in hospitality organizations that result from career development programs.

For the organization:

- identification of human resources with promotional potential
- more qualified and skilled pool of human resources
- an increase in the amount of cross training
- improvement in retention and a decreased turnover
- reduction in recruiting expenses for highly trained personnel
- minimization of performance problems resulting from job dissatisfaction and frustration
- teamwork is encouraged
- communications improve between management and work force

For the employee:

- greater sense of job satisfaction
- realistic expectations about promotional opportunities, with a clearer sense of direction
- opportunities to develop talent potential
- assistance and coaching in the development of his or her careers
- opportunity to take responsibility for individual growth and development
- recognition as an individual

Development programs can be a powerful motivation and retention tool for human resources managers. You will read in the section on coaching and team building that the manager plays a very vital role in the development process. Assisting our human resources with personal development is a serious challenge for a hospitality organization and must be conducted with care and concern for all involved participants.

How Does a Career Development Program Work?

A hospitality organization is composed of individuals, and for it to succeed, there must be a commonality of ideas and goals. The design of development programs must take into consideration the mission statement of the enterprise and the organizational goals. The development paths of our human resources cannot be separate from the development path of our hospitality organization. The individuals in our organization must be able to relate to company goals.

Identifying the personal goals of employees requires an atmosphere of trust and open communication. Through communication with our human resources we can identify their interests and concerns that will assist us with their career development. Development programs place you in the role of counselor and coach to help employees identify their goals and career aspirations. Remember that our dishwashers are the only ones in possession of their aspirations. As a manager with human resources responsibilities, our role is to assist the dishwashers in identifying those aspirations and then gear their development program in a direction in which those aspirations can be met. Not all career development must lead to promotional opportunities. When it does we refer to the activity as **career pathing,** and the information is used by the hospitality organization in succession planning.

Every individual is distinct in their values, interests and work goals. Hence, successful human resources development stems from communication efforts that accurately identify individual needs and behavior. **Career planning** is the process by which the individual's short- and long-term career goals are identified. Part of this process includes identifying the individual's work values by asking the employee what is important to them in the individual's work. No two employees will come up with the same list of work values. As career counselor, you then analyze the

---

Table 8-2. Steps in a Development Program

---

1. Identify mission statement and goals of hospitality organization.
2. Assist employee in determination of personal goals and needs.

   - appraise current skills and knowledge
   - define career progress

3. Obtain information pertaining to organizational needs and priorities.
4. Develop action plan matching employee's needs with organizational needs.
5. Provide feedback and guidance to carry out action plan.

---

employee's job to see if any of these work values are missing.

A development program begins by assisting the employee in determining individual development goals and needs (Table 8-2). These are based upon the employee's interests, abilities and attitudes. Next the human resources manager as career counselor obtains information about the employee's job and the organizational goals and needs. This includes data on available job opportunities, skill requirements of jobs and the employment needs of the hospitality organization. An action plan is then formulated that will match employee needs with organizational needs. The action plan translates into the development plan for that individual human resource.

For development programs to be effective, feedback must be continuous. Your employees must understand that participation in this process does not mean automatic promotion. The only individuals who will be promoted are those individuals who are ready to be promoted. This brings us to another point that we wish to emphasize. Participation in the development programs must be optional, not mandatory. The initiative for development must be employee driven to be successful. The desire to grow comes from within each of our human resources with the hospitality organization providing the support and tools for personal growth.

The Development Review

The development review is a tool that will assist you in managing the potential of your work force (Figure 8-1). While we have already stated that feedback should be continuous, the review supplements the feedback program. The development review is a meeting between you and the employee during which the employee's aspirations and potential are assessed in light of the needs of the organization.

To maximize the effectiveness of the development review it is useful to have each employee fill out a form that will provide background information. Personal background information would include work history, education and training, both external and internal to the current organization. The development review provides an opportunity for each employee to make sure that the information is current.

Approach	Goal
1. ACTIVE LISTENING	Hearing and clearly understanding what is being said, by concentrated involvement in the communication process with the employee.
2. REFLECTING	Mirroring the subordinate's message content with an estimate stating what his/her feelings and attitudes are believed to be.
3. PARAPHRASING	Demonstrating an understanding of a worker's ideas by restating them in your words.
4. CLARIFYING	Getting employee elaboration on feelings or attitudes to benefit understanding.
5. INTERPRETING	Dealing with cause-and-effect relationships, apparent from the supervisor's own knowledge and the worker's comments, to understand the implications.
6. QUESTIONING	Using inquiry to help pull together the interaction.
7. SILENCE	Intentional pauses that help adjust the pace of interaction.
8. ENCOURAGING	Supportive statements or gestures that let the employee know that the supervisor can accept or empathize with his or her approach.
9. TENTATIVE ANALYSIS	Partial conclusion based on initial public testing of one idea expressed by the worker.
10. SUMMARIZING	Tentative overall conclusion of what has transpired in the interaction, to check levels of agreement and understanding by the participants.

Figure 8-1. Techniques and Goals for Effective Career Enhancement by Supervisors. Reprinted from *Personnel Administrator,* March 1986, Copyright 1986, American Society for Personnel Administration, Alexandria, VA.

Your role in the development review is that of coach and career counselor. You have the ability to assess the employee's potential for advancement, need for additional training as well as helping the individual keep his or her expectations realistic in terms of the employee's abilities. The review focuses on the needs and career of the individual employee. In development planning, consideration is given to their personal interests, strengths and weaknesses, and objectives. To assist the employee in identifying individual career interests and strengths, a career development form is filled out jointly by the employee and manager (Table 8-3).

The development review involves two-way communication between you, the manager in your role of career counselor and the employee. The discussions should revolve around employee growth, which might not be

---

Table 8-3. Career Development Form

Name _____ Job Title _____

Employee's Career or Job Goals (Outline each goal.)

_____

_____

_____

_____

Employee's Career Strengths

_____

_____

_____

Employee's Job or Career Development Needs (Identify the experiences the employee needs to achieve the job or career goals.)

_____

_____

_____

---

the same as employee advancement. The career development form helps guide the direction of the career discussions as well as assisting the employee in formulating career goals. Again, we emphasize career goals are not always vertical in direction.

Action plans are the result of the development review. Action plans provide a timetable for the accomplishment of the employee's goals along with a way of best meeting those goals. The action plans must be driven by the employee's goals and not those of the organization, if career development programs are to be successful. The more self-assessment tools you provide the employees with, the more successful they will be in identifying their interests and skills. This will provide you with the best information possible to assist in the preparation of the action plans.

Selecting a Development Program

As we have seen, development programs provide a type of career ladder, either lateral or horizontal, for hourly human resources. There are several different approaches to implementing the development process. Each provides a slightly different focus on the intended outcome of the development program. Many hospitality organizations use a combination of the techniques that we will now discuss.

Mentor Programs

According to the Greek mythologist Homer, Mentor was the man whom Odysseus selected to train his son while he was away fighting the Trojan war. As Mentor was known for his sensitivity and wisdom, the word "mentor" has come to mean a trusted and wise advisor.

In development programs mentors are the individuals who guide the employees in their personal and career development. One of the advantages of mentoring programs is that the person being mentored receives individualized attention. Mentors know the hospitality organization, its mission and goals, hence, particularly in complex, large organizations, those mentored learn how the system operates from someone who participates in it on a daily basis.

As with all development programs, both the mentors and those mentored will require information and training on how the program operates, what they can expect from each other, problems that they might encounter and what benefits each will obtain from the mentor program. Mentors are not substitutes for the employee's manager, and these distinctions must be clearly drawn. While there has to be a mutual trust between mentor and the person being mentored the relationship cannot conflict with the authority between the supervisor and subordinate relationship.

Management Development Committees

These programs are used primarily for development reviews of managers. The committees consist of high-level management personnel that work jointly with individual managers in the achievement of the managers career goals. The progress reports that stem from these reviews are used in recommending job moves, either lateral or horizontal.

We feel that there is no reason why a committee approach to development would not work for our hourly human resources, as well. In the hospitality industry, it is not uncommon for our employees to report to more than one manager. Different managers work different shifts, and shift changes among hourly human resources are common, also. All managers to whom the employee has reported should be involved in the development review. Care should be taken that the employee does not feel that he or she is being "ganged up on," but rather that the entire management team is interested in assisting the employee achieve their personal and career goals.

We have stated throughout this chapter that development is not always a vertical path. Advancement is in the eye of the beholder, not the eye of management. In the hospitality industry we are always in need of good followers, those human resources that want to do a good job in their hourly job positions. If our entire staff wanted to be managers we would indeed be in for some serious trouble.

If what your hospitality organization needs is good followers, then your development program should be set-up so that good followers are cultivated.[1] In other words, being successful is not only for those who wish to become managers, being successful can occur for human resources at all levels in the hospitality organization. Managers and followers can both be a success, the only difference is in the job tasks they perform. In development programs that cultivate followers, employees are counseled on improving their followship skills, not their leadership skills.

Many hospitality organizations use a combination of these themes in their development programs. Job enrichment and positive reinforcement programs are other approaches to employee development. A fundamental technique that can underlie each of these methods is the concept of coaching and team building. Coaching is more than just another type of development approach: it is the strategy used in the development review. Let's now examine coaching and team building as development strategies that are being used more and more frequently in the hospitality industry.

Coaching and Team Building

Development activities require the manager to perform a nonvaluative role of counselor. One of the best techniques in career development counseling is that of coaching. Counseling and coaching are part of a manager's job in a hospitality organization. Before we look specifically at this management role we must first examine the topic of motivation.

Motivation as an Element in Development

The ability to motivate is a critical building block in the development process. Just look around you in the world today at all of the motivational speakers that promise to inspire you to greatness by showing you how to motivate your work force. Individuals such as Zig Ziglar (*Born to Win*), Tom Peters (*In Search of Excellence*) and Ken Blanchard (*The One-Minute Manager*) travel around the country as motivational speakers. Since Dale Carnegie wrote his book *How to Win Friends and*

Figure 8-2. Good coaches, like good hospitality managers, have the ability to motivate their teams to victory.
Photo by Mike Jula

Influence People in 1936 managers have sought to increase productivity through the ability to motivate.

Before you can motivate your staff you must first understand *what* motivates each employee in his or her specific job position (Figure 8-2). We know that differences exist between what motivates hourly and management employees.[2] What makes a job interesting to a group of hourly employees is different from what makes a job interesting to a group of managers. Furthermore, what one employee may find interesting may not be of any interest to another employee. We also know that no matter what we do there will be some jobs in the hospitality industry that just cannot be made interesting.

Motivation Theory

What do we mean when we say that we are going to motivate someone? We mean we are attempting to change the individual's behavior, and thereby influence his or her performance through some type of external stimulus. The questions that now arise are: Which types of external stimuli should be used? Which behavior do we wish to modify? How do we want the performance to be influenced? The answers to these questions will provide the motivational goals in your development program. Let's briefly examine what the motivation theorists have come up with throughout the years.

The Pygmalion Effect. The Pygmalion Effect states that the expectations your human resources have of themselves will determine how they perform. If you expect great things, great things will happen. If you expect mediocre performance, mediocre performance is what you will get. Also known as the self-fulfilling prophecy, this effect was discovered by Robert Rosenthal of Harvard University.

By emphasizing the positive and what employees *can* do your employees begin to believe strongly in themselves. This requires vocalizing your belief in their abilities. The more they hear you tell them how successful they can become, the more competent they will be. If you set high performance and quality standards and tell your employees that you believe that they can rise to the occasion, the self-fulfilling prophecy says that they will. Positive expectations equal positive results.

Maslow's Hierarchy of Needs. In the 1950s, Abraham Maslow identified the "whys" of motivation theory. His theory states that man is motivated by satisfying a set of needs common to all individuals. In ascending order of importance these are:

1. Physiological needs (food, clothing, shelter).
2. Safety/security needs (freedom from fear of losing job, clothing, shelter).
3. Acceptance needs (to belong and be accepted by others).
4. Esteem needs (status, prestige, power).
5. Self-actualization needs (maximize one's potential).[3]

Maslow believed that until the physiological needs are satisfied the other needs would not serve as motivators. Furthermore, once a need was met it no longer acted as a motivator, and another need took its place. One of the problems with Maslow's theory is that while it worked in life situations, it was not applicable to work settings. Clayton Alderfer, in an attempt to apply Maslow's theory to the work place, reduced the five levels down to three: existence (pay and security), relatedness (social aspects of work), and growth (personal development).

Hertzberg's Two-Factor Theory Hertzberg's theory identified job satisfaction and job dissatisfaction as separate elements that are not polar opposites of each other. The two-factor concept states that job factors that are generally regarded as motivators should actually be divided into two groups; one consisting of motivation factors (or satisfiers) and one group consisting of maintenance factors (dissatisfiers or hygiene).

Since job satisfaction and job dissatisfaction do not balance each other out, the elimination of a dissatisfier does not necessarily lead to job satisfaction. Motivation factors include such conditions as recognition, achievement, advancement and responsibility. Hygienic factors include working conditions, company policies and salary. One of Hertzberg's major conclusions was that money was not a motivator.[4]

Hertzberg believes that if motivation factors are present in the work place that employees will be motivated, and if they are not present, then motivation will not occur. If hygienic factors are present then employees will be satisfied with their work, and if they are not present then employees will be dissatisfied. Hygienic factors in no way affect motivation, whether they are present or absent.

To relate Hertzberg's theory with Maslow's Need Hierarchy you will note that Maslow's lower-order needs correspond with Hertzberg's hygienic factors, and that the higher-order needs correspond to the motivational factors. For Maslow, a satisfied need does not motivate. Therefore, the need for money is not as effective of a motivator in times of financial prosperity. For Hertzberg money was not a motivator but needed to be present for job satisfaction to occur.

Theory X–Theory Y Douglas McGregor generalized two assumptions about human behavior. Theory X assumes that people are generally lazy by nature and must be pushed into productive behavior on the job. Theory Y assumes that people can enjoy work and be self-motivating if the right set of conditions exist. McGregor believed that most people's natures conformed to Theory Y, while most management styles were Theory X. Furthermore, the problem with using Theory X in the work place was that it was likely to become a self-fulfilling prophecy.[5]

Expectancy Theory Victor Vroom's Expectancy Theory is one of the more implementable motivation theories. The theory states that a person will be motivated when the individual perceives a link between what he or she is doing and the expected reward. The higher the effort, the greater the reward and vice versa. It is important that the reward is attainable and that your human resources will feel rewarded for the effort they produce.[6] Pay-for-performance compensation systems operate on this principle as you will learn in chapter 10. Fixed hourly wages or flat salaries do not motivate because there is no link between effort and reward. For the reward to operate as a motivator, the employee must value attainment of the reward, the employee must see a link between his or her work efforts and receiving the reward, and the individual must possess the abilities and skills to do the job.

Money as a motivator The motivational value of money may change after a person's basic needs have been reasonably well satisfied. Since human beings have a way of continually redefining their needs, whether money will motivate is to some degree a matter of the amount involved and the amount the employee is already earning. Therefore, while some people will be more highly motivated to work for money, practically every employee has making money as one motive for working.

In the hospitality industry, with the large number of hourly employees on our payroll, establishing a link between performance and pay can have a motivating effect. Incentive programs are frequently used with this theory as their basis. When you reward a waitstaff employee for selling the most appetizers in a shift, or a housekeeper for cleaning the most rooms while meeting quality standards, you are attempting to motivate your human resources to improved performance through money. Let's face it, those hourly employees are working for that paycheck at the end of the week, and the greater the relationship they see between pay and performance, the greater a motivator money becomes.

Job enrichment In 1968, Hertzberg proposed the idea of job enrichment as a reaction to the KITA (kick-in-the-ass) motivational approach that he found most managers practicing. Job enrichment is based on his belief that "The only way to motivate employees is to give them challenging work in which they can assume responsibility."[7] This strategy includes modifying jobs so that they are more meaningful and give the employee an opportunity for recognition and greater responsibility.

Motivational Effectiveness

It should be clear from the above discussion that there is no consensus on how best to motivate your work force, despite thirty years of study. As a human resources manager, consideration needs to be given to several factors that involve human resources functions other than development. Selection procedures need to be effective so that individuals are placed in job positions that they are capable of performing. Training programs must be effective in ensuring our employees have the necessary skills, and evaluation procedures must be in place to monitor their performance. Compensation practices need to be developed that link performance and pay. Furthermore, these practices must all be viewed as fair; that poor performance is not tolerated while high performance is recognized.

If your work force is to be motivated they must believe that extra effort and superior performance is of benefit to them. Rewards do not have to be monetary. Flexible work hours, recognized achievement, increased responsibility, and the opportunity to develop their personal and career goals work directly towards a motivated work force. The environment of the hospitality work place has to create desire, commitment and confidence in your employees. Communication channels have to be open, and organizational goals clearly defined.

Once the environment is conducive to the development of a highly motivated work force, the techniques of coaching and team building can be implemented.

The Human Resources Manager as Coach

Coaching is a method that is used to increase the effectiveness of your development program. The coach is a very powerful motivator in the world of sports. Just as an athletic coach's motivational techniques lead to a greater sense of team spirit, so can a manager as coach motivate his work force to perform as a team.

We think that you will agree with us that part of your job as manager is to assist your human resources in the achievement of desired performance standards. We use training to teach basic skills and the techniques of progressive discipline to correct the marginal performer. The focus is on deficiencies in performance levels, where corrective action is taken to improve the job situation.

Coaching is a directive strategy that enhances employee motivation for individual development and improved job performance. The focus is on future performance, in assisting the employee to become the best that he or she can be.

INDUSTRY EXPERTS SPEAK

Coaching—Developing

A good coach (human resources manager or general manager) must have a *belief in talent*. The great coaches in all sports have an eye for the individual who is blessed with a natural ability to excel in a certain area. The great hospitality managers (coaches) have this "eye" also. They are able to see, for example, that in addition to simply making drinks, a certain bartender always has his customers laughing. A certain waitress is asked for by name. A certain cook's finished product always looks great.

A certain waitress was able to sell more wine than any of the other servers. As managers, we knew that Denise had a certain knack for dealing with what can be a confusing and

208

frustrating area of suggestive selling. When we kicked off a wine sales contest, we knew Denise would win hands down. Rather than have our "all star" capture a commanding lead in the contest, we asked Denise not to participate for the prize, and, instead, become the contest coordinator and wine coach for the other servers! We gave Denise a separate reward for her efforts, and the contest was a big success.

Here was a case of recognizing talent and letting that talent grow into a coaching position. The other servers were benefitted as their sales (and tips) increased by using what they saw as tricks-of-the-trade from one of their own.

On the other hand, one new manager, fresh out of a major university hospitality program and a graduate of his company's training program, did not realize that some employees have talent and skills in certain areas that exceed even the manager's. Our new manager had responsibility for the bar area and soon began to feel threatened by the abilities of the restaurant's lead bartender. Rather than take the bartender's advice on technical issues, the new manager demanded things be done his way. Feeling very frustrated, the bartender finally gave notice and went to work for the competition whose happy hour sales went up appreciably. Not because they had better prices or products, but because a loyal following left along with the bartender.

The moral of the story? Being a good coach means also knowing when not to coach a strong performer. As a manager, you must rely on your in-house experts. Do not feel threatened because you have not been a cook or bartender or front desk person for as many years as some employees. Solicit opinions and ask questions. Let them help solve the operation's problems. There are far more employees than managers in all hospitality operations. As a manager, use your coach's savvy to guide the talented employer down the field.

—Hugh Murphy, Chili's

Coaching skills are quite different from counseling skills. Counseling provides advice, assistance, support and guidance in career development. The counselor listens, clarifies, understands and helps. Coaching is more forceful, more motivational, more active in its implementation than counseling. The coach prepares, initiates, pushes and encourages. Coaching is done on a day-to-day basis.

The athletic coach comes to practice each day with a set of challenging objectives for each player. At the beginning of practice each player is told what is expected of him, and throughout the practice is informed of individual progress. Feedback is immediate! When performance is improved and objectives are met positive reinforcement is used, perhaps a reduced practice period. The outstanding performers are designated as team captains. How is the coach rewarded? Every time his or her team wins a game or match!

As a manager you come to work each day. Do you prepare a list of challenging objectives for your employees? You could, and start each shift with a brief team meeting outlining the objectives. Throughout the shift you recognize improved performance, frequently letting each employee know how well he or she is doing. If objectives are met during the shift, positive reinforcement is provided, perhaps going home 30 minutes early and getting paid for the time. How are you, as the coach–manager rewarded? Your staff's successful efforts are a reflection on your abilities as manager. In addition, we guarantee you a great deal of personal satisfaction in watching your human resources grow and develop and seeing them accomplish objectives that they didn't think were possible.

Coaches develop commitment in their players, a critical component of the staff in a successful hospitality operation. They do so by clearly indicating the performance expected to all players. While players are selected by coaches because of their skills, the hospitality work place differs in that we select people that we feel can be trained in the required skills. It is therefore our responsibility to see that the required training occurs because without it, we can never expect to have employee commitment.

Coaches also consistently communicate their faith in their players' ability to perform successfully. Perhaps this is the Pygmalion Effect at work. High expectations of player performance yields high performance. Coaches know what motivates each player and what is most important to them individually. Reprimands are not uncommon when players' performance is poor and can range from extra laps to not being allowed to play in a game. When players cannot meet expected performance standards they, too, are terminated in the form of being traded to another team or released to fend for themselves.

Coaching assists in the development of your human resources. A great coach can get his people to go beyond their self-imposed limits to do what they never thought possible. Becoming a career coach for your employees can be enormously self-satisfying. Remember that your role is to be supportive, not evaluative, that the atmosphere has to be receptive to open two-way communication, and that the coaching process is done on a day-by-day basis.

Building Your Hospitality Team

One of the benefits of implementing a coaching strategy into your development process is that is also fosters a sense of teamwork. When you place an emphasis on development and improvement, employees tend to become more comfortable working together, communication is increased and anxieties are reduced. The common goals become clearer to everyone, and the work force works together to see that they are carried out. While it might sound like a contradiction, encouraging independence helps to stimulate teamwork.

Team building became a buzz word in the work place in the mid-1960s, and was considered a very humanistic management approach. Team building advocates say that it will:

- reduce conflict among your work force
- act as a motivator
- improve the quality of decision making
- assist you in managing cultural diversity
- decentralize the power base
- refocus management as a development role
- increase involvement thereby increasing commitment
- improve two-way communication

Creating a Team Spirit

Motivation, coaching and team building go hand-in-hand as one strengthens the others. It is impossible to create a team spirit unless you have a highly motivated work force. It is hard to motivate a work force that views itself as a loser. That is where development programs enter the picture. By setting attainable career goals for your human resources , you give them the opportunity to taste winning. Winning teams are always more highly motivated to work hard to repeat their successes (Figure 8-3).

Identify your top performers and work with them in becoming team captains. People improve when they associate with individuals who strive to be their best, not with those who look for the shortest route to completing their jobs.

A lot of team spirit will be generated from your attitude. Before a team can win, they first have to want to win. Second, they have to make the commitment to doing what it takes to win. This requires that you believe in them and their abilities. If you have a positive self-image, this will transfer to your work force.

Decision-making needs to be delegated. It's hard to get people to work as a team if you retain all the decision-making powers. When employees can make decisions for themselves they are much more likely to be committed to carrying out the choice they made.

Figure 8-3. A team spirit can create an atmosphere of good feelings.
Courtesy of FIU Athletics

Team building is a process, which when effectively implemented, allows the work force to go beyond what any of its individual employees could accomplish by themselves. Teamwork also stimulates motivation and gives development programs the opportunity to maximize their full potential.

Conclusion

Development programs provide you, the human resources manager, with a process in which you can help your employees succeed. Through development activities you can assess your employees' ambitions, interests and goals. Career goals and developmental activities can then be identified. Progressive hospitality organizations encourage their em-

212

ployees to pursue career development and to take advantage of the opportunities available to them.

Career development programs benefit the hospitality organization as well as the individual employee. Their very structure stimulates communication between management and employees as well as among departmental managers. They force the organization to refocus on its human resources, its most valuable assets.

Development programs stimulate motivation by providing your human resources with opportunities in which they can be successful. Positive work experiences translate into a stimulated work force. Motivation can not only change behavior, it can also improve job performance.

Coaching and team building have been found to be effective motivational strategies. Through coaching, human resources are stimulated to become their best. Through team building, hospitality organizations encourage creativity and innovation. We now turn our focus to the evaluation of job performance and improving employee retention.

Case Problem 8-1

You are the human resources manager of a medium-size resort on the West coast. The resort is owned by a single proprietor who leaves you and the remainder of the management team to manage the resort as you desire, as long as the bottom line is satisfactory. You have been employed at this resort for over six years, with two years in your current job position.

Shortly before you took your job as human resources manager you trained a busperson in the resort's dining room, which operates only at dinner. This individual, who is 16 years old and just finishing the junior year of high school, feels that he or she would like to become a hospitality manager. The resort has a development program which can be tailored to meet the career needs and aspirations that your human resources may have. Specifically, what guidelines would you suggest to maximize the busperson's success of obtaining his career goal? How realistic do you feel the busperson is being? What steps could you take to help ensure the busperson's success (identify both short-range and long-range plans)?

If the busperson had come to you with no career aspirations, how might you have assisted him or her in identifying career interests and expectations? Do you think that the busperson's career aspiration of becoming a hospitality manager makes career counseling harder or easier than a diswasher who just wants to become the best dishwasher they can be? In one or two paragraphs defend your response.

Case Problem 8-2

Cindy is a counter server in a coffee shop located at a busy international airport in a major city in the Southeast. Cindy is a high-school drop out, but due to the unionization of your operation is receiving an hourly wage that is quite high. While Cindy's job performance is satisfactory, it is hard to get her excited about anything, least of all her job. In Cindy's words, "Life is just kinda a drag. You get up. You go to work. You go home. You go to bed. You get up. You go to work. You go home . . ."

You have always prided yourself in your ability to motivate your human resources. What's your strategy for motivating Cindy? You have a team of enthusiastic players in your operation. Cindy's attitude is beginning to effect your ability to motivate the rest of the team, especially new employees who work during Cindy's shift. You've decided it's time to spend some one-on-one coaching with Cindy. What's your strategy for motivating her and stimulating her to become a member of your upbeat hospitality team? Relate your strategy to one of the "classic" motivation theories. Will you be able to use pay as a motivator? As a coach one of the things you want to do is build commitment in your players. How would you help Cindy to build a stronger commitment to your organization?

214

RECOMMENDED READING

Blessing, B. 1986. Career planning: five fatal assumptions. *Training and Development Journal* 40, (9): 49–51.

Crosby, P. B. 1988. *The Eternally Successful Organization* New York: McGraw-Hill Book Company.

Jackson, T. and Vitberg, A. 1987. Career development, part 2: challenges for the organization. *Personnel* 64, (3): 68–72.

Jackson, T. and Vitberg, A. 1987. Career development, part 3: challenges for the individual. *Personnel* 64, (4): 54–57.

Keidel, R. 1985. *Game Plans Sports Strategies for Business* New York: E.P. Dutton.

Mellow, C. 1988. Getting the corporate rear in gear. *Human Resource Executive* 2, (8): 3543.

Merchant, J. E. 1988. Motivating entry-level service employees. *Management Solutions* 33, (3): 43–45.

Quick, T. L. 1985. *The Manager's Motivation Desk Book* New York: John Wiley & Sons.

Roberts, L. H. 1988. Building a winning team spirit. *Restaurants USA* 8, (10): 15–18.

Schweiger, D. L. and Ivancevich, J. M. 1985. Human resources: the forgotten factor in mergers and acquisitions. *Personnel Administrator* 30, (11): 47–48, 50–51, 53–54, 58–59, 61.

Slavenski, L. 1987. Career development a systems approach. *Training and Development Journal* 41, (2): 56–60.

END NOTES

1. Kelley, Robert E., "In Praise of Followers," *Harvard Business Review,* 88, (1988, 6): 142–148.
2. Kovach, Kenneth A., "What Motivates Employees? Workers and Supervisors Give Different Answers," *Business Horizons,* 30, (1987, 5): 58–65.
3. Maslow, Abraham H., *Motivation and Personality.* (New York: Harper and Row Publishers, Inc., 1954).

4. Hertzberg, Frederick, *Work and the Nature of Man.* (Cleveland: World Publishing Company, 1966).
5. McGregor, Douglas, *The Human Side of Enterprise.* (New York: McGraw-Hill, 1960).
6. Vroom, Victor H., *Work and Motivation.* (New York: John Wiley, 1964).
7. Hertzberg, Frederick, "One More Time: How Do You Motivate Employees?" *Harvard Business Review,* 46, (1968, 1): 53–62.

215

DISCUSSION QUESTIONS

1. Development programs have recently gained importance as human resources tools in hospitality organizations. What factors and conditions do you think are responsible for their increased popularity?
2. List the steps in the career development process. In your own words, briefly describe each.
3. What do you feel are the two most important ingredients of a successful development review?
4. Discuss two different types of development programs. Which do you feel is most appropriate for a hospitality organization? Why?
5. Identify and describe three different theories of motivation.
6. What happens when employees don't get satisfaction from their jobs? What do you think is the reason why career development programs improve retention?
7. What can you do as a manager to increase motivation in a work area, such as the dishroom, where motivation is low, despite good pay, benefits and working conditions?
8. Explain how coaching can assist you implementing development programs.
9. Discuss how team building could be used as a retention tool.
10. Why would you want to develop coaching and team building strategies in your hospitality organization?

CHAPTER 9

EVALUATING PERFORMANCE AND EMPLOYEE RETENTION

INDUSTRY ADVISOR   *Anonymous, Manager, Food and Beverage*
Company Anonymous

> **"There is something that is much more scarce, something rarer than ability. It is the ability to recognize ability."**—ROBERT HALF

KEY WORDS

appraisal instrument
appraisal interview
Behaviorally Anchored Rating
Scales (BARS)
critical incident method
development appraisal
entitlement trap
halo effect
incident file

incentive programs
job previews
management by objectives
performance appraisal process
performance evaluation
performance goals
performance planning guide
recent behavior bias
retention

INTRODUCTION   Now that you have recruited, hired, oriented, trained and initiated a development program for each of your human resources, you must evaluate the performance of each. Evaluating the performance of your human resources is a very powerful tool that serves both the needs of your hospitality organization and the needs of your human resources. If properly implemented and performed, the performance evaluation can assist in assuring that each human resource is successful in his or her job. This personal success leads to high retention rates that will become critical to the success of the hospitality organization. The human resources goals, to attract and retain, continue in their importance as we discuss evaluating performance.

At the conclusion of this chapter you will be able to:
1. Identify the purpose of performance appraisal as a human resources management tool.
2. Describe where performance appraisal fits into the human resources management process.
3. Discuss how performance appraisal information is used.
4. Describe the conflicting roles of judge and coach in the performance appraisal process.
5. Identify the basics of "how to" appraise an employee's performance.
6. Define the different methods of evaluating performance.
7. Identify the most common mistakes evaluators make when conducting a performance appraisal, and how to avoid them.
8. Increase your effectiveness when appraising the performance of human resources.
9. Understand different ways to improve the longevity of your work force through various retention methods.

Evaluating Performance

Performance reviews, assessments, evaluations, ratings and appraisals are all terms that refer to the task of assessing the progress of our human resources. Think of it as a feedback system that provides you with information relating to the achievement of your manpower plan. Performance appraisals (the term we have elected to use) will tell you how well each of your human resources is progressing in his or her individual development as well as how each is progressing in meeting the goals of the business plan. We will define **performance appraisal** as a process for determining how well each of your human resources is doing in achieving the criteria considered essential for success in his or her job position. The term *performance appraisal* is generic, that is it is used to describe a variety of types and methods of evaluating the performance of your human resources. This can only be done after an inventory of human resources skills has been conducted, and a plan for improvement developed. Progress can then be assessed.

Think for a moment about a useful analogy that each of you can identify with. In the classroom, professors assess students by testing their performance in various subject matters, such as accounting, menu planning, food production and computers. This assessment leads them to an appraisal of the student's growth and knowledge levels that eventually translates into a grade given for the student's performance level in a particular subject matter.

In the hospitality work place, as managers, you will assess human resources by conducting performance appraisals of their work behaviors

218

and skills. This appraisal will be used to make a number of human resources management decisions regarding wage increases, promotions and training/development needs for your hospitality operation. Just as in academia, appraisals may be conducted on any level of employee, from hourly wage earners to salaried managers. In all situations, the process of appraising performance is for the purpose of distinguishing among levels of performance. Table 9-1 presents a more detailed comparison between the employee and student in performance assessment.

The Purpose of Performance Appraisals

Performance appraisals will let you and your human resources know how well they are doing their jobs and what steps should be taken if performance improvement is needed. Everyone has a need and desire to know how well they are doing their job. Remember as a student how much better you felt when your professor provided you with frequent feedback so that you knew how you were doing, as opposed to professors who provided minimal feedback so that you didn't know how you performed until you received your grade card in the mail.

Table 9-1. Major Determinants of Performance Assessment Methodology

	Subject of Assessment	
	Employee	**Student**
Measurement purpose	To differentiate among levels of performance (successful vs. unsuccessful)	To differentiate among levels of performance (high achievers vs. low achievers; masters vs. nonmasters)
Decisions	Administrative personnel decisions: Selection Promotion Retention Demotion Transfer Termination Salary increase	Administrative and instructional decisions: Screening Diagnosis Classification/placement Formative Summative
Actions	Counsel to improve motivation Train to improve skills	Prescribe appropriate instructional program or treatment Certify License

Reprinted from *Performance Assessment Methods and Applications,* Ed. Ronald A. Berk, with permission of John Hopkins University Press, 1986.

There are many purposes for the appraisal process. They are:

- to assess the quality of job performance
- to provide feedback to your human resources regarding job performance
  - feedback consists of either recognition of good performance or notification of performance deficiencies.
- to plan future performance goals and objectives
- to improve job performance through recognition and counseling
- to establish a better knowledge of the employee so as to understand what motivates him or her

Importance of the Appraisal Process

Everyone likes to know where they stand with respect to their performance levels, even when that information might indicate that improvement is needed. Have you ever worked for a manager who never let you know how you were doing? Did you ever feel unsure of what management's expectations were of you? Fortunately, most hospitality organizations have begun to recognize the importance of letting their human resources know where they stand and, as you will learn in our discussions about compensation, rewarding human resources as their performance improves (pay-for-performance).

The appraisal process, when conducted effectively and fairly, yields many benefits to human resources managers. These benefits include:

- an open two-way system of communication between management and each human resource
- an objective set of criteria to measure job performance
- improved job performance
- a basis for modifying poor work habits
- a means of gathering employee suggestions for improving performance, methods or morale
- a more immediate awareness of problems
- a stronger commitment to the organization
- improved job satisfaction
- an effective motivational tool
- a way of demonstrating concern
- a source of documentation in the event of litigation
- a basis on which to determine promotions and wage increases
- a means to seek alternatives to termination
- future direction for employee improvement and development

These benefits are based upon the assumptions that your human resources have a desire to improve their performance, that feedback

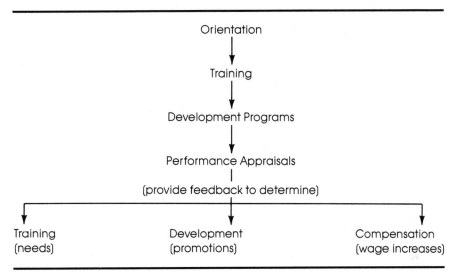

Figure 9-1. Role of Performance Appraisal in Human Resources Management.

regarding job performance can affect performance levels and that job satisfaction (and a happier work force) stem from improved job performance.

The Role of Performance Appraisal

Where does the performance appraisal process fit into the human resources management system? Figure 9-1 illustrates the relationship of performance appraisal to the other human resources function activities. As you can see, the information obtained from performance appraisals serves multiple purposes.

Relationship to Performance

We appraise our human resources in terms of the results and performance levels we expect them to accomplish. Our human resources management plans become the basis for our appraisal system as they define accountability. We said earlier that our manpower plans could be used as motivators and agreed that all of our operational objectives would need to be supported by performance standards. It is the performance standards that we established as an integral component of our human resources plan that become the basis for performance appraisals. The performance standards are what you will use to differentiate between good and bad performance, as well as among various levels of good.

Relationship to Communication

We also said that our plans would be communication devices, and they are, in the process of performance appraisal. Misunderstandings are prevented when the performance standards are clearly communicated to the human resources that are accountable for the results defined by your manpower plan. As your hospitality organization grows and your human resources develop, planning evolves.

Relationship to Development

Your appraisal process should emphasize the development of qualified human resources from within your hospitality organization to fill the opportunities that are constantly being developed in a growing organization. A successful development plan will integrate the needs and goals of the individual with the needs and goals of the hospitality operation. Appraisals assist in linking the individual's goals with the organizational goals.

Relationship to Training

Performance appraisals identify deficiencies in job performance. These deficiencies can frequently be traced to the individual's inability to perform the job according to standards. In these situations training needs are identified and training sessions can be scheduled to correct the performance problem.

Relationship to Compensation

Performance appraisals have been used as a basis for wage determination and wage increases for a very long time. Unfortunately, some managers view this activity as the sole purpose of performance appraisals. While the level of performance should certainly have some relationship to the amount of compensation received, you are overlooking a valuable tool if this is the only reason you conduct appraisal activities. The relationship of compensation to performance is of particular concern in the pay-for-performance and merit compensation plans.

When used for compensation decisions the performance appraisal is used to discriminate between high and low performers based upon established criteria. Compensation scales are established that are commensurate to each performance level. A further discussion of job grading can be found in chapter 10.

When selecting which appraisal process to use in your hospitality organization, it is essential that you have a clear understanding of the mission of the hospitality enterprise. The roles of the performance appraisal will be clearly indicated to you by the organizational goals that stem from the mission statement. You can then develop appropriate operational objectives for appraising performance that are in keeping with the needs of the enterprise.

Judge versus Coach

As we have seen, there are numerous roles that performance appraisals assume. One of the major problems with performance appraisals is the inherent conflict among these roles. The primary conflict lies between the appraisal's role as a determinant of compensation decisions, and the appraisal's role in improving job performance and human resources in development. In the first situation, the appraiser must act as judge and in the later as the coach. Even though this dual conflict has been identified for over twenty-five years,[1] the problem still exists. We will discuss ways to avoid this problem in a future section of this chapter.

Let's look at how these dual roles can create a conflict in practice. We have an employee, Beth Doolittle, who has been with our 100-room lodging facility for two years. The time is approaching for Beth's performance appraisal meeting, at which time you will discuss with her 1) how she is performing her job,and what needs you mutually see for training and development; 2) what her goals may be and whether they have changed; 3) how you can assist her in satisfying those needs and goals, and 4) what her wage increase, if any, will be.

If you provide Beth with a list of training and development needs and then give her a wage increase, she is likely to be confused. Why must she undergo more training if you are satisfied enough with her present job performance to give her a raise? If, on the other hand, you tell Beth that she will not be receiving an increase because of unsatisfactory job performance, then she is not likely to hear what plans you have for her development and training. The two dialogues simply don't belong in the same appraisal meeting. Your human resources, as well as you, are likely to be very confused as you constantly switch from your judge hat to your coach hat.

The solutions to this dilemma will be discussed throughout the rest of this chapter. The first thing you can do is institute a system that provides two different appraisal interviews. In one, called the **development appraisal,** you will wear your coach hat and let your employee know how much you value his or her contributions to the organization. You mutually agree upon training and development needs that assist the employee in achieving the goals that are most important to him or her. The decisions made in this interview become the basis for the retraining that we discussed in chapter 7 and for the individual development programs we discussed in chapter 8.

In the second appraisal interview, called the **performance evaluation,** you will wear your judge hat and provide the employee with information on his or her successes and failures in the hospitality organization. Has the employee met the operational objectives based upon the business plan of the organization? What have been the individuals accomplishments? This information then relates to decisions pertaining to wage adjustments and promotions.

223

Obviously, these two roles have to be connected to be effective for both the hospitality organization and the employee. While the performance evaluation is controlled primarily by the needs of the organization, the development appraisal is a process controlled by the employee. The performance evaluation provides the employee with a means of achieving the extrinsic rewards the organization has to offer. The development appraisal provides the employee with a means of achieving the intrinsic rewards: challenging work, opportunity for growth and being recognized for a job well done. An effective performance appraisal process provides a method for satisfying the needs of everyone involved in the hospitality organization.

How To Appraise Performance

Performance appraisal is a term either dreaded or loved by management and employees, alike. For both, it can be either a painful or rewarding experience. It is not pleasant to tell or be told that you are not doing a good job and improvements need to be made. On the other hand, some employees look forward to their appraisals, especially if they respect the manager giving it. Have you ever been the recipient of a performance appraisal? If so, we are sure that you can identify with some of these feelings.

The last thing we want the performance appraisal to do is to demotivate our human resources. When a problem with performance or behavior exists, it is our job as an appraiser to convince that individual that 1) a problem does exist, and 2) that they need to improve.

INDUSTRY EXPERTS SPEAK

Our industry advisor takes this opportunity to relate a performance appraisal strategy to you: "Whenever I have a performance review to give an individual, I always tell him or her a few days in advance that the individual will be receiving it. This allows the employee time to collect his or her thoughts relative to the review and to form well defined questions if desired. Besides, this permits the employee to become emotionally prepared for the process, if it is anticipated to be strenuous.

I recall one case in particular with a relatively new manager when I was apprehensive as to the content and outcome of the upcoming review. Based upon the individual's actions I felt that the employee's heart was not in the job, and, that as a result, the individual's performance and work groups were suffering.

The strategy that I had mapped out was to discuss organizational goals, then the individual's performance as it related to the goals for an introduction to the individual's level of performance. I felt that this would, as amicably as possible, illustrate the manager's shortcomings and lead into a discussion of "Where do we go from here?" My opinion had already been formed based on the manager's skills and attitude that this person was not in the right job. This meant that try as the employee might, the individual would likely never excell in the present job, and that my best bet, both for the organization and the person, was to place the employee in a job that better meshed the person's skills and desires.

To my delight and suprise when we came to the point of deciding "where to go," the employee suggested the job I had in mind. It resulted in a career change and a very successful saving of a valuable person for me. This only served to reinforce in my mind the value of searching for the most appropriate niche for each employee within our company. If the first job doesn't fit, instead of discharging or discouraging the person, the challenge to me and my staff is to find a job that does. Then both our organization and our people benefit."

We now turn our attention to the elements that make up an effective performance appraisal process.

Goal Setting

The first statement we will make about the design of a performance appraisal process is keep it simple! The process we design will be used to both develop and evaluate performance. It logically follows then that the best place to start is by identifying the job standards and responsibilities. If our human resources know what is expected of them in the performance of their jobs, they are more likely to be successful (Figure 9-2).

For a human resource to know what is expected of him or her, the employee must understand the functions and responsibilities of the job as well as how he or she should go about achieving those functions and responsibilities. These elements are contained in the goals that are jointly developed by the manager and the employee together.

Goal setting occurs for new employees after their orientation and training period, and for current employees at the conclusion of their performance evaluation. The goals become the criteria for determining acceptable quality and quantity work levels. They are based on both the business needs, as identified in the business plan, and on the employees'

226

Figure 9-2. The goal-setting meeting is an important component of the appraisal process.
Courtesy of Strongbow Inn, Valparaiso, Indiana

career aspirations, strengths and weaknesses. Thus, they serve as performance criteria for both the development appraisal and the performance evaluation.

Goals are based upon your job descriptions and are the starting point for an effective performance appraisal process. We recommend that they meet the following criteria for maximum effectiveness:

- Logical. They evolve from an accurate job description and job specification that indicate duties, responsibilities and accountability.
- Specific. The goals cannot be stated in vague or general terms.
- Realistic. The goals must be clearly achievable. This does not mean that they should not be challenging, but they must be attainable.
- Measurable. The employee must be able to ascertain his or her progress toward the goal and know when the results have been obtained. This keeps the appraisal process objective as opposed to subjective.
- Time sensitive. The employee should clearly understand when this goal is to be achieved.
- Results oriented. This is not the time to discuss the method or activities used to complete the goal, but the time to define the results to be accomplished. The results should be observable by others.

- Mutually committed. The goals should be committed to by every person who has an affect on the employee's performance.

Performance goals include the performance expected of the human resources in your hospitality organization. A performance planning guide will provide you with a written record of the performance expectations that you and the employee agreed upon. This record can be used throughout the appraisal process when conducting either development appraisals or performance evaluations.

The Appraisal Instrument

Remember that the performance appraisal should be based on the employee's job performance related to the job description. The instrument should contain certain basic information, such as the employee's name, job position, date of the interview, period covered by the appraisal and who is conducting the appraisal interview. Table 9-2 is an example of a performance appraisal rating form used in the appraisal of hourly employees.

The specific type of information you include on the appraisal instrument is highly dependent upon the method of performance appraisal used by your hospitality organization. While these specific methods will be discussed later in this chapter, there are certain elements that all appraisal instruments must contain, regardless of the particular method.

First, and foremost, you can stay out of costly litigation resulting from discriminatory appraisal methods by using an instrument based upon a job analysis. According to our industry advisor management must be trained to use this instrument. The results of the job analysis must then be used to develop an instrument that is both valid and reliable. The appraisal instrument typically contains some type of rating system that permits you to rate each employee with as much objectivity as possible.

Consideration must be given to the number of levels you will use to rate your human resources. It is probably safe to say that all employees can be classified into three categories: poor, average and superior. The difficulty in using just three rating categories is that most managers are uncomfortable being forced to distinguish among employees in such a restrictive way and will rate most employees as average. How would you like to be told you were *average?* There is no agreement as to the optimum number of rating levels, although most hospitality organizations use between four and seven levels, and most industry advisors concur that three is not enough.

Defining the criteria for each level is more important than the number of levels. Care must be taken to develop performance criteria that allow the appraiser to distinguish between levels of performance. Wording must be clear and unambiguous to be of value. If you are

Table 9-2. Performance Appraisal Rating Form

Name _____ Date _____

Job Position _____ Last Review Date _____

Hire Date _____ Rated by _____

Type of Review: _____ 90 Day _____ Annual-Year

(Check appropriate box in each category)

1. KNOWLEDGE OF WORK (How well does employee know the job? Consider knowledge of job gained through experience, education, prior or on-the-job training.)

Well informed on all phases of work.	Knowledge to work without assistance.	Adequate grasp of job. Some assistance.	Requires considerable assistance.	Inadequate knowledge.

2. QUALITY OF WORK (How well does employee do the job? Consider how well their work measures up to operation's standards.)

Exceptionally accurate, practically no mistakes.	Acceptable Usually neat occasional errors.	Seldom necessary to check work.	Often unacceptable, frequent errors.	Too many errors.

3. QUANTITY OF WORK (How much work does the employee do and what percentage of the workday is spent working?)

Rapid worker Unusually big producer.	Turns out good volume.	Average.	Volume below average.	Very slow worker.

4. INITIATIVE (Does the employee make decisions that are independent and sound? Does he or she require much supervision?)

Initiative results in frequent savings in time and money.	Very resourceful.	Shows initiative occasionally.	Rarely shows any initiative.	Needs constant prodding.

working for a hospitality organization that does not have rating forms already developed, be sure and get plenty of input from the line supervisors. They will be able to tell you if the instrument you develop will assist or hinder their own job performance.

Keep the forms simple, so that the person doing the appraisal does not have a lot of writing to do on the form. Too much written text can be confusing and only should be used to support or clarify the appraisal form. If you have done your homework you should be able to state the performance standards and objectives precisely. With a well-developed rating scale, the appraiser should not have to do extensive writing on the appraisal instrument. This means that the form will have numbers or letters to insert or boxes to check.

So far in the appraisal process we have established the employee goals, determined the performance standards against which the goals will be measured and through the development of a rating scale we now have our definition of what constitutes superior performance. We are now ready for the appraisal interview. Since we discussed the development appraisal in chapter 8 we will focus on the performance evaluation here.

The Appraisal Interview

You should give the employee plenty of advance notice before the interview so that the individual can prepare a self-evaluation of his or her performance to bring to the session. You, as the appraiser, also have much to do before actually conducting the interview.

As the appraiser, you must carefully review the employee's job description and specification so that you are familiar with the individual's job function. A review of the performance standards, employee achievements and the performance planning guide is also necessary. You should have been keeping a file or journal on the employee's accomplishments during the review period. These files are oftentimes referred to as critical incident files. **Critical incident files** contain a written message for each accomplishment or failure that an employee has had. Before the appraisal interview these should be reviewed.

If you are anxious about conducting an appraisal interview it is important that you work through these feelings before confronting the employee. The person might perceive your anxieties as an indication that the review he or she is about to receive is going to be negative. Care must be taken not to bring into the interview session any feelings of anger or hostility that you might have towards a particular individual. This assessment must be kept objective and fair.

At the beginning of the interview you will need to establish a positive and comfortable atmosphere that will be conducive to honest, two-way communication. Explain to the employee immediately what the procedure will be for conducting the interview. If this is his or her first appraisal, the employee is likely to be nervous and have no way of knowing what to expect.

Remember that this interview is for two-way communication, which means that you and the employee should each talk about half of the time. Introverted individuals might have a hard time talking about themselves. The self-appraisal they filled out before the interview will be useful in drawing the person into the conversation. The focus of the discussion should be on the goals and results. Pull out the performance planning guide and discuss each goal separately.

Criticisms that need to be made should be specific and performance related. Do not focus on personality or character traits, but on the goals and the reasons why they were not achieved. Give specific examples instead of generalities. Stay calm and do not get into an argument with the employee. Your focus should be on providing feedback to assist the employee in improving his or her performance, not on the actual rating itself.

Take as much time as you feel is necessary. Do not plan a tight schedule into which you will attempt to work in an appraisal interview. Depending upon the individual, the length of the interview will vary. Seek employee feedback especially on projected goals. It is important that the employee feel that he or she is an integral part of the process and can key in to the ideas. Before concluding the interview summarize the employee's strengths and the areas in which improvement is needed. Provide solutions and guidance on how he or she can improve in these areas. Emphasize your commitment to assisting the employee in reaching higher levels of performance. Work with the individual to establish new goals for the next review period. You will continue to use the performance planning guide for this purpose. The focus at the conclusion of the interview should be on the future performance, not the past.

Documentation is an essential part of this process. Feel free to take notes during the session and complete the file shortly after the appraisal session ends, while the discussions you have had are still fresh in your mind. Have the employee sign the appraisal forms and provide them with a copy.

Methods of Appraising Performance

There is no one method of appraising performance that is suitable to all organizations. The particular method used in your hospitality organization will be dependent upon the mission statement of the enterprise and the existing corporate culture. We will now discuss some of the more frequently used appraisal methods.

Critical Incident Method

The critical incident method focuses on the behavior of the human resource that is to be evaluated. As we have discussed, the two of you have already met to mutually agree upon the goals that the employee would work on attaining during this review period. During the course of the review period it will be up to you, the manager with human resources responsibilities, to maintain an incident file. An **incident file** is an ongoing record of the employee's behaviors, both positive and negative, during a specified review period.

When it is time for the appraisal interview, you have a file of both poor and outstanding performance for each of your human resources. For this type of appraisal to be successful, it is important that you give the employee feedback continuously on their critical incidents. That means when an employee does something outstanding, you immediately tell the person verbally to reinforce that behavior, as well as making a note in the employee's file. Additionally, poor performance should be discussed soon after the occurrence so that the employee can immediately correct the behavior. Remember, your role is as a coach and judge. You are not sitting on the sidelines just waiting for your employees to do something wrong. But when they do, they need to know that you are there and are willing to assist them in getting back on the right track.

Behaviorally Anchored Rating Scales

Behaviorally Anchored Rating Scales, or BARS, as they are more commonly called, require that a job analysis has been conducted that has identified the types of behavior that is appropriate for various levels of performance. For example, a Level I behavior might be an extremely accurate worker, rarely makes mistakes; a Level II behavior might be consistently accurate, makes few errors that are seldom repeated; a Level III behavior might be work is consistent with job standards, errors are infrequent and so forth.

The BARS method has the advantage of being objective as each human resource is rated against a predetermined specific set of behaviors that have been identified on a job-by-job basis. While the BARS instrument is highly reliable it is time consuming. Oftentimes, the expense required to perform a detailed job analysis to determine the behavior criteria is too great for some hospitality organizations.

Management by Objectives

This method of appraising performance was first proposed by Douglas McGregor in the 1950s. Instead of focusing on behavior, this method focuses on the results of the behavior. Specific, written goals are developed by the subordinate and supervisor at the beginning of the review period. At the end of the period, the performance is evaluated based on how many of the goals the employee has achieved.

While this approach is supposedly more objective than some of the other methods of performance appraisal, many people believe that this method can be abused by unfairness, just like any other method. The primary weakness in the process is the ability to establish realistic, yet challenging goals. Many supervisors that know their own evaluations will be based upon how well their employees meet their goals, will establish more obtainable and less challenging goals for their subordinates. Why establish a difficult goal if you know that your evaluation will suffer if you don't achieve the goal? Management By Objectives (MBOs) can usually support other appraisal systems as opposed to being used as a stand alone.

There is no one perfect system. The best approach is the one that works for your particular situation. It is much more important that your human resources receive consistent, objective feedback, that communication channels are open and that the method is understood by all who will be using it, than it is that you stick with one particular method and not waiver from it. We now look at some things to avoid in evaluating performance.

Mistakes to Avoid in Conducting Performance Appraisals

One of the major problems in assessing an individual's performance is the bias of the appraiser. Either negative or positive biases can result in a nonobjective and unfair performance appraisal. A variety of factors can affect even the most well-intentioned appraiser's judgment about the performance of one of his or her human resources.

The halo effect is one of these conditions that can cloud appraiser judgment. The halo effect results when limited information about an event influences the interpretation of subsequent events. For example, a positive halo may occur if the employee scored very high on a preemployment skills test. Employees come into the work place with the manager expecting great things of them because of their high test score. Everything they do in the performance of their job is weighed against these high expectations. If a poor performance is seen by management, the manager might assume that this person is just having a bad day, that this performance is not typical. No consultation about the poor performance is held. This reinforces the idea in the employee's mind that this performance is acceptable. As you can imagine, the longer this occurs the lower the performance. If this positive halo carries over into the performance appraisal then the evaluation of this employee's performance will be elevated to meet the high expectations of the appraiser. The opposite result occurs when a negative halo surrounds an employee. No matter what performance levels the individual achieves, the performance will probably not be good enough. High standards of information gathering before the appraisal can reduce these effects.

Recent behavior bias is a by-product of the time frame that precedes the performance appraisal. All of us tend to remember the most recent behavior of the individuals we know. Think of your best friend, and without taking a lot of time to think, write down one adjective that you would use to describe the person. We predict that whether that adjective was negative or positive was largely influenced by your interaction the last time you were together. In the work place, our human resources tend to be evaluated on their behavior in the past several weeks, rather than on their average behavior over the appraisal period. If employees are aware of this, they will strive to improve their performance just before the evaluation interview. This points out the great need for management education of the appraisal process.

233

Another bias to avoid is comparing the employee to yourself and weighing the person's performance against what you would do if you were working in the individual's job position. It is natural for each of us to favor those people who remind us most of ourselves, but to do so in the performance appraisal results in an unfair evaluation. This could also cause a problem from a discrimination perspective.

The development of an appraisal system that none of your people understand can create problems of job dissatisfaction. For the process and method you select to be effective it must be clearly communicated and understood by all who will be effected.

The entitlement trap occurs when the appraiser socializes too much with the human resources that the manager is responsible for evaluating.[2] We are sure that many of your professors have already cautioned you against the dangers of making personal friends with your subordinates. We point it out here because it will directly affect your ability to objectively and fairly evaluate your employees. If your employee/friend is not doing a good job will you be able to tell the person so?

Other problems with evaluating performance are:

- Insufficient time to properly review materials and documentation.
- The appraiser's inability to rate people as outstanding or poor, but rather evaluating all human resources as average.
- Performance goals that are either vague or conflict with one another.
- Performance appraisals that are only used as a control mechanism rather than also as a development tool.
- An organizational structure that does not reward management for the development of their human resources.

Increasing the Effectiveness of Your Performance Appraisal Process

We want to take this opportunity to summarize what you, as the human resources manager, can do to assure that your hospitality organization has an effective performance appraisal process:

- Performance expectations must be clearly identified and communicated to all individuals involved in the process.
- While the appraisal process is ongoing with continuous feedback, periodic, systematic performance evaluations are held with each human resource.
- There is a method by which the employee can respond to his or her performance evaluation as well as a formal system of appeals.
- Performance appraisals evaluate the individual's behavior, not the person.
- The hospitality enterprise provides a supportive organizational structure.
- Performance evaluations are candid and specific, they both critique and compliment.
- Appraisers have the training necessary to conduct appraisal interviews. This is a skill and can be taught and learned.
- The performance appraisal process provides for both individual development and sound human resources management decision making.
- Your human resources should know specifically what the consequences are of a poor performance evaluation.
- Use the appraisal interview as a tool to find out how well you are doing your job.

Retention

The word retention has been brought up repeatedly throughout this text because every human resources function that we have discussed so far impacts upon the retention of your human resources. We will define **retention** as the maintenance of a high quality work force through programs that seek to decrease turnover and thereby maximize the longevity of the hospitality organization's human resources. According to a recent survey of human resources professionals, retention and recruiting were identified as the two most important human resources activities in the next three years. Ninety-one percent of the respondents identified retaining key people as their priority.[3]

Turnover rates in the hospitality industry have always been notoriously high, with some segments and geographic regions of the country reporting as high as 200–300%! By this time you have a full understanding of the labor market and demographic changes that make the continuation of these percent figures not just unacceptable, but impossible, if you hope to have people to staff your hospitality operation when you graduate. What can you, as future hospitality human resources managers, do when you are out in industry?

To begin with you will have to be receptive to innovative and nontraditional approaches to human resources management in the hospitality industry. Too frequently we hear students, upon learning about new human resources management methods, say that it won't work; the industry just isn't set up to work that way; "you wouldn't get management to buy into that where I work"; and endless other reasons why the new method will fail. Creativity and adaptability will have to become part of your management style if you are to be successful in facing the challenges "the next chapter" will be bringing to you. So keep your minds open while we present some of the innovative approaches planned with retention as their goal that are working in the hospitality industry today!

235

Turnover

A good place to begin discussing retention is to examine some of the reasons that high turnover exists in the hospitality industry. One of the realities in our industry is that it is not seen as an attractive place to work. Let's face it, the work is physical, the hours long, the working conditions frequently poor, the times we're busiest are weekends and holidays when the rest of the world is off and our pay scales have been hovering around minimum wage, or less, when we can get away with it. Sometimes it seems as if we are almost boastful of the sacrifices it takes to work in a foodservice operation or lodging property. How many times have you heard it said that everyone must "pay their dues" in hospitality? At this point, you are probably wondering what you are doing working on a degree in hospitality administration! The point we are trying to make is that this thinking is very outdated. Working within a sector of the hospitality industry does not have to be like the scenario we just described.

Retention Methods and Programs

The number of hours worked, wages, the scheduling of work hours, training, promotions, physical job demands, benefits package, treatment by management, job challenge, work environment: each of these job-related concerns can be the reason our human resources stay with our hospitality operation, or it can be the reason they leave. A human resources tool frequently used to determine the reasons why people leave our organizations is the exit interview. Upon termination, either voluntary or involuntarily, an interview is conducted to determine the specific causes that resulted in losing an employee. A turnover report is then compiled with this information, and management then seeks to eliminate the reasons why these individuals left.

The problem with this logic is twofold: first, it assumes that the reasons people stay are the opposite of why people leave, and second, it assumes that the people who stay do so because there is a high degree of job satisfaction.[4] In either case, the assumption is likely to be invalid. A more innovative approach would be to study why the human resources in your hospitality organization are staying, and if they are happy working in your operation or if they remain because there is no opportunity for them elsewhere.

Recall that our definition of retention includes "a high quality work force." This means that your human resources are with you for a long period of time because that is where they want to be. Your job, as human resources manager, is to find out what causes people to want to stay with your hospitality organization and then institute retention programs that reinforce those reasons.

Job Previews

Job previews are a procedure in which new employees are told about the undesirable aspects of the job before they are made a job offer. The preview is given to the new employee before he or she actually begins working in the job position. The logic behind job previews is that turnover will be reduced if employees are given a realistic picture of all aspects of their job, both the positive and the negative.

They can be used either at the time of recruitment or at the time of orientation when employees are gaining familarity with the hospitality organization and specific operation that they will be working in. As you might note, job previews represent a very different approach from traditional recruitment and orientation methods. Why do they work in reducing turnover? Research provides us with a number of reasons.[5]

Haven't you dreaded going some place or doing some activity (maybe giving a presentation in front of the class) only to discover that once you were doing it, it wasn't nearly as bad as you had thought it was going to be? The same psychology plays in presenting employees with a realistic job preview. Once they are actually performing the job tasks they find that they aren't really as bad as they had imagined.

Another reason job previews reduce turnover is that some people will leave the job position at the recruitment or orientation stage when they hear the negatives. Others who stay and experience the negative aspects of the job are more comfortable with them because they knew what to expect ahead of time. They did not feel that management deceived them just so they would accept the job.

All of these reasons for the success of realistic job previews make a lot of sense, so why are they not used more frequently? One reason is that the approach is innovative. Another, more important reason for you to consider, is that sometimes job previews can increase turnover rather than reduce it. Particularly in industries such as hospitality where some entry-level job positions pay minimum wage, there is a tight labor market, and the industry is perceived negatively as a place to work.

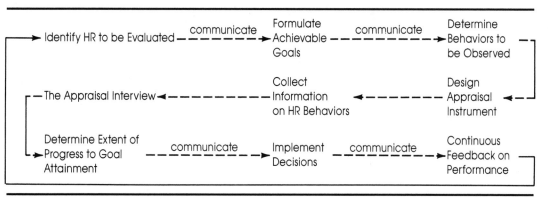

Figure 9-3. The Process of Evaluation

Research shows that a critical factor in the successful use of job previews is to ensure that a strong binding occurs between the individual and the organization.[6] We talked about the importance of socializing when we discussed orientation procedures in chapter 7. The more loyalty you can create in the individual, the more likely the success of job previews as a retention tool.

Employee Incentives

Many hospitality organizations are using incentive programs with great success as both retention tools and as performance motivators. Actually, high motivation levels in your human resources staff will translate into strong retention and reduced turnover.

What kinds of incentives could you use in your operation? Cash awards, trips, small gifts (such as watches), seminars for which expenses and wages are compensated and company outings. The key to using incentives as retention tools is that they need to be tied to longevity. The longer a human resource is with your organization, the more the individual stands to lose by leaving your organization. For example, Mississippi Management Inc. (MMI) rewards its hourly employees with a trip anywhere in the United States after fifteen years of service, after twenty years they get a Caribbean cruise for two.[7] Employees are not likely to leave after fifteen years of service for insignificant reasons. MMI has done a good job of rewarding service and creating loyalty in their staff.

Conclusion

The process of evaluation is summarized for you in Figure 9-3. After you identify which human resources are to be evaluated, the process begins by formulating achievable goals and determining the appropriate behaviors to observe to effectively measure job performance levels. It is critical that each stage in this process is communicated to all involved.

The appraisal instrument needs to be designed and information collected on the appropriate human resources behaviors. During the appraisal interview the extent to which the goals have been attained are mutually agreed upon by the employee being evaluated and the appraiser. The decisions made in the interview are implemented, and feedback is supplied to the employee on his or her job performance. The cycle then begins again with the feedback assisting in the formulation of achievable goals.

At its best, the performance appraisal is a difficult process. Some human resources managers are never completely comfortable with discussing negative and positive aspects of performance with the employee on a one-on-one basis. Remember, however, that people do respond to constructive criticism, just as you as a student perform better when you receive feedback as to your progress in the classroom. One of the most important aspects of the performance appraisal is that it shows your human resources that you care about them. What an effective motivator this can be!

Performance appraisals can be one of your most valuable tools in the management of your human resources. They tie many of our human resources functions together with the mission statement and goals of the hospitality organization. As we continue to reduce turnover and improve the longevity of our work force, the benefits of a good performance appraisal process will allow both management and its human resources to spend their time working together in improving both themselves and the hospitality organization.

If properly implemented, performance appraisals will lead to increased productivity, higher job satisfaction and an improved work environment. All activities, plans and programs associated with the performance appraisal process must be directed towards operational needs. The dollars spent on these programs must make a visible difference in the operation of the hospitality property, be it in the lodging or food service sector of the industry.

You are the manager responsible for the performance appraisals for all of the human resources paid hourly in an all suite, independent hotel located on the outskirts of Atlanta. You have been asked to review the performance appraisal system for this operation.

In the course of your review you make the following observations:

- Performance appraisals have been conducted on a sporadic basis. Some employees have been appraised annually, some biannually, and a few have never been through a formal review. At least you can find no records indicating a performance appraisal in some of the employees personal files.
- No follow-up is made after the performance appraisal interview has been conducted and the forms have been filled out.
- Suggestions for overcoming performance deficiencies are well identified in the performance appraisals that have been completed.
- There are no signatures on the completed performance appraisal forms and in many cases no indication of who filled out the appraisal form.
- Managers of this operation, in general, feel uneasy about conducting performance appraisals.
- Comments on some of the performance appraisal forms indicate a lack of cultural awareness and sensitivity.
- Recognition of good performance is generally received by the employees.
- After talking to the employees, you feel that all would like to have a better indication of their performance quality levels.
- Ninety percent of poor performance appraisals end up in terminations or resignations.
- Goal setting (performance) is usually initiated at a meeting at the conclusion of the employee's on-the-job training.
- Floor supervisors are unaware of employee's personal performance goals.
- Job descriptions and specifications are well written.

What are some of your initial observations about the performance appraisal system used by this operation? What do you feel has been the purpose of the performance appraisal in this operation to date? While performance appraisals are suppose to be geared to improve job performance, there is no indication that this is their purpose in this all-suite property. What changes would you make to ensure that this objective of performance appraisals is met? What other uses would you make of the performance appraisal system in this operation?

What changes would you recommend to top management that would have to be made to make this a viable system? Which of these changes would have to take place immediately and which would be long-term changes?

Do you see any danger of litigation occurring due to the way performance appraisals are presently conducted? If so, why? Which performance appraisal method would you use for this lodging operation? What are your reasons for selecting this approach?

RECOMMENDED READING

Berk, R. A., Ed., 1986. *Performance Assessment Methods & Applications.* Baltimore: The John Hopkins University Press.

Cayer, M.; DiMattia, D. J.; and Wingrove, J. 1988. Conquering evaluation fear. *Personnel Administrator* 33, (6): 97–98, 100, 102, 104, 106–107.

Frumkin, P. 1988. Employee incentives pay off. *Restaurant Business* 87, (12): 126, 128–129.

Herlong, J. E. 1989. "How am I doing, boss?" *Restaurants USA* 9, (1): 14–16.

Kirkpatrick, D. L. 1986. Performance appraisal: your questions answered. *Training and Development Journal* 40, (5): 68–71.

Latham, G. P. and Wexley, K. N. 1981. *Increasing Productivity through Performance Appraisal.* Reading, Massachusetts: Addison-Wesley Publishing Company.

McGregor, D. 1987. An uneasy look at performance appraisal. *Training and Development Journal* 41, (6): 66–69.

Patten, T. H., Jr., 1982. *A Manager's Guide to Performance Appraisal.* New York: The Free Press.

END NOTES

1. See Meyer, H. H., Kay, E., French, J. R. P., "Split Roles in Performance Appraisal," *Harvard Business Review,* (1965, Jan.–Feb.): 123 for this classic article.
2. Mahoney, D., "How Not to Evaluate People," *Newsweek,* CXII, (1988, 12).
3. Hay Group. "Facts and Figures," *Human Resource Executive,* 2, (1988, 8): 58.

240

4. Hughes, C. L. "Why Employees Stay is More Critical Than Why They Leave," *Personnel Journal,* 66, (1987, 10): 19, 22, 24, 28.
5. Meglino, B. M. and DeNisi, A. S. "Realistic Job Previews: Some Thoughts on Their More Effective Use in Managing the Flow of Human Resources," *Human Resource Planning,* 10, (1987, 3): 157–166.
6. Ibid.
7. Richman, T. "Mississippi Motivators," *Inc.,* 8, (1986, 10): 83–84, 86, 88.

241

DISCUSSION QUESTIONS

1. What are some of the reasons why many human resources managers dislike performance appraisals?
2. Explain the differences between the development appraisal and the performance evaluation.
3. How much impact should the employee have in setting his or her performance goals? Discuss the reasons why.
4. Discuss what activities need to take place and what information you need to collect to prepare for the appraisal interview.
5. What information should be on the performance planning form?
6. Identify the steps in the appraisal interview.
7. Describe two different methods of performance appraisals. Which do you prefer? Explain why, be specific.
8. Discuss three mistakes that you might make in conducting performance appraisals and how each could be avoided.
9. Explain how job previews might be used as a retention tool. What are their advantages and disadvantages?
10. Think of eight different incentive programs you might use in the hospitality operation you are managing. List them and tell why each would help increase the longevity of your work force.

SECTION 4

REWARD SYSTEMS

CHAPTER **10**

COMPENSATION

INDUSTRY ADVISOR   *Richard Ysmael, Corporate Director*
Foodworks Management Services, Motorola Inc.

"... equity is in the eye of the beholder."—DAVID BELCHER, 1978[1]

KEY WORDS

Age Discrimination Act of 1967	incentives
base pay	job evaluation
bonuses	job grading
Civil Rights Act of 1964	job pricing
Cost of Living Adjustments (COLA)	merit rating
	merit systems
Commissions	nonexempt personnel
comparable worth	pay-for-performance
compensation	profit sharing
compensable factors	salary
compensation planning	salary grades
compensation surveys	salary ranges
compensatory time	service charge
employee stock ownership plans	tip
Equal Pay Act	wage
Executive Order 11246	wage compression
exempt personnel	wage expansion
Fair Labor Standards Act (FLSA)	wage grades
gain sharing	wage ranges

INTRODUCTION

A major component of the reward systems designed for your hospitality enterprise will include the plans for compensation for both hourly and management human resources. As was true for each of the human resources functional areas discussed previously, the compensation plan must also be linked to the mission statement and organization goals. The specifics of your compensation plan will vary based upon such considerations as the type of investment strategy employed, the types of products and services offered and whether your hospitality organization operates on a profit or not-for-profit basis.

At the same time, compensation plans must be linked together with your organization's benefit program to assure a harmonious relationship between the two. The variety and complexity of benefit programs offered by hospitality organizations has greatly increased since the mid-1980s. With increasing frequency you will discover that prospective management candidates are selecting the particular hospitality company they wish to work for on the basis of the benefit program it offers as opposed to the compensation plans. In "the next chapter" this trend is likely to continue for the hourly human resources you will be employing.

As all service industries are competing for the same pool of unskilled and semiskilled human resources, compensation structures are becoming more innovative and competitive in their approaches. Keeping abreast of the changes and innovations in the administration of these programs will be increasingly important to your personal success as a manager with human resources responsibilities.

At the conclusion of this chapter you will be able to:
1. Understand the importance of compensation planning to sound human resources practices.
2. Distinguish between exempt and nonexempt personnel.
3. Develop a compensation plan for a hospitality organization.
4. Plan a job evaluation for a hospitality organization.
5. Plan an external compensation survey.
6. Identify the elements that are critical in the development of pay grades and rates for a hospitality organization.
7. Identify the effects of a collective bargaining agreement on your compensation plan.
8. Explain the philosophies behind the tipping versus service charge debate.
9. Describe the role of compensation as a motivator in the service sector.
10. Discuss the advantages and disadvantages of a pay-for-performance compensation plan.
11. Distinguish between the various types of incentive programs.
12. Maintain an awareness of the legal issues pertaining to compensation in a service enterprise.
13. Identify the trends and changes in compensation planning.
14. Administer a compensation plan for a hospitality organization.

A Management Philosophy of Work and Compensation Planning in the Hospitality Industry

The development of a sound compensation plan is critical to the credibility of your hospitality management team. The compensation plan translates into the policies and procedures that will be used to implement and administer the compensation component of your total reward system. It is imperative that a great deal of care and thought go into compensation planning as no other plan in your organization will be examined as closely for inequities in the structure.

The compensation policies that you initially develop will set the precedent for all actions taken with respect to wages and salaries. These policies and procedures will serve as a decision-making guideline for the operational managers. In large hospitality organizations, where compensation decision making occurs at a multitude of levels, it is these policies and procedures that help to assure consistency in implementation.

247

Additionally, compensation planning involves a large portion of your hospitality operations budget. Labor costs continue to increase along with legislation raising minimum-wage levels. So for management credibility, improved decision making and sound budgetary considerations your compensation plan (i.e., policies and procedures) must be carefully coordinated, communicated, integrated and administered to assure consistency.

This chapter will discuss practices and policies commonly used in the hospitality industry today in the establishment of equitable compensation plans. It is important for you to remember that wage and salary policies are individually based upon your company's own needs and operational objectives. For a hospitality enterprise, however, to be successful in compensation planning, it is critical that all compensation policies and procedures are well planned, fully developed and carefully articulated to the human resources within your operation.

Exempt vs. Nonexempt Personnel

INDUSTRY EXPERTS SPEAK	The terms *wage* and *salary* are not used operatively in the industry. Rather, the term *salary* is used to cover all compensation plans. According to Richard Ysmael, most companies do not like to make an obvious distinction between wage and salaried employees. Only in salary or wage structure and how they are paid (i.e., hourly, semiweekly, weekly) is this distinction used. Operationally, wages and salaries are the same and mean the same.

A mutual understanding of the terminology as we will be using it in the remainder of this chapter must be reached. Please note that this terminology is used for the purpose of explaining the different pay struc-

248

tures that exist in the hospitality industry. In the context of this chapter **wage** is money that is paid to your hourly employees regardless of whether their skill level is unskilled, semiskilled, or skilled. **Salary** is paid to those employees who work for a weekly, monthly or annual rate of pay. While you probably think of salaried employees as management, in the hospitality industry our skilled personnel (such as chefs) are also frequently compensated on a base salary. And in other, less frequent situations, you will find management that are compensated on a hourly basis.

The terms *compensation* and *pay* will be used generically to include all human resources employed by our organization. We will define **compensation** as the rate of pay (or award) given to human resources in the hospitality industry for the performance of work or the provision of services. In previous chapters we have used the terms hourly and salaried to make distinction between management and nonmanagement resources. While that distinction was sufficient for previous and future discussions the topic of compensation requires specific terminology.

When establishing a compensation plan for your human resources it becomes important, for Fair Labor Standards Act (FLSA) classification, to distinguish not between management and nonmanagement, but rather between exempt and nonexempt personnel. These terms stem from federal and state minimum wage and overtime regulations that specifically define the legal requirements that must be adhered to if you wish to exclude a category of employees from overtime pay.

Exempt personnel are those employees to whom, under Section 13(a)(1) of the federal minimum wage law, you are not required to pay overtime. According to the law, any employee employed in a bona fide executive, administrative or professional capacity is considered exempt from both minimum wage and the overtime provisions of the law. We therefore say that these employees are exempt from overtime pay. Typically, these exempt employees hold managerial positions, however, just because an employee is classified as management does not necessarily mean he or she is excluded from overtime pay. Employees must meet several requirements or tests for exemption that are outlined in the law before exemption is presumed. Modifications are periodically made in the specific terms and conditions for exempt status. We suggest, therefore, that you check with the nearest Office of the Wage Hour Division for the most current information on specific exemptions. **Nonexempt personnel** are those to whom overtime hours must be compensated. We say then that these employees are nonexempt from overtime pay.

Considerations in Developing a Compensation Plan

The compensation plan for your hospitality organization must fit into the overall manpower plan. As is true in the development of any human resources plan, the place to begin is with the objectives. What are the objectives of your compensation plan? These stem directly from the mission statement of the hospitality enterprise and the organizational goals.

Think for a moment about what you feel might be some possible objectives for a good compensation plan. Job satisfaction on the part of your human resources would be one objective, as would a reduction in grievances, a fair pay structure, a system rewarding seniority and a plan that will attract human resources to your hospitality organization. Each of these objectives could be the basis of a compensation policy or procedure. The point we are trying to make is that the objectives of your compensation plan are unique to the mission and goals of your operation.

Now answer another question. From management's viewpoint, what do you feel is the most important consideration in the internal pay structure of your hospitality company? As a manager with human resources responsibilities you will be expected to assist in the control of labor costs. This means your pay structure must take into account the overall financial goals of the organization. Compensation costs make up a large percentage of operational expenditures. Sound management practices require that you pay competitively, but not excessively. If you pay excessive wages and salaries you may be assured of enough labor, but your labor costs would skyrocket. This situation would be similar to the decision to only purchase prime ground sirloin when ground chuck would satisfy your needs. The amount of discretion you will have in determining the compensation plan for your particular hospitality operation will be determined not only by external job factors, but internal factors as well.

What do you think your employees will feel is the most important characteristic of the compensation plan you develop? If your answer is that it be equitable or fair you are absolutely correct! There is no way you can prevent your employees from comparing the compensation they earn with those of others. And not only will this comparison be among employees in your operation, but with other operations as well. Think for a moment about the period of time when you will be interviewing on your campus for your first post-graduation job. We guarantee that you will know the starting salaries for most of the companies interviewing on campus whether you personally interviewed with them or not. And part of the decision-making process that each of you will use in determining which job to accept will include a comparison, and ultimately a determination, of whether the salary being offered to you is equitable. If you do not feel an offer is fair, you will not accept that offer.

There is nothing that can destroy the morale of a group of employees faster than the belief that the pay structure is inequitable. That belief will occur if your employees feel that they are doing the same work (or more) as another employee that is getting paid more money. Skilled employees may feel that the quality of their work is higher than that of a

Opportuco-worker, and that the pay structure has not taken their talents and experience into consideration. If this attitude of inequity persists, it will permeate your operation, and low morale along with higher turnover may be the result. Table 10-1 identifies the outcomes of a sound compensation plan in the hospitality industry.

One of the considerations that you need to take into account in the development of a compensation plan is that of equity. An external consideration that you must take into account involves the pool of available labor for each skill level that your hospitality enterprise requires. How much competition is there for the available labor supply? The low levels of unemployment in some market areas means that established pay rates must be competitive for recruitment and selection procedures to be effective. How attractive are your job openings as compared to the restaurant, hotel or catering operation down the street from your property?

A related external consideration is how your hospitality company or organization is viewed as an employer. Do you have a reputation as a low-wage company? Pay must be set high enough to attract the human resources you need and still allow the company an opportunity to meet its labor expense budgets. While the rate of pay is very important in attracting and retaining employees, do not forget that it must be considered as part of the total reward system that also includes benefits, ability for advancement and quality of the work environment. A planned process for individual growth and career development through promotions becomes an integrated component of a sound rewards system.

Internal considerations in the development of an equitable compensation plan include any collective bargaining agreements that might be in existence, whether you establish a single rate of pay or a range of rates for each job, if and how cost of living adjustments (COLA) will be

---

Table 10-1. Outcomes of a Compensation Plan in the Hospitality Industry

The Goal:

To Reduce the Inequities among Wages and Salaries

Intended Outcomes:

Increased Motivation
Improved Job Performance
Advancement Opportunities
Reduced Absenteeism
Employee Retention
Employee Job Satisfaction
Attract Best Employees
Career Development

maintained, and if and how seniority will be rewarded. The needs and expectations of your human resources in "the next chapter" will be dynamic rather than static. A compensation plan should stimulate your people to work for pay increases through improved performance. Later in this chapter we will further discuss the pay-for-performance compensation plan.

In the hospitality industry, the largest single cost factor is that of wages and salaries. Both management and nonmanagement employees have a vested interest in assuring equitable compensation policies and procedures. To have a uniform centralized compensation plan is simply good human resources management.

Job Evaluation

There is no single approach to determining appropriate wages and salaries. Decisions now need to be made regarding how much you are going to pay your employees. These decisions must take into account both your management philosophy of compensation and the internal and external considerations discussed previously. What other factors are important in wage and salary determination for the hospitality industry? How do you decide how much to pay? For those of you who will be entering existing hospitality operations, how will you find out whether you are paying appropriate wages? Why is it necessary to establish a wage and salary scale?

An established wage and salary structure will assist you with labor cost containment and the administration of the compensation plan. Actually, you have already collected the information you need to begin the process of wage and salary determination. The job analysis provided us with information concerning job content that we then used to write job descriptions and job specifications. In a job evaluation this information is used to categorize the jobs and establish a job hierarchy.

The process of job evaluation examines the internal pay relationship within an organization. We will define **job evaluation** as a process that assesses the relationships that exist among job positions within a hospitality organization to provide a set of criteria for differentiating jobs for the purpose of wage determination. Job evaluation will assist you in maintaining internal equity in the pay rates among jobs.

In the job analysis process we did not analyze the employee's performance level, but rather the duties and responsibilities associated with each job in your hospitality operation. So it is with job evaluation, the job analysis information assists you, the manager with human resources responsibilities, in grading the jobs by job families so that a pay rate can be assigned to each job grade level. In some hospitality organizations wage or salary ranges are used instead of one rate per job grade. At this stage, however, we are not attempting to determine what an employee's actual amount of pay should be within that range.

Compensation Surveys

The amount of money, before deductions, which is paid to an employee to perform a specific job is known as the **base pay** of that job. Earlier, we discussed one of the external considerations in developing a compensation plan, your competition. To ensure the competitiveness of your compensation structure external surveys are conducted. Local area compensation surveys provide you with information concerning pay rates for the specific segment of the hospitality industry that is of concern to you. This data will give you the ability to determine the competitive position of your pay rates in comparison to the level of compensation provided by other companies for comparable jobs.

In order to attract and retain the human resources your operation needs it is important to know what other companies pay for comparable jobs. If your pay structure is too low, employee dissatisfaction may result in high turnover, excessive recruitment efforts, and high orientation and training costs. To maximize the benefits from a compensation survey you must determine first if your operations are really comparable to the operation in the survey. This includes an examination of the duties the employees perform. If dishwashers are being paid $8.00/hour you need to find out what their job descriptions require. A second consideration is an evaluation of the total reward system, including the benefit packages of your competitors. Your hospitality operation might be effective in attracting and retaining employees as a result of the benefits package you offer, even though your wage and salary levels are somewhat lower.

Hospitality operations should be viewed by you as competitive if:

- They are geographically close (although management jobs are competitive on a national basis)
- They provide similar products and/or services
- They draw employees away from your operation

Job Grading

The first step towards determining the value of each job is job grading. Once the job descriptions have been written the jobs can be compared and evaluated against each other. **Job grading** can be defined as a method of establishing a job hierarchy through a comparison of job content. To do this the jobs are categorized in terms of compensable factors obtained from the job analysis: the skill level required, job responsibilities, effort, working conditions and job requirements such as educational background and prior work experience. These compensable factors enable you to rank jobs by placing one job at a higher level or grade than another job in the hierarchy.

The judgments made by you and your management team will determine which compensable factor(s) will place a job at a higher point on the hierarchy scale. The philosophy, mission statement and organizational goals will also influence which factors are weighted more than others. It is important to recognize that there is no one set of factors, but rather a group of factors that vary in their individual importance relative to their contribution to the overall success of your particular operation. As the mission statements of each hospitality enterprise vary, so does the importance of the various compensable factors that will be used to rank the jobs within the enterprise. If you can distinguish between the important and unimportant aspects of a job, the result is a means by which jobs within your hospitality organization can be compared.

253

Let us use the job description for a line server that we discussed in chapter 4 and identify what the relevant compensable factors would be for a food service operation. We believe that those would be:

Skill Level/Job Requirements
- Education
- Experience
- Training required
- Knowledge of materials and processes
- Judgement and initiative
- Time required to learn job

Effort
- Concentration
- Physical demand
- Physical fatigue

Job Responsibility
- Monetary
- Methods and procedures
- Contact with guests
- Public relations
- Cooperation
- Safety
- Supervision of others
- Dependability
- Coordination
- System to master

Working Conditions
- Danger from equipment
- Heat
- Shift hours

Remember, our evaluation process involves the job of a food service worker, not any one particular individual that is performing that job. For each of our compensable factors we need to determine a standard scale. Let us look at two of the compensation factors under skill level and see how this would be applied.

Education:

No high school diploma	5 points
High school diploma	15 points
Some college education	20 points
Bachelor's degree	25 points
Master's degree	30 points

Time required to learn the job:

0–1 week	5 points
2–3 weeks	10 points
4–8 weeks	15 points
9–26 weeks	20 points
27–52 weeks	25 points
1–2 years	30 points

Our job of food service worker requires a high school diploma, equal to 15 points and 2–3 weeks to learn the job, which equals 10 points. This accumulation of points needs to be done for each of the other compensable factors so that we have a total number of points for the food service worker job in our food service operation.

Hospitality organizations frequently use the job-classification method of job evaluation that classifies jobs into a number of grades. These grades then become the basis of compensation administration. After the jobs are quantified according to the compensable factors we just discussed, each job in the organization is classified into a grade level. The result is job clusters or families, each with its own grade level number that remains consistent throughout the organization. Table 10-2 shows you an example of job grades used by Stouffer Hotels and Resorts.

Statistical analysis procedures can be used for the purpose of job grading. Once a system is established, historical data from your hospitality operation can be used to update your job grades as operational changes cause job descriptions to be modified. With the aid of a computer, statistical techniques remove some of the subjectivity associated with traditional job grading methods and, hence, better assure equitable internal pay relationships among jobs. And as we will discuss later, equity is critical in improving human relations and for using compensation as a motivational tool in human resources management.

Job Pricing

The next step in job evaluation (after job grading) is job pricing. We will define **job pricing** as a method of setting the range of pay or rate of

Range	Min	1st Qtr	Mid	3rd Qtr	Max
	Table 10-2. Stouffer Hotel Company Salary Ranges				
1	800	900	1,000	1,100	1,200
	9,600	10,800	12,000	13,200	14,400
2	864	972	1,080	1,188	1,296
	10,368	11,664	12,960	14,256	15,552
3	933	1,050	1,166	1,283	1,399
	11,196	12,600	13,992	15,396	16,788
4	1,007	1,133	1,259	1,385	1,511
	12,084	13,596	15,108	16,620	18,132
5	1,088	1,224	1,360	1,496	1,632
	13,056	14,688	16,320	17,952	19,584
6	1,175	1,322	1,469	1,616	1,763
	14,100	15,864	17,628	19,392	21,156
7	1,270	1,429	1,587	1,746	1,904
	15,240	17,148	19,044	20,952	22,848
8	1,371	1,543	1,714	1,886	2,057
	16,452	18,516	20,568	22,632	24,684
9	1,481	1,666	1,851	2,036	2,221
	17,772	19,992	22,212	24,432	26,652
10	1,599	1,799	1,999	2,199	2,399
	19,188	21,588	23,988	26,388	28,788
11	1,727	1,943	2,159	2,375	2,591
	20,724	23,316	25,908	28,500	31,092
12	1,866	2,099	2,332	2,565	2,798
	22,392	25,188	27,984	30,780	33,576
13	2,015	2,267	2,519	2,771	3,023
	24,180	27,204	30,228	33,252	36,276
14	2,177	2,449	2,721	2,993	3,265
	26,124	29,388	32,652	35,916	39,180
15	2,351	2,645	2,939	3,233	3,527
	28,212	31,740	35,268	38,796	42,324
16	2,539	2,857	3,174	3,492	3,809
	30,468	34,284	38,088	41,904	45,708
17	2,742	3,085	3,428	3,771	4,114
	32,904	37,020	41,136	45,252	49,368
18	2,962	3,332	3,702	4,072	4,442
	35,544	39,984	44,424	48,864	53,304

Table 10-2

Range	Min	1st Qtr	Mid	3rd Qtr	Max
19	3,198	3,598	3,998	4,398	4,798
	38,376	43,176	47,976	52,776	57,576
20	3,454	3,886	4,318	4,750	5,182
	41,448	46,632	51,816	57,000	62,184
21	3,723	4,193	4,663	5,133	5,603
	44,676	50,316	55,956	61,596	67,236
22	4,013	4,525	5,036	5,548	6,059
	48,156	54,300	60,432	66,576	72,708
23	4,325	4,882	5,439	5,996	6,553
	51,900	58,584	65,268	71,952	78,636
24	4,662	5,268	5,874	6,480	7,086
	55,944	63,216	70,488	77,760	85,032
25	5,025	5,685	6,344	7,004	7,663
	60,300	68,220	76,128	84,048	91,956
26	5,417	6,135	6,852	7,570	8,287
	65,004	73,620	82,224	90,840	99,444
27	5,838	6,619	7,400	8,181	8,962
	70,056	79,428	88,800	98,172	107,544
28	6,293	7,143	7,992	8,842	9,691
	75,516	85,716	95,904	106,104	116,292
29	6,783	7,707	8,631	9,555	10,479
	81,396	92,484	103,572	114,660	125,748
30	7,311	8,316	9,321	10,326	11,331
	87,732	99,792	111,852	123,912	135,972

Source: Stouffer Hotel Company

pay for each job grade. Decisions now need to be made to determine what your organization is willing to pay for each grade level. How much a job is worth is determined by several variables. These include the job information you have gathered through your job grading process, the external labor market data collected in your local compensation surveys and any collective bargaining agreements that your hospitality organization may be guided by. You are now faced with the task of establishing wages and salaries alluring enough to attract quality people and simultaneously assuring them of a fair internal pay structure in order to maximize retention.

A decision that needs to be made is whether you will use a pay structure made up of different grades. This will depend on the number of jobs that are in your hospitality organization and how similar they are to each other. The most common practice in the hospitality industry is to use a wage or salary range that contains a minimum, standard and maximum rate. This enables employees to be financially recognized for the special skills, experience and personal characteristics that they possess and bring with them to the job. In addition, a pay range permits your employees to advance to a higher rate of pay while remaining in the same job-grade level.

When establishing pay ranges you must determine the minimum and maximum rates of pay to be assigned to each job grade, and how much overlap will exist between grade ranges. The establishment of grade ranges may be done for both managerial and nonmanagerial positions. The minimum rate of pay for a grade is the lowest you will pay to an employee for a particular job. These are likely to be employees with no experience or a relatively small work history.

The standard or midpoint rate of pay is what the typical experienced employee that performs his or her work satisfactorily is worth to your hospitality enterprise. This is what you learned other hospitality companies were willing to pay for that job. The specific rate of pay that a particular employee earns usually varies around the standard rate commensurate with the individual's experience and performance level. For example:

Grade 8:

Minimum	First Qtle	Midpoint	Third Qtle	Maximum
$15,000	$17,300	$19,500	$21,700	$24,000

The maximum rate of pay is the most your hospitality enterprise is willing to pay for the performance of a particular job grade. You should recognize that the actual implementation of rate ranges is subjective regardless of the guidelines you establish in your compensation plan. Proper administration of the compensation process, however, will assure that the flexibility built into your plan through range rates is not abused in practice.

What do you need to take into consideration when you determine the pay differences within your hospitality operation? What considerations are those based upon? The determination of pay differences is a human resources management decision. One of your decisions includes where you want to be with respect to your local pay structure. Do you want to pay wages and salaries that are higher than your competition to attract employees away from your competitors? What type of a public relations image do you want to portray with respect to compensation? The competitiveness of the market, the quality of the human resources available and what your need is for quality people in your hospitality operation will be the basis for determining starting wage and salary rates. These decisions all must take into account the effect of any collective bargaining agreements, along with a thorough understanding of the legal issues and laws pertaining to compensation administration.

258

In the hospitality industry the type of people we hire is as important to the success of our operation as the work that they perform. Table 10-3 identifies some of the people characteristics that may affect the level or amount of wages you decide to pay particular individuals. In particular, our industry has recognized the commitment of its people to the organization and hospitality industry at large. This is reflected in compensation plans that reward previous industry experience and length of service. Hospitality has been an industry proud to take care of its own and provide opportunities for advancement and career growth.

As our human resources become scarce, your compensation plans will need to be innovative in providing for the long-term needs of your people. Later in this chapter we will discuss some of the trends in compensation planning that are occurring in order to accomplish this goal. In the hospitality industry, the pay structures reflect the organization's belief that when an individual is hired, consideration should be given to what the long-term abilities and contributions of that individual will be to the operation, rather than what he or she can actually do on the day that the individual is hired.

What other traditions exist in the hospitality industry with respect to wage and salary differences? One factor may be the particular segment of the hospitality industry you will be working in. Another difference will relate to the specific department your employees are in. And within departments there are the differences that we have already discussed that exist among the jobs themselves. And even among the employees working in the same job, pay differences exist based upon the individual's length of service with the industry, with the company, the employee's personal performance record, working conditions and whether the company is unionized. Perhaps the "graveyard" front desk shift is paid higher than the more desirable daytime shifts. Or the night server in a

Table 10-3. Characteristics of the Individuals You Hire That May Affect the Level of Compensation

- Skill level
- Education
- Length of service or seniority (industry and organizational commitment)
- Experience

24-hour restaurant might be paid higher wages to compensate for fewer tips and a less desirable working environment.

As you have learned in this discussion, compensation plans and policies are heavily dependent upon the job analysis and job descriptions developed in chapter 4. Providing both external and internal equity in your wage and salary structure is a vital component of your job as human resources manager. If your wage and salary structure is to be accepted, the results of your job evaluation process must be clearly communicated to human resources at all levels of your hospitality enterprise. Equally important will be the administration of the compensation program.

Effects of Collective Bargaining

A trade union operation requires that you, as the human resources manager, are fully aware of all collective bargaining agreements. The conditions pertaining to wage determination, increases and incentive-type programs are as a general rule very specific. It is your responsibility to conduct all compensation planning within the framework that is established by those agreements.

Since one of the union's major concerns will be with the equity of your pay structure, representatives will sometimes be willing to assist in the job evaluation process. Several conditions that might encourage employee interest in unions are tied to compensation. These include unequitable wages, wages that are inappropriate for the work performed, employees feeling that there is no flexibility or incentives in their wage earning capabilities, inadequate benefits and employees who feel that they are not recognized for their performance on the job. This profile of compensation-related conditions shows again the importance and value of sound compensation decision making.

Tipping or Service Charges?

The compensation our staff receives from tips is a long-standing tradition in our industry in the United States. Servers are paid less than the minimum wage standards required by the Fair Labor Standards Act (FLSA) because the difference is compensated by tips received. **A tip** is a gratuity given by a customer to an employee. This is quite different from the hospitality industry in many European countries where it is not unusual for an automatic service charge to be added to your bill. **A service charge** is an amount added to a customer's check by the employer. The amount is usually a fixed percentage of the check total.

Changes in government regulations in 1988 required employers to pay the 7.51 percent social security tax (FICA) on all reported tip income over $20 a month. Restauranteurs and hoteliers alike increasingly began evaluating the value of instituting a service charge system in their operations. The promotion of the service charge system is supported by a consumer advocate group that vehemently opposes the tipping system.

Proponents of the service charge system argue that for too long our industry has permitted our customers to compensate the waitstaff instead of paying them their fair wages. It is true that no other service industry historically has relied on tipping to compensate its employees. While the theory of tips is that they are to serve as a reward for good service, they have long lost this attribute as customers routinely leave tips with little or no regard to the quality of the service received.

According to the law, when hospitality organizations institute a service charge system into their hospitality operations, that money is considered part of the operation's gross profit. As such, it can be used by the employer to pay any business expense, including paying waitstaff the full minimum wage. The argument in favor of the service charge system states that if we want to treat our human resources as professionals, then it is time we start compensating them professional wages.

A tip, according to the 1959 definition provided by the Internal Revenue Service, must be solely at the discretion of the customer. Furthermore, the customer must have the right to determine the amount of the tip and to whom the tip shall go. None of these factors can be determined by company policy. Those in favor of retaining the tipping system believe that the system does reward, with the highest gratuities, those human resources that provide the best service. As such, the system of tipping does motivate the staff to sell more products and provide better service.

In hospitality operations using the tipping system, the division of gratuities among employees varies from company to company and from operation to operation. While some properties permit the employees that received the gratuity to keep all of it, some company policies require a pooling and division of all gratuities at the end of a designated shift. Even the procedures for dividing the gratuities vary.

In some properties, all employees share in the division, with service and production staff considered equals. In other properties, the sharing of gratuities remains within the group of waitstaff only. Sometimes the pool is shared equally, other times the division is based upon the sales of each individual. Obviously, there are positives and negatives for each of the alternatives pointed out here. Perhaps each of you can think of different procedures that you have encountered when you held service positions in the hospitality industry. The decisions that you make with regard to the policies and procedures for handling gratuities in your hospitality operation reflect your own philosophy as a manager with human resources responsibilities. It is important for you to recognize that the policies you establish will become an integral part of your overall compensation plan.

The hospitality industry has historically not been known for its high rates of pay. Some of that reputation stems from undesirable

260

working conditions in the form of late hours, weekends and holidays. Let's face it, we have each selected a career in an industry that works its hardest when others are at play.

To maintain a competitive edge with other service industries who are competing for the same human resources, your compensation rates must be periodically reviewed. Does the company you work for, or own, want to be viewed as a good employer? The community's perception of your operation and the hospitality industry as an employer is largely reflected in the compensation policies and procedures you develop.

261

Compensation as a Motivational Tool?

Do you believe that money is a motivator for the people who report to you? Can wages be effective as motivational tools? Would you still work if you did not need the monetary rewards? In the United States, historically, most individuals would answer yes to that question.[2] So, if money is not the main reason you go to work, what does motivate you? Each of you undoubtedly came up with a somewhat different answer to that question, which is why a discussion on theory of pay as a motivational tool can become so complex. Once the basic individual needs in each of us is met, there is no single source of satisfaction that will motivate all of us.

The ability to understand why people behave as they do and the ability to motivate them to behave in a specific manner are two interrelated managerial qualities that are essential for effective human resources management. The process of goal setting can be directly related to motivational theories. Goal setting emphasizes the importance of investing an individual's mental and physical resources in the areas that have the highest potential for payoff. Therefore, the more clearly a goal and its rewards are visualized, the greater its motivational pull. This is equally true for all human resources, regardless of where they fall in the job hierarchy.

The basic premise in our discussion of pay as a motivator is that your compensation plan does satisfy the employee's basic needs of food, shelter and clothing that Maslow identifies in his Needs Hierarchy. When those needs are not met, pay becomes, according to Hertzberg, a dissatisfier in the work place. Hertzberg's theory states that pay is not a motivational factor, but rather a hygiene or maintenance factor. According to these theories on motivation and others found in literature, the motivational value of money may change after a person's basic needs have been satisfied. Since human beings have a way of continually redefining their needs, whether money will motivate is to some degree a matter of the amount of pay involved and the amount of pay the employee is already earning. Therefore, while some human resources will be highly motivated to work for money, other compensatory factors, such as recognition for seniority, might be more motivational for other employees in our hospitality operations.

In traditional compensation plans, using the job evaluation technique discussed previously, equal job positions are usually slotted in the same pay range or grade. In such systems, job grade level and the assignment of an employee to that job are the basis for pay determination. The determinant of pay was established by the labor market and what that job was worth compared to all other jobs in the hospitality enterprise. In "the next chapter" you will be faced with a number of alternatives to this traditional way of thinking about compensation planning. The concept of pay-for-performance including a variety of individual and group incentive plans such as gain sharing, commissions, bonuses, profitsharing and employee stock ownership plans are some innovative compensation plans being used by other industries. The hospitality industry is now turning towards some of these ideas. Let's examine some of the key elements in each of these concepts.

Pay-for-Performance

Some of the long-standing customs regarding pay structures in the hospitality industry will be changing as human resources become increasingly scarce. Historically, wage rates were structured to reward the employees with the highest skill levels with the higher wages. Oftentimes, the level of skill required by the job was determined to be more important (i.e., higher wage) than the contribution of the particular job to the achievement of the operation's objectives.

Take, for example, a food-and-beverage operation that serves 1000 covers a day during lunch and dinner. While this operation may be able to operate effectively (i.e., meet its operational objectives) for a day when the executive chef calls in sick, the operation's effectiveness is seriously reduced without the dishwasher performing his or her job for that day. Less status, less pay has frequently been the rule in the hospitality industry. But when unskilled and semiskilled human resources are more difficult to recruit and retain, your philosophy as a manager with human resources responsibilities is apt to change. In "the next chapter," the jobs that are critical to the success of the organization will reflect the greatest amount of pay increases. Hence, there will be less disparity in compensation among unskilled, semiskilled and skilled employees. More important than level of skill will be the level of the performance.

To motivate and retain our valuable human resources, hospitality organizations are trying to develop methods of determining who should be and who should not be rewarded. Many of these programs are based upon the idea of basing rewards on the level of performance each human resource obtains along with the value of that performance level to the overall success of the hospitality enterprise. Those that contribute the most to the achievement of the organizational goals and operational objectives are compensated with the largest reward. Those who do not make a significant contribution to the organization's success receive a proportionately lesser reward.

It is in pay-for-performance compensation plans that pay has its greatest influence as a motivator. People usually like to know what they can expect in return for their level of performance. In such a system, the staff knows what to expect regarding the level of effort that they must achieve in order to receive a desired outcome or reward. Rewards serve to motivate performance by satisfying the needs of our human resources that relate to work.

For compensation to be effective as a motivator, your human resources must believe that good performance will lead to greater pay, and, at the same time, that minimal performance levels will not be rewarded. Too often in traditional compensation plans, the employees perceive that no one recognizes extra effort and that even marginal performance levels will receive the same percentage pay increases each year. According to Richard Ysmael, this will depend upon your merit budget and whether or not management can distinguish between good and bad performance and reward as such.

A pay-for-performance system is based upon established performance goals that are designed to be challenging, but obtainable. Here, risk taking is encouraged through a nonpunitive appraisal process that is based upon both quantitative and qualitative performance measures. This approach tends to foster both creativity and team spirit among your human resources. In addition, such programs have been found to increase productivity levels. While it is appealing to most people to believe that their pay is tied directly to their performance, there are some problems in implementing pay-for-performance plans. As a result, a number of hospitality organizations have been reluctant to use performance-based systems.

The major obstacle for most hospitality organizations, especially those with several decentralized levels of management, is the difficulty in accurately and objectively linking pay levels to performance. These companies feel that the potential for subjectivity could result in increased legal liability.

In addition, pay-for-performance plans must be clearly communicated to your employees, or they will lose their effectiveness. While these programs are increasingly being used, studies still show that most employees do not make the connection between their performance levels and the amount of pay received.[3,4] Even in companies that clearly communicate their performance-based systems, the employees are somewhat skeptical about the sincerity of their employers.

The term *merit-based pay systems* is frequently used as analogous to performance-based pay systems. Merit rating, however, is used to compensate for above-average performance levels. Merit ratings are tied to merit increases. The basic rate, or lowest grade, would be used for new hires that meet the minimum job requirements as indicated in the job specifications. For potential employees with more than minimal experience, a higher grade pay rate may be assigned. This type of system is not typically used on a new-hire basis. More often the method assists in compensating current employees that have demonstrated performance. Each employee then has the opportunity to advance to a higher grade level in the same job as he or she gains experience. **Merit rating** can be defined as a system that permits and encourages job proficiency through a process of increased compensation in the same job.

Let's now look at a few of the compensation plans that take into account job performance and see how each of them differs in its approach to basing pay on the measurable achievements of its human resources.

Individual and Group Incentive Pay Programs

Incentive plans relate increases in compensation to increases in performance based upon a set of established performance criteria or standards in an endeavor to directly reward above average performance. Standards might be based upon amount of time saved, sales volume generated, breakage reduction in glassware and china, improved customer service or improved safety records. In hospitality production operations, such as in-flight feeding kitchens, a piece-rate plan can be established.

For an incentive program to be effective, it must be based on performance only, and there must be a clear relationship between what your employees do and what they receive for doing it. Everyone likes to get rewarded for a job well done. This behavior pattern begins when you are a small child. You quickly learned that when you did something right, you received a reward in the form of a cookie, hug or praise. The reward followed the performance immediately.

Individual incentive programs have been found to have a greater motivational effect on performance than do group incentive programs. This is due to the fact that in group incentive programs the reward is tied to the performance of the group rather than individual efforts. The larger the group, the less motivational the incentive program becomes. Group incentive programs aid in the development of cooperation and teamwork within your hospitality organization. The pros and cons of individual versus group incentive programs will need to be carefully weighed in light of your organization's goals.

There are a great variety of incentive plans that you might want to consider implementing in your hospitality organization. These might include contests, achievement/recognition awards (good safety records), gifts, prizes, merchandise, travel incentives (least glassware broken over a specified period of time), earned time off, commissions or bonuses, profit sharing, gain sharing and employee stock ownership plans. We will now briefly discuss a few of these options with which you may not be familiar.

Commission plans. Commission plans relate pay directly to the amount of sales generated. On a straight commission plan, your human resources must sell or they will receive no compensation. In the hospitality industry, a modification of the traditional commission plan can be used to relate rewards to performance. For example, your waitstaff could receive a percentage of the total wine sales or dessert sales they generate over a specified period of time. We just need to expand our thinking to include a greater number of employees who can be called sales persons.

Bonus plans. Bonus plans or lump sums are offered on a periodic basis to human resources that achieve a high level of performance. These may be used in the hospitality industry instead of the annual raise used in traditional compensation planning. The message given by awarding bonuses is much different from the message given by annual pay raises. Pay raises are expected by each of your employees, independent of the level of performance they have maintained throughout the year. Bonuses, given for the achievement of specific performance levels, indicate to your human resources that mediocrity will not be accepted in your hospitality organization. This has the effect of reducing the friction that is created by across-the-board increases. These increases actually penalize your high performers and create burnout and frustration when their contributions to the organization's success go unnoticed. Bonuses allow the outstanding employee to still earn the maximum in his or her pay range, while nonperformers are static at the midpoint in their salary ranges.

Profit sharing. Profit sharing is a program by which all human resources that elect to participate in the program receive a portion of the hospitality company's profit at the end of the year. If profits are raised through the contributions of all employees then all share in the rewards. The distribution of these profits is sometimes deferred until the employee retires, or it may be annually distributed. The motivational factor behind profit sharing is that the employees will become more conscious of the effect their performance has on the bottom line, and, therefore, will be motivated to work towards the success of the hospitality organization. For this to occur, your employees need to be made aware of how their individual performance can affect profits.

Gain sharing. Gain sharing is a more sophisticated approach to profit sharing that is used as a group rather than as an individual incentive plan. Gain sharing distributes a portion of the company's profit based upon the contributions of specific employee groups to specific stated objectives. The implementation of gain sharing can contribute to a team-building atmosphere within the hospitality organization.

Employee stock ownership plans. Employee stock ownership plans (ESOP) are offered to employees by a number of corporations such as Marriott and Motorola. An employee stock ownership plan gives employees the option to buy stock in the company that they work for. The specific guidelines for stock purchase vary from company to company. The idea behind ESOP is that they give your employees a chance for ownership in the company, thereby improving performance levels, increasing loyalty and assisting in the development of a sense of teamwork.

Summary. The idea of paying for an individual's contribution to the hospitality organization rather than merely his or her length of service is the heart of the pay-for-performance compensation system. This system is most effective when improved efforts can be related directly to improved performance. Although care must be taken in developing objective performance standards, the hospitality work environment provides numerous occasions for such a system to be successfully applied. The motivational effect of these plans—improved morale and better communications—are all advantages in a well administered and implemented system.

Incentive programs have been created in an effort to motivate our human resources to reach new heights in production and efficiency in service. Incentive programs alone, however, do not make our human resources high achievers. In order to be effective, these programs have to be clearly communicated so that all people affected understand the opportunities the programs provide for their financial advancement. Do your human resources know what performance is rewarded by additional pay? Incentive programs are most successful when the employee can readily see the relationship between what the individual does and the reward he or she receives. Whatever incentive program you select to implement, it must be administered accurately, with the performance levels being measured objectively to maintain the equity of your compensation planning.

Legal Issues in Compensation Administration

The decision-making process you use in compensation planning will be closely governed by federal and state regulations. While it will be up to you to investigate the appropriate state laws that govern where your hospitality operation(s) is or are located, we will discuss the federal legislation that will affect compensation decision-making.

Fair Labor Standards Act

The Fair Labor Standards Act (FLSA) is a broad federal statute that includes information and regulations on the following compensatory areas:

- Federal minimum wage law
- Employee meals and meals credit
- Equal pay

- Child labor
- Overtime
- Tip, tip credits and tip pooling procedures
- Uniform and uniform maintenance
- Recordkeeping
- Exempt vs. nonexempt employees

This act was first passed in 1938 and has been amended several times for the purpose of raising the minimum wage rates and expanding the groups of employees covered under the act. The act is enforced by the Department of Labor that maintains regional offices of the Wage and Hour Division throughout the country. It is our recommendation that any specific questions you may have concerning your hospitality operations' compensation plans be addressed directly to their closest office.

Compensatory time is a spin-off of the FLSA provisions regarding overtime. The use of compensatory time practices has been common in the hospitality industry, where the nature of the business requires shifts longer than eight hours and some weeks longer than 40 hours. "Comp time" is then given to these employees instead of overtime pay. Generally, this is practiced on a voluntary basis. For example, the food service operation you are working in is busier than usual on a Saturday afternoon, and you ask one of your waitstaff to work a double shift. If the person agrees to work the double shift, you promise him or her an extra day off next week. Even though the double shift will put that employee over a 40-hour work week, you compensate by giving the individual an extra day off the following week.

The problem with this situation is that according to the Fair Labor Standards Act, you are in violation of not paying overtime. The extra hours your waitstaff employee worked in the first week cannot be offset by reduced work hours in the second week. Doing so is a dangerous practice. If an employee reports such policies to the Wage and Hour Division of the Department of Labor you will be required to pay overtime rates (1.5 times the hourly rate of pay) for all hours worked over 40 in one week. (These regulations are different in California.) Overtime, however, is not paid on hours worked over eight in a given day.

Equal Pay Act of 1963

The Equal Pay Act was passed to prohibit companies from paying wage and salary differentials on the basis of sex. Jobs that require the same skill level, effort, responsibility and working conditions must be paid at the same rate of compensation.[5] Seniority systems and merit or pay-for-performance systems can legally result in differentiated pay scales even though skills and responsibilities are the same. All employers who are governed by the FLSA are also covered by the provisions in the Equal Pay Act (EPA). The EPA is enforced by the Equal Employment

Opportunity Commission (EEOC). While the EPA stipulates that pay rates must not discriminate between sexes, a pay differential still exists between the sexes.

Comparable Worth

In the early 1960s, the cry was one of "equal pay for equal work." The passing of the Equal Pay Act in 1963 and a year later of the Civil Rights Act was a response to the discriminatory practices that existed at that time in the United States. The hospitality industry, which historically has been dominated by white male employees, was no exception. During the 1980s, the slogan changed to "equal pay for comparable worth" and while still not covered by any laws, it continues to be a hotly debated issue. The proponents of comparable worth feel that jobs should receive the same rate of pay if they contribute equally to the success of the organization. Jobs of equal value are said to be of comparable worth to the organization.

The Civil Rights Act of 1964

The Civil Rights Act of 1964 contains Titles I through VII. Title VII, which established the Equal Employment Opportunity Commission (EEOC), deals with a number of compensation-related elements. Title VII makes it unlawful for an employer to discriminate with respect to hiring, compensation, conditions, privileges or terms of employment "on the basis of race, color, creed, sex or national origin."

Executive Order 11246

While executive order 11246 is not a piece of legislation, it is an order issued in 1965 under President Lyndon Johnson. This order established affirmative action programs for all employers covered by the order (government contractors and subcontractors with ten or more employees and $10,000 in contracts). Employers who meet these criteria are subject to review by the Office of Federal Contract Compliance Programs (OFCCP), and, if found guilty of compensation discrimination, are subject to paying back wages with interest.

Age Discrimination Act of 1967

Just as Title VII prohibits discrimination on the basis of race, color, creed, sex or national origin, the Age Discrimination Act prohibits discriminatory employment practices on the basis of age for those individuals between the ages of 40 and 69. The EEOC is the agency that administers this act. An amendment to this act in 1978 raised the age limit of mandatory retirement programs from 65 to 70. For hospitality organizations with a senior and, therefore, more highly compensated group of human resources, labor costs will be impacted.

Figure 10-1. Compensation planning sessions are a necessary component of sound human resources management.
Courtesy of Motorola, Inc.

Legal Miscellaneous

There are many legal constraints imposed upon hospitality companies by the legislation already discussed. In addition is the Social Security Act of 1935 that requires employers' as well as employee contributions to the plan. Typically these funds must be paid at least quarterly.

State legislation should be thoroughly investigated for all states where you have a responsibility towards a hospitality operation. Worker compensation, unemployment insurance laws, discrimination laws and even minimum wage standards could differ significantly from what federal legislation requires.

Trends in Compensation Planning

Compensation planning has become one of the key human resources functions (Figure 10-1). Approaches and methods are becoming innovative tools to assist you in attracting and then retaining the people you need at all levels in your hospitality organization. We have identified six of the trends that you should keep informed of as you enter the hospitality industry.

1. Your employees are no longer willing to sacrifice leisure time for extensive overtime hours. This does not mean that they are

unambitious or not hardworking, but rather that they want to enjoy life today as well as when they retire.[6]

2. To accommodate the change in attitude, your compensation plan will need to be flexible as opposed to rigid.

3. As pay becomes more closely related to an individual's performance level and/or contribution to the hospitality enterprise, tools to measure performance standards and contribution levels will become more reliable and more widely available. The increasing use of computers in the work place, to handle data, will assist in the progression.

4. The entrepreneurial paycheck concept strives to retain entrepreneurial employees within the folds of the organization. This idea has been used for several years in high-tech companies, but it is finding its way into no-tech companies as well. A company located in Boston, Au Bon Pain, has a program that permits revenues to be shared with store managers.[7]

5. As the hospitality industry becomes more global and as individual companies expand their markets across the United States, compensation plans will need to become more considerate of the regional, as opposed to the national, rate of pay.[8]

6. The changes in compensation programs will increase the likelihood of hourly employees making more money than their supervisors. A watchful eye will need to be kept on the effect this occurence will have on the traditional subordinate-supervisor relationships as the number of pay levels included in the compensation plan are reduced.

Compensation Administration in the Hospitality Industry

The success of a compensation plan lies in its credibility and how well it is maintained as both the hospitality enterprise and hospitality industry changes and grows. So far in this chapter, you have succeeded in developing an equitable plan, one that is based upon well written job descriptions. All of your compensation policies should be formalized into a written manual and made available to all employees. Once, however, this has been accomplished, it does not mean that you can forget about the compensation component of your total reward system. On the contrary, all elements of your reward system need constant attention in order to maintain their effectiveness in attracting and retaining the best human resources available.

If your compensation plan, along with the bonus, merit pay and other incentive programs you have established in your hospitality operation are to be effective as motivational devices, they must be constantly presented as such to your employees. Once your employees have been hired and have fallen into the job routine, they will need to be reminded of the opportunities that your compensation package provides for them. Promote the rewards that are offered and give your employees time to think about the incentives they are working towards.

Once an employee has earned a reward, take an opportunity to issue the reward where other employees can honor the recipient. Not only does this give the employee receiving the reward a chance to be recognized for his or her contribution, but it also allows other co-workers to be reminded that rewards are obtainable for them as well.

The degree of autonomy you will have in compensation decision making will depend on the size of the hospitality organization you are working in. In large organizations, there will be a compensation department with staff personnel whose job is to administer the compensation plan. In very large corporations, these departments will include individuals who are experts in compensation. These compensation professionals may or may not have worked in a hospitality enterprise previously, but rather have developed competencies in the areas of compensation, benefits, pension plans, job analysis and merit pay systems. In these large hospitality companies the compensation professionals work with the line managers to obtain the compensation objectives of the hospitality enterprise.

In smaller hospitality organizations, compensation administration and decision making rests with the general manager of the food service or lodging operation. This would include decisions in the job evaluation process that we discussed earlier in this chapter, as well as decisions regarding changes in any of the established pay grades or pricing structures. Compensation surveys should be conducted periodically (we suggest no less frequently than once a year, although significant changes in the local labor market may require more frequent review) to assure that your hospitality organization's pay structure remains competitive. If it does not, you will find yourself losing some of your most valuable human resources over pay differentials to neighboring hospitality operations. COLA, or cost of living adjustments, are provided for by some hospitality organizations to counter the effects of inflation in our economy.

As your hospitality organization is dynamic, not static, it grows larger, or perhaps even smaller in size. The jobs within your operation are similarly altered. Job re-evaluation must be conducted to take into consideration the changes that will be reflected in the job descriptions. None of the human resources management tools that we have described to you are firmly fixed in cement, never to be changed.

Maintaining the accuracy of the job descriptions is one of the most useful functions performed by a human resources manager. New jobs are likely to be created that will require evaluation, and efforts will need to be made to assure the continued equitability of your compensation plan.

As periodic adjustments are made in the pay structure over a period of time, wage compression or expansion is likely to occur. This has the potential of affecting the internal equity you have worked so hard at building into your compensation plan. Wage expansion occurs when there is an increase in the difference between job-grade midpoints. Wage compression occurs when there is a shrinking in the difference between grade midpoints.

As changes in the wage and salary structure influence both human resources development and recruitment, the administration of compensation is a vital human resources activity. As human resources become scarce commodities in the service sector, keeping pay levels competitive will be a major challenge you face in "the next chapter."

Conclusion

Compensation development, implementation and administration in hospitality organizations is a vital human resources management activity. The satisfaction of your work force and, in essence, the success or failure of the operation, is heavily dependent upon an equitable compensation plan that both attracts and retains the caliber of human resources required by the mission statement of the hospitality enterprise. In "the next chapter," changes in the labor market will play a large role in determining the relationship between job hierarchy and pay structure. Pay is still used to satisfy our basic physical needs, but also assists us in recognizing our star performers and allows us to give our human resources a sense of accomplishment, no matter what job they perform for us in the hospitality operation. It is very difficult for a hospitality organization to keep all of its employees happy and satisfied, which is why it is so important that your selection of rewards is keyed to satisfying the needs of your employees. Of all the rewards an organization can offer to its employees, the wages and salaries are the most visible reward.

If you were to develop the ideal compensation plan for your hospitality organization what would you want to provide?

- Competitive pay rates that would attract qualified, competent human resources.
- A reward for longevity with your company that would encourage retention among the employees.
- A promotional incentive that would motivate your human resources to seek the opportunities your hospitality organization has to offer.
- A reward for quality work to show all human resources that your organization strives for excellence in the goods and services it provides.
- An equitable system that all human resources view as fair.

- Procedures that permit a uniform approach to compensation changes that maintain the integrity of the reward system.
- An effective method for controlling compensation costs. This, in effect, is based upon the organization's ability to pay.

We now turn our attention to compensation's partner in the reward system: benefits.

273

Case Problem 10-1

You are the human resources manager of a 150-room, nonunionized hotel. The property offers food service on a continuous basis from 7:00 a.m.–9:00 p.m. in its one restaurant. Alcoholic beverages are served in the dining room; there is no bar or lounge on premises. The hotel is owned by a group of investors with no current plans to franchise. The investors do want to show a profit margin each year. There is one other hotel property in the area that is close enough to be competitive with your property for wages. They provide similar services to those offered in your hotel. Frequently you have employees who leave your operation to work in your competitors. However, you do upon occasion hire employees who have, in the past, worked for your competitor.

This hotel has never linked compensation directly to performance appraisals or productivity levels. Due to the impending labor shortage and high labor costs you believe that a pay-for-performance compensation plan (for nonexempt employees) would address all of these issues.

The general manager, however, feels that you will encounter a number of difficulties in switching to a pay-for-performance plan. How will you convince the general manager that a pay-for-performance plan will be best for the long-term operation of this particular hotel? Although the relationship between benefit planning and compensation planning is critical in this, as in all hospitality operations, it should not be a consideration in answering this case problem.

A detailed plan should be prepared to present to the general manager. What could be some of the reasons that your employees leave to work at your competitors? Present solutions related to compensation planning which might entice your employees to stay. While there are presently no signs of union activity, one of your objectives in compensation planning is to a remain nonunion organization. A complete job evaluation has been conducted that you feel is accurate.

Case Problem 10-2

You are a strong advocate of adding a service charge to every guest check. You feel that tipping is not an effective method of compensation for service employees. You are the food-and-beverage manager of a 300-seat dinner house. This is a chain with ten properties located throughout the eastern seaboard. The two individuals who own this chain of dinner houses strongly resist the idea of implementing a service-charge system. They believe that tipping is a preferred system. The chain is six years old and presently uses a tipping system. The only exception is that a 20%

service charge is added to parties of twenty or more. These parties are notified of this policy at the time they make their reservations.

How will you convince the two owners that a service-charge system is the wave of the future? Prepare a written report that you will present to them to convince them to switch from the current system of tipping. Be logical and thorough in your ideas.

OR, take the position of the owners and prepare a written report that will convince the manager of this operation that the tipping system should prevail. Be logical and thorough in your ideas. (Just because they own the operation does not mean they are dictators when it comes to establishing operational policies.)

275

RECOMMENDED READING

Ameci, G. 1987. Bonuses and commissions: is your overtime pay legal? *Personnel Journal* 64, (1): 107–108, 110.

Bookbinder, S. M. and Seraphin, R. M. 1987. Making pay for performance work. *Personnel* 64, (9): 66–69.

Cissell, M. J. 1987. Designing effective reward systems. *Compensation and Benefits Review* 19, (6): 49–55.

Citron, Z. 1989. Waiting for nodough. *The New Republic* 200, (1): 9–10.

Foegen, J. H. 1988. Tip talk. *Restaurant Hospitality* LXXII, (3): 38–39.

Frumkin, P. 1988. The service charge system. *Restaurant Business* 87 (15): 75–76.

Henderson, R. I. 1979. *Compensation Management: Rewarding Performance.* Reston, Virginia: Reston Publishing Company, Inc.

Kanter, R. M. 1987. The attack on pay. *Harvard Business Review* 65, (2): 60–67.

Main, B. 1987. Strategic bonuses. *Restaurant Business* 87, (5): 84, 86.

McAdams, J. 1988. Performance-based reward systems: toward a common-fate environment. *Personnel Journal* 67, (6): 103–104, 106, 108, 111–113.

National Restaurant Association and Laventhol & Horwath. 1988. *Survey of Wages and Benefits for Salaried Employees and Executives in the Food Service Industry–1987.* Washington D.C.: National Restaurant Association.

National Restaurant Association. 1988. *Waitstaff Compensation: Tips vs. Service Charges.* Washington D.C.: National Restaurant Association.

Reyer, N. S. 1988. To tip or not to tip. *Restaurant Hospitality* LXXII, (10): 12.

Waldman, S. and Roberts, B. 1988. Grading "merit pay." *Newsweek,* (November 14): 45–46.

END NOTES

1. Belcher, David W., "Wage and Salary Administration," In C. E. Schneier and R. W. Beatty (Eds.), *Personnel Administration Today: Readings and Commentary.* (Reading, Mass.: Addison–Wesley, 1978): 426.
2. Belcher, David W., "Toward a Behavioral Science Theory of Wages," In M. S. Wortman (Ed.), *Creative Personnel Management: Readings in Industrial Relations* (Boston: Allyn and Bacon, Inc., 1969): 202–218.
3. Kleiman, Carol, "Does Hard Work Lead to a Raise?", *Miami Herald,* (June 19, 1988): 2F.
4. Waldman, Steven and Roberts, Betsy, "Grading 'Merit Pay'," *Newsweek* 112, (1988, 20): 45–46.
5. U.S. Department of Labor, "Equal Pay," *WHD Publication 1320.* (Washington D.C.: Government Printing Office, 1974.)
6. Bennet, Amada, "The Baby-Busters," *The Wall Street Journal,* CCXII, (1988, 82): 1, 10.
7. Kanter, Rosabeth Moss, "The Attack on Pay," *Harvard Business Review,* 65, (1987, 2): 60–67.
8. Levine, Hermine Zagat (Ed.), "Compensation and Benefits Today: Board of Members Speak Out, Part I," *Compensation and Benefits Review,* 19, (1987, 6): 23–40.

DISCUSSION QUESTIONS

1. Describe the process involved in compensation planning.
2. What is the one most important characteristic of a compensation plan?
3. Explain the concepts of external and internal pay equity.
4. List the intended outcomes of a sound compensation plan.
5. Describe the job evaluation process. List several examples of compensable factors important in the grading of jobs in your hospitality organization.
6. Present a brief argument for both tipping and a service charge system.
7. Describe how a hospitality organization can develop a pay-for-performance compensation plan. How does this differ from traditional compensation plans?
8. Do you believe that pay can motivate performance in the hospitality industry? Why or why not? Identify some of the compensatory incentives an employer in the hospitality industry could offer to you that would personally motivate you to perform at a high level.
9. Differentiate among the following incentive programs: bonus plans, profit sharing and gain sharing. Why might each of these programs fail to motivate improved performance?

10. Discuss how wage compression among unskilled, semiskilled and skilled human resources might effect the morale of the work environment. Identify both negative and positive effects.
11. What is the key focus of the FLSA? Discuss the legalities of compensatory time.
12. Identify potential compensation problems in hospitality organizations.

CHAPTER 11

BENEFITS

INDUSTRY *James F. Moore, President*
ADVISOR   *Far West Concepts*

"Money is the seed of money, and the first franc is sometimes more difficult to acquire than the second million."
—JEAN JACQUES ROUSSEAU

KEY WORDS

benefits
benefits menu
benefits planning
cafeteria benefits program
Consolidated Omnibus Budget
  Reconciliation Act, (COBRA)
cost containment
cost sharing
day care
defined benefits plan
defined contribution plan
educational assistance plan
elder care
Employee Retirement Income
  Security Act, 1974 (ERISA)
Employee Stock Ownership Plans
  (ESOP)

flexible benefits programs
flextime
Health Maintenance
  Organizations (HMOs)
income deferral
long-term care
long-term disability
pension plans
Preferred Provider Organizations
  (PPOs)
profit sharing
retirement plans
social security
thrift plans
Worker's Compensation

INTRODUCTION   Benefit planning is compensation's partner in the achievement of an equitable, attractive, competitive reward system. As with all of the human resources functions we have discussed thus far, the topic of benefits is changing rapidly. This is an area where you are only limited by your creativity in the types of programs you can develop to satisfy the needs of the human resources in your particular

279

hospitality organization. The price tag associated with the various types of benefits programs you may select ranges from the very inexpensive to the high priced. Regardless of how small or large the operation you are responsible for, you will have an abundance of benefits plans from which to select that will not be beyond your organization's means.

The most notable trend in benefits planning is the concept of flexible or cafeteria programs. In these programs your job as the human resources manager will be to select a "menu" of benefit plans from which your employees can select the options that best suit their personal needs.

At the conclusion of this chapter you will be able to:
1. Describe the contribution that the benefits program will make to the total reward system in your hospitality organization.
2. Differentiate among benefits, incentives, pay and employee assistance programs.
3. Understand the effects of changing social demographics on benefits planning.
4. Distinguish among the different types of benefits plan offerings.
5. Select types of benefits for a program in a hospitality organization.
6. Understand how to plan a benefits program for a hospitality organization.
7. Maintain an awareness of legislation affecting benefits planning.
8. Describe the concept of a flexible benefits program including its advantages and disadvantages.

The Role of Benefits

Benefits are a complimentery component of the total reward system you develop for your hospitality organization. In most cases, the reward system will already be in place when you join an organization, and your task as manager with human resources responsibilities will be to effectively communicate, monitor and administer the program. If, however, you find yourself in a position of designing a benefits program, you will also need some information on its planning and implementation.

In this chapter, you will need to view yourself as a benefits manager. As you will see, the scope of benefits planning is expanding and changing rapidly. Much of the volatility in this area is due to the government's ever changing position on benefits, which is reflected in the variety of laws and regulations being proposed and approved. Hospitality corporations find that benefits experts are crucial to understanding this complex arena.

Benefits differ from incentives and pay in that they are not tied to an employee's performance. At one time, benefits were referred to as *fringe benefits,* but that term is no longer appropriate as benefits are no longer a negligible component in your reward system. In hospitality organizations today, benefits can make up a serious 19 percent of payroll expenditures, if you exclude FICA, unemployment and disability. We will define **benefits** as a favorable allowance provided by the employer for the employee in addition to wages and/or salary that subsidize auxiliary employee needs and services.

Benefits programs are used by hospitality organizations as recruitment, motivational and retention tools. If they are to be effectively used as such, it is important that your human resources view the benefits you offer as part of their overall reward for being members of your hospitality organization.

The role of benefits has changed largely due to a shift in employee demographics, expectations and costs to both employer and employee. In the 1970s, traditional benefits programs were developed based on the structure of the family unit. At that time, most families were supported by a single wage earner, the male, who supported a nonworking spouse and dependent children. Benefits needs focused on medical insurance for the employee's dependents and himself or herself. Benefits were truly fringe rewards, initially only offered by the most innovative organizations. In the 1980s, not only did the structure of the family unit change, but now employees expected that benefits were part of their rewards package. The organization they worked for now owed these benefits to them. The family structure of the '80s was composed of two incomes, more women in the work force and the need for benefits that accommodated these changes. Cafeteria plans emerged to address the changing demographics and the new needs of employees.

Trends and Innovative Approaches in Benefits Programs

No one organization offers all of the benefits identified here to all of its human resources. Each organization must carefully plan its benefits program so that it meets the goals of the organization while at the same time maintaining a competitiveness with other organizations vying for the same job candidates. Additional differences exist between the benefits offered to hourly or salaried human resources. In the hospitality industry there is a relationship of the proportion of compensation to benefits expected. For example, operational managers on salary expect to receive basic benefits while to a server making very high tips, low benefits would be acceptable.

INDUSTRY EXPERTS SPEAK

According to Mr. Jim Moore, president of Far West Concepts, "As long as we offer a competitive health care program that is likewise competitively priced, we will be able to attract and

282

retain a sufficient supply of employees to meet our needs. As employees progress through the organization and take on additional responsibilities (i.e., families, homes, etc.) and are no longer working solely for cash compensation in order to put "bread on the table," there develops a need to broaden the benefits offered. It is a very delicate balancing act to juggle the needs of the employees with the cost to the company while keeping both eyes on the competition within the restaurant industry, general industry and the bottom line. It is a constant battle of weighing perceived benefit value vs. cost."

Knowing which benefits are right to select, implement and administer in your organization depends upon a thorough understanding of benefit developments in the 1990s. A discussion on the most commonly found benefit offerings in the hospitality industry follows, in alphabetical order.

Child Care

Child care could be provided as a benefit for either hourly or salaried human resources. The increasing need for quality child care is a direct result of women entering the work force and a change in the traditional child rearing patterns (Figure 11-1). The lack of quality child-care facili-

Figure 11-1. Employer-sponsored day care is an important benefit for the working parent(s). Courtesy of Concordia Lutheran School

ties in the communities have prompted employer-sponsored child-care programs. And the demand for these programs is growing. You will see an increasing number of human resources making employment decisions based upon whether such programs are available or if benefit options include assistance with child care expenses.

The Bureau of Labor Statistics identifies that 72 percent of mothers with school-age children and 57 percent of the mothers of preschool children are currently in the work force. Table 11-1 is a breakdown of the types of child-care benefits offered by the 10.1 percent of U.S. companies with 10 or more employees that offer such benefits.

The need for child care is not only important for dual income marriages, but it is critical to single-parent households. Increasingly, men are left with child-care responsibilities. Note that there is even a cartoon strip now about the man being the "houseman." According to recent studies, men are experiencing the stress of trying to balance both career and family life. While it is usually acceptable for women to miss work due to child-care responsibilities, it has been less accepted for men to miss work to care for their children.[1]

Benefits that can reduce the stress levels experienced by both men and women in the care of their children can make your human resources more satisfied with their jobs as well as reducing the amount of absenteeism in your hospitality organization. Such programs can include:

- Company child care facilities
- Parental leave, unpaid
- Financial assistance with child care
- Babysitting allowance
- Parenting seminars
- After-school programs
- Summer camps

Table 11-1. Child Care Benefit Offerings

The Bureau of Labor Statistics figures that about 10.1 percent, or 113,928 of the estimated 1,128,000 U.S. companies with 10 or more employees, offer child care benefits.

A breakdown of the types offered:

Employer-sponsored day care	18,048
Assistance with child care expenses	34,968
Information and referral services	48,504
Counseling services	47,376
Other child care benefits	10,152

Note: Many employers offer more than one benefit type.

Source: Bureau of Labor Statistics 1988

- Sick-child centers
- Vacation care

The lodging segment of the hospitality industry has a great opportunity to provide company child-care facilities on property. The rooms needed to provide such a benefit to their employees already exist, and with moderate renovations lodging facilities could readily become child-care facilities. With the need for such facilities increasing, watch for lodging operations to turn their company-provided facilities into revenue producers for other companies in the community, as well as for hotel guests travelling with children.[2] Child-care centers are more difficult to implement for the restaurant operator given the geographic dispersion of work locations. Contracting with existing child-care facilities to negotiate a more favorable group rate for your employees is a pliable solution. Be sure to check into the costs, especially that of the additional insurance coverage for liability, which you will need to carry.

Educational Assistance

Benefits plans that provide financial educational assistance for our human resources in the hospitality industry are certainly not new, although their availability is increasing. The offerings of these plans vary from company to company. The most common is to provide tuition paybacks to employees who have satisfactorily completed course work. These plans typically require that an employee work a specific number of hours and maintain a designated grade-point average in order to be eligible for the assistance. Far West Concepts offers educational assistance to all salaried employees after one year of employment. The reimbursement is up to $500 per year if a passing (C) grade is obtained.

Some of the more innovative forms of educational assistance include providing low-cost educational loans for the children of your employees. In some organizations, consideration is being given to offering college tuition subsides for employees' children as a benefit option. Retraining programs are also being offered in an effort to combat the increasing labor shortages. Human resources who want to move to another department or division within the hospitality company are being retrained at the organization's expense. Seminars are no longer being restricted to management, but include the hourly unskilled and semiskilled work force in an effort to prepare them for job openings within the company.

Educational assistance benefits are costly, but are based on the theory that the hospitality organization will receive a return on its investment. To prevent employees from accepting these benefits in order to obtain a better job at another organization, some companies have required their employees to sign a promissory note agreeing to pay back the costs if they leave. Companies have been successful in obtaining court settlements when employees leave before the specified time period.[3]

Elder Care

As our society is aging new concerns regarding the care of our elderly parents and other relatives come into play. While acceptability is increasing for men and women who need leave time to care for children, acceptance of the need to care for our senior citizens has been slow. The concept of elder care can become an important benefit to both hourly and management employees who are faced with the care of an elderly relative.

A variety of innovative methods are being developed to assist our human resources in caring for the elderly. Some programs, such as long-term care insurance, permit the employees to use their benefits for elderly relatives if they elect to do so. This provides the employee with additional flexibility in the use of his or her benefits without significantly increasing the cost to the employer. Caring for an elderly relative can be highly time consuming and stressful. Elder care strives to alleviate some of these problems.

Financial Planning Service

As the complexities of benefits planning and possible options increase, our entire staff could use some assistance in managing the benefits they receive. Research studies have shown that many employees bring their financial worries with them to the work place and this affects job performance.[4] Financial planning assistance will gain popularity as a benefit offering in hospitality organizations as we approach "the next chapter."

Flextime

Allowing our human resources to vary their work hours, to better accommodate their personal lives, has a enormous potential in the hospitality industry. For decades we have promoted the idea of split shifts. Flextime conforms to the peaks and valleys that typify our business patterns. After we define critical work hours, our human resources are then given the opportunity to determine which hours will complete the remainder of their workweek. The more innovative applications of flextime permit job sharing, with two part-time employees sharing one job. This opportunity also accommodates the employees who have child care or elder care responsibilities as well as the employee who simply seeks more leisure time.

Long-Term Care

Nursing home bills can rapidly impoverish an employee's life-time earnings. As the cost of long-term care increases so do the number of hospitality employers that offer insurance to help pay the cost of nursing home stays. During the late 1980s, employees had to pay the entire cost of the premiums for this type of coverage. Today, more companies offer long-term care insurance as a benefit option, with the company paying either the entire or the majority of the premium expense.

Restrictions and conditions under which the long-term care benefits are to be paid vary widely. The more coverage, the higher the cost to the company and/or the employee. Some programs cover nonmedical custodial care for victims of Alzheimer's disease, the severely handicapped and retirees who live at home but require care. Whether they are employee funded or company provided, long-term care benefits reflect the needs of the aging work force.

Long-Term Disabilities

Most of the human resources we have working with us in the hospitality industry depend upon their jobs as their primary means of financial support. An injury or illness that disables an employee from working temporarily or permanently could destroy his or her ability to earn a living. Long-Term Disability benefits (LTD) are offered to protect our employees' earning power by making them eligible for all, or a portion, of their pay should they become disabled and unable to work. Pay continuance plans such as these provide protection above what the employee might be entitled to through Worker's Compensation or social security disability.

Worker's Compensation provides disability benefits due to a work-related injury or illness. These benefits vary state-by-state. Social security disability benefits are paid when an employee is not able to perform any work that is available and reasonable, given the individual's work experience and education level. Social security typically does not begin paying until the sixth month of disability. That's why there are advantages to an income protection plan for your human resources.

Pay continuance plans typically expire after a stated period of time. For disabilities that last an extended length, group Long-Term Disability (LTD) plans are offered. LTD plans are typically elective benefit options. That is, the employee must elect to participate in the plan and also support the premiums. The advantage of this option is that the group plans are much less expensive than the individual disability plans. LTD plans cover all forms of disability with an offset for benefits provided under Worker's Compensation, social security or the Railroad Retirement Act.

Medical Plans

The rapid escalation of health care costs has placed medical care beyond the ability of most of us to pay for a serious illness or injury, especially if hospitalization is required. Medical plans, one of the oldest benefits employers have offered to their human resources, are designed to protect employees from financial disaster due to their expensive medical needs or those of their family members. Comprehensive cover-

286

age of medical expenses resulting from an injury or illness are handled by the medical plans offered by your hospitality organization. Table 11-2 gives you an example of the types of life/medical/dental coverages offered by The Restaurant Enterprise Group.

Table 11-2. Portions of Group Life/Medical/Dental Plan for Salaried Employees of the Restaurant Enterprises Group, Inc.

Eligibility

You are eligible to enroll in the Group Life/Medical/Dental Plan one month from your date of hire if you are regularly scheduled to work 25 or more hours per week. In addition, your spouse and dependent children (from birth to age 19, or age 23 if a full-time student) are eligible to enroll in the medical and dental plans at the same time you enroll.

Life Insurance

Your coverage equals two (2) times your base annual pay, rounded to the next higher $1,000 to a maximum of $250,000. You must be enrolled in the Group Medical Plan or an HMO to receive this coverage.

Group Medical Plan—Prudential

The following general coverages are available to you and your enrolled dependents:

- Calendar Year Deductible . . . . . $200 per person with a $600 family limit.
- Out-of-Pocket Maximum . . . . $2,500 per person per calendar year with a $7,500 family limit.
- Maximum Lifetime Benefit . . . . . . $1 million per person
- Hospital/Surgery . . . . .80% of reasonable and customary (R&C) charges, after the deductible is met. Hospital Preadmission Review required (see following section).
- Choice of Hospital . . . . $500 deductible if not a Pru-Net
  Pru-Net hospital, except for emergency or if a Pru-Net hospital is not within 25 miles.
- Office visits . . . . .80% of R&C, after the deductible is met.
- X-Ray & Lab . . . . .80% of R&C, after the deductible is met.
- Prescription Drugs . . . . .80% of R&C, after the deductible is met.

Dental Plan

You must be enrolled in the Group Medical (Prudential) Plan or an HMO to qualify for dental coverage. Your group dental benefits are through Prudential. The following general coverages are available to you and your enrolled dependents:

- Preventive/Diagnositc . . . . .100% of R&C with no deductible
  (check-ups) applied.
- Routine Restorative . . . . .75% of R&C after the deductible is met.
  (fillings, etc.)

(continued)

- Major Restorative . . . . .50% of R&C after the deductible is met.
  (crowns, bridges, etc.)   You must be enrolled for the prior 12
                                                 months.
- Orthodontics (braces) . . . . .50% of R&C after the deductible is met
                                                 to a $2,000 lifetime benefit maximum.
                                                 You must be enrolled for the prior 12
                                                 months.
- Calendar Year Deductible . . . . .$50 per person with a $150 family limit
- Calendar Year Benefit
  Maximum . . . .$1,000 per person

Optional Group Insurance Plans

The Company provides three optional group insurance plans to full-time salaried employees: Supplemental Life Insurance, Short-Term Disability and Long-Term Disability Income Plans.

Source: Far West Concepts

The costs of health care have risen steadily since the late 1970s. For hospitality organizations that provide health care for their staff this has translated into double-digit increases in insurance premiums. Much of the increased expense is due to the price inflation of the services covered by the typical health care plan. Price inflation is due to a number of factors including malpractice suits, reduction in payments from Medicare, a reduction of in-patient care stimulated by the increase of Health Maintenance Organizations (HMOs), more expensive technology and medical procedures such as transplants and a rise in catastrophic cases due in part to the AIDS epidemic.

The 1980s found benefits managers experimenting with cost containment measures to control the rising premium costs. Unfortunately, some of the measures contributed to the inflation in prices. These include the shift from inpatient care services to outpatient care, and a steady rise in state-mandated benefits. Legislative trends indicate that by the mid-1990s the federal government will have mandated medical benefits for all employees.

A survey conducted by the National Restaurant Association (NRA) in 1987 focused on the status of health care plans provided in the restaurant industry.[5] A surprising number of small (sales volume under $500,000) operations provided no health insurance coverage for their employees. The NRA calculates that federally-mandated insurance would cost these operators approximately 4 percent of gross sales, a considerable amount for these restaurant companies.

So far, the picture we have painted regarding the outlook for health care benefit plans does not look very promising. What measures can be taken in further attempts to combat rising health premiums? Cost containment!

INDUSTRY EXPERTS SPEAK

Mr. Jim Moore explains, "Cost containment, particularly as it applies to medical care expenses, is and continues to be the most important factor affecting benefits planning and administration in the 1980s and 90s, given the impact that double-digit medical care inflation has on our bottom line. I view cost containment as the following four independent yet interrelated components:

1. Cost sharing/shifting
   a. Employee contributions
   b. Deductibles
   c. Copayment levels
   d. Out-of-pocket stop loss level
   e. Caps on certain types of benefit provisions (e.g., substance abuse, outpatient psychiatric care, etc.)
2. Plan design and administration
   a. Hospital preadmission review
   b. Second surgical opinions
   c. Hospitalization concurrent review
   d. Hospital bill audit
   e. Preferred hospital networks
   f. Eligibility requirements
3. Managed care programs
   a. PPOs
   b. HMOs
   c. Hybrid PPOs/HMOs/indemnity plans
4. Employee communication/education
   a. Wellness programs
   b. Health care consumer education
   c. Employee incentives for low utilization"

Let's expand on a couple of Mr. Moore's ideas. **Preferred Provider Organizations** (PPOs) are one type of managed care program. If PPO plans are to be effective, employees must have some incentive for selecting the preferred provider over a provider of their choice.

Another approach to cost containment that has been proven to be effective for hospitality organizations is that of cost sharing. **Cost sharing** refers to a plan that requests a larger employee contribution to the health care benefit expenses. While it is unreasonable to expect our human resources to shoulder the entire burden of health care increases, there will be an increase over the copayments seen in the late 1980s.

Cost sharing also has proven to make employees more cautious when visiting medical facilities. If their share of copayment is negligible, there is likely to be a higher abuse of services, than if they had to pay $15 to $30 for each visit. In line with cost sharing are incentive programs for those employees with limited utilization of their health care benefits in a given year. By rewarding these human resources with smaller copayments, the abusers of medical benefits would hence be penalized.

Just what type of provisions are contained in health care packages? The following is a list of some of the options that you might want to consider including in a plan for your hospitality organization. Just remember that for every option your package provides there is a corresponding cost:

- Major medical and hospital
- Psychiatric
- Stress-related care
- Alcohol and drug abuse
- Maternity
- Outpatient services
- Home health care
- Newborn child care
- Vision plans
- Prescription drugs

Each of these options will contain varying conditions of eligibility, costs and benefits provided. It is up to you, the manager with human resources responsibilities, to keep current with the latest trends in health care benefit management as cost containment continues to be the buzzword throughout "the next chapter."

Retirement Plans

Health care benefits are not the sole contributor to escalating benefit costs. As our population ages, the hospitality organization's expenditures for retirement plans increases. This situation is further impacted by a reduction in the size of the work force that contribute their earnings to these programs. An increase in withdrawals and a decrease in contributions result in the need to carefully manage your organization's retirement plans.

Retirement plans come in a variety of forms, but the basic purpose of these plans remains the same: to provide retirees with a proportion of their income. These programs are a supplement to social security and other savings plans to which your employees may have contributed.

An accompanying service provided in connection with retirement plans is preretirement planning programs. Typically, these programs are offered in the form of seminars, meetings or carefully prepared written materials explaining the retirement plans offered by your hospitality company and postretirement financial planning. As plans for retirement become more complex, and the retirement age declines, this is an important auxiliary service that your company can provide at a relatively low cost to employees at all age levels.

The trend in retirement planning is towards less reliance on government (as viewed in the tightening of social security restrictions) and a shifting of responsibility to the individual worker. We will now explore some of the retirement programs available for our human resources.

Pension plans. The traditional pension plan is referred to as a *defined benefit plan*. This plan makes up the majority of all types of retirement programs. Based upon a formula, the employer agrees to pay the employee a specific amount of income upon retirement age. This money is contributed by the employer as tax-deferred income. Upon retirement, the employee can elect to withdraw the pension in monthly payments or as a single lump sum. The amount of contribution made to the pension by the employer is typically based upon length of service and an average income during the last few years of service to the hospitality organization.

The Tax Reform Act of 1986 has affected the attractiveness of this type of pension plan by reducing the tax advantages. Most hospitality companies and a large number of other employers are moving away from defined benefit plans to defined contribution plans. The advantage of these programs is their ability to calculate more closely what your employees will actually be receiving for their retirement income.

Defined contribution plans are established so that both employer and employee may make contributions to the plan. Some of these plans are only employee supported while profit sharing plans are typically employer only supported. The amount the employee contributes is placed into a tax-deferred account and is matched by an employer contribution. Although the use of defined contribution plans is less common than defined benefit plans, their implementation is increasing. These plans work well for low-wage earners as well as higher paid management personnel. They are readily acceptable as they are easy for your human resources to understand. Typically, annual statements are mailed so that the employees can see exactly how much of their contribution is in the plan.

Thrift plans are specific types of defined contribution plans where the employer guarantees to match a percentage of the employee's contribution to the plan. These act as a retirement savings account and are based upon an employee's voluntary contribution to the plan. The benefit of these plans is a tax advantage known as income deferral. **Income deferral** allows your employees to reduce their current income tax liability by setting aside a portion before it is taxed. Their gross income is reduced by the amount of their income deferral so that less tax is paid. Payment of this tax is made when distribution from the accounts is received by the employee. Most organizations provide payroll deductions

291

so that is quite easy for your human resources to make contributions to thrift plans. Generally, a number of investment options are provided to those participating in these plans. These investment options include:

- Equity funds. Assets invested in stock and securities; high return, risk may be high or low depending on the portfolio mix.
- Money market funds. Assets invested in short-term instruments such as treasury bills; earnings should approximate rate of inflation.
- Balanced fund. Assets invested in both equity and fixed-income investments, fixed-income portion is directed to guaranteed investment opportunities such as bonds; minimizes risk over straight equity fund arrangements.
- Company stock fund. Assets invested entirely in the employer's common stock; perhaps high risk.

Profit sharing is another type of defined contribution plan that permits the employee to share in a portion of the hospitality company's profit. These are defined contribution plans where the employer's contribution is determined by the company's profitability. Thus, the contribution will vary from year to year.

The formula developed to calculate an individual employee's earnings generally determines the amount of total contribution that is distributed to individual employee accounts based on annual earnings. An employee right to his account typically vests over a period of time, which builds loyalty. Most defined contribution plans have a vesting schedule.

Employee stock ownership plan (ESOP) operates as defined contribution plans as well. In these plans, the hospitality company makes contributions to its employees in the form of company stock. The maximum annual company contribution is determined by federal law and divided among eligible employees in proportion to their annual compensation. These plans may be used for both hourly and management human resources, although at time of going to press these plans were not currently in vogue due to taxation rules.

Vacation Time

Vacation policies vary widely from operation to operation based upon the different business needs of each. Vacation time is accrued based upon the length of service of each employee with your hospitality company. Some policies permit employees to carry over vacation time from year to year; other policies allow a portion of earned time to be held over, while other organizations believe that their human resources need to use the time off during the year it is earned. Which policy your organization has or will establish is dependent upon the hospitality enterprise's mission statement, goals and operational objectives.

Unique Benefit Offerings

The types of benefits that you, as the manager with human resources responsibilities, may select for your hospitality organization's benefit plan can be placed in five categories:

- Retirement Related
  - Pensions
  - Preretirement counseling
  - Savings/thrift
  - Cash deferred
  - profit sharing
- Insurance Related
  - Health related
    - Medical
    - Dental
    - Prescription drugs
    - Vision
    - Mental and psychological
  - Disability income
  - Life insurance
    - Group
    - Survivor security
    - Employees over 65
    - Retirees
- Time not Worked
  - Holiday
  - Vacation
  - Leaves of absence
    - Parental
    - Sick
    - Personal
  - Meal periods
  - Days off
- Financially Related
  - Educational assistance
  - Child care
  - Financial counseling
  - Social and recreational
  - Credit unions
  - Employee meals
  - Uniforms/drycleaning
  - Parking assistance
  - Legal counseling
  - Service awards
- Legally Required

294

A Summary of Marriott Corporation's
Benefit Package

1. **Medical**
   The Multi-Med Health Plan provides comprehensive medical care coverage through any of four Multi-Med options.

2. **Dental**
   The Dental Care Plan covers both routine and special treatment.

3. **Long-Term Disability/Salary Continuation**
   The plan provides an assured source of income in case you become disabled and cannot work for an extended period of time.

4. **Life Insurance**
   Life Insurance is available to both employees and their spouses at low-cost group term rates. You may select coverage of one to four times your base annual salary, with an insurance maximum of $400,000.

5. **Profit Sharing Plan**
   The Profit Sharing Plan provides retirement, disability, and death benefits; a convenient tax sheltered way to save money; and, of course, an opportunity to share in the company's profits.

6. **Stock Purchase Plan**
   The Stock Purchase Plan allows employees to buy shares of the company's common stock, without brokerage fees, at a fixed price set at the beginning of each year or the price at the end of January of the following year, whichever is lower.

7. **Credit Union**
   The Marriott Corporation Credit Union, is located at the Corporate Headquarters, is open to all employees and provides financial planning services, loans at reasonable rates, and a convenient way to save through payroll deductions.

8. **Bene-Trade**
   Bene-Trade is a program which allows you to make use of unused vacation and sick leave balances by trading a portion of your unused sick leave balance and vested vacation to help pay your contributions to the medical, dental, and disability plans.

9. **Vacation Leave**
   Hotel employees are eligible for three weeks paid vacation after one year of continuous service.

10. **Sick Leave**
    After six months of continuous service, paid sick leave is offered to full-time employees for four days a year.

11. **Gift Shop Discounts**
    All Marriott employees receive a 30% discount in all corporate Marriott Hotel Gift Shops.

12. **Hotel Discounts**
    All Marriott employees receive a generous discount on available rooms at most Marriott Hotels and Resorts.

13. **Tuition Reimbursement**
    All full-time employees are eligible for educational assistance after one year of service. This benefit provides up to $1500 of tuition and registration fees for business related course work.

Figure 11-2. A summary of Marriott Corporation's benefits package
Courtesy Marriott Corporation

- Worker's Compensation
- Social security
- Unemployment insurance
- State mandated

One of the benefits-planning decisions that will need to be made is the determination of what benefits will be company sponsored and which will require a contribution from your employees, if they wish to participate. Some benefits (health plans) can be funded with pretax contributions of employee money, thus saving taxes for both the employee and employer on amounts contributed. Generally, for our employees' convenience, these contributions are deducted automatically from their paycheck by the payroll department. Figure 11-2 shows an example of the benefit package offered by Marriot Corporation.

Special Concerns of Benefits Plan Design

As you have already seen, rewards to your human resources are not always received in the form of pay. As you choose from the multitude of benefit offerings you must take care to provide a balanced program for your employees. Part of your human resources responsibility will be to be on the lookout for ways to improve the plans already established. Benefit plans might be improved by suggesting changes that would make them more cost effective. Improvements might be suggested that would make the existing benefits plan better understood by the employees that participate in them. Don't feel as though your hospitality organization doesn't need your ideas regarding benefits plans simply because they already exist. Benefits plans design is one of the most proactive, evolving and expensive human resources functions in the 1990s.

Benefits Planning

Since benefits have become such a integral part of your total reward system, care must be taken so that your benefits plan fits into the organizational goals of the hospitality enterprise. One way to assure this is to prepare operational objectives for your benefits plan, and then design the plan so that it will meet those objectives. Table 11-3 identifies some of the considerations in benefits planning.

Communication becomes a critical component of benefits planning. The more alternatives your plan provides for your human resources, the better your communication system has to be. Many people have a difficult time understanding the financial planning provisions and variety of medical insurance options. The rapid changes in legislation tend to perpetuate this confusion. In addition, your plan has to be flexible enough to accommodate changes based upon employee needs. Getting your human resources involved in the design or redesign phases of benefits planning can lend valuable insight into just what their needs are (Figure 11-3).

Issues in the 90s

Health care insurance has been offered by hospitality organizations for decades in an effort to attract and retain quality employees. Once our valuable human resources wish to retire, retiree health care benefits are sometimes provided. No one expected the increasing expense of maintaining these benefit offerings. With medical costs increasing and our populace of employees aging and retiring earlier (more retirees to provide for) the future of this benefit is unsure. While a number of measures are being taken in an attempt to make costs more manageable, in some cases these benefits are being severly restricted or even cancelled entirely. This raises serious questions about the medical care of our aging society and who will maintain financial responsibility for their care.

The AIDS issue will gain attention throughout the 90s as medical expenses for patients can rapidly wipe out their life savings. The expense for insurance companies is enormous and can mean financial ruin for smaller insurance companies or employers who self-fund their medical benefits. An increasing concern is AIDS-infected mothers and children. Again, the question is raised: who will take the financial responsibility for their care?

Rising expenditures for benefit plans make cost containment the issue in "the next chapter." To assist with this and other benefit issues consulting companies have emerged that specialize in benefits. These firms have the knowledge and information regarding various insurance companies, legislative changes and interpretations, as well as the skills to negotiate with pharmaceutical companies, all in an effort to reduce the costs in providing these benefits to the employee. As the benefits arena continues in its complexity more hospitality organizations may find themselves relying on benefits specialists.

Table 11-3. Considerations in Benefits Planning

- Availability of labor
- Corporate mission statement
- Demographics and needs of your employees
- Different groups have different plans
  (full-time vs. part-time, hourly vs. salaried)
- How much the hospitality organization can afford to pay
- Number of part-time employees
- Organizational goals
- Potential short- and long-term costs
- What the competition is doing
- Who should participate (eligibility)
- Whether employees will have a choice in benefit selection

Figure 11-3. A benefits package is being explained to a group of employee's at Far West Concepts.
Courtesy Far West Concepts

Effects of Legislation

Throughout our discussion we have referred to the legislative environment that surrounds benefits planning. Much of this legislation is sending mixed signals to both employers and employees. The federal government, particularly the Reagan administration, called for a self-reliance position for the American people. This posture was taken largely as a result of the weakening social security system established by the Social Security Act of 1935. For a large portion of participants, these retirement benefits are no longer completely tax free. While the government would like to see a lesser dependance on social security it has simultaneously reduced the tax incentives for doing so.

In the past twenty-five years much legislation has been approved that imposes restrictions and/or administrative policies in the benefits arena. The Employee Retirement Income Security Act (ERISA) of 1974 was established to protect employees from failing pension plans that are maintained and operated by companies, including hospitality organizations. Standards have been established in this act that must be met for the company to be eligible for tax deductions for contributions made to the pension plan. The Internal Revenue Service and the Department of Labor can provide you with the additional information you will need to assure that your hospitality company is meeting the requirements of ERISA.

The passing of ERISA was a response to move away from government supported retirement plans, such as social security, (making this a mandatory benefit program). Both employees and employers contribute to the social security funds. This tax was established by the Federal Insurance Contribution Act (FICA). As of 1989, the amount required by the employer is 7.51 percent that matches the employee's contribution of 7.51 percent of the first $45,000 in pay. Frequent amendments to this act result in the increase of contributions, by both employer and employee.

Some of the legislation that has passed is aimed at reducing the disparity in benefits between highly paid executives and hourly wage earners. The Tax Equity Fiscal Responsibility Act of 1982 (TEFRA) limits the amount of pension benefits that executives can receive with tax advantages.

In 1986, the Consolidated Omnibus Budget Reconciliation Act (COBRA) was passed that required employers to meet certain conditions to provide extended health care benefits to retirees, employees who voluntarily or involuntarily quit, and divorced or widowed spouses and dependent children of present employees.

After COBRA, employers were faced with the famous Tax Reform Act of 1986 that imposed numerous significant changes in the tax laws effecting a number of employee benefits. Effective January 1, 1989, provisions were added to the act in section 89 that attempted to further restrict executive benefits at the expense of the employer. Equal benefits for all employees is the main purpose of the additional restrictions. What all this means for you, the manager with human resources responsibilities, is more paperwork and more complexity in understanding what your legal responsibilities are surrounding benefit programs.

Flexible Benefits Programs

The concept of flexible or cafeteria benefits programs grew in popularity throughout the 1980s. As the name implies, these programs identify a list or "menu" of benefits options that the human resources in your hospitality organization may choose from. This has the advantage of allowing the employees to select the benefits that they need the most and eliminates the expense of employer-supported benefits that are not used.

Again, it is the changing demographics that are largely responsible for the increasing popularity of these plans. Two-income families in traditional benefit programs typically end up with dual coverage for the same benefits plans. Single people with no dependents end up subsidizing their co-workers with families. Younger employees have different needs than do those nearing retirement. Single parents have needs revolving around their children. Life-styles have changed and the baby boomers are enjoying their leisure time, the time off from their job duties and responsibilities. While some of our older workers wish to retire later in life, many are opting for earlier retirement and time to enjoy life. There no longer exists the average American worker. The diversity in our work force will continue to increase along with the diversity of needs.

Flexible benefits programs began in the 1970s. They were first introduced by the Educational Testing Services (ETS). These progressive programs have grown in number since then, and in 1988 it was estimated that some 20 percent of companies offered this type of benefits program.[6] The Internal Revenue defines a cafeteria plan as "a written plan under which all participants could choose among two or more benefits or cash, property or other taxable benefits." In 1986, the Tax Reform Act eliminated those plans with cash options.

A flexible benefits plan may consist of a core of key benefits that are provided for all employees and a menu or a listing of alternative benefits plans from which the employee may select. Many recent plans do not have a core, and participants may elect freely among benefits offered. An important part of designing these programs is careful determination of the benefits to be included in the plan. Consideration, therefore, must be given to the characteristics of your work force so that the benefits you select meet the needs of your employees. Getting the input of your human resources can be a valuable approach when designing such a program. Once the benefits list has been developed, a determination must be made as to how much, or what part of, the plan will be funded by the hospitality organization, and how much by the employees themselves.

The operation of the flexible benefits plan is simple, however, the administration can be a nightmare requiring added communication. Each employee is allocated "benefit dollars" that may be based upon pay level, hourly vs. salaried, and/or length of service. The most common arrangement is to differentiate hourly and salaried. Your human resources may then take these "dollars" and use them to select benefits from the menu you offer them. In some plans employees may take a salary reduction and "buy" more benefits, if they feel they need the coverage. Some hospitality companies require that a minimum amount of health care, life and/or disability insurance be purchased. In other plans, choices are completely unrestricted. That means that care must be taken to make sure that your human resources understand the benefits: what is good for them and what is not. It appears as though most employees do, for in a study reported in 1987, medical coverage was the first choice of benefits selected in flex plans followed by life insurance, dependent-care coverage, long-term disability, dental, 401(k) plans, vacation time and short term disability was ranked eighth.[7]

What are some of the advantages that hospitality organizations have discovered through offering flexible benefits plans? Recent studies and experience indicate that cost containment is not achieved. Since, however, a flexible benefits plan meets the specific needs of your human resources, greater employee satisfaction is produced. Because of these advantages, employers also see greater company loyalty, improved retention and an attractive recruitment tool. Typically, employees like the plan because it gives them a sense of control over their lives.

300

Flexible benefits plans are not without disadvantages. Foremost is the initial expense to convert from a traditional benefits program. The design and implementation of flex plans requires much time and energy. The transition phase must be carefully planned with open communication between employer and employee. If your employees do not fully understand the new program they are likely to perceive that you are taking away something that is rightfully theirs. Remember that in the 1990s benefits are expected as part of the reward system you offer.

Other problems with these programs stem from unions that are generally not supportive, and with small companies who can't afford the extended bookkeeping that is required to keep track of who receives which benefits. While tax laws have so far been favorable to these types of plans, changes in legislation may make them less attractive in the future. A potential problem is that an employee could choose a totally inappropriate package resulting in a serious financial loss.

Despite the disadvantages, the increasing popularity of flexible benefits plans is expected to keep growing in the upcoming years. The hospitality companies that have adopted these plans find high employee acceptance. Although they represent greater administrative challenges and require closer communication efforts, flexible benefits plans also offer a more productive, happy work force.

Conclusion

Benefits programs are the second component in the reward systems that you design, implement and administer in your hospitality operation. They have become an important component in the attraction and retention of quality employees for human resources managers. As we proceed through the 1990s, this role is not likely to lessen in its importance in the operation of hospitality establishments.

Twenty years ago, profit sharing was the most important element in a progressive benefits program. Since then, benefits programs have expanded to include provisions for dental care, preventative care, paid vacations and pension portability. The changes in benefits planning stem from changing demographics in American society, the rising costs of providing retirement and health care coverage, as well as the effects of legislation and mandated benefits. Table 11-4 compares the distinction between traditional and participatory reward systems.

While no longer a supplementary component of compensation the goals of benefits programs have remained consistent. They remain:

Table 11-4. Appropriate Reward System Practices		
	Traditional or Theory X	**Participative or Theory Y**
Reward System		
Fringe benefits	Vary according to organization level	Cafeteria—same for all levels
Promotion	All decisions made by top management	Open posting for all jobs, peer group involvement in decision process
Status symbols	A great many, carefully allocated on the basis of job position	Few present, low emphasis on organization level
Pay		
Type of system	Hourly and salary	All salary
Base rate	Based on job performed; high enough to attract job applicants	Based on skills; high enough to provide security and attract applicants
Incentive plan	Piece rate	Group and organization-wide bonus, lump sum increase
Communication policy	Very restricted distribution of information	Individual rates, salary survey data, all other information made public
Decision-making locus	Top management	Close to location of person whose pay is being set

Source: Reprinted with permission from Fombrun, Tichy, and Devanna: *Strategic Human Resources Management* John Wiley and Sons, Inc., New York. 1986, p. 146.

- To create a climate for improved human relations
- To attract and retain human resources
- To provide an incentive for increased performance through job satisfaction
- To install a sense of partnership between employee and the hospitality organization
- To protect the financial resources of employees
- To provide security
- To reward loyal service and
- To improve general morale

To be effective in meeting these goals the benefit programs require periodic review and modification. They require an understanding of existing legislation and awareness of new legislation. They need to be employee driven and well communicated.

302

INDUSTRY EXPERTS SPEAK	According to Jim Moore, one of the major weaknesses in hospitality organizations today is their failure to communicate. And most of all, they must be responsive to the needs of the human resources in your hospitality organization. Mr. Moore also stresses, "The focus in benefits planning is on the relationship of perceived benefits value vs. cost to the company. We are in the business to make money and in a labor intensive industry, such as the hospitality industry, every little change in benefits programs translates to a significant monetary expense or savings that ultimately effect the company's profitability."

Case Problem 11

Develop a benefits plan for the hospitality operation that you described in Case Problem 1. Part of what you should include in this benefits plan is a cafeteria program. How will you determine which offerings your cafeteria program will include? Present the menu of cafeteria offerings, justifying why you have included them in your program. How will you incorporate cost-containment measures into your benefits program? (Hint: You will need to provide some demographic information on the makeup of the work force in the area.) Remember that one of the goals of benefits planning is to have a happy, satisfied work force, while at the same time keeping the benefits program cost effective.

RECOMMENDED READING

Baker, C. A. 1988. Flex your benefits. *Personnel Journal* 67 (5): 54, 56–61.

Cohn, B. 1988. A glimpse of the "flex" future. *Newsweek* CXII, (5): 38–39.

McCaffery, R. M. 1983. *Managing the Employee Benefits Program.* New York: AMACOM.

Montana, P. J. 1985. *Retirement Programs: How to Develop and Implement Them.* Englewood Cliffs, New Jersey: Prentice-Hall, Inc.

Morrison, M. H. 1984. Retirement and human resource planning for the aging work force. *Personnel Administrator* 29, (6): 151–159.

Newman, J. D. 1987. Giving long-term disability benefits a shot in the arm. *Personnel Journal* 66 (6): 134, 136, 139.

Rosenbaum, M. and McCallen, J. 1988. The do-it-yourself advantage. *Cashflow* 9 (3): 44–45.

Rosenbloom, J. S. (Ed.) 1988. *The Handbook of Employee Benefits Design, Funding, and Administration.* Homewood, Illinois: Dow Jones-Irwin.

Ryland, E. K. and Rosen, B. 1988. Attracting job applicants with flexible benefits. *Personnel* 88, (3): 71–73.

Stiteler, A. 1987. Finally, pension plans defined. *Personnel Journal* 66, (2): 45–53.

Tane, L. D. 1988. How to get more bang for your benefits buck. *Financial Executive* 4 (4): 48–52.

Wells, K. 1988. Hotels and resorts are catering to kids. *Wall Street Journal* CCXII, (29): 29.

Zoghlin, G. G. 1988. Defined benefit plans: old fashioned or new wave? *Cashflow* 9, (3): 35–37.

304

END NOTES

1. Trost, Cathy, "Men, Too, Wrestle With Career-Family Stress," *Wall Street Journal* CCXII, (1988, 86): B1.
2. Huffman, Lynn M. and Schrock, Jay R., "Corporate Day Care: An Answer to the Labor Shortage," *Cornell Quarterly* 28, (1987, 1): 22–24.
3. Miller, Annetta and Springen, Karen, "If the Boss Pays, You Stay," *Newsweek* 112, (1988, 14): 41.
4. Fritz, Norma R., "Helping Employees Manage Their Finances," *Personnel* 65, (1988, 2): 6–9.
5. Mills, Susan, "A Review of Industry Health Insurance Plans," *Restaurants USA* 7, (1988, 8): 42–44.
6. U.S. News and Word Report, "A Cafeteria of Benefits," *U.S. News and World Report* 104, (1988, 12): 68.
7. McKendrick, Joseph E., "Cafeteria Plans—What's on the Menu?," *Management World* 16, (1987, 2): 16–17.

DISCUSSION QUESTIONS

1. Briefly discuss the role of benefits in the development of a total reward system in the hospitality industry.
2. Explain the difference between benefits and incentives.
3. Describe how the changes in family structure have affected the selection of benefits offerings in the hospitality industry.
4. Briefly define the following benefits options: child care, educational assistance, long-term care and retirement planning.
5. Explain the use of flextime in a hospitality operation.
6. Identify and describe two cost containment measures aimed specifically at the rising cost of health care.
7. Describe legally required benefits.
8. How can hospitality managers better communicate to their human resources about benefits programs?
9. What are the most significant effects of the legislation surrounding benefits?
10. Select five benefits options that you strongly feel should be part of a benefits plan (other than legally required). Defend why you feel so strongly about these choices.
11. Would you support letting all human resources determine their own benefits package? Why or why not?
12. What are the values and problems in establishing a flexible benefits plan?
13. What are the objectives of a benefits program in the hospitality industry?

CHAPTER 12

PROGRESSIVE DISCIPLINE, COUNSELING AND EXITING THE ORGANIZATION

INDUSTRY ADVISORS

Anonymous, Director, Menu Planning & Development
Company Anonymous

and

Anonymous, Regional Director of Human Resources
Company Anonymous

"The Fault, dear Brutus, is not in our stars,
But in ourselves, that we are underlings." — SHAKESPEARE

KEY WORDS

Age Discrimination in
   Employment Act
discipline actions
discipline policy
Employee Assistance Program
   (EAP)
employee-at-will
employee performance records
employee exit checklist
exit interview

nonpunitive approaches
performance counseling
positive discipline
progressive discipline
resignation
rules of conduct
suspension
termination
wrongful discharge

INTRODUCTION

How many of you have had the unpleasant task of disciplining or terminating an employee that worked for you? Do you remember how you felt the first time you fired someone? We do. And we imagine every hospitality manager remembers the feelings of anxiety he or she felt before that termination meeting. We have had to discipline our human resources for being late, for not showing up for their shift, for poor performance, for being rude to the guests in our operations and even for not using proper hygiene before they came to work. The emotions that build up inside you are dreadful, you find yourself filled with anxiety, uneasiness and concern. While you will never look forward to disciplinary and termination actions, we hope that in this chapter we will be able to provide some insight into transforming discipline from punishment to constructive criticism. Constructive for both the human resources we manage and the hospitality operations we have a responsibility towards.

At the conclusion of this chapter you will be able to:
1. Describe the rights of both management and employees in a hospitality organization.
2. Identify the purpose of rules of conduct and a fair treatment policy for a hospitality organization.
3. Implement the steps in the discipline process.
4. Discuss the purpose of a discipline policy for a hospitality organization.
5. Explain the benefits of progressive discipline to hospitality organizations in the 1990s.
6. Describe the roles of performance counseling in the discipline process.
7. Plan a performance review for one of your employees during counseling.
8. Implement termination procedures.
9. Explain of the legal implications included in wrongful discharge lawsuits.

Progressive Discipline

For as long as our human resources are human a discipline policy will need to be part of the Standard Operating Policies (SOP) of our hospitality organizations. If our human resources always abided by the rules we developed for the operation of our properties, and if they never performed below the established performance standards, there would be no need for disciplinary actions. But unfortunately, until that day, a sound human resources text book must include this chapter.

The purpose of the information in this section is intended to provide you, the manager with human resources responsibilities, with general guidelines for the establishment and implementation of disciplinary procedures. It would be impossible to include all of the potential situations in which you will find yourself, in the hospitality work place. Everything we discuss in this section needs to be tempered with your discretion as manager. There are few disciplinary situations that are either black or white. In most situations, you will need to carefully weigh all the facts before reaching any conclusions that might have an adverse effect on both the individual(s) involved and your credibility as a fair, impartial human resources manager.

Management Rights and the Rights of Our Human Resources

Management has the right to expect employees to abide by the rules of conduct and to meet the hospitality organization's performance standards. While we would like our human resources to be conscientious and cooperative at all times when in our employ, it is necessary to develop rules of conduct, such as the example found in Table 12-1. These rules guide our employees in maintaining positive relationships with our guests, the management team and with each other. These rules also help to ensure a safe work environment for all concerned.

The consequences of infraction vary with each rule, as some are more critical to the safety of persons in the hospitality operation than others. Possession of a weapon, fighting, possession, use or sale of an illegal substance and failure to follow safety procedures are all violations that could result in personal harm or injury to either other employees or guests. The consequences of these violations might possibly include suspension pending investigation, possible termination or in the case of illegal substances, prosecution.

Insubordination, tardiness, no-shows and violation of some property rules (such as smoking in nondesignated areas) could carry less severe consequences. The recent "employment at will" litigations, however, have found otherwise. Tardiness and absences are usually covered in a separate company policy statement. For other rule infractions, the severity of the

---

Table 12-1. Rules of Conduct

The following rules and regulations have been adopted by this company to insure your health, safety and welfare as well as that of our guests. They represent the kind of conduct that is not permitted and will subject you to disciplinary action.

1. Falsifying production or other records.
2. Careless or willful destruction of company property.
3. Fighting or hitting another employee, or similar disorderly conduct during work hours.
4. Sleeping on the job.
5. Smoking in restricted areas or in any part of the operation where there are guests.
6. Unauthorized removal or punching of another employee's time card.
7. Unauthorized possession of company property, including the removal of china, silverware, flowers, food, linen or office supplies.
8. Failure to maintain safety and sanitation standards.
9. Excessive tardiness and absenteeism.
10. Failure to follow a supervisor's instructions.
11. Conviction of a felony.
12. Willful restriction of production.
13. Taking excessive breaks.
14. Being in nonpublic areas of the operation on your day off without management's permission.
15. Working overtime without authorization from your supervisor.
16. Possession of weapons on hotel property.

---

violation is taken into account and normal disciplinary procedures established for your hospitality organization would be put into effect.

Before a hospitality organization can expect its employees to obey the rules that govern their behavior, the rules must be:

- Developed in a consistent manner
- Written clearly
- Communicated clearly to all human resources
- Middle management must be trained to understand the disciplinary procedures for each rule infraction and administer them consistently

Consistency and communication are required if you are to successfully implement any disciplinary procedures for rule infractions. Without these two elements, disciplinary procedures that lead to termination could easily result in a wrongful discharge suit being filed against your hospitality organization by the disgruntled employee.

Hospitality management also has the right to expect job efficiency from each employee. Here is where the rights of our human resources and several other human resources functions come into play. The employee needs to be placed in a job that is compatible with his or her abilities and skills. In addition, each employee should have been adequately oriented and trained for his job tasks. Your employees also are entitled to a fair and timely appraisal of their performance. When these systems are in place, the need to discipline for poor performance levels is greatly reduced. At times, however, failure to meet performance standards will result in disciplinary actions.

What else do our human resources have a right to expect from us, their managers and employers? They have a right to have any complaints and problems listened to in an impartial manner, and to have these complaints and problems promptly resolved. If employees do not feel that the matter has been satisfactorily resolved by the immediate supervisor, then the employees have a right to express their concern to a higher management level while simultaneously following the appropriate chain of command.

The Discipline Process Applied

One key to successful implementation lies with a well-written discipline policy. This written policy will be located in the human resources policy manual. A second key aspect, and one over which you, the manager with human resources responsibilities has control, is to handle all potential disciplinary problems as soon as they occur. Since the discipline function is so distasteful, hospitality managers have a tendency to put off these activities. Frequently, we recognize that a problem exists, but we fail to act upon it quickly. Delaying disciplinary actions can only magnify a problem situation and make it worse.

Perhaps we notice that Jennifer in the salad department has been late in preparing for dinner, or that Tony did not show for his job at the front desk. Instead of asking Jennifer what the problem is the first time she is late, we might wait thinking that the problem will not reoccur. And we fail to ask Tony the next day if everything is all right and tell him how much we missed having him at his post. Before too long, Jennifer is never on time preparing for dinner, and when you do confront her she is angry and upset. "Why haven't you said something sooner? I didn't think it was creating a problem for the waitstaff, or you would have told me." And Tony, thinking no one notices—or even worse, cares—when he calls in sick, starts missing one day a week. By the time we call him in, we are upset and frustrated because of the extra work load it has placed upon the rest of the front desk staff. We now have to justify the overtime on everyone's timecards and are angry because this might reflect on our personal evaluations.

We can only blame ourselves. We must be timely and efficient in our human resources management responsibilities. You can't ignore a problem and expect it will go away. It won't! Good communication skills and practices go a long way in reducing the need for implementing disciplinary policies. Another good method for avoiding the need for discipline is employee meetings. At these sessions, the concerns of our human resources can be voiced. Frequently, we are unaware of some of the problems that can exist. These meetings also provide us with a forum for explaining new procedures and policies as well as soliciting suggestions from the employees.

Remember that the purpose of the discipline policy for your hospitality organization is to provide the management with guidelines when communicating with an employee who fails to meet your organization's standards of conduct or performance. These guidelines provide a means for consistently applying and enforcing the established rules of conduct and performance standards.

The Steps to Implementation

When an employee violates the organization's rules of conduct or performs at a substandard level, there is a series of disciplinary actions that might take place. As noted earlier, there are certain, serious violations that could result in immediate suspension or termination.

Any action to discipline is a serious management decision and should be preceded by a careful, thorough investigation. As the manager with human resources responsibilities, you must be careful not to make a decision regarding either the incident or possible disciplinary action until you have gathered all the facts. Acting without full knowledge of the conditions surrounding the incident may result in the disciplinary action being overturned by arbitration (if your organization is unionized) or in a court of law. If the incident requires the employee to be removed from his or her job, the employee should be suspended, pending the investigation. Never should an employee be terminated immediately. Oftentimes, situations are not as they really appear at first. Immediate termination puts your hospitality organization at risk for a wrongful discharge suit.

Part of your investigation will include the identification of any other employees or other persons involved. Each of these individuals should be questioned in the presence of another management person in addition to you. The person being questioned should also be permitted to have someone else present with him or her. If the investigation includes a guest or guests, it is useful to obtain a written report of the incident directly, including an identification of the employee(s) involved. If a police investigation is called for (theft or illegal substance), then you will need to provide space for them to conduct their interviews. A thorough investigation and questioning of persons involved is needed for both performance and rules of conduct violations.

Next, a meeting is called with the employee to present the results of your investigation. The names of other employees whom you questioned are never revealed. The focus of this meeting is to be on the problem, not on the person. The meeting should be conducted in private with no interruptions. The following events occur during the meeting:

- **Identification of problem**
- **Identification of specific rule or performance standard that was violated** It may be that the employee did not know or understand the rule or standard. Remember that it is management's responsibility to present rules of conduct and performance standards in a clear manner and to ensure that they are both communicated and consistently enforced throughout the hospitality organization. Your human resources should not only understand what your expectations of them are, but what the consequences are of not meeting those expectations.
- **Listen to the employee** Remember that the goal of this session is to correct the problem, not humiliate or punish the employee. While you have facts obtained from other individuals you still need to hear from that employee the reasons for consistently being late for work, or why the individual was rude to a guest the evening before. At this time you can also make sure that the employee understands the importance of being on time, or what constitutes unacceptable behavior with the guests in the hospitality operation.
- **Reach a mutual agreement or solution** Here the alternatives are explored for resolving the problem. The focus should be on getting the employee to modify his or her behavior so that it

meets management's expectations. A plan of action should be developed that would result in a solution to the problem. Once this has been accomplished, you ask the employee to:

- **Summarize** both the problem and the mutually agreed upon solution. By requesting that the employee summarize what just occurred you have an opportunity to confirm that he or she has a clear understanding of the events of the disciplinary meeting. A time should be established when the two of you will get together to evaluate the progress of the action plan.
- **Notify employee of necessary formal actions that need to occur** Even if this is the employee's first violation, documentation still needs to be made of your disciplinary meeting. The extent of the documentation depends upon the severity of the violation. If the violation is minor and a first time occurence, a handwritten note in the employee's file stating the date, incident and action plan established is sufficient. This information can serve as a reminder of what was agreed upon by both parties when the evaluatory meeting is held to review action plan progress.

311

Follow up and reinforcement of the action plan should take place after the disciplinary meeting takes place. The role you assume is now one of performance counselor. The action plan has been developed, but you must assist the employee through counseling activities in guiding the individual's behavior towards acceptable standards.

Too frequently, in day-to-day operations, we forget to acknowledge acceptable behavior. If we see that the employee is back on target and successfully fulfilling the requirements of the action plan, we fail to communicate that message. It is no wonder then that our human resources perceive discipline as punishment. Acknowledging desired performance and behavior would go a long way in changing that perception. Table 12-2 identifies the components of an effective disciplinary meeting.

Table 12-2. Requirements for Effective Disciplinary Meeting

Timeliness: meet as soon as possible following the alleged infraction.

Objectivity: focus the meeting on the behavior and not on the individual.

Investigation: be certain to interview witnesses and obtain all the facts.

Discipline: be sure disciplinary actions taken are consistent with prior incidents.

Document: make accurate notes defining the infraction and action(s) taken.

The Discipline Actions

The specific actions that you design into the disciplinary policy of your hospitality organization should be carefully selected in view of the mission statement, goals and objectives that guide the decision-making process for policy determination. The procedures used vary from hospitality organization to hospitality organization. Table 12-3 contains an example of this type of policy.

Disciplinary action steps typically number between three and five ranging from a series of verbal warning(s) to a series of written warnings. Termination should only be taken as a last resort after all other alternatives have been exhausted, or when the violation is too serious for other options to be considered. Written warnings are issued after a verbal warning has been documented and the behavior or performance does not improve. The written warning is prepared using a format similar to the one shown in Table 12-4. The policy for disciplinary actions provides management with guidelines for the implementation of the actions.

The Purpose of Discipline

The intent of disciplinary actions has changed along with the increasing labor shortages and our ever increasing need to retain, not dismiss, our human resources. Fifteen years ago our disciplinary actions were seen merely a way to document "bad" employees and to prevent a lawsuit. It was not uncommon for managers, wanting to rid themselves of an employee, to initiate disciplinary actions to justify the intended termination of that employee. While this was never viewed as cost effective (recall from our discussion of training that even the short-term employee has a cost investment made in them), it was a simplified way of "cleaning house." Good human resources management? No. Not then and certainly not in "the next chapter."

Today, our progressive disciplinary policies and procedures are designed to assist our human resources in correcting unacceptable behavior or performance levels. A hospitality operation has to rely upon standards of conduct and performance to meet its organizational goals.

Table 12-3. Progressive Discipline Policy

The Company endeavors to follow a progressive discipline policy to provide employees with notice of infractions and an opportunity to improve. Whether to follow the progressive discipline procedure and a specific level of discipline in a particular case, however, remains in the Company's discretion. Although the discipline often depends on an employee's work history and the nature of the infraction, the Company retains the discretion to discharge an employee immediately if it believes it appropriate.

Table 12-4. Employee Performance Record

Employee's Name: _____

Manager's Name _____ Date: _____

1. Describe what the employee did. Include dates and events (who, what, when and where).

2. Describe what action is planned (except in cases of commendation or termination). This should include a description of the corrective steps to be taken: actions, responsibilities

3. How many written warnings has this employee had in the last twelve months,

including this one? _____

4. What is the next disciplinary step if correction does not occur satisfactorily?

5. Circle the type of action which was taken:

| COMMENDATION | VERBAL WARNING* | WRITTEN WARNING** | SUSPENSION (NOT TO EXCEED THREE DAYS) | TERMINATION |

_____   _____

MANAGER'S SIGNATURE   DATE

_____   _____

EMPLOYEE'S SIGNATURE   DATE

  * No employee signature is required.
** If the employee refused to sign a written warning, suspension, or termination notice, a witness should sign to indicate the form was read to the employee.

RETAIN THIS FORM IN THE EMPLOYEE'S PERSONNEL FILE

Managers with human resources responsibilities must assume that an understanding of acceptable norms rest with them.

If one of our human resources has violated a rule of conduct by smoking in a nondesignated area and further not washed his or her hands before returning to the job of food preparation, what is it that we, as managers, want to have occur? Do we want the person to be punished for his or her behavior? Or do we want the behavior to change to fit in with the accepted norms of the work environment? Similarly, if our bellperson can never be located when a guest is ready to be taken to his or her room, what do we want to have occur? Is it more important that the bellperson is verbally or more formally punished for his or her behavior, or that the next time a guest checks in that the bellperson is ready and waiting to show the guest to his or her room?

We think that most of you will agree that we want the deviant behavior to be altered so that it conforms with acceptable levels of conduct and performance. In order for that to occur, we need to obtain a commitment from the food preparer and the bellperson that a change in behavior will take place. Before they can make that commitment, an understanding needs to be made concerning both the problem and the action plan necessary to correct it.

Putting the Progressive into Discipline

The discussions in this chapter have been describing a corrective action, progressive discipline or positive discipline program. These are terms for similar styles of discipline that emphasize constructive criticism and the return of the employee to the work environment as a productive human resource. These programs seek to avoid actions that could demoralize an employee and cause the work force to perceive management as cruel and unfair.

The concept of progressive discipline was first discussed in 1964.[1] Twelve years later, Performance Systems, Inc., was started in Dallas, Texas specializing in the implementation of nonpunitive approaches to discipline in organizations.[2] Positive discipline is a three step approach:

1. Verbal warning
2. Written planning
3. Decision-making leave (day off with pay)

While a day off with pay sounds like an unusual disciplinary action, Performance Systems, Inc., firmly believes in its effectiveness. During this day off, the employee is expected to decide whether to continue employment with the organization under the established rules and standards, or to terminate employment with the organization. If the employee decides to return, but if the behavior does not change, dismissal is the next action step.

It is this type of innovative approach to human resources management, which you, in "the next chapter," must be alert to. The problem with traditional, punitive approaches to discipline is that they fail to foster commitment to organizational goals. They are typically viewed as unfair by our human resources and are often susceptible to union arbitration. It is hard for unions to argue against a system that provides the employee with a paid day off. In addition, traditional systems perpetuate managers' fear and distaste of the disciplinary process, which means that problem areas are not likely to be acted upon as quickly as they are brought to the attention of management. By using a more innovative approach to discipline, we can stop viewing the process as a way to document for eventual termination, but rather as a way to save valuable human resources for our hospitality organization.

Classification of Discipline Problems

A word needs to be mentioned about the different types of discipline problems you will encounter. So far in our discussion we have treated problems in behavior or performance as though there existed a typical human resource that acted and reacted to the work environment like all other typical human resources. People are not alike, and, thus, the motivations for their behavior or performance problems will vary. Thus, not only do you need to keep the severity of the violation in mind as you apply the disciplinary process, but your investigation should also attempt to seek the reason the problem occurred. Problems occur within three frameworks:

- Employee knows what is required, but chooses to ignore the requirements.
- Employee breaks the rules, but does not understand the rules or have the training necessary to meet required standards.
- Employee tries or intends to meet requirements, but is incapable of doing so due to circumstances that he or she cannot control.

Employees in the third situation need our help and understanding so that they can return to being functioning members of our work force again. Some of these individuals need to be referred to the Employee Assistance Programs (EAPs) that we will be discussing in chapter 13. These programs are designed to assist human resources with mental, personal and medical problems such as alcohol or drug dependency. The help required by these employees goes beyond what we are trained for as hospitality managers. The best help we can provide is our support and referral to professionals that can assist these individuals in overcoming their problems.

There are other reasons that might be responsible for employee misconduct that will require our careful attention. Is the employee late because the individual lost his or her driver's license and now has to rely on public transportation? Does the employee have a chronic illness such as asthma that is unsettled by the particular work location the person is in? Does the employee take longer-than-required breaks because he or she needs to take medication on a recurring basis? These are all situations that once understood by management can lead to productive human resources that follow your hospitality organization's rules of conduct routinely.

316

Performance Counseling

Regardless of the cause of the problems, job performance is often negatively affected. Troubled employees affect both performance levels and the quality of service you offer in your hospitality operation. Problems can also account for increases in absenteeism, tardiness, an increase in job-related accidents and increased sick leave, all of which result in rising costs for the hospitality enterprise.

So what can we do in the hospitality industry to help our people? Since very few of us are trained professionals in the area of counseling, we have to be careful not to get involved in situations that we are not trained to handle. If the hospitality organization where you work does not have an established Employee Assistance Program then you should be aware of the public services available in your community. But before you can direct your problem employees to available help, you must first be astute enough to recognize that undesirable behaviors and performance levels are problem related. While you might secretly wish for the behavior and performance to magically improve so that you won't have to deal with it, problems don't just disappear or resolve themselves. By constantly monitoring the performance of our human resources, we are likely to capture any problems shortly after they occur.

Counseling as Part of the Discipline Process

Progressive discipline attempts to alter the employees' performance or behavior so that they may retain their position in the work force. The method through which this is accomplished is performance counseling. The idea of counseling is a theme found throughout human resources management in "the next chapter" as we strive to find innovative ways to retain our valuable human resources.

Since these individuals are human, problems that affect job performance will occur while they are in our employ. When this happens, the disciplinary process emphasizes counseling in an effort to get the employee back on the right track. Figure 12-1 shows you where counseling fits in the discipline process. Let's examine each of the steps in the process.

Problem Identification and Analysis. Problem identification should be initiated by the human resources manager as soon as signs of negative

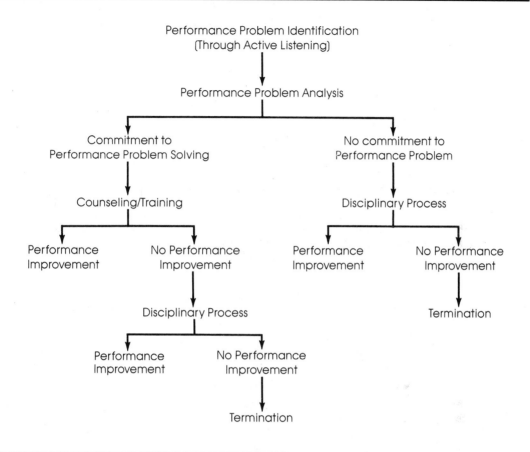

Figure 12-1. Relationship of Counseling in the Disciplinary Process

behavior or reduced performance levels are exhibited by the employee. The employee may easily be put on the defensive, so care must be taken in your initial approach. Open-ended questions, a comfortable atmosphere, an understanding that you are sincere in wanting to help the person and active listening may help the employee feel as if he or she can confide in you. Active listening requires that you not make judgments about what the employee is telling you so that you really hear what the individual has to say.

It is not always easy to be a good listener. The problems you will identify will either be job related or personal. Again, if the problem is something that you are not trained to deal with, refer the employee to your EAP or to some other professional. Problem analysis requires empathy and an open mind. Some of the information the employee is sharing with you might very well be your responsibility to correct. What if the employee talks of inadequate equipment, facilities that are poorly designed, work group members that are uncooperative, a lack of skills training, nonexplicit instructions or hazardous working conditions? Aren't these problems really management problems? Do not overlook the possibility that the low performance of your human resources is the result of management failings.

Determining Commitment. The next step in the counseling process is to determine if the employee is committed to improving performance so that it conforms with acceptable standards. Not all employees are going to recognize that a problem exists, or, if they do, are willing to make the effort to improve. In areas where labor is tight, this can be a particular problem if the employee believes that you simply cannot afford to suspend or terminate his or her employment. Not all employees are model citizens.

Table 12-5. Self-Appraisal Form for Human Resources in Performance Counseling

---

Job Design and Satisfaction
> Do you feel you are well placed in your present job assignment?
> Do you have a clear understanding of the expectations your immediate supervisor has for you in your present job?
> Do you have a clear understanding of the goals of the work unit to which you are assigned?
> How do you feel about the kind of work you are doing in your present job?
> How effectively do you feel you have met the responsibilities of your job position?

Performance Appraisal
> How worthwhile was your last performance appraisal in helping you to improve your performance?
> Summarize the overall strengths and weaknesses you have demonstrated in performing your present assignment.
> Does your immediate supervisor give you the necessary information to enable you to know how you are getting on with your job?

Development
> How do you feel about the progress you have made thus far in performing your job?
> How confident are you that your career aspirations can be met by remaining in this hospitality organization?
> Do you feel you have potential beyond your present job assignment? How have you demonstrated this potential?
> How much assistance have you been given by your supervisor in planning your career development?

Communication
> Do you receive enough information to perform your job effectively?
> Do you receive enough information to understand the relationships among your job, the work unit to which you are assigned and the mission of your hospitality organization?

They bring their anger, resentments and grievances with them to the work place. If these employees are not willing to work with you and make a commitment to improved performance, you have little choice but to continue the disciplinary process.

For employees who want to work with you towards solving the problem and improving their performance counseling is initiated. Together, the two of you write an action plan that is geared towards performance improvement. The self-appraisal form found in Table 12-5 includes examples of some of the types of questions the problem employee might ask himself or herself during the counseling session. The answers to these questions provide some direction for problem resolution. At each session, a performance review is made in writing by both you and the employee. An example of such a review is seen in Table 12-6. The review format should be modified to best meet the needs of the specific problem that the two of you are working on resolving.

Remember that the goal of the counseling process is to reverse the behavior or performance pattern into one that is in keeping with the goals of the hospitality organization. Feedback is an important element of this process. When the employee's performance improves, it is necessary to recognize it so that the employee better understands the type of behavior that is acceptable. Once the performance has improved, the counseling process continues to provide a monitoring mechanism of the employee's performance. Once the problem has been resolved to the satisfaction of both parties, the counseling period ends.

Exiting the Organization

So far in this chapter, numerous alternatives to the termination, dismissal, firing, letting go or "canning" of your employees have been presented. This is due to the fact that the hospitality industry is facing a serious labor shortage, and that we have a serious investment in each of our human resources with respect to hiring, placement, orientation and training expenditures. The last thing in the world that we want to do is to have all of our efforts result in a termination or in a resignation.

Despite all of our retention efforts, sometimes we have to terminate an employee, or they need to resign from our employment. There is no list to show you that contains all the factors that need to be present before you decide whether to retain or terminate an employee. Each case must be judged on its own merits. This is when you, as the manager with human resources responsibilities, must use your own discretion and judgment.

Termination

If you decide that termination is the last alternative available to you, then certain procedures must be followed or you will quickly find

Table 12-6. Form for Performance Review of Human Resources in Counseling

Name of Counselee _____ Work Unit _____ Job _____

Adjustment Progress and Problems	Analysis by Unit Mgr.	Analysis by Counselee
What progress has been made by the counselee during the review period in making the following adjustments:		
Job Adjustments?		
Behavior Adjustment?		
Work Unit Adjustment?		
Personal Adjustment?		
What are the obstacles to achieving adjustment expectations in the areas listed above?		
What comments should be made on the *results* achieved for each of the adjustments listed above?		
In what areas has the counselee made the MOST progress in adjustments? The LEAST progress?		
Do the adjustment expectations need to be revised?		
What are the plans and priorities for achieving adjustment expectations?		

Signature of Counselee _____

Signature of Unit Manager _____

Date of Review _____ Next Review Date _____

your hospitality organization involved in a wrongful discharge lawsuit. Ask yourself the following questions:

- Was the employee informed of the rule violation or substandard performance levels?
- Was the employee given an opportunity to correct the behavior/ performance?

- Did the employee understand the consequences of not correcting his or her behavior/performance?
- Has the rule/performance standard been consistently enforced?
- Has the rule/performance standard been applied in a nondiscriminatory manner?
- Has a thorough investigation of the situation been conducted?
- Has the investigation and disciplinary process been adequately documented?

Consistency, communication and documentation appear to be the key words when faced with a decision to terminate. Improper terminations can result in lawsuits against the hospitality organization that destroy employee morale, motivation and a sense of job security. All terminations should take into account the underlying reason(s) for the employee's behavior or substandard performance, and only take place after careful review of all facts and pertinent information. You should have a carefully outlined procedure for handling all involuntary terminations.

The Exit Interview

The exit interview is used to provide the hospitality organization with information regarding attrition. For voluntary terminations, exit interviews can be particulary useful in determining why the employee is leaving your organization. Whenever an employee leaves your employ, there are a number of issues to resolve such as paycheck, benefits, rehiring privileges and unemployment compensation. As managers, we hope to use the information from these interviews to uncover weak human resources practices, to provide us with an evaluation of hiring practices, to indicate a noncompetitive compensation plan, to locate specific sources of job dissatisfaction or supervisors that do not follow the policies and procedures of the hospitality organization (Figure 12-2). If we know why our employees are unhappy, we will be able to do a better job of reducing unwanted employee turnover.

Exit interview practices vary widely among hospitality organizations. Table 12-7 is an example of an exit interview form. The specific content of the interview questions should be modified to obtain the information that you feel is most useful for your hospitality organization. Why the employees are leaving, in the case of voluntary terminations, is of particular interest to us in our retention attempts. Sometimes, asking the employee what could be done to get him or her to stay yields a more productive response than merely asking the person why he or she is leaving. One of the biggest weaknesses of the exit interview is that the information obtained is only as valuable as the honesty of the employee responding. Sometimes the employee is reluctant to give completely honest answers.

322

Figure 12-2. The exit interview can yield information that can lead to the improvement of your retention methods.
Photographer: Michael Upright

Exit interviews should not be conducted on the last day of employment, as that can be a distractful day for the employee. On the last day, however, an employee checklist is completed similar to the one shown in Table 12-8. This is a good policy to establish, particulary if the employee has keys, uniforms or other property that belong to the hospitality organization.

If turnover is to be controlled, the real reasons why employees leave must be discovered and communicated to the management team. It simply does not make good human resources management sense not to conduct exit interviews.

Wrongful Discharge

Throughout this chapter there has been a repeated emphasis on the importance of documentation. We cannot overstate this point. It is also important that certain pieces of this documentation have the signature of the terminated employee. Counseling and disciplinary sessions should be documented with the employee's signature on the documentation. If an employee refuses to sign, ask another manager to witness and sign the document. Documentation must contain behavioral facts. Take care not to label employees ("John is a drug addict") or state your opinion regarding the behavior. If the termination is due to unacceptable behavior,

Table 12-7. Exit Interview Form

NAME: _____ LENGTH OF TIME EMPLOYED: _____

POSITON: _____ DATE: _____

A. INITIAL ORIENTATION TO COMPANY

323

   1. Were the employee benefits adequately explained? _____
_____

   2. Were the conditions of employment, salary, promotions/transfers, etc. adequately explained? _____

   3. Was the pretraining you received adequate to perform a good job? If not, please explain how could it have been improved: _____
_____

   4. Was the training and development after job placement adequate? Please explain how it could have been improved. _____
_____

B. SUPERVISION

   1. Describe, briefly, the type of communications you had with your:
     a. Restaurant Manager(s) _____
     b. District Manager(s) _____
   2. How could your supervision been improved? _____

C. EMPLOYEE RELATIONS

   1. What did you like most about your job? _____
   2. What did you dislike about your job? _____
   3. Do you have any suggestions that would improve our employee relations and/or working conditions? Please explain. _____
   4. Would you ever consider working for _____ again? _____
Please explain. _____
   5. Have you accepted or been offered other employment? _____
If so, with what company or industry (i.e., restaurant, manufacturing, banking, etc.)? _____
   6. Was your separation from _____ handled to your satisfaction?
_____ Please explain. _____
_____

   7. Please list in order of priority the reason/s for your leaving.
     a. _____
     b. _____
     c. _____
     d. _____
   8. ANY ADDITIONAL COMMENTS? _____
_____

_____
HUMAN RESOURCE SIGNATURE

Table 12-8. Employee Exit Checklist

Employee Name: _____

SS# _____ Last Day Worked _____

W-2 Address (if different from present address):

    Street: _____

    City, State, Zip: _____

Employee Exit Checklist

____ Keys Returned—List: _____

____ Uniform, Name Tag Returned—List: _____

____ Other Items Returned—List: _____

____ Exit Interview Completed (if applicable)

____ Outstanding Wage Advances, Loans or Other Monies Reimbursed to the

    Company—List: _____

    _____

____ Other—List: _____

    _____

To Be Completed By The Employee

Reason for Leaving: _____

_____

_____

Signatures

Manager	Date	Employee	Date

which was seen by other employees, get a written notarized statement from the witnesses.

Due to recent legal rulings you should also review all human resources policies and procedures manuals for any statements that limit your right to discharge an employee-at-will. Courts have viewed human resources documents as implied employment contracts between the hospitality organization and the employee. Many states have altered the traditional employee-at-will concept, which states that the term of an individual's employment is discretionary or may be terminated at any time by either party.

With the increase of AIDS and drug testing, more employees that have been terminated are filing for wrongful discharge. Some states have passed legislation requiring that certain notices be given employees who are about to be terminated; other states have said that terminations have violated an implied contract initiated at the time the individual was hired. Caution your staff not to make any oral or written statements in which a contract is implied. Otherwise, you are likely to find yourself on the losing side of a wrongful discharge suit filed for breach of contract. Not only are these employees winning reinstatement, but they are also entitled to back wages. Following the guidelines we have established throughout this chapter will help in keeping you out of the courtroom and in your hospitality operation where you belong.

325

Age discrimination suits have also come of age in the 1990s. Their frequency in the courts is likely to increase as the population ages. The Age Discrimination in Employment Act was passed in 1967 with the purpose of protecting employees in the 40 to 65 age group from bias in hiring or in firing. In 1978, the cap was raised to 70, and in 1986, the cap was eliminated in most occupations. In addition, many states have passed legislation prohibiting mandatory retirement.

Another interesting area of wrongful discharge relates to the subject of off-duty terminations. Can you terminate an employee for dating another employee? Can you terminate an employee for marrying another employee at one of your hospitality competitors? Can you terminate an employee for committing a crime? For using drugs and getting drunk and obnoxious while not on your time and not in your operation? The answer to these questions used to be an absolute "yes," however, today the courts are less likely to view what employees do on their own time as any of your concern.

One of the major issues facing our industry (and others) is drug testing. While the use of drugs is clearly illegal, the argument is that an employee's life-style outside the work place has no relation to job performance or behavior on the job, and therefore cannot be viewed as grounds for termination. The individual's right to privacy is increasingly being supported by recent court rulings. Again, the legal concern is tied into the employment-at-will concept. Can employers fire employees without job-related cause? Is that an invasion of privacy or the employer's right to terminate at will? These are questions that will require your close monitoring in "the next chapter."

The Effects of Exodus

There is no doubt that firing an employee is the most difficult and emotional job that hospitality managers have to face. But what about the employees being terminated? And what about remaining employees who are still at work in your hospitality operation? What can you do to assist them?

You have a responsibility to assist the human resources left in your employ in dealing with the loss. You are likely to be viewed as the "bad guy," especially by the terminated employee's friends and co-workers. They are likely to see that individual from a different perspective than you did as his or her supervisor. These employees will need you to provide them with an opportunity to vent their anger. Explaining to them that you did everything you could in the way of counseling and training sessions to assist that individual in getting back on the right track might help. Oftentimes, your staff will simply need to be assured that their own jobs are safe, and that they are not in jeopardy of being terminated. Care must be taken not to "bad-mouth" the terminated employee, or you might be subject to a defamation claim.

Conclusion

Progressive discipline is an action taken against an employee for violating a rule of conduct or falling below the specified performance standards you have established. This is not a punitive action, but one taken to correct the behavior or performance problem. The counseling process is used for those human resources who are willing to accept that a problem exists and want to make a commitment to self-improvement and problem resolution. Problem-solving sessions are held with the employee, action plans are developed and mutually agreed upon. When the performance or behavior improves, the employee is praised and the improvement is duly noted. Feedback is continuous until you both agree that the problem has been resolved.

When there is no other recourse to take, termination becomes the avenue you must choose, despite its unpleasantness. Care must be taken to temper the resentment and confusion that remaining employees may harbor. The key words throughout this chapter have been consistency, fairness, and documentation.

Now we will turn our attention to a more detailed discussion of Employee Assistance Programs.

Case Problem 12

Relating to the hospitality operation you described in Case Problem 1, you have established the following rules of conduct, which are only a sampling of the complete list:

- no smoking in restricted areas or in any part of the operation where there are guests
- failure to maintain safety and sanitation standards
- unauthorized possession of company property, including the removal of china, silverware, flowers, food, linen, or office supplies

For each of the three progressive discipline situations discussed below, describe how you will handle the situation.

- What disciplinary action(s) would you take? Identify, for each, the steps in the discipline process.
- In which situations, if any, would you use performance counseling techniques?
- Plan a performance review for each of the employees that you would use during counseling.
- For which situations do you feel it is necessary to implement termination procedures?
- Identify these procedures for the appropriate discipline situation(s).

Do not forget the legal implications involved in a wrongful discharge lawsuit. Make your discussions specific to the hospitality operation you described in Case Problem 1. (Note: The specifics of the hospitality operations discussed below have intentionally been left vague so that you can adapt them to **your** specific hospitality operation.)

Progressive Discipline Situation 1

January 2, 1990: Larry had been cleaning up the operation after the **very** hectic holiday season. This was the first day since prior to Thanksgiving that you were not operating at 100 percent. Larry was in a guest area that was unoccupied at the time he decided to have a cigarette. Your assistant manager found him, cleaning while a cigarette was hanging out of his mouth as she brought a potential guest into the area Larry was cleaning.

February 15, 1990: The assistant manager walked into a guest area which Larry had just finished cleaning. She noticed a smoke smell and upon further investigation discovered a cigarette burn in the carpeting.

Progressive Discipline Situation 2

April 3, 1990: Susan had prepared the roast turkey for a meal function that evening. The meat was cooked, sliced, and ready to serve. You discover that the meat had been overcooked and was dry. The temperature was room-temperature, and the appearance of the product was unappealing. Susan was going to serve this product to the guests, but you substituted a processed, ready-to-serve turkey product instead.

May 1, 1990: Your chef opened up the kitchen only to find that Susan had not properly cleaned up the kitchen when she closed. The chef found food left unwrapped in the refrigerator and freezer, in addition to a prime rib that was left on the counter at room temperature; $200.00 worth of food had to be thrown away.

Progressive Discipline Situation 3

March 9, 1990: Kevin was taking out trash to the dumpster when you walked by and noticed that the bag seemed to be unusually heavy. You asked Kevin to take the trash bag back inside and dump it out so that you could examine its contents. Upon doing so, you discovered eight dinner knives, six dinner forks, three salad forks and four spoons were mixed in with the trash.

May 7, 1990: Kevin has gathered up all of the employee uniforms for pick-up by the uniform company. This is a service that, twice weekly, picks up dirty uniforms and leaves a clean supply. You notice that there are clean tablecloths (or bed linens) mixed discreetly in with the dirty uniforms. Kevin knows that the uniform company does not clean these items.

RECOMMENDED READING

Boyle, K. 1987. Effective employee discipline requires keeping in close touch. *Restaurants USA* 7, (10): 26–28.

Campbell, D. N.; Fleming, R. L.; and Grote, R. C. 1964. Discipline without punishment—at last. *Harvard Business Review* 42, (4): 62–69.

Drost, D. A.; O'Brien, F. P.; and Marsh, S. 1987. Exit interviews: master the possibilities. *Personnel Administrator* 32, (2): 104, 106–110.

Griffith, T. J. 1987. Want job improvement? Try counseling. *Management Solutions* 32, (9): 13–19.

Harvey, E. L. 1987. Discipline vs. punishment. *Management Review* 76, (3): 25–29.

Homer, J. 1989. A manager's toughest job. *Working Woman* 14: 67.

Matejka, J. K.; Ashworth, D. N.; and Dodd-McCue, D. 1986. Discipline without guilt. *Supervisory Management* 31, (5): 34–39.

Pitone, L. 1986. *Absence & Lateness.* Madison, Ct.: Bureau of Law and Business, Inc.

Redeker, J. R. 1983. *Discipline: Policies and Procedures.* Washington D.C.: The Bureau of National Affairs, Inc.

Reibstein, L. 1988. Firms find it tougher to dismiss employees for off-duty conduct. *Wall Street Journal* CCXI, (61): 33.

Schwartz, A. E. 1988. Counseling the marginal performer. *Management Solutions* 33, (3): 30–33.

Woods, R. H. and Macaulay, J. F. 1987. Exit interviews: how to turn a file filler into a management tool. *The Cornell H.R.A. Quarterly* 28, (3): 39–46.

END NOTES

1. Huberman, John, "Discipline Without Punishment," *Harvard Business Review* 42, (1964, 4): 62.
2. Jacobs, Bruce A., "An Approach of Non-Punitive Discipline," *Industry Week* 231, (1986, 3): 123, 126.

DISCUSSION QUESTIONS

1. Distinguish between the rights of management and the rights of employees in hospitality organizations.
2. List twenty (20) possible rules of conduct for a food service operation.
3. Define the purpose of a fair policy statement.
4. What are the critical factors for the successful implementation of a discipline policy?
5. List the steps in the implementation of a discipline policy. In your own words, briefly explain what each step accomplishes.
6. What is the purpose of a progressive discipline policy in a hospitality organization?
7. Identify the problems of traditional discipline approaches.
8. Describe the use of performance counseling as an alternate route in the discipline process.
9. What is the goal of performance counseling?
10. When do you use termination procedures in a hospitality organization?
11. Discuss two different ways you could be brought up in a wrongful discharge suit by one of your terminated employees.
12. What are the most important items to remember when implementing disciplinary, counseling, and/or termination procedures?

SECTION 5

HUMAN RESOURCES
SUPPORT SYSTEMS

CHAPTER 13

EMPLOYEE ASSISTANCE PROGRAMS

INDUSTRY   *Jim Tye, Director of Employment*
ADVISOR   *Furr's/Bishop's Cafeterias, L.P.*

"Man's mind, once stretched by a new idea, never regains its original dimensions."—OLIVER WENDELL HOLMES

KEY WORDS   Acquired Immune Deficiency
Syndrome (AIDS)
contracted-out EAP
Employee Assistance Program
(EAP)
human immunodeficiency virus
(HIV)

in-house EAP
intervention
personal problems
substance abuse
"troubled" employee

INTRODUCTION   Employee Assistance Programs (EAPs) are rapidly becoming a valuable management tool in the hospitality industry in our quest to retain our human resources. Innovative companies such as Furr's/Bishop's Cafeterias, L.P., Friendly Ice Cream Corporation, Sheraton, Harry M. Stevens Inc. and Hardees are just some of the companies that have established EAPs for their employees.

Employee assistance programs work in tandem with the progressive discipline and counseling programs we discussed in the previous chapter. Together, these programs help in the retention of the "troubled" employee. As you will soon see, the problems EAPs assist with are very diversified.

At the conclusion of this chapter you will be able to:
1. Define an Employee Assistance Program and its role in human resources retention.
2. Identify problems that you think could be handled by an EAP.
3. Describe the differences between in-house and contracted-out EAPs.
4. Describe the development and implementation of an EAP in a hospitality organization.

5. Identify the evaluation methods used to determine the cost effectiveness of an EAP.
6. Explain the role of employee assistance programs in the human resources management plan for a hospitality organization.
7. Understand the effects of AIDS in the hospitality work place.

334

The Philosophy of Employee Assistance Programs

Jeffery has been with your hospitality organization for over ten years, and you have come to know him as an employee that is both reliable and trustworthy. While Jeffery's job position is storeroom clerk, the responsibilities he has gained throughout the years include receiving and inventory. Recently, you have heard your other employees complaining that supplies are not being maintained as they should be. Frequently, the other employees tell you they do not have the supplies to perform their job duties, and this is beginning to reflect upon their own job performance. Checking the inventory sheets you find that supplies are up to par and that there is no indication of ever running out of any supplies. You suspect that Jeffrey has been stealing. What do you do?

If your hospitality organization has an established employee assistance program and you have had training in dealing with employee problems, your approach with Jeffery is likely to be one of intervention as opposed to the all too frequent confrontation approach. What if Jeffery has a substance dependency? What if Jeffery's wife left him with three children to feed and clothe? What if Jeffery's mother is a victim of cancer or if he has a friend in his care with AIDS? Do any of these situations condone Jeffery stealing from your storeroom? Would you have more compassion for Jeffery if his wife had left him than if he had a substance dependency or was caring for an AIDS victim?

None of these situations, which are just a sample of the type of personal problems your employees might bring with them to the work place, is a justification for stealing. On the other hand, Jeffery has been a valued employee; all of his performance appraisals for the past ten years reflect that. When you intervene in the situation you find out that, indeed, Jeffery has a chemical dependency. That afternoon he enters into a 28-day treatment center for addicts.

What we have just presented to you is an oversimplification of how having an EAP in your organization can assist you in retaining your valued employees, and help another human being get his life back on the right track (Figure 13–1).

A Historical Perspective

In the 1920s, occupational counseling programs were established in companies to help employees deal with personal problems that were

Figure 13-1. EAPs provide assistance for a variety of personal problems.

causing deficient performance in the work place. Substance abuse programs, in particular those dealing with alcoholism, can be found at Dupont in the 1940s. The establishment of Alcoholics Anonymous (AA), the promotion of using performance evaluations to discover alcoholics at an early stage and the recognition by the American Medical Association (AMA) of alcoholism as a disease in the late 1960s all helped to support the need for employers to assist the alcoholic employee with recovery.

The drug-abuse crisis of the 60s and 70s brought drug- and alcohol-abuse programs together under the auspices of "substance" abuse. During the same time period, the changing demographics in the U.S. saw a weakening of the family structure, and more single-parent households resulting in family, child, legal and financial personal problems for many of the nation's employees. Mental and emotional problems were seen as illnesses, not as a social stigma.

Any one of these problems can, and does, cause impaired job performance in the hospitality industry, as well as every other industry in the U.S. today. The term Employee Assistance Program, first used in the seventies, broadened the scope of problems covered. Table 13-1 identifies some of the problems that can be included in an EAP. Employee assistance programs of the 90s are for all employees in the work place.

Table 13-1. Problems Covered by an EAP
• Alcohol abuse
• Alcohol dependency
• Career development difficulties
• Children/adolescent
• Depression/burnout
• Domestic violence
• Drug abuse
• Emotional difficulties
• Family issues
• Gambling, compulsive
• Legal problems
• Literacy
• Marital difficulties
• Life transition
• Personal financial problems
• Psychological
• Stress-related problems

What Is an Employee Assistance Program?

We will define the **Employee Assistance Program** in the hospitality industry as an employer-provided program that is used as a management tool to assist employees in dealing with personal problems before they seriously impair job performance. Employee assistance programs do not claim to be a panacea for performance deficiencies, nor do they claim to turn every employee with personal problems into a full-fledged contributing member of your work team.

For the employee that is willing to admit his or her problems and seek assistance in their resolution, EAPs provide a means by which the employee can do so, and still keep working. For the employee who is at the early stages of a potential problematic situation, EAPs offer a place the employee can turn to for advice and counseling without fear that doing so will result in the loss of his or her job. For the employer, EAPs provide a course of corrective action and disciplinary procedures that can protect the employer from a lawsuit if the situation results in a termination. It also becomes another retention tool in a period when loosing an employee with personal problems can create operational problems.

The skyrocketing costs of health care make EAPs a complementary component of the entire benefits package. A strong emphasis is placed on the preventive aspects of the EAP. By creating an attitude in the work place environment that says—"everyone has personal problems, and we realize that those problems will affect your job performance if you don't seek help as quickly as possible; here is a program that is designed to do that for you"—your employees are more likely to seek help before they reach a crisis stage with their problem.

INDUSTRY EXPERTS SPEAK	Jim Tye, Director of Employment for Furr's/Bishop's Cafeterias, L.P., is involved with his company's EAP and offers the following thoughts: "Anyone who has been in the hospitality industry for any length of time will tell you that one of the greatest satisfactions comes from seeing the growth and development of others. At the same time, the very nature of our business affords us an incredible opportunity to help others. Employee Assistance Programs carry that mission a step further: the commitment by a corporation to formally and systematically assist employees with specific problems becomes a very human statement, as well as having long-term effects on productivity and profitability for the company. One need only witness families re-united, troubled children returned to heathful, productive activities from a bout with drugs or alcohol or financial counseling aid a family deeply in debt to really appreciate the human side of what we can do."

Why Should I Provide an EAP?

Clearly, EAPs convey an "I care" message to the human resources working in your hospitality organization. They are humanistic and serve to exemplify sound human resources management practices. In addition, they encourage your employees to improve their life-styles by confronting their problems early on. For employees whose personal problems have already reached crisis proportions, the EAP provides them with an opportunity to get their lives back on the right track, while it allows them to remain employed.

Perhaps some of you are thinking "this all sounds nice, but let's get real. Who has the time and money to fool with a goody-goody program like an EAP? Besides, the chances of an employee having a personal problem so bad that it affects his or her productivity is slim. Furthermore, if an employee has a problem it's the employee's problem, not mine. I get paid to manage this operation, not hold someone's hand!" To address some of these issues that you might be raising let's first look at how extensive the problems are, and then examine what the "troubled" employee costs U.S. businesses each year.

The Scope of the Problem

A recent estimate by the federal government states that one out of every four Americans regularly uses drugs. Between 10 percent and 23 percent of American employees use drugs while on the job. Drug abuse

Table 13-2. Indicators of Chemical Dependency in the Workplace

Place an "X" next to behaviors exhibited by employee, or reported to you by others. More than four "Xs" should alert you that some problem exists. You may want an evaluation conducted at this time. Call Glenbeigh Hospital of Miami at 558-9999 for a free confidential evaluation.

JOB PERFORMANCE

[   ] Frequent Monday or Friday absences.
[   ] Longer or more frequent absences.
[   ] Multiple instances of unauthorized leaving work site.
[   ] Excessive morning or noontime tardiness.
[   ] Increased number of "cuts" during work day.
[   ] Difficulty in concentrating.
[   ] Difficulty in recalling simple instructions.
[   ] Increased inability to learn from or recall previous mistakes.
[   ] Alternating periods of high and low work performance.
[   ] Marked inattention to detail.
[   ] Increased overt boredom, tiredness or disruptive behavior.
[   ] Marked decline in productivity.
[   ] Missed deadlines.
[   ] Increased excuses for incomplete, missing or unacceptable work.
[   ] Increased signs of disorientation; frequent instances of loss of train of thought.
[   ] Sleeping on the job.
[   ] Less responsible about doing assignments.

SOCIAL

[   ] Decreased interaction with peers and family.
[   ] Change in peer groups.
[   ] Hypersensitivity to perceived or actual criticism.
[   ] Withdrawal from previous friends.
[   ] Drastic changes in personality.
[   ] Co-workers or friends talking to you about employee's behavior or attitude changes.
[   ] Drastic change in taste of music.
[   ] Defending the right to drink or to smoke marijuana.
[   ] Irritability or lack of emotion.
[   ] Extreme, rapid mood swings without apparent reason.
[   ] Inappropriate emotional responses.
[   ] Loss of previous goals.
[   ] Consistent reports of lost, borrowed or stolen belongings.

PERSONAL GROOMING AND HEALTH

[   ] Change in eating or sleeping habits.
[   ] Decreased attention to personal hygiene.
[   ] Appearance of rash around mouth or nose.

(continued)

[   ] Inappropriate clothing (long sleeves or jackets on warm days, lightweight attire in cold weather).
[   ] Frequent instance of stiff or painful arms.
[   ] Inappropriate, sudden and unprecipitated sweats.
[   ] Increased coughing, post-nasal drip or sore throats.
[   ] Continual symptoms of flu or gastrointestinal upset.
[   ] "Needle tattoos" caused by carbon residue from heated syringe or substances.
[   ] Selling of personal belongings, with no evidence of proceeds.
[   ] Dark glasses often and inappropriately worn indoors.
[   ] Nicotine spots on thumb and index finger, particular to pot smoker.
[   ] Change in taste of dress or clothing.

FAMILY

[   ] Are you missing money or other valuables from your home?
[   ] Is child less responsible about doing chores?
[   ] Do you catch your child in lies?
[   ] Is there an increase in family arguments?
[   ] Do you disapprove of your child's choice of friends?
[   ] Does your child become unresponsive to discussions about drugs and alcohol?
[   ] Is there open defiance regarding family rules?
[   ] Has your child ever run away from home?
[   ] Has there been violence or hostility toward family members?

Source: Glenbeigh Hospital of Miami

includes both illegal and legal drugs. See Table 13-2 for a list of indicators of chemical dependency in the work place.

Alcohol abuse is another work-related problem. Documentation from the hospitality industry suggests that usage might be higher for our human resources. Some of the reasons for this include the consistent availability of alcohol, working conditions that include exposure to high temperatures, the different working hours our employees work, the demeaning nature of some of the jobs and an all too frequent acceptance of drinking by management.[1]

Mental distress affects 25 percent of the population with 10 to 15 percent of the population needing mental health treatment.[2] Mental wellness has become an important goal of industry.

Costs of the "Troubled" Employee

Why does this matter to you, the manager with human resources responsibilities? Employees working under the influence of drugs or alcohol function at approximately two-thirds of their potential. Substance abusing employees are three times as likely to use sick leave benefits, three times as likely to have accidents on the job, use their health benefits four times more often then other employees, miss work five times more frequently and lower the overall productivity of the work force.

It has been estimated that the personal problems that employees bring to the work place result in a $102.3 billion per year loss. That breaks down to alcohol abuse costing $54.7 billion, drug abuse costing $26 billion and mental illness $21.6 billion.[3]

In addition to the personal problems already identified is the nation's AIDS crisis and the effect it is having on the hospitality industry. The impact of this disease continues to be devastating and will continue to be so until a cure is found. Indirect costs include lost productivity while

Figure 13-2. A successful EAP assists in maintaining a happy and healthy work force.
Courtesy of Furr's/Bishop's Cafeterias, L.P.

health care expenses are escalating due to intensive care needs and premature mortality.

Attendance, productivity, use of health care benefits, safety, behavior and work quality are all affected by the personal problems our human resources bring with them to the hospitality work place (Figure 13-2). We hope that you now are in agreement that the development of an employee assistance program could benefit your hospitality organization. We will now look at the types of EAPs most commonly found, and then discuss how to develop and implement a program.

In-House vs. Contracted-Out EAPs

Employee Assistance Programs vary in their approach among hospitality organizations. Despite this diversity, they all maintain the same goals of identifying employees with personal problems that may be affecting their job performance, providing an avenue for those employees to seek counseling and help and maintaining the confidentiality of the employee(s) participating in the program.

Even the smallest hospitality company can implement an EAP. The most popular method for companies that can't afford to operate their own program and are too small to have a contractor come in and provide one for them is the consortium. In a consortium, several small hospitality companies or operations would band together, possibly structuring themselves as a private, nonprofit corporation. Each of the member companies would pay a flat rate based upon its average use of the EAP per employee.

In-House EAPs

Hospitality organizations that provide in-house EAPs have to be large enough to support a professional counselor and, if necessary, a counseling staff. The remainder of the human resources management staff will also require some training and education as to the use of the EAP in established human resources practices, such as progressive discipline procedures.

One of the greatest disadvantages of operating an in-house EAP is the potential lack of confidentiality. For the EAP to be successful, the confidentiality of the employee using the services has to be guaranteed. Information from any part of the EAP, including the counseling sessions, never becomes part of the employee's personnel file. If your human resources do not believe that confidentiality will be maintained they will not fully use the services the program offers to them.

The advantage of operating an in-house program is that you will have greater management control over the program itself. Your company will hire the counseling staff, and they will become members of your hospitality organization.

Contracted-Out EAPs

Just as with any contracted service, the EAP provider offers assessment and counseling services for a fee. These services are offered in a location outside of the work site, assuring confidentiality. To be of maximum benefit, however, the off-site location must be accessible to your work force.

Usually, the service will also include telephone counseling that is aimed at crisis intervention. This crisis intervention uses a hot-line style and it offers complete anonymity to the troubled employee. Counselors discuss the problem with the employee and, if they feel therapy is needed, the employee is referred to an outside resource.

The costs of these programs vary depending on the number of employees using the program and the types of services the contractor provides. Fees typically range from $12 to $35 per year per employee.

Caution must be exercised when selecting an outside contractor to provide EAP services for your employees. It is important that the contractor understand the hospitality industry, its unique pressures and stresses. The hours our human resources work can oftentimes be straight around-the-clock with no days off. The contractor you select must be willing to meet the needs and schedules of your staff. EAP specialists and professional counselors should be licensed or certified. You do not want amateurs counseling your valued human resources. Contract services are increasing in number. Use the same care and consideration you would use before entering into any type of contractual arrangement with a service provider.

Setting Up an EAP

An effective EAP provides a system of education for all human resources in the hospitality organization. This serves to explain how the EAP works and stresses its confidentiality. Supervisors are taught how to identify performance deficiencies that may be due to personal problems. An emphasis is placed on not diagnosing or judging the employee. Rather, the supervisors are taught to refer the troubled employee to the appropriate resource.

Development

Development begins with an assessment of the needs of your organization and takes into consideration the following elements:

- Review of organizational profile.
- Review of current benefits program. (After all, an EAP should be a new benefit).
- Review of human resources policies and procedures.

- Determine extent of start-up program, what type(s) of assistance will be provided.
- Determine test market. Ideally, you would identify test units (in each region/division) to determine employee acceptance and to work out any problems, before implementing company wide.
- Determine resource requirements. Will extra staff be needed? What role will operations play? What is the approximate cost?

343

Once your hospitality organization has determined its needs and the extent of the EAP, an action plan must be initiated. The action plan will:

- Schedule activities.
- Assign responsibilities.
- Update administration.
- Reinforce management commitment and support.

Implementation

The core of the implementation process is the establishment of a policy statement on the EAP and how it will operate. This policy must be written, published and distributed to all employees. This communication is critical to the acceptance and success of the program. Employees must view the EAP as a benefit, not as an invasion of privacy.

Specific procedures need to be developed with respect to:

- Supervisory referral
- Self-referral
- Confidentiality

A choice needs to be made based upon your company's needs and objectives as to whether you are going to select an in-house or contracted-out type of program. Supervisory training and employee orientation then follow.

Determining the Cost-Effectiveness of Your EAP

Compared to the costs of other benefits, EAPs are relatively inexpensive. This is largely due to the small proportion of employees who use the program. You should check into your health insurance plans to assure that they will accommodate the occasional employee who needs extensive treatment and hospitalization.

The literature contains much information on the effectiveness of EAPs. This effectiveness ranges from reduced absenteeism to improved retention to literally saving lives. What hospitality operator wouldn't enjoy knowing that there will be fewer employees calling in sick, quitting or coming to work late?

Employee assistance programs can also serve to reduce the rising cost of health care and Worker's Compensation claims. Better job performance is frequently the end result. Compared to the high cost of termination, EAP expenses are nominal.

Some of the ways you might measure or evaluate the effectiveness of your EAP would be:

- Usage
- Direct feedback
- Comparative costs/cost containment
  - Turnover/retention
  - Health benefits
  - Absenteeism
  - Safety

Historical data is a necessity in order to make a significant comparative cost-savings analysis.

Use of an EAP

Once your EAP is firmly in place, clearly communicated to all employees, and training has been conducted for all persons involved, how does a troubled employee take advantage of the program? There are basically two paths. In the first, or 80 percent of all cases, the employees contact the program directly. The remainder of the cases are referrals by supervisors that notice a decline in performance levels.

On-line supervisors are the best persons to notice a change in performance or personal behavior, since they observe employees on a daily basis. When a decline in performance or behavior occurs, the supervisor confronts the employee in an attempt to determine the cause. This intervention is an important component of the EAP, as it frequently works to break the pattern of denial in which many troubled employees are trapped. As we noted in the previous chapter, performance decline can be caused by factors other than personal problems. If the condition appears to be related to personal problems, the employee is referred to the EAP staff (Figure 13-3).

Once you have attempted to assist the employee through the corrective interview, it is your responsibility to continue monitoring performance. The employee can take one of two paths: seek help and improve performance or refuse assistance, in which case standard disciplinary practices are implemented. At each stage of the discipline process, EAP

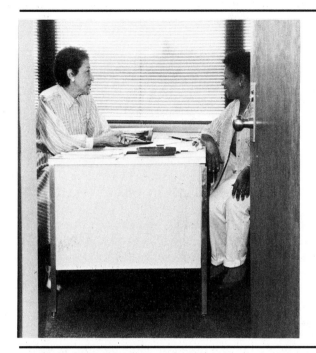

Figure 13-3. EAP counselors ensure that total confidentiality is maintained. Photo by Michael Upright

participation is offered, again in an attempt to break the denial pattern. Participation in the EAP is not a substitute for maintaining acceptable performance standards.

AIDS in the Work Place

The AIDS epidemic affects us all. For the hospitality manager, as with managers in all types of businesses throughout this country, a knowledge and understanding of AIDS is critical for your success. What will you tell the housekeeper who won't clean a room because he or she fears the person(s) staying there might have AIDS? What do you tell your server that refuses to wait on a table for the same reason? What do you say to the guest that asks if any of your cooks have AIDS? What if an employee cuts himself in the kitchen, and the other workers are afraid of contracting AIDS? What do you tell an employee that comes to you in fear that he may have AIDS? AIDS is and will continue to be one of the personal problems your employees may seek help with through your employee assistance program. The confidential nature of the EAP provides a natural setting and a valuable counseling tool in dealing with the depression employees face that receive a positive antibody test, the loss of a friend or family member or an AIDS diagnosis themselves. It is for these reasons and because of the many misconceptions about AIDS that we include this section.

The Facts

346

AIDS, or Acquired Immune Deficiency Syndrome, is a virus that destroys (makes immune) the body's defense system against disease and infection. It is transmitted through sexual contact, an injection with infected blood, shared needles (commonly associated with drug addiction) or passed by infected mothers to their newborn babies. These are the only documented methods by which the AIDS virus has been contracted.

AIDS cannot be spread by casual contact. Did you know that according to federal food safety officials, AIDS cannot be transmitted through the preparation or service of food? Food simply cannot be contaminated with the AIDS virus.[4] According to C. Everett Koop, former Surgeon General of the U. S. Public Health Service, no AIDS cases have occurred from using swimming pools or hot tubs, sharing linen or touching toilets or telephones.

If this is true, then where has all of the hysteria come from surrounding the AIDS epidemic? The fact that, to date, there is no known cure is part of the reason. The other scary aspect of AIDS is that the virus that causes AIDS, the human immunodeficiency virus (or HIV) is a "sleeper." That means that it can lay dormant inside a human carrier for years before it begins to attack the nervous system. Carriers can pass the disease for years before they know they have it, unless they seek a specific blood test to determine if HIV antibodies are present. It also means that the exact scope of the AIDS epidemic is, at present, still unknown. In 1988, the U. S. Centers for Disease Control (CDC) estimated that from one to five million people in the United States were currently infected with the HIV virus.[5]

The Hospitality Manager and AIDS

How does this affect you, the manager with human resources responsibilities, in a hospitality operation? Only through education can you intelligently and accurately answer the types of questions your employees might ask you, questions similar to those we asked you at the beginning of this section. Table 13-3 gives you addresses where you can obtain further information on AIDS.

The education, however, does not stop with you. Part of your responsibility will also be to educate the human resources working for you, and in some cases the educational process will extend to the public that enters your establishment with its own fears and concerns. The work place provides an excellent setting for this type of education. The National

Table 13-3. Sources of Additional Information on Aids

AIDS Action Council
729 Eighth Street, S.E.
Suite 200
Washington, D.C. 20003

American Council of Life Insurance
1001 Pennsylvania Ave., NW
Washington, D.C. 20004-2599
• Educational materials

American Foundation for AIDS Research
40 West 57th Street, Suite 406
New York, New York 10019-4001

American Hotel and Motel Association
1201 New York Avenue, NW
Washington, D.C., 20005-3917
• "Dealing with Legal Issues Raised by AIDS in the Work Place."
• "AIDS: Questions and Answers for Lodging Industry Employees"

American Red Cross AIDS Eduction Program
(202) 639-3223 or contact your local Red Cross chapter

InterAmerican Research
1200 E. North Henry Street
Alexandria, VA 22314
• Pamphlet "AIDS and Your Job"

National Restaurant Assocation
1200 17th Street, NW
Washington, D.C. 20036-3097
• Two-part set of videotapes
• "The Facts About AIDS"

San Francisco AIDS Foundation
333 Valencia Street
4th Floor
San Francisco, CA 94103

U.S. Department of Health and Human Services
Public Health Center
Center for Disease Control
P.O. Box 6003
Rockville, MD 20850
• "Understanding AIDS"

U.S. Public Health Service
Hubert H. Humphrey Bldg.
200 Independence Ave. S.W.
Washington, D.C. 20201

Restaurant Association and the American Hotel and Motel Association have both responded to the need for information. Each organization has produced educational materials for both you and your employees.

One of the key points that both associations make is that there is nothing unique about AIDS in the hospitality industry. Hospitality is facing this crisis along with all other industries. Educational programs and operating procedures cover all communicable diseases. Current disinfecting methods and sanitary food-handling procedures already in effect in the hospitality industry guard against all forms of communicable diseases, including AIDS.[6]

In addition to the information your national industry organizations provide you with, you should be aware of state, county and municipal laws when dealing with AIDS. While there is no one policy, the federal Rehabilitation Act of 1971 forbids discrimination against any person that has a contagious disease that fits the legal definition of a handicap. The courts, to date, have ruled against companies that have dismissed employees that have AIDS. They have viewed AIDS as a handicap and, therefore, protected from discriminatory actions under the law. Futhermore, you cannot ask your employees or job applicants if they have AIDS, or require them to take tests for AIDS.

The other arena in which AIDS will affect all businesses is in benefits planning and design. For AIDS victims, medical coverage becomes a number one concern. While victims cannot be fired under the law, they still require medical coverage when the disease leaves them physically unable to work. Laws such as the 1986 Budget Reconciliation Act require that companies with over 20 employees that offer group insurance rates continue coverage for up to 18 months after the employee leaves the company.

What all of this means is that hospital and medical rates and insurance premiums will continue to rise. Hospitality companies that try to self-insure could, potentially, be wiped out by one AIDS victim. All insurance companies are struggling for ways to best deal with the situation. One approach has been to permit payments to hospices and other care facilities, that care for AIDS victims that do not require hospitalization, but still need round-the-clock assistance.

Estimates state that by the year 1991, $56 billion in lost productivity will be a direct result of AIDS.[7] That is perhaps one of the saddest statistics pertaining to the AIDS crisis. Education is our most effective weapon in reducing the potential hysteria that can be created. The National Restaurant Association has outlined the following four steps in a crisis program:

1. Assemble a crisis team. This is done before a crisis strikes. The team is trained to handle any crisis that the operation may face, be it a fire or AIDS.

2. Develop an AIDS policy statement. This explains the company's position for both employees and guests.
3. Educate your employees.
4. Develop an AIDS communication strategy.

There are many problems relating to AIDS that you will have to deal with in the work place. These range from rising health benefits costs to emotional distress to possible discrimination suits to guest hysteria. The more you read and learn about AIDS, the better prepared you will be to handle these situations.

INDUSTRY EXPERTS SPEAK

According to Jim Tye, "As the hospitality industry continues to grow amid what will surely be a shrinking labor pool, the role of a basic Employee Assistance Program will become increasingly important. Employee Assistance Programs, when properly developed, implemented and evaluated have shown the potential for dramatic impact on a company's financial position when considered only in the areas of employee retention, safety and productivity. Of course, there is the very important benefit, almost an intangible, of knowing that the company is genuinely interested in helping others."

Conclusion

To management, and in particular to human resources management, the dollars and cents logic in support of EAPs clearly speaks for itself. Conservative estimates place the cost to industry from personal, employee-related problems to be in excess of $50 billion per year with, in addition, as much as 25 percent productivity lost at all levels. One major corporation with a well-established assistance program has seen a five to one return on its investment, a 49 percent decrease in the use of health benefits and a 61 percent decrease in on-the-job accidents. In today's competitive, cost-conscious business environment, figures such as these indeed become very significant. With the impending impact of AIDs yet to have reached its full potential, future human resources professionals in our industry must be ready to assume these responsibilities.

The goal of any EAP is to return the employee to full productivity, whenever possible. An effective EAP will catch the personal problems at a very early stage and, in many, cases be able to prevent more serious concerns from occurring. Your human resources are your most valuable asset. Employee Assistance Programs convey that message.

Case Problem 13-1

As a manager of a medium-size resort property located in a secluded geographical area, you are in the middle of a very busy season, having been able to attract several small conference groups.

One morning after a particularly busy weekend, your executive housekeeper comes to you with a problem. Her housekeepers have told her that they will not clean several of their assigned rooms, as they strongly believe that the guests staying in those rooms could have AIDS. Your executive housekeeper is not sure what to do. Getting employees to work at your location is very difficult and the housekeeping department is filled with good, reliable staff. The executive housekeeper tells you that she would clean the rooms herself, but she is not entirely sure that she might not be putting herself at risk.

There are several options that you, as the manager with human resources responsibilities have available to you. Identify each of them and then discuss which of the alternative courses of action you would choose. (Hint: You have two issues that you are dealing with in this case problem. The first is the immediate concern of getting the rooms cleaned. You have all rooms reserved for this evening. The second issue revolves around the lack of information and misconceptions your staff has about AIDS and its transmission from person to person.)

Case Problem 13-2

You are the district human resources manager of a regional chain of cafeteria foodservice operations. Many of the operational managers have indicated over a period of time that no-shows and absentee turnover ratios have been gradually increasing. The president of the company has asked you to investigate the possibility of establishing an employee assistance program in an effort to curb this trend. She has asked you to prepare an initial three page report that will provide her with the following information:

- a goal statement for the EAP
- an itemized list of the personal problem areas that this EAP would cover
- whether you would recommend an in-house or contracted-out EAP
- a defense for the role an EAP would have in the human resources management plan for your hospitality organization
- your personal view of EAPs

RECOMMENDED READING

Lehr, R. I. and Middlebrooks, D. J. 1986. Legal implications of employee assistance programs. *Employee Relations Law Journal* 12, (2): 262–274.

Moffie, R. P.; Moffie, D. J.; and Tower, R. B. 1985. Auditing the troubled employee. *The Internal Auditor* XLII, (4): 30–36.

Moomaw, P. 1988. AIDS how the industry can cope. *Restaurants USA* 8, (11): 12–13.

Schumacher, L. A. 1985. Employee assistance how to help victims of domestic violence. *Personnel Journal* 64, (8): 102, 104–105.

Stevens, P. J. 1986. How to set up an EAP. *Restaurant Business* 84, (8): 191–192.

Straussner, S. L. A. 1988. Comparison of in-house and contracted-out employee assistance programs. *Social Work* 33, (1): 53–55.

Waldo, W. S. 1987. A practical guide for dealing with AIDS at work. *Personnel Journal* 66, (8): 135–138.

END NOTES

1. Peters, Jim, "How to Set Up an Employee Assistance Program," *Restaurant Business* 87: (1988, 15): 81–83, 90, 99.
2. The President's Commission on Mental Health, *Report to the President* 1, 2, 4 (Washington D.C.: U.S. Government Printing Office, 1978).
3. Morrall, Katherine (Ed.), "Assistance Programs Tackle Employees' Personal Problems," *Savings Institutions* 109: (1988, 1): 70–71, 73.
4. Gatty, Bob, "Washington Report on the AIDS Epidemic," *Restaurant Management* 1: (1987, 5): 66.
5. Aid Association for Lutherans, "Growing AIDS Epidemic Affects Us All," *The Correspondent* 86: (1988, 546): 16–17.
6. Bell, Doreen, "AIDS Prevention Practices," *Lodging Hospitality* 44: (1988, 2): 92.
7. Aid Association for Lutherans, (1988). "Growing AIDS Epidemic Affects Us All." *The Correspondent,* 86: (546): 17.

DISCUSSION QUESTIONS

1. What is an Employee Assistance Program?
2. Identify several personal problems that you think could be handled by an Employee Assistance Program.
3. How do EAPs fit into the progressive discipline process?
4. Describe the differences between an in-house and contracted EAP. Which do you prefer? Why?
5. Describe the development and implementation process for an Employee Assistance Program in the segment of the hospitality industry you hope to work in.

6. Are EAPs cost-effective? Explain your answer.
7. What is the effect of AIDS in the work place? What is the best tool against AIDS?
8. Would you implement an EAP where you work? Why or why not?

352

CHAPTER **14**

LABOR RELATIONS

IN THE HOSPITALITY INDUSTRY

INDUSTRY   *Regynald G. Washington, Senior Vice President*
ADVISOR   *Concessions International, Inc.*

"Decide on what you think is right, and stick to it." — GEORGE ELIOT

KEY WORDS

American Arbitration Association
American Federation of Labor
  (AFL)
arbitration
arbitrator
Clayton Act (1914)
closed shop
collective bargaining
Congress of Industrial
  Organizations (CIO)
craft unions
Federal Mediator Conciliation
  Service
grievance procedure
Hotel and Restaurant Workers
  and Bartenders International
  (HRWBI)
Hotel Employees and Restaurant
  Employees International
  (HERE)
industrial unions
injunction
labor relations

Labor–Management Relations Act
  (1947) or Taft–Hartley Act
Labor–Management Reporting
  and Disclosure Act (1959) or
  Landrum–Griffin Act
mediation
mediator
National Labor Relations Act of
  1935 (NLRA or Wagner Act)
National Labor Relations Board
  (NLRB)
negotiations
Norris La Guardia Act of 1932
organized labor
right-to-work laws
Service Employee International
  Union (SEIU)
strike
trade unions
unfair labor practices
union
union shops
yellow-dog contracts

INTRODUCTION

U nions, negotiators, grievances, mediation, arbitration, labor law, and collective bargaining: how do all these organizations, people and processes that we call "labor relations" affect you in your role as a manager with human resources responsibilities? Based upon your current knowledge of labor relations, what are your feelings about unions? Do you think that they are only for the benefit of the worker and are a detriment to the hospitality organization? Do you think that they protect incompetent workers and make it almost impossible to fire anyone? Do you believe that unions are filled with corruption, that negotiators are unfair and inflexible, that union contracts prevent you from really doing your job as manager and that strikes have unnecessarily hurt a lot of companies? Have unions outlived their usefulness? Are they historic dinosaurs that should be put to bed?

Many of you will, at some time in your careers, have managerial responsibilities in a hospitality organization that is a union shop. Your success will come largely from how well you understand what unions are, the strategies used by union negotiators, the processes of mediation and arbitration, how union organizers can enter your nonunion shop and what your rights and obligations are in dealing with the organizers. Although you could take several courses in unions and their management, we have compiled for you the most critical information to assist you in becoming a successful hospitality manager.

At the conclusion of this chapter you will be able to:
1. Describe what a union is.
2. Discuss the major historical developments that have influenced unions.
3. Maintain an awareness of the laws regulating labor relations and union activities.
4. Identify the reasons why people join unions in the hospitality industry.
5. Explain the importance of positive union relations as it relates to the impact of human resources management.
6. Describe how unions organize employees so that you can prevent unionization in a nonunion hospitality organization.
7. Identify negotiable demands that either union or management could request during the process of collective bargaining.
8. Describe the grievance procedure.
9. Explain the processes of arbitration and mediation.

The Changing Face of Unions

A **union** is nothing more than a group of employees that feel that they can obtain, from management, what they want more effectively as a group than as individuals. By bargaining as a group, they feel they have more power and that management is more likely to listen to them. Throughout history, in the form of federal and state legislation, employees have been given certain rights that permit them to bargain collectively, that is, bargain as a group as opposed to each individual bargaining separately with his or her supervisor.

Whether you are pro-union, anti-union or neutral; whether you believe that unions have outlived their usefulness or that they are facing a new revitalization, one fact that cannot be challenged is the numerous changes that unions have undergone in the past several years. American organized labor, in the hospitality industry as well as all others, will face many challenges in "the next chapter" as it tries to find its place in a changing society. Before we look at where organized labor is heading, the factors behind the changes in union efforts and its role in the work place, let's take a brief historical journey into unions.

To understand the union of the 1990s, you must understand the reasons for its inception and the legislation protecting and governing union activities. Many of the historical events serve as precedents for the types of actions you should take when assuming human resources responsibilities. As we discussed in the first chapter, the climate is such that both our guests and our human resources are more knowledgeable about the service sector. Not only will our guests be demanding improved service, our human resources will be demanding a work environment, compensation and benefits that are comparable to the improved level of service. As you are about to read, it was poor working conditions, low compensation and non-existent benefits that provided unions the impetus for their inception.

Union Beginnings

The efforts to organize unions in the United States began with the journeymen, who were tired of harsh treatment, poor working conditions and no say in decisions made by their trade masters. If one wanted to learn a specific trade, both the apprentices and journeymen were completely at the mercy of their masters.

The first unions formed were local trade unions representing the shoemakers, printers and carpenters. Bargaining, as we know it today, did not exist, although the unions did strike. Their primary complaints revolved around wages, the number of work hours and how many apprentices were permitted into a specific trade.

In 1886, the formation of the American Federation of Labor (AFL), under the leadership of its first president Samuel Gompers, sought the eight-hour work day. The AFL had a unique strategy for organizing. Instead of organizing based on specific trades, the AFL sought to form craft unions that were made up of people performing similar tasks, such as bakers.

The power of unions was increased by the Clayton Act (1914), which enabled employees to strike legally while simultaneously making it

356

easier for employers to obtain an injunction (a law stopping anyone from doing something such as strike). The period of the '20s represented an intensive campaign by management to discourage the growth of the labor unions. Benefit and recreational (social) programs were established by companies. Welfare programs for employees were considered good management practice. Yellow-dog contracts were common. In these contracts, the employee agreed, at the time of hire, not to join a union.

The Norris La Guardia Act of 1932 drastically reduced the conditions under which an injunction in a labor dispute could be issued by specifying the following five conditions that must prevail:

- Unlawful acts must have been threatened or occurring.
- Substantial damage to property must be seen as likely.
- The damage or injury must be greater if the injunction is denied.
- No adequate remedies in damages.
- Local police are unable or unwilling to provide protection.
- Norris LaGuardia also made yellow-dog contracts unenforceable.

Labor Laws Affecting Us Today

There are three federal laws that will affect you today in your labor relations in the hospitality industry. The National Labor Relations Act of 1935 (NLRA) is also called the Wagner Act. This was a pro-union act that established the National Labor Relations Board (NLRB). The act sets forth "unfair labor practices" governing the conduct of employees, unions and their agents.

The simplest explanation of the Wagner Act is that it describes the conditions under which collective bargaining may take place and guarantees employees the right to act together, as a group, rather than as individuals. This act had a significant impact on increasing union membership.

The National Labor Relations Board administers this act. It conducts union elections, certifies the results, and prevents both management and workers from committing unfair labor practices. An **unfair labor practice** is a violation of the law by either a union promoting unionization or an employer opposing unionization. Interrogation, threats, spying or firing an employee for union activities would be considered unfair labor practices as would any practice that interferes with the right of the employee to organize or discriminates against your employees for participating in union activities. Table 14-1 gives you some additional examples of unfair labor practices that you might encounter in the hospitality industry.

By 1941, there were two major national labor federations: the AFL that as we stated previously, was made up of craft workers, and the Congress of Industrial Organizations (CIO) that was composed of a

---

Table 14-1. Examples of Unfair Labor Practices by Union and by Management

Management cannot:

- offer a promotion or salary increase to an employee if he or she stays out of a union.
- discriminate against an employee in any manner for joining a union.
- refuse to hire a person because he or she belongs to a union.
- not bargain in good faith over union demands.
- harass an employee that files a grievance with the union.
- give wage increases to employees that are considering a union.

Union cannot:

- make harmful threats to a nonstriking worker.
- fire union members for crossing a picket line in an unlawful strike.
- cause an employer to discriminate against an employee.
- make acts of force, violence or threats.
- coerce an employer on his or her choice of representation.
- charge excessive or discriminatory dues as a condition of union membership.

---

group of industrial unions. Industrial unions were made up of workers from an entire industry, regardless of their occupation. A good example is the Hotel and Restaurant Workers and Bartenders International (HRWBI) that is a major union for the food service industry. Industrial unions are vertical unions as they cover all skill levels from the top to the lowest. As you recall, craft unions were made up of people that shared a common craft, regardless of the particular industry. An example might be all bakers: it would not matter if they worked in a restaurant or in a local bakery or for a large manufacturer of baked-good products.

The Labor–Management Relations Act or Taft–Hartley Act was passed in 1947 as an amendment to the Wagner Act. This amendment was considered to be mostly pro-management as it extended governmental intervention into labor relations.[1] The Taft–Hartley Act also made closed shop agreements illegal, although it permitted union shops, except where prohibited by state laws. This resulted in a number of the right-to-work laws that many states still maintain today. A closed shop was an organization that stipulated that a person must join the union prior to being hired. Union shops require that a person must join the union within a specified period of time after being hired, typically after a 30- or 60-day probationary period.

The second amendment to the Wagner Act was the Labor–Management Reporting and Disclosure Act of 1959, Public Law 86-257 (more commonly known as the Landrum–Griffin Act). This amendment is considered to be a union Bill of Rights as it sought to protect the rights of union members. The act defined specific ethical standards and codes of conduct that all labor organizations are to adhere to. This act helped to alleviate some of the abuses towards employees by both union officials and management. Essentially, power was taken away from the unions and given back to the employees, whose interests the unions were supposed to be looking out for.

The three basic purposes of the Landrum–Griffin amendment are:

- To regulate the internal affairs of the unions and reduce the possibility of labor racketeering.
- To insure union democracy by preventing unethical collusion between the company and the union.
- To protect union funds and prevent misuse by union leaders.

The power of the unions increased rapidly after World War II with union membership soaring. Union demands for welfare and benefit programs were aggressive and strikes were bitter. The Taft–Hartley Act was, in large, a public response to the unions' growing power and influence. Even with the passage of the Taft–Hartley Act, union membership grew and in 1955 the two major labor federations, the AFL and CIO merged.[2]

State labor laws. State labor laws vary widely, so it is always best that you check with your regional labor offices to assure that you are in compliance with the law when dealing with labor relations matters in your hospitality organization. State right-to-work laws are just one example.

Right-to-work laws are not highly thought of by unions, as they forbid contracts that require workers to join unions when they are hired. Since unions must, by law, represent all employees in an organization that is unionized, the right-to-work law prohibits them from collecting dues from all people in the bargaining unit. Unions rely upon their dues to meet operating expenses. If an operation has a large number of nonunion members in a bargaining unit, the union's effectiveness can be hindered. While in a democratic society most people believe it is wrong to require union membership of employees, the nonunion and union employees both benefit equally from union negotiations for pay increases and better benefits packages. What do you think? Should employees be required to join a union that represents them and pay dues as a requirement of employment?

Labor laws, both state and federal, are subject to change. Those of you that will be employed by a large hospitality organization will find that you are likely to have a labor-relations consultant or attorney working for your company. If you work for a smaller organization, these experts are still available to you, for a fee, to answer your questions. It is usually best to consult with them before you take any actions of which you are unsure.

Labor Unions Today

The sixties saw the unionization of public, professional and farm personnel with the issuance of Executive Order 10988. This changed the face of union membership. The traditional industrial and craft unions have since seen a decline in membership.

The hospitality industry has historically only had a small percentage of its workers join unions, with the early seventies being the period of highest membership. In 1981, only 14 percent of hospitality workers were unionized, with the Hotel and Restaurant Workers and Bartenders International (HRWBI) ranking as the 14th largest union in the United States.[3] Of the four million restaurant and hotel employees in the U.S. in 1984, only 10 percent belonged to the Hotel Employees and Restaurant Employees International Union (HERE).[4] Growth in union membership in hospitality industry has remained fairly stable for the past ten years with only a slight decline.

Effects on Unions in the 1990s

Whether unions will prosper or decline in the next decade is a matter of great debate. There are many that feel that unions have outlived their useful purpose and are dying. Other labor-relations experts believe that by the year 2000, the union movement will be reborn in this country as unions rise to meet the needs of the new American worker.[5] It is clear from reading these two diametrically opposed positions that union leaders are not presenting a united front.

Just what challenges does organized labor face in obtaining and retaining membership in its local and national organizations? Many of these challenges are the same as those that have been presented to you in previous chapters. For one, the composition of the work force. The first union members were primarily native white males, who worked full-time as the sole heads of households. More women, immigrants and part-timers are in the labor force and have different needs from the white male in the work place. Unions will need to meet the new needs of its new labor force if they hope to entice them into becoming dues-paying members.

Typically, women and minorities are found in the low-wage, low-status job positions. Look for unions to promote upward mobility for minorities and women. The concerns that these new groups of workers will have are likely to differ greatly from their native male counterparts. For many, English is a second language, or one that they don't speak at all.

With minimum wage increases being mandated by state and federal laws, the hourly employee's ability to pay union dues also increases. Who you hire also becomes more important, as you will be forced to pay higher rates of compensation. Teens and unskilled labor become less attractive when you have to pay them more. Teens are less likely to join unions because they view the jobs in hospitality as temporary. Hence, the increase in minimum wage could have the potential effect of increasing the type of individuals that would find joining unions attractive, if the union leaders seek them. It could take away the need for one of organized labor's basic bargaining items: higher wages.

The change in the U.S. economy from an industrial society to a service society means that unions will try to attract hospitality employees more so in the '90s than ever before. The base has switched from manufacturing to service, and so, too, the unions must adjust their recruiting strategies as millions of new jobs are being created in the service sector. Look for unions such as the Service Employees International Union (SEIU) and others to attempt to organize the virtually untapped and unorganized service workers.

Will unions be phased out by the year 2000? Will they become merely fraternal organizations as opposed to bargaining units? Will there be a rebirth of unions with service workers leading the way? While we can't answer any of these questions for you today, all are worth taking note of. No matter what direction unions take, they will, more than likely, at some point in the future have some affect on your human resources responsibilities.

Why Do People Join Unions?

Perhaps by examining some of the reasons why workers join unions you can be better prepared to keep your employees from feeling the need to join organized labor. You will recall that unions originated because of bad working conditions, low wages and abusive treatment by management of its workers. Federal legislation has come a long way in assuring our human resources that we won't underpay them, that we will maintain a reasonable work week length and that we will provide a safe and healthful work environment for them in which to perform their job duties and responsibilities. For many of our human resources though, unions can provide job security, increases in compensation, extensions in benefit offerings, protection from arbitrary management decisions, reasonable work loads, and a process to grieve what they feel are unjust practices.

Think for a moment about our discussions on motivation, and how throughout each chapter the human resources functions you perform relate directly or indirectly to the retention efforts of your hospitality organization. The theme that all of the industry experts have stressed to you is protection of your valuable human assets. Unions seek to protect and promote the interests of their members. If you, in performing your human resources responsibilities, do not keep the interests of your human resources foremost in your mind, chances are good that a union will be able to easily unionize your hospitality organization. Table 14-2 identifies some conditions that could encourage employee interest in unions.

Table 14-2. Conditions Encouraging Employee Interest in Unions

- Wages inappropriate
- People feel there is no flexibility in their earning capabilities
- Unpleasant working environment
- Inadequate benefits
- Job insecurity
- Employees feel that management does not respect them
- Discrimination
- Favoritism
- Inconsistent discipline
- Employees do not feel that they are truly a part of the hospitality organization
- Employees feel that management is taking advantage of them
- Employees have no pride in their work
- Failure to recognize individual efforts and performance
- Poor communications

In some hospitality organizations, union membership is compulsory according to the union agreement. This means that a new hire must join the union and pay dues if he or she wants to obtain the job. Present employees must join the union and pay dues if they want to keep their jobs. Unionized organizations that do not have union agreements requiring compulsory membership permit employees that do not join the union to share in the benefits of the union-bargaining activities. Hence, some employees could get a "free ride."

INDUSTRY EXPERTS SPEAK

Regynald G. Washington points out the fact that "a union is a business operated for a profit and, therefore, unions are not particularly interested in mom-and-pop operations, but aggressively pursue large hospitality facilities with large numbers of employees. Additionally, union officials are elected by the members of the union, and popularity as well as response to employee complaints play a major role. Union officials usually handle employee complaints quickly and aggressively in order to maintain their popularity that will eventually end up as a vote."

Effective Collective Bargaining Management

What are some of the things that you can do, as a human resources manager, to avoid the unionization of your hospitality organization? Let's walk through each of the human resources functions covered in this text.

362

- Hiring process. Always go for the absolute best person you can. In the hospitality industry, personality can often be the key to success.
- Orientation/training. Make sure your people are comfortable and knowledgeable about their new work environment and company. Tell people your expectations.
- Performance appraisal. The system for appraisal must be clearly communicated, understood and fair.
- Development. Your human resources see a way to move up and into other job positions.
- Positive counseling. Troubled employees have opportunities to resolve personal problems and turn their performance records around without fear of punishment.
- Compensation. Both current and future pay must be viewed as equitable.
- Open communications. You can't manage from behind your desk; you have to be available to your people. There are positive benefits to management and employee daily communications as it relates to the vehicle for positive labor-relations management.
- Consistency in management. This is the best policy for keeping you away from union activity.When you go into arbitration unions will look for inconsistencies in management.

| **INDUSTRY EXPERTS SPEAK** | Regynald G. Washington relates the following story: "A recent union case was lost by management due to inconsistency in management. A cocktail server was terminated for overcharging customers for drinks. Management learned of the problem from a co-worker of the terminated cocktail worker. Management sent unannounced service shoppers into the bar and found that the overcharging problem was true. The beverage manager, however, of the operation had permitted special arrangements (requested days off) for the cocktail server that had tipped off managment to the overcharging problem in the lounge. The cocktail server that tipped off management to the overcharging problem had many personal problems with her husband who battered her, sick kids who had too often to be taken to the doctors, etc. The beverage manager had received similar requests from other cocktail servers that worked the same shift in that same lounge and were denied schedule adjustments. Although service shoppers caught the cocktail server overcharging the guest, the arbitrator ruled in favor of |

the employee due to the favoritism shown to the terminated cocktail server's co-worker. Several cocktail servers were subpoenaed to testify that they had been denied unusual schedules requested because of personal problems. Inconsistency in management was key to the loss of the arbitration."

Table 14-3 identifies some other ways for preventing union unionization in the hospitality industry. As you will notice, most of the suggestions relate to simply fair and sound good management practices. One of the major reasons that people join unions is for job security. If a hospitality organization does not provide security for its human resources through the areas identified above, then unionization can more easily occur.

In addition, many establishments maintain a "no solicitation" rule. This means, that in addition to keeping unions from soliciting your employees, the rule must be enforced equitably for every group from the Girl Scouts to the United Way or it will be viewed as an unfair management labor practice.

The Union Campaign and Election

The union may approach your hospitality organization either internally or externally. Internally, one of your employees may be contacted to assist the union in organizing your employees. Table 14-4 shows some potential signs of union activity. Or, your employees might be angry with management and collectively (or as a select group) decide to call in the union for help. Externally, a union organizer might enter your operation and sit at the bar and talk to the bartender about how he or she likes working for you, or

Table 14-3. Methods of Union Prevention

- Establish credibility between management and employees
- Promote open door policies
- Encourage employees to report problems
- Take employee complaints seriously
- Keep commitments to employees in a timely manner
- Understand the need for appreciation
- Know how to give positive feedback
- Maintain high standards
- Allow employee participation programs
- Provide a positive work environment
- Open channels of communication
- Listen to employees

have lunch and talk to the server. Due to the nature of the hospitality business, it is quite easy for a union organizer to infiltrate your organization.

During the covert campaign, the union organizers will be attempting to win union recognition (Figure 14-1). Petitions and authorization cards will be passed among your employees. As a manager, you don't want to look at anything a union organizer has to give you, especially union authorization cards. Looking at them will oftentimes commit your company to that union's organization efforts.

Once you know that a union is attempting to organize your employees, get help! Hire a labor lawyer when dealing with unions if your hospitality organization does not have such a person already on staff. This area of law is a tough one, and you, as manager, are going to be limited in the actions that you can take. Your best approach is to listen and document everything that goes on, on a day-to-day basis.

The Election

To file for an election, 30 percent of your employees need to have to be organized. About two weeks after the petition is filed for an election, a hearing is held. A hearing is very much like a court proceeding, with each side, management and the union agent, testifying.

The election is usually held 30 days after the hearing. To win a union election, you need a 50 percent vote plus one of all voting employees. It is unlawful for an employer to recognize a union that does not represent a majority of the employees. Once the union becomes certified, you are legally bound to negotiate with that union. If the union looses the election, then no union can attempt to organize your employees for a period of one year.

The Collective Bargaining Agreement

After the union has won the recognition election and is legally recognized as your organization's bargaining unit, the collective-bargaining

---

Table 14-4. Signs of Union Activity

- Presence of unfamiliar faces
- Anyone making a list of employee names
- Groups of employees that are deep in conversation until you approach
- New informal groups with emerging group leaders
- Business being conducted during breaks or lunch
- A sudden increase in questions about company policy, procedures and benefits
- Anticompany graffiti in employee restrooms and break areas
- A number of small gatherings of employees
- Gossip among disgruntled employees

364

agreement is negotiated by representatives of both the union and management. The process through which this agreement is developed is called **collective bargaining.** Items that can be bargained for are guided by numerous labor laws, but generally include working conditions, pay, human resources management practices (such as hiring, promotions, sick leave, benefits and disciplinary procedures), grievance procedures and length of agreement. While the union attempts to bargain for its position, management must bargain in good faith, but management does not have to accept the union's position. Each side has its own list of demands. The bargaining process is give-and-take on the part of both groups.

INDUSTRY EXPERTS SPEAK	Mr. Washington points out, "Unions usually discredit management and perform character assassinations on various members of the management staff. This is used as a weapon to positively influence an arbitrator to rule in favor of the union. Therefore, it is necessary to focus on how management develops credibility and respect with the union. This leads to effective labor-relations management. It is important that management have total involvement in labor contract-negotiations."

Figure 14-1. Small groups of employees discussing "secret" agendas is often a sign of union organization.
Photo by Michael Upright

It is important for management to enter the bargaining process with a list of its own demands. Can you think of things, which if in a union shop, you would like the union to either give up or adopt? What about the following:

- fewer vacation hours
- fewer sick leave hours
- fewer paid holidays
- a restriction on accrual of sick hours and vacation hours to be used during the current year
- shorter breaks
- restriction on personal calls made on the company phone
- laundering of uniforms done by employees
- increase in the probationary hire period
- temp-help to eliminate overtime

These are just some items that you might want to demand from the union. Remember, the process of collective bargaining is one of negotiation. Neither party enters the negotiations expecting to receive its entire list of demands. Some items are even included as "throwaways," those items added strictly for the purpose of negotiating.

The point we would like you to remember is that you are always better off entering the negotiations with a demand list of your own. The alternative is simply to counter the union's demands, which does not permit you to bargain from a position of utmost strength. You should not view the negotiating process as merely a place to minimize your losses!

The Contract

At the end of collective bargaining, the union contract is signed by both management and the union. During the life of the contract, numerous interpretations will need to be made as incidents occur between employees and management. Effective labor relations stem from a willingness on the part of both the employees and management to make the union contract work. Large hospitality organizations, such as Walt Disney World, have a staff of employees whose job is to troubleshoot between the employees and management. In other companies, union officers or stewards are elected to assist in resolving problems between employees and their supervisors. While it is the steward's job to protect the rights of the employees as specified in the union contract, stewards do not have managerial authority or responsibility.

It is critical that, as a hospitality manager in a union shop, you learn the union contract! It is customary for union officials to hold union-contract educational seminars at the local union hall. These sessions usually are conducted by the union's attorney and union officials. Ongoing contract training is administered to all shop stewards. Management personnel cannot effectively manage union employees when the union

366

employees are more informed regarding contract issues then management people. A labor-relations lawyer can assist you and other management team members. Typically, you would use the lawyer who negotiated the contract since the contract is written in legal language.

Most union contracts specify a grievance procedure, which is used to resolve complaints and disputes between employees and management. This formalized procedure makes it easier for management to deal with the union in an open forum. It also makes it easier for employees that want to bring up complaints against management. When grievances cannot be resolved by this process, the grievance goes to arbitration.

Arbitration and Mediation

While it is always better for both parties to resolve conflicts in-house, a peaceful arbitration with a third party is still a better alternative than a strike or lockout. The arbitrator and mediator are neutral umpires selected by the mutual agreement of both union and management. An **arbitrator** is the final judge, his or her decision is final and binding. A **mediator** has no power other than the opportunity to use persuasion.

In the process of mediation, the mediator sits down with both parties and identifies the issues that are preventing agreement. It is the mediator's job to try to get each side to fully see the other side's position on a given issue. The mediator then attempts to get the two parties to agree to develop some alternative solutions to the problem that had not been thought of before. Finally, the mediator tries to get both parties to agree to a solution that is fair to everyone involved. If a solution is found to which both parties agree, the grievance is resolved, although nothing the mediator does or says is binding on either party. The two parties must mutually agree to a solution. If no solution can be agreed upon, the mediation fails.

Arbitration takes place only after mediation has been tried and has failed. Since the decision of the arbitrator is by law binding on both parties, the selection of this individual is of utmost importance. Sources for arbitrators include the Federal Mediator Conciliation Service, which maintains a panel of certified arbitrators as does the American Arbitration Association. These arbitrators are paid daily fees that can be quite high. The cost is shared equally by both parties. Arbitration is an expensive process. In addition to the arbitrator, both sides will want to have legal counsel representing them during the proceedings. Therefore, issues do not go to arbitration routinely or unless the issue is an important one to the union.

At the end of the arbitration, one party will have won, and one party will have lost. Why then would either party want to go to arbitration? Remember, we said that arbitration only took place after mediation had failed. Thus, only when you have reached an impasse over a grievance or the contract. If this impasse is not resolved, then a strike or work slowdown is likely to be the result. It is best to avoid arbitration if you can. Very seldom does management win in cases that pair the big corporation against the little employee. Arbitration costs money.

Conclusion

In the past several years, many companies have taken a union avoidance posture. Management has done this by encouraging such practices as self-management, employee involvement, co-participation with management, participative decision making, quality circles, team problem solving, better communication with employees (including keeping them informed about organizational changes) as well as instituting some of the retention methods we have been discussing throughout this text. This approach keeps management and employees talking to each other rather than establishing a "them" vs. "us" type of mentality.

Although service industries have not historically been heavily unionized, there is a chance that this may change in "the next chapter." With demographic changes and economic shifts, unions will be looking at the new labor force in the service industry as potential members. An additional human resources responsibility that you will need to assume is an awareness of union activities in the hospitality industry.

CASE PROBLEM 14

Case Problem 14-1

You have noticed the following events occurring in the hospitality operation you described in Case Problem 1:

369

- gossip among disgruntled employees
- business being conducted during lunch
- an employee making lists of employee names
- unfamiliar faces around the premises
- increased questions about company policies

Based upon these events you strongly suspect that an attempt at union organization may be occurring within your hospitality organization. Currently you operate a nonunion operation.

As a hospitality manager, discuss in two to three paragraphs your feelings about these suspected union organization activities. Do you wish to attempt to legally stop union organizational efforts? If your answer is no, explain why you feel that unionization of your hospitality organization would be a benefit. Be specific. Identify both short-term and long-term benefits of unionization. If your answer is yes, you wish to attempt to stop unionization, identify the steps that you can take to nullify these organizational efforts. Again, be specific.

Regardless of your response to unionization, identify eight conditions that could have prompted union organizational efforts in your hospitality organization. Be specific. (Hint: This will require that you present some additional descriptive information about the hospitality organization that you described in Case Problem 1. This description should provide the reader with information about management styles, operating techniques, and behaviors.)

Case Problem 14-2

The union's organizational efforts identified in Case Problem 14-1 have paid off—for the union. One of your employees was contacted by the union to assist in organizing the other employees. Petitions and authorization cards were passed among your employees, and you were careful not to look at any of these materials. Doing so could have committed your company to the union's organization efforts. A petition was filed for an election signed by 50 percent of your employees. A hearing was held two weeks later with both union and management testifying. The election was held 30 days after the hearing carrying 85 percent of the employees who voted. The union is now certified, and you are legally bound to negotiate with that union.

370

You are now ready to negotiate the collective bargaining agreement. One of the first decisions you made was to hire an excellent labor relations attorney. It is the responsibility of this individual to represent the company's interest in collective bargaining. You, however, as part of the management team in this hospitality organization have an obligation to identify a list of items and conditions that are and are not acceptable. Prepare an outline of items that can be bargained for by your lawyer. At a minimum this outline should consider working conditions, compensation plans and benefit packages.

For each of the conditions that you specify, indicate if this is a negotiable or nonnegotiable item. What other issues will you want to specify for the labor relations attorney? Prepare a general listing of these additional items.

RECOMMENDED READING

Begin, J. P. and Beal, E. F. 1985. *The Practice of Collective Bargaining.* Homewood, Illinois: Richard D. Irwin.

Florey, P. 1985. A growing fringe benefit: arbitration of nonunion employee grievances. *Personnel Administrator* 30, (7): 14, 16, 18.

END NOTES

1. Office of the General Counsel, National Labor Relations Board, "A Guide to Basic Law and Procedures under the National Labor Relations Act," (Washington D.C.: U.S. Government Printing Office, 1978).
2. Bernstein, I., "The Growth of the American Unions," *American Economic Review* 44, (1954): 303–304.
3. Tiegs, Carol Lynn, "Unions Gear-up Activity in Fast Food Industry," *Restaurant Business* (November 1, 1988): 68.
4. Kohl, John P. and Stephens, David B., "On Strike: Legal Developments in Labor–Management Relations," *The Cornell Hotel and Restaurant Administration Quarterly* 25, (1985, 4): 71.
5. Thompson, Donald, "New Role for Labor Unions," *Industry Week* 232, (1987, 3): 30–33, 35, 38.

DISCUSSION QUESTIONS

1. What is a union? Are you pro-union, anti-union or neutral? State the reasons why you took that position. Did you feel differently before reading this chapter?
2. Have you ever worked in a union shop? If so, describe how it was different from a nonunion shop. If not, describe how you believe it would be different based upon what you read in this chapter.

3. Describe the three major pieces of federal legislation that affect labor relations today and their impact on the union movement.
4. What are some of the reasons that people join unions? How, in the 1990s, can human resources management affect unionization in a nonunion hospitality organization.
5. Describe some of the challenges facing organized labor in the 1990s.
6. Describe the events that occur in a union campaign and election.
7. Explain the collective bargaining process and the union contract.
8. Discuss the differences between mediation and arbitration.

371

APPROACHING
THE YEAR 2000

CHAPTER 15

COMPUTER APPLICATIONS
IN HUMAN RESOURCES MANAGEMENT

"A journey of a thousand leagues begins with a single step."
—LAO-tZU

KEY WORDS

automation
computer applications
data base
hardware
Human Resource Information
  System (HRIS)

integrated systems
Management Information
  Systems (MIS)
microcomputer
software
vendor software

INTRODUCTION

The computerization of human resources management has extended into arenas only imagined a decade ago. Today, few human resources departments are found without a microcomputer. This can be attributed, in part, to the rapid advancements in computer technology. Hardware, in particular desktop computers, have decreased in cost and that has made these small systems affordable for even the smallest hospitality operation. Software that supports the human resources functions is also available. These programs can generate reports, perform various kinds of data analysis and simulate a variety of "what if" scenarios.

For hospitality managers with human resources responsibilities in "the next chapter," an understanding of computer applications will be a necessity. As you will see in this chapter, such an understanding will not only simplify your job, but will assist in the organizational effectiveness and decision-making process of the hospitality enterprise. Top management is depending more and more on the information provided by the human resources department.

At the conclusion of this chapter you will be able to:
1. Explain the applications and use of software within the human resources functions.
2. Define a Human Resource Information system (HRIS).

3. Understand the importance of conducting a needs-assessment prior to purchasing software.
4. Explain how to successfully introduce computers in your hospitality organization.
5. Describe the differences between vendor-selected software and designing your own software.
6. Identify the benefits of computer applications in hospitality human resources management.

Computers and Human Resources Management

In a people oriented business such as hospitality, computers can allow managers to become more people oriented. While guest service is something that only your people can do, automation gives you more time to focus on the heart of your business: the guest! Recall that in the first chapter we said that sound human resources skills and tools would allow you to maintain your commitment to high quality products and excellent service. Computers should be thought of as simply another human resources management tool, like your development program, your placement process or EAP, which when used properly, can help you maximize the quality of the products and services you offer.

The ultimate purpose of the computer for hospitality managers is to improve the quality of the service. It achieves its purpose by freeing you from time-consuming paperwork and giving you more time to interact with your guests. The speed at which information can be processed and reported expedites decision making. The advances in desktop publishing serve to improve communications throughout the hospitality organization.

Computers, with their enormous capacity for storing, maintaining and retrieving information in a usable format have helped human resources departments in becoming the information center for hospitality organizations. What could be more important to management decision making than information about the hospitality organization's most critical resource, its people? Which department is responsible for information on people? The human resources department, division, office, manager: wherever and whoever in your hospitality organization assumes the human resources responsibilities.

The computer is not a substitute for managerial expertise and experience, but it does have the capability of providing valuable analytical data and decision-support information to improve your effectiveness when carrying out human resources responsibilities.

What the Computer Can Do

Computers support you as a manager as you carry out your human resources responsibilities by performing a variety of time-consuming tasks. For example, much of the work in the human resources office is clerical in nature. Many of the routine tasks can be automated, reducing the number of individuals required for these tasks. Think back upon the human resources functions that we have discussed. Select any one of those functions and think through the amount of information gathering and paperwork that goes into the successful completion of that particular human resources function. Perhaps, if your hospitality organization is very small, the amount of time spent in clerical tasks will not seem too overwhelming. The larger the hospitality organization, however, the greater the complexity of the data gathered and, more importantly, the greater the chance for error.

In large organizations, one of the biggest problems is the maintenance of a current file on all of your human resources. If there is a backlog in information gathering, or even in the recording of the information, inappropriate decisions could be made. For example, let's examine career development and succession planning for a relatively large hospitality organization. This operation has done a good job of information gathering. That is, all of the performance appraisals are current as well as the individual development planning sessions. The backlog has occurred in updating the files in the human resources office.

An executive planning session has been called to conduct the annual review of the succession plan. You, having assumed the responsibilities of human resources manager, have been asked to bring information pertaining to the career development progress of all human resources currently in the succession plan, along with all others that management might want to consider for inclusion. If your human resources files are not up-to-date, you will be presenting top management with inaccurate information on the human resources currently in the succession plan. Furthermore, there will be no way for you to prepare a report on potential candidates for the succession plan, since your information is outdated.

Unfortunately, even though you have been diligent in your duties and responsibilities in gathering the information, the volume of the data has kept your clerical staff from being efficient.

In addition to automating clerical tasks, the computer can also be used in the development of standardized reports. Take out a piece of paper and identify the many reports the manager assuming human resources responsibilities must generate. Think through each of the human resources functions we have discussed and the federal legislation that governs each of them. Many of the standardized reports you will generate are required to show federal compliance.

Now compare your list with the following areas that require standardized reports, either for purposes of federal compliance or for management decision making:

- Attendance analysis (sick leave, vacation leave, etc.)
- Immigration tracking
- Training history (job, safety and sanitation)
- Training, types (what cross training does each human resource have, which job positions are they qualified to fill from a training/job knowledge perspective)
- Retention/turnover analysis
- EEO and AA compliance
- Job applicant tracking
- Payroll
- Career development/promotions
- Skills inventories
- Manpower analysis (how many human resources are in which departments)
- Educational assistance program utilization
- COBRA compliance
- Accident reporting
- Applicant search expenditures (cost per hire)

How many more examples of reports generated from human resources functions did you think of?

Computers can assist you, first, with routine clerical tasks and, second, in the generation of standardized reports. These two uses of computers are handled by routine data-processing systems, those that assist you in day-to-day operations. Computers give you the ability to streamline these routine, yet important, tasks. Just ask your employees how important it is to process their payroll checks! Or check with your lawyer about the fines for not maintaining federal reporting requirements!

A third general application of the computer is to provide management with the information it needs to make decisions. Better management decision making translates into improved organizational effectiveness for the hospitality enterprise. Since the computer can supply information more rapidly than manual procedures, feedback is provided on a more frequent basis. Table 15-1 provides you with a list of the more general applications of the computer in dealing with human resources responsibilities. Let us now look at some of the more specific applications within some of the human resources functions that have been discussed previously.

The Computerization of Human Resources Functions

Imagine for a moment that the hospitality organization you are working for has not incorporated any of its human resources functions into the existing automated information system. Suppose that you have been asked by your boss to identify areas, within the scope of your human

**Table 15-1. The Use of Computers
in Human Resources Management: General Applications**

- Clerical functions
- Record keeping
- Federal and state compliance
- Desktop publishing
- Career pathing
- Skills inventories
- Compensation administration
- Benefits administration
- Short- and long-term planning

resources responsibilities, which need to be automated. Which human resources functions do you feel should be among the first to be computerized?

How many of you answered payroll? There is no question that compensation plans, with their increasing complexity and federal regulations, can best be implemented and managed through a computerized system. The priority in which human resources functions are computerized for any one particular hospitality operation is hard to determine. A needs assessment and additional information about the size of the operation is required. For those hospitality operations that provide a variety of services and options for their human resources, the order in which the specific human resources functions are discussed in this chapter will typically make the most sense for purposes of implementation.

Compensation administration. Compensation administration involves not only payroll record keeping and paycheck issuance, but the development of pay grades, ranges and wage amounts. The effect of wage increases and the impact of merit increases can be pretested by asking the computer to answer a number of "what if" questions. Increases in compensation can have a far-reaching impact on the hospitality organization's future. Without computerization, it is almost impossible to determine the effects of such increases.

In addition to handling these needs, Human Resource Information Systems (HRIS) can be developed that can integrate performance evaluations with salary adjustments and/or career development progress. Compensation levels could be determined by bringing in appropriate data from the job evaluation process.

Combined or integrated human resources systems are oftentimes advantageous for a hospitality organization. While the functions of compensation, benefits, career development and job evaluation are quite different, they use much of the same information. Instead of having each function entering the same data repeatedly, human resource information systems are designed so that the data only needs to be entered once, yet all functional areas have access to it when the data is needed. HRIS applications will be discussed later in this chapter.

In pay-for-performance compensation plans, computerization becomes even more important. Before your people can be rewarded for their performance, accurate human resources information is a must! Mistakes in rewarding performance due to inadequate or faulty information could be disastrous to the morale and motivation of your staff.

Benefits administration. Much of benefits administration deals with maintenance decisions. The computer can save enormous amounts of time when dealing with the "paper trail" required to meet federal compliance and the support needed to offer flexible benefits. Think about the maintenance involved in a hospitality operation that has a flexible benefits plan that allows participants to select from four different health care plans, two different dental plans and, three different pension plans, in addition to day care, life insurance, elder care and educational-assistance benefits offerings. How will you keep track of health insurance and pension accruals, tuition reimbursements and day care contributions? How will you keep track of which employee has selected which health care, dental and pension plan? How will you administrate who is entitled to what under which plan? Does all this seem a bit confusing and overwhelming? Without computerization it would not only be an administrator's nightmare, but the potential for inaccuracies and mistakes is enormous!

It has been estimated that a company can save between 1.5 percent to 3 percent of its payroll expenses by using a flexible benefits plan in coordination with IRS Section 125. Both employer and employee save money in social security payments, Worker's Compensation payments and taxes by using Section 125.[1] As was pointed out in the chapter on benefits, there are many advantages for your human resources when a hospitality organization offers a flexible benefits plan. The biggest disadvantage for the employer is the record keeping that accompanies the implementation and administration of these types of benefits plans.

This is where the computer enters into the benefits picture. Software has been developed that can track the choices your employees make, make the appropriate payroll deductions and provide you with a report of the costs.[2] Stouffer Hotels and Resorts successfully makes use of such a system.[3]

Even for hospitality organizations that choose not to offer flexible benefits, software is available to assist you in updating your personnel files. Benefits plans most typically operate based on information supplied by your human resources when they are first hired. People's lives are seldom fixed; they get married or get divorced, they have children or their children grow up and leave their home. All of this information must be modified in the employee's personnel file so that the company only pays for benefits that they actually should be providing.

Human resources planning. Effective human resources planning also requires an almost insatiable supply of information. Programs that can link human resources supply-and-demand analysis with its costs and benefits, programs that can assist in forecasting and those that can generate decision information on alternatives to achieving strategic human resources plans are all ways that the computer can assist in human resources planning activities.

Succession planning can also make use of computer capabilities to identify progression paths that focus on key human resources and their replacements. These systems can better track the individuals in the succession plan to ensure continuity in vacated positions. Systems capable of coordinating skills-inventory data with succession planning could be of great value to larger hospitality organizations. Typically, succession plans are developed only for top managerial positions. Expanded data base fields could permit succession planning to be carried to lower position levels in the future. Computers have the capacity to identify qualified internal candidates for vacant job positions: a great asset to a hospitality organization.

The application of computers in manpower planning has barely touched the surface. As this function becomes of increasing importance to hospitality organizations in "the next chapter," watch for a greater sophistication in the use of computer systems to assist in human resources planning decisions.

Recruitment and selection. Suppose that you have a job opening in your hospitality organization. You have been successful in your recruiting efforts and now, in front of you, is a pile of applications and resumes. Now, imagine that you can turn to your desktop computer. You enter the qualifications of all the applicants along with the job description and specification for the open position. Next, you request a list of the best candidates and the computer generates one, prioritized, of course!

A computerized recruitment system could handle this selection task with ease, along with other elements of the recruitment process. For example, just with the applicant data that is already stored, your system has built up a pool of applicants that could be recalled at the touch of a fingertip any time a job opening occurs.[4] The longer the selection capacities are used, the more data you will have to analyze the selection results. Is there a particular applicant profile that best fits a specific job position? What is the turnover rate of the applicants selected by the computer? What are the performance records of those individuals? Knowing the answers to questions such as these will enable you to further refine the selection system.

The selection procedure used by the computer, described above, also requires that you enter information about the vacant position. As you already know, the information necessary to make a valid selection decision is found in the job description and job specification. If this data is entered into the computer system for all job positions, you have the ability to recall, almost immediately, the job details for any vacant position. Reduced is the "paper trail" of required information that can sometimes delay the recruitment process.

382

Such an automated system also gives you the capacity to track the applicants as they go through the recruitment process. The applicant-tracking flow chart could be generated at any given moment and tell you exactly where the applicants stand in the process. Have they had their second interview? Are their letters of recommendation on file? Have the reference checks been completed? Is preemployment testing required and, if so, what is its status? If the automated system is tied into a word processing system, offer and rejection letters could be generated to the appropriate applicants.

Once you automate the recruitment process, you will have a greater ability to keep track of the costs associated with obtaining a new hire. An analysis could be made to determine the most cost effective advertising media. Monetary figures, such as cost per hire and cost per applicant, could easily be generated. All of this information translates into better administration of the entire recruitment process, from placing the first ad to selecting applicants to interviewing to making a job offer. Effectiveness in making the right applicant selection is also improved. All of these factors translate to a cost savings.

The technology exists, at present, to use computer information systems in all of the applications just discussed. Confidentiality can be protected by restricting levels of access into the system.

Training management. There are a variety of uses for the human resource information system in training program management. Once you have a data base, the system can match the specific training requirements of various job positions with the training needs of your employees. The identification of training needs can be a time consuming process when handled manually. Additional paperwork is involved in monitoring the progress of your human resources as they participate in various training programs.

A safety program is offered in many hospitality operations. Not only will automatization establish records for purposes of Occupational Safety and Health Administration documentation requirements, the system could be tied into your accident reports to troubleshoot problem areas. For example, your accident reports indicate an increase in the number of falls on wet floors. Your safety training program can then immediately be modified to emphasize the proper procedures and policies for mopping floors. The result could be a reduction in the number of accidents.

Training program management software systems can also be tied into development programs, performance appraisal systems and succession planning. The information from each of these areas could be combined to assure that the training needs of all your human resources are met as the hospitality organization progresses towards the target goals and objectives identified in the strategic human resources plan. Career development plans can also be integrated so that the computer can identify weaknesses in an individual's profile that could be rectified through appropriate training or education. From the perspective of the hospitality organization, the computer can alert you to weaknesses in the company's current work force or even identify potential career paths for your employees. Since the computer operates with total objectivity, it can provide you with a better assessment of the talent that exists in your operation.

Other human resources uses. The automation of human resources functions yields some additional capabilities. The record keeping and reporting component of the Equal Employment Opportunity Act (EEOA) maintains strict requirements. With the data base you established during the recruitment and promotion process, accurate information can be readily provided on ethnic identities, race, religion and sex.

383

Record keeping is also required to meet the regulations established in the Employee Retirement Income Security Act (ERISA) and the Consolidated Omnibus Budget Reconciliation Act (COBRA). Very specific timetables have been established by the federal government with stiff financial penalties for failure to comply.[5]

Computerization also allows for the analysis of data. Some examples of such usage in human resources management would include turnover, attendance and patterns of sick leave. In addition, software is available that will produce organization charts and safety statistics, assist in negotiations planning, tie performance appraisals to merit payments, monitor management development and conduct budgetary analysis.

These applications are just beginning to enter into human resources management in the hospitality industry (Figure 15-1). Now, let

Figure 15-1. Information systems are a valuable asset to the hospitality manager with human resources responsibility.
Photo by Michael Upright

us turn our attention to defining what a human resource information system is and how we might implement it, or other software packages, into our hospitality organization to assist us with our human resources management responsibilities.

Human Resource Information Systems

384

A computer is nothing more than an electronic device which can only operate under the control of a software program or programs. Software programs are written by people for the purpose of manipulating data in a specified manner. The data which is to be manipulated is gathered and entered into the computer by people. The accuracy of the program is only as accurate as the programmer and the data. The computer has no way of determining the accuracy of its output. In other words it does not know the difference between "real" data and bad data, nor can it tell you whether the program it's operating under is "right" for the particular application you have in mind. GIGO spells garbage in-garbage out, which is exactly what will happen to you and your credibility if care is not taken in software selection, data gathering and data entering.

There is no "typical" computer or software system for human resources functions in the hospitality industry. Actually one of the advantages of computer (hardware) and software systems is their flexibility and adaptability. You can select both the hardware and software which fits your specific purposes.

Management Information Systems (MIS) revolutionized personnel management in the 1960s. These large scale management tools provided a wholelistic look at the hospitality business environment.[6] An information system refers to information or data which is integrated for the purposes of decision-making. The logic is that the integrated data will serve to improve the decision-making process. An information system which is designed for the purpose of maximizing human resources decision-making is known as a *human resource information system or HRIS*. These systems can be centrally maintained to report on information related to all human resources in your organization. You have already read some of the ways in which HRIS can enhance human resources decisions.

Human resource information systems have the capability to store vast amounts of data from a variety of input sources. The HRIS is designed to retrieve discrete pieces of data, about human resources and jobs, and translate it into useful information rapidly and without error. These systems need to be thought of as a management tool which can be used to make a hospitality organization more efficient and productive. Most HRIS's are designed to be interactive. This means that they permit managers to view the output on their computer monitors as it is being manipulated. This permits the manager to make instant alterations, as they are required. Once the data and the format are satisfactory, the report can be printed into a "hard copy".

Implementation of a HRIS

Most human resource information systems are implemented using the hospitality organizations mainframe computer. What if your company is small and does not have a mainframe? Increasingly common is the use of microcomputers, such as the IBM PC or Apple IIE's or any one of a number of such systems which are available on the market today. To be most effective these microcomputers should be dedicated exclusively to human resources management activities. But wait, let's backtrack for a moment and see how the world of computers with human resources applications has evolved.

A Study of Past Events

As was the case in the development of a number of the human resources functions such as training and preemployment testing, the military and government were the first to apply computer technology to applications in human resources management.[7] It was actually the finance department that first computerized payroll systems in the early 1950s.[8] These systems ran on big mainframe systems, usually so large that entire rooms were devoted to them. The systems were so complex that computer professionals, not human resources managers, operated them. Typically, requests from the human resources departments were given low-priority status.

It was during the late 1970s that computer technology began to be used to manage the challenges faced by human resources management. The revolution of the microcomputer increased the availability of hardware along with reducing the costs. The 80s brought with it the personal computer and an enormous reduction of cost. This triggered an avalanche of software programs, gradually improving in user friendliness. Computers were stored on desktops and no longer required computer specialists to operate them.

Today, software systems include not only complete Human Resource Information Systems, but functionally specific programs as well. As the number of software vendors increases with each passing year, the manager with human resources responsibilities must be prepared to understand the proposed applications of the software he or she is choosing among.

The Purpose of a Needs Analysis

The particular work environment of a hospitality organization will determine the requirements of the automated human resource informa-

386

tion system. No two human resource information systems are identical. Software designed for specific applications all have their limitations. There are somewhere between 300–400 software packages for human resources applications for the microcomputer alone![9] How do you know which software will perform optimally for your hospitality organization? Should you select a complete Human Resource Information System or several individual packages designed for specific applications?

The software or system that will work best is the one that is based upon the human resources information needs of your particular operation. We talked earlier in the text about the importance of establishing human resources goals and objectives. Your information needs should reflect those objectives. The software that you select should be designed to fulfill the hospitality organization's information needs. In other words, the human resources objectives determine the software applications you require. Don't let the software vendor convince you that your objectives should be modified to meet the capabilities of the software they are selling.

System and Software Decisions

Once your information needs have been identified, you need to determine whether you will need a complete HRIS or software with separate applications. This decision will depend upon the size and computer capabilities of your operation. If your organization already has a HRIS running on a mainframe or microcomputer, you will need to provide human resources information to supplement the data already contained on the system.

It is now time to make software decisions. Even though there is an abundance of software with human resources applications on the market, sometimes nothing less than custom-designed software will match your particular information needs. Making sure that you have the right software is critical! Designing software is not a skill mastered by most hospitality managers. It is well worth the money to hire a computer technician with programming capabilities to do the design and development. Make sure all the "bugs" are worked out before the technician leaves.

Selecting special-application software already available on the market is probably the quickest, most inexpensive and easiest alternative. Great care should be taken when reviewing all of the products available on the market. The key objective is that the software matches the requirements of your hospitality organization. If you discover that the needs of your operation are unique and not met by any of the shelf software, you might be forced to develop (or have developed) a custom package.

As you select software, you might want to consider if the software has the capability to generate information in formats different from the standardized report form the software is programmed to generate. Some software packages permit you to generate ad hoc, or specialized reports, on an as-needed basis to fulfill a specific human resources function requirement. It is often quite useful to have the capability of building specialized reports from information in the data files. Another consideration might be the format in which reports are presented. Are they easy to read and interpret? Are they similar to what the staff is already used to seeing? Are they in a tabular or narrative format? How user friendly are the input and retrieval processes? What are the upgrade capabilities? What is functional today, might be outdated tomorrow. These are just a few examples of considerations that need to be taken into account when selecting software.

After your software has been selected, and only after your software has been selected, can you shop for hardware. Some software can only run on specific hardware, so care must be taken in the selection process. Work with a knowledgeable individual whom you trust, when making hardware selections.

Always remember that software and hardware selections must be based upon the human resources information needs of your particular hospitality operation. Define what specific applications your operation requires and make your selection decisions accordingly.

The Computer and the Manager with Human Resources Responsibilities

Software with specific applications for human resources functions have been available on the market for some time now, while the HRIS, or integrated systems, are relatively new. One of the advantages of a rapidly advancing technological society is that computer applications have become cost-effective for even small hospitality operations.

Justifying the investment in an automated system requires that you evaluate both the tangible and intangible savings generated. Most companies realize a short pay-back period in their computer investment with savings in the future.

"Computerese" has evolved a long way in the hospitality industry, since point-of-sale cash registers (probably the first computer) were introduced. From large hospitality corporations to entrepreneurs, the personal computer has been an important ingredient for success. Listed below are some of the benefits of computerization:

- Gives management more control over their data
- Improves the accuracy of information
- Provides for timeliness of information
- Offers savings on reduced clerical efforts
- Provides new capabilities for record maintenance and reports

388

- Permits human resources applications in new areas that require detailed analysis
- Can manipulate numerous variables simultaneously
- Provides consistency in report formats
- Permits the human resources arena to provide greater service to operational management
- Allows savings over manual methods of collecting, maintaining and reporting information
- Allows human resources to play a greater role in organizational decision making
- Offers improved communications between human resources and operating divisions

Managers with human resources responsibilities are more stimulated as there is less busy work and more creative thinking involved in their jobs. If you still need a convincing selling point for automation, ask a manager with a computerized information system if he or she would switch back to the old methods. We predict that the answer will be a resounding "no!"

Conclusion

Human resources applications using the computer go far beyond their origins in record keeping. Automation continues to find solutions to the daily problems encountered in human resources management. In recent years, great strides have been made in using computer potential for the accumulation, manipulation and reporting of data relating to human resources management. Computers are no longer merely electronic filing cabinets. Human resources management has just recently entered the new technological age, giving human resources functions a new respect and place of importance in the hierarchy of the hospitality enterprise. One of the most significant developments for hospitality organizations has been the development of the desktop or personal computer.

The computer has become a multipurpose tool in the effective management of our valued human resources. The manager with human resources responsibilities does not have to be a programmer in the 90s, but will need an awareness of how computer capabilities can make the manager more effective in his or her job. Changing managers' work habits is not easy. Nor is it easy for all seasoned managers to trust the strange, new machinery. Each of you has an enormous advantage upon entering the hospitality management work force in the 1990s. Most, if not all, of you have been exposed to the computer at some point during your education. You will make use of the benefits of the computer with much greater ease than many managers who have been in the field for several years. As computer technology improves, and software becomes more friendly, computer fear will hopefully subside, and all managers with or without human resources responsibilities will take advantage of this incredible tool that is available to them.

There can be little doubt, after reading this chapter, that the computerization of human resources functions is an asset to any manager charged with human resources responsibility. In "the next chapter" there will probably be a software package available for every human resources function that has been discussed. As the hospitality organization continues to rely on the human resources arena for more accurate information, the need will increase for improved human resource information systems. As the information needs of the organization change, the systems that organize that data will grow and adapt to fit the needs. For the next several years, however, a great need will continue to exist for adequate training in both the use of computers and the software that runs them. The future of human resource information systems lies in the training of individuals that are knowledgeable about human resources to also become computer literate. At the present time, there are many who continue to resist the information society of the 1990s.

Remember that you don't work for the computer, it works for you to facilitate the storage, manipulation, and retrieval of large amounts of information on a multitude of people. If you become tied to your computer, instead of using it to free you from time spent in the office, you will be taken away from your guests. Used effectively, the computer can save you time in the performance of your human resources responsibilities, providing you with new ways to organize and execute your responsibilities, while at the same time, saving your employer(s) money. If a manager systematizes the routine data gathering tasks involved in human resources management, the manager assuming human resources responsibilities takes on an elevated position in the hospitality organization. Human resource information systems give hospitality managers better ways of managing human resources.

Top management increasingly looks toward the human resources arena for credible data that can assist it in cost containment measures, in minimizing legal risks, in dealing with the everchanging government policies and regulations and in improving retention. Unreliable, outdated and inconsistent information can carry a high price for the hospitality enterprise of "the next chapter." Management decision making, where alternatives explored are based on sufficient and accurate data, can give hospitality organizations a competitive edge. Computer applications have traveled a long way from their origin in payroll record keeping!

Case Problem 15

Anytime a hospitality manager finds himself or herself in a new job position, challenges and opportunities abound. When that management position includes human resources responsibilities, both the opportunities and challenges increase. The changes in technology can be thought of as both a challenge and an opportunity. The challenge that is presented in this case for your consideration and discussion mirrors that found currently in many hospitality environments.

The management position that you recently assumed can provide you with the opportunity to share your knowledge of computer applications in the hospitality industry with the existing management team. The job position might be the first one you assume after graduation. Or, it might be a job that you find yourself in later in your hospitality career.

Select the hospitality environment that you see yourself in the future, or perhaps the hospitality management job that you have now. It does not matter whether the job is in the lodging, foodservice, or tourism sector of the hospitality industry. The common condition that exists is a lack of computer applications for human resources management functions. You are convinced, based upon your knowledge in this area, that the hospitality operation could benefit by the implementation of a HRIS.

While this is an opportunity for you to shine and become a valued member of the management team, your challenge is to convince the other members of the management team who have no knowledge about HRIS. Develop an outline that you will use in making an oral presentation to the management team. Discuss your ideas for a HRIS. At a minimum this outline should include a definition of what a HRIS is, along with any other definitions you feel the management team must understand in order to benefit from your presentation. An overview of the software applications for human resources functions, a needs assessment, and an identification of some of the benefits of computer applications in your hospitality operation should also be included.

Remember that you will need to be convincing in your presentation. The other members of the management team have been successful in resisting computer applications up to this point. What can you do to change their minds? In order to be competitive, computers are a necessity, not merely an ammenity. You will need to present some specifics of the hospitality operation you are working in. You will also need a justification of the cost investment.

RECOMMENDED READING

Anderson, K. J. 1988. Putting the "I" in HRIS. *Personnel* 65, (9): 12, 14–15, 18, 20, 22–24.

Berger, F.; Evans, M. E.; and Farber, B. 1986. Human-resources management: applying managerial-profile databases. *The Cornell H.R.A. Quarterly* 27, (3): 44–50.

Frantzreb, R. B. 1986. Microcomputer software for human resources: a directory. *Personnel Administrator* 31; (7).

Luck-Nunke, B. 1988. Easing your company into the computer age. *Personnel Administrator* 33, (6): 190–191.

Oleksinski, M. and Oleksinski, W. A. 1989. The case for payroll software. *Restaurants USA* 9, (4): 38–39.

Pasqualetto, J. 1987. Computers no more us vs. them. *Personnel Journal* 66, (12); 60–67.

Plantamura, L. M. 1985. Choosing an HRIS vendor. *Personnel Administrator* 30, (11); 18, 20, 22.

Restaurants and Institutions. 1988. The byte stuff. *Restaurants & Institutions* 98, (13); 185–186, 188, 190.

END NOTES

1. Travis, William I., "How to Justify a Human Resources Information System," *Personnel Journal* 67, (1988, 2): 83–86.
2. Walker, Alfred J., "New Technologies in Human Resource Planning," *Human Resource Planning* 9, (1986, 4): 149–159.
3. Berger, Florence; Evans, Martin E.; and Farber, Bonnie, "Applying Managerial-Profile Databases," *The Cornell Hotel and Restaurant Administration Quarterly* 27, (1986, 3): 44–50.
4. Travis, William J., "How To Justify a Human Resources Information System," *Personnel Journal* 67, (1988, 2): 83–86.
5. Miller, Lawrence R., "Law and Information Systems," *Journal of Systems Management* 28, (1977, 1): 21–30.
6. Griffin, John F., "Management Information Systems—A Challenge to Personnel," *Personnel Journal* 46, (1967, 6): 371–381.
7. Kaumeyer, Richard A., Jr., *Planning and Using Skills Inventory Systems,* (New York: Van Nostrand Reinhold Company, 1979): 10.
8. Blair, Edward, "Bootstrapping Your HRIS Capabilities," *Personnel Administrator* 33, (1988, 2): 68–72.
9. Leote, Dennis M., "Piecemeal Planning Hinders HRIS Performance," *Personnel Journal* 67, (1988, 3): 65–69.

391

DISCUSSION QUESTIONS

1. Rank in terms of priority of need, the major uses of a computer in a hospitality organization that has never been computerized. Limit your responses to human resources responsibilities.
2. What is the role of the computer in decision making in a hospitality organization?
3. Discuss the importance of conducting a needs analysis prior to the implementation of a computer system.
4. Why would you want to design your own software as opposed to purchasing vendor supplied software?
5. Identify several benefits to the automation of human resources functions.
6. React to the following statement: "Using computers to monitor human resources responsibilities and functions reduces the need for direct personal contact between management and employees."

392

CHAPTER 16

THE NEXT CHAPTER...

"It is our duty as men and women to proceed as though limits to our abilities do not exist."—PIERRE TEILHARD DE CHARDIN

"Success is easy if you believe. But first you must believe."—
PETER PAN

INTRODUCTION

Human resources management is no longer referred to as "personnel" in most hospitality organizations. The change is more than merely one of nomenclature. It represents a change in attitude, a change in conception, a change in status.

Personnel functions were considered primarily related to record keeping and administration. Personnel offices were located in out-of-the-way places in the hospitality operation, down by the employee lockers and "break" room. The human resources office is no longer hidden. With employees being viewed as an asset with a direct impact on the bottom line, hospitality companies are recognizing that properly managed human resources can give them a competitive edge. Human resources professionals are seen at top-level strategic planning sessions, and more COOs and CEOs are using human resources positions as the avenue to the top.

At the conclusion of this chapter you will be able to:
1. Discuss how the human resources arena will be important to organizational effectiveness.
2. Explain the future role of the human resources manager in the hospitality industry.
3. Identify the most likely developments and trends in the hospitality work force in "the next chapter."
4. Make three predictions regarding human resources management in the hospitality industry in the year 2000 from each of the industry advisors.
5. Obtain advice (we hope you will use) from each of the industry advisors as you enter the hospitality work force.

394

Figure 16-1. Sound human resources management practices make the hospitality environment a great place to work for all employees.
Photo A by Michael Upright; photo B courtesy of Marriott Corporation

The Increasing Importance of Human Resources Management

The issues that you, as a manager with human resources responsibilities, will be facing are much more complex than those of your predecessors. The impact that your role will make on the hospitality organization will be much farther reaching in its implications. In a survey reported in 1987, it was found that CEOs expect the human resources division to:

- Understand and support the needs of the business
- Play a major role in the use and development of talent
- Formulate cost containment measures
- Formulate productivity improvement measures
- Help both shape and communicate corporate values[1]

These expectations indicate that human resources management is going to have a much greater impact on the hospitality organization's strategic plan. Everything that is done will revolve around the mission statement, organizational goals and operational objectives. Human resources programs will not be developed merely for the sake of the human resources division, rather managers with human resources responsibilities will serve as support for the operational managers. Strong support in areas of problem solving and decision making can be given. The human resources arena is the information center for the organization's most valuable asset: its people (Figure 16-1).

A hospitality organization still needs its human resources policies and procedures to ensure consistency and continuity. This will still be an important role for human resources management in "the next chapter." Imagine if every operational manager and supervisor were permitted to set his or her own wages, discipline according to their own whims, run recruitment ads whenever the manager felt it was needed and hire at random. The point we want to stress is that human resources responsibilities will be expanded well beyond these traditional boundaries. Human resources systems planning must become part of a hospitality organization's business plan.

Looking through the literature, you can see that having human resources managers serve as advisors to the executive board is not a new idea.

> *"If he is truly to function as an adviser to top management, the personnel executive will have to live down the stereotype of a hail-fellow-well-met trying to keep everybody happy by administering a variety of employee benefits and services. These may still be important, but they are not of first importance today."[2]*

Forgetting for the moment that Myers only talked about the "personnel man," it is clear that even thirty years ago the insignificant role of personnel was being challenged.

> *"The point of view expressed here is that people as an organizational resource, are at least equally important with the others, and that ignorance, neglect, waste or poor handling of this resource has the same consequences as ignorance, neglect, waste or poor handling of money, materials or market."[3]*

Historically, part of the problem with human resources management is that it has always been difficult to fix a dollar amount on the return on investment from costly employee programs. A change in how personnel functions are viewed occurs when employees are thought of as an asset, rather than as an expense item. Human resources functions can then be recognized for their contribution to the bottom line. Human resources management can then become a profit center. Cost savings are not only tangible. What about the nontangible cost savings that occur when a union grievance does *not* occur? How much is saved when ERISA, OSHA, EEO or AA penalties do *not* have to be paid? What is it worth in dollars and public relations *not* to have a lawsuit filed against you by a disgruntled employee?

Criticisms of the personnel function have not always related to costs. Many have felt that personnel responsibilities were insignificant to the overall effectiveness of the organization. In the early seventies, the following criticisms were pointed out:

- "The personnel function is not management oriented.
- The personnel function is not adaptable to change.
- The personnel system is absorbed in relatively unimportant tasks like record keeping.
- In general, administrative offices function at low levels of productivity and are measured against inappropriate standards."[4]

If human resources management is no longer to be perceived as playing merely a mechanical, bookkeeping function, then the manager who assumes these responsibilities will need to adapt new strategies to meet the challenges of "the next chapter."

The Human Resources Professional

As we pointed out in the first chapter, every hospitality manager has human resources responsibilities. The importance of these skills is not only reflected in a review of the literature, but in the increase of course offerings related to human resources functions in colleges and universities. Regardless of the advancements made in computer technology, human resources management will still require the skills and labors of people! Not only will human resources departments and divisions within the hospitality organization take on greater prominence, the human resources professional will enjoy a much greater status. People will still need to be recruited, hired, trained, developed, motivated, counseled, disciplined and possibly terminated. The ability, however, to understand the hospitality business outside of the human resources functions will also become critical to the human resources professional in "the next chapter."

With labor shortages in the forecast, maximizing the productivity of the human resources already in your hospitality operation will become more important. Top management will be turning to the human resources professional to assist them in achieving this goal. In larger corporate organizations, human resources people are reporting directly to the top and assuming senior-level executive positions. Respect for the human resources professional is on the rise.[5]

Opportunities for advancement for the human resources professional will be more prevalent in "the next chapter" for the right human resources people. What skills do the right people possess? More management and finance oriented than human resources professionals in the past, they will understand a balance sheet and what affects it. These individuals understand the total business environment of the hospitality industry and their organization. They see the effect of human resources management on the bottom line.

As human resource information systems become more integrated into the hospitality environment, the human resources professional will be proficient in computer skills. These individuals won't necessarily have programming abilities, but he or she will be familiar with word processing and spread sheets such as the Lotus 1-2-3.

The human resources professional in "the next chapter" will be as comfortable discussing business strategy as he or she will be explaining the benefits package or in strategic human resources planning sessions. The ability to attract, develop and retain a highly motivated work force will still be critical job responsibilities. A forward looking, strategic and integrated approach to human resources issues will be of equal importance. With these skills and abilities, the human resources professional will find the potential high for career growth and mobility.

397

Challenges of the Future

What forces will be affecting you as you assume human resources responsibilities in "the next chapter"? We have already taken into consideration many of these forces as we discussed the various human resources functions. While many of these forces will challenge us, many will make our jobs more exciting and rewarding. Let's take this opportunity to summarize some of the challenges and changes facing us in "the next chapter":

- Extensive planning to meet tomorrow's work force needs in light of a worker shortage
- Continued search for ways to use our human resources more effectively
- Accelerating demand for better trained human resources
- Increasing sophistication in technology leading to improved human resource information systems
- More use of participatory management
- A decentralization of decision making
- Strategic human resources planning will seek input from the employees
- Better working relationships between unions and management
- Greater governmental influence and control through legislation
- Greater increase in the availability of human resources support services offered (EAPs, child care, etc.)
- Business-education partnerships
- More creativity in attracting and retaining our human resources
- Greater increase in the diversity of our work force
- Innovative changes will be required in compensation and benefits plans
- Communication will become instantaneous
- Jobs will be redesigned to integrate new skills

- Career paths will run horizontal as well as vertical
- Health care costs will continue to rise
- Compensation plans will become competitive and performance driven
- A constant need for training will be created
- Increase in the number of employee involvement programs

In 1988, the National Restaurant Association conducted a study using the Delphi method to determine what the food service industry would be like in the year 2000. Table 16-1 presents you with a list of what the panelists felt were the ten most likely developments in the work force. It is interesting to note, the two least likely developments that the panelists identified were: a decrease in employee turnover and that entry-level employees will be less educated.

Predictions for the Year 2000

Having access to our own panel of experts—the industry professionals who served as advisors to the chapters you have read—allowed me to ask them to make their own predictions. What follows is their response to this statement: "Make three predictions about human resources management in the hospitality industry in the year 2000."

Elaine Grossinger Etess, President, Elaine G. Etess Associates:

"1) The human resources shortage will be a critical problem for our industry to solve. Recruitment, training and retention will be the key to

---

Table 16-1. Top Ten Most Likely Developments in the Work Force

1. More emphasis will be placed on increasing employee productivity.
2. The industry will provide more training programs for its employees.
3. More specialized areas of study will be available in hotel, restaurant and institutional degree programs.
4. Industry management will be more highly educated.
5. More cooks and chefs will have formal culinary training.
6. The average foodservice employee will be older than today's average employee.
7. Greater emphasis will be placed on developing career foodservice employees.
8. The industry will employ a larger proportion of minorities.

9/10. Industry employees will be more likely to work a five-day work week.
9/10. The industry labor shortage will worsen.

Reprinted from *Foodservice Industry 2000* Published by the National Restaurant Association.

solving this problem. If we are not creative and innovative in our processes and procedures, our businesses will not be able to compete in the global marketplace.

2) By the year 2000, travel and tourism (of which hospitality is an integral part) will be the nation's number one employer, with one out of every seven workers employed in it. The lodging industry alone will need up to 800,000 more employees.

399

3) To insure the financial investment in a property, a formalized, aggressive human resources development program will become imperative for survival."

Michael Hurst, Owner, 15th Street Fisheries and Vice-President, National Restaurant Association:

"1) Hiring for personality rather than age will become more prevalent.

2) Part-time employees will be even more important in the year 2000. We must appreciate that our work is secondary to their outside responsibilities.

3) Management must lead! It means that simple administration will not get the job done. It's going to take exemplary performance. Customer-focused management will score big victories and grow and prosper as a result. Profit-oriented management will find that it is possible to go out of business with good food and labor costs."

Joel S. Katz, Director, Human Resources Development, ARA Services:

"1) In the next five years, as quality human resources become more scarce, companies will expend a large amount of resources to recruit people away from one another. The most successful companies, however, will be those that find and develop completely new resources: disabled workers, re-entering homemakers, homeless people, exiting military and other nontraditional workers.

2) As companies realize the value of quality human resources, they will begin to practice 'human resources accounting.' The expression 'our people are our most important asset' will become more than just rhetoric. Companies will place a value on their human resources much as they do for their equipment, inventories, real estate and other assets. And, Return on Investment (ROI) will become the key measure in human resources management.

3) In the 70s and 80s, the competitive playing fields were technology and marketing. In the 90s, companies will compete on the human resources playing field. The companies that are able to develop and implement strategies for recruiting, developing and retaining high-quality employees will walk away with the trophies."

David R. Murphy, Former Director, Corporate College Relations, Marriott:

"1) The hospitality industry, in order to competitively attract quality managers, will adjust the present excessive hours of work.

Figure 16-2. "The focus will be on the training and retention of employees."
Courtesy of Stouffer Hotels and Resorts

2) Most major companies will have graduates that have spent progressive summers in their employ.

3) Women will dominate the graduating classes of major Hotel Restaurant Institutional Management schools."

Cathy Conner, Manager/Recruiting, Gilbert/Robinson, Inc.:
"1) A better quality of life will be even more of an issue than it is now. We'll probably see more flex time, four-day work weeks and permanent or semipermanent schedules. For example, the nursing field schedules.

2) As the quantity of applicants continues to diminish, "high touch" will become critical. The focus will be on training and retention of employees (Figure 16-2).

3) Future managers will have to be true leaders and have charisma and integrity. They will have to have enough self-confidence to empower their employees and allow them autonomy to make decisions."

Nicholas F. Horney, Ph.D., Director Training and Development, Stouffer Hotels and Resorts:
"1) Human resources managers will be stronger business partners with operations and marketing than currently perceived.

2) Human resources managers will have leaner corporate staffs that require greater decentralization of the human resources function.

3) Operations management will be more involved and better educated in human resources management."

Hugh Murphy, Former Vice President Human Resources, Chili's, Inc.:
"1) Dramatic shifts in the demographics of the labor pool will force operators to reevaluate traditional selection techniques.

2) The low-supply-and-high-demand labor market will result in a shift in the classical decision making process. The labor market will be a key determinate to a company's growth strategy.

3) Operators may adapt the Japanese employment-for-life concept

as a viable alternative to turnover or short staffing. The incremental expense will probably end up a savings."

Anonymous, Manager, Food and Beverage:

"1) As our economy becomes more service oriented the service sector will try and adopt production and manufacturing logic in dealing with employees. As a result, service standards will initially decline until a complete understanding of quality control is grasped by management.

2) The work environment for employees of the service sector will be pressured to be on a par with manufacturing (i.e., work week, pay, benefits and physical environment). As a result, luxury service environments will become very expensive to provide. Fewer people will be able to afford them.

3) The skills required by the professional manager in the hospitality industry will be increased. Mom-and-pop operations will diminish as chains replace them. Competition for management skills will increase greatly."

Richard Ysmael, Corporate Director Foodworks Management Services, Motorola Inc.:

"1) Training and development of personnel at all levels will be essential to success. Our industry must commit the financial resources to achieve this critical task.

2) Productivity: the tight labor market we are experiencing today will continue through the next decade. Improvements in equipment and design layout will have to accelerate significantly. Operating techniques and systems will focus on productivity enhancement.

3) Part time employees: Flextime and day care will require continued evaluation and emphasis."

James F. Moore, President, Far West Concepts:

"1) We will see increased government regulations on total employee compensation mandated to operating companies.

2) There will be a severe labor shortage in both hourly and management employees.

3) The result of the aforementioned practices will paradoxically result in more restaurant concepts showing up that have the following ingredients:

Larger in size than present (but not built from the ground up) that use primarily part-time help, are priced moderately, give less service but provide outstanding quality products. These concepts will find a uniqueness generally absent from the present marketplace. These new operations will place great emphasis on the customer and the customers' needs.

The next decade will move away from the cost cutting and automation for their profits and will focus on the customer as their base philosophy."

Jim Tye, Director of Employment, Furr's/Bishop's Cafeterias, L.P.:

401

"1) Shrinking labor pool with fewer quality players; fewer people with even basic reading, writing and arithmetic.

2) Increasing legislation and regulation, particularly in the area of benefits administration.

3) Major demographic and cultural impact."

Regynald G. Washington, Senior Vice President, Concessions International, Inc.:

"1) In the 90s, hospitality management personnel will receive stronger and more competitive compensation packages thus creating an environment of greater professionalism that allows for fewer mistakes and the need for the implementation of systematic and proactive management techniques.

2) Collective bargaining in the hospitality industry will continue to exist through the 90s. Union business managers will be highly skilled and extremely competent regarding union affairs and contract negotiations.

3) With mandated employee benefits becoming a fact of the future, unions will look for additional perks to include in union contracts, thus costing management more money and possibly smaller profits."

Advice From the Industry Experts

The industry advisors were asked to provide you with some additional information. "What is one piece of advice you would give students who are about to graduate and enter the hospitality work force"? Their suggestions follow.

Elaine G. Etess: "No matter which area of the hospitality industry you choose, it is essential that you have an acute awareness of human resources. People make the difference. The manager that focuses on human resources development will undoubtedly be the most successful."

Michael Hurst: "The hospitality business has always been about people. The primary target is our customer. Keep score. Did you beat last year at breakfast? Lunch? Dinner? Play the customer game! To win, you soon realize that location, facility, pricing, presentation are all given factors. The facet that brings it all together is the server. These individuals make or break our business. All positions exist in the organization to make that server look absolutely great to our guest. Staff supports the front of the house, and we all focus on doing a better and better job for the guest. Keep your eye on the target! Understand that your job is customers (Figure 16-3) and the way you get them is by an excited, knowledgeable staff."

Joel S. Katz: "Human resources management would be very easy if it weren't for people. This is somewhat of a facetious comment, but there is much truth to it. Because human resources management involves

402

Figure 16-3. "Understand that your job is customers. . . . "
Courtesy of Strongbow Inn, Valparaiso, Indiana

people—that bring to the work place their needs, problems, hopes, joys, abilities and disabilities—there is very little, if any, science in it. There are few rules, principles or laws of nature that can be relied on in a consistent way. And so, successful human resources management requires a level of knowledge, skill and judgment that exceeds most other business disciplines. These competencies can be acquired through reading and training, but most of all through experience."

David R. Murphy: "Be realistic about expectations in your first-year environment. Plan part-time work experience wisely. Get involved in school and industry functions. Make a full-time job out of getting a job upon graduation."

Cathy Conner: "Take care of your employees. A "my way or the highway' or similar attitude won't make it in the 1990s. Managers will have to take a leadership vs. a 'police officer' role. We'll need to get involvement out of our people and feel comfortable empowering them to be successful, ourselves."

Nicholas F. Horney: "Look around you at the people that are able to persuade others to accept their opinions and influence them to take action. Remember that influence is power. Regardless of the job that you hold, the more influential you are, the more power and greater contribution you can make to your organization."

Hugh Murphy: "Give it time! At the initial operating level, the hospitality business is extremely demanding, challenging and frustrating at times. Keep in mind what great restaurateurs like Norman Brinker (Chili's chairman of the board) have know for years: you will succeed only to the degree that your employees want you to succeed! Believe it."

Anonymous: "You should set high goals for yourself. And then you should expect to have to work hard to achieve your goals. You shouldn't just expect things to happen without effort on your part."

Richard Ysmael: "There are no shortcuts that will provide long-term success in this business. Pay your dues. The many tasks one must learn to manage people and operations effectively require dedication, time and energy. While you are doing all this, don't forget the customer, for that's what drives this business. Commit yourself to these initiatives, and you will be on your way to a rewarding career."

James F. Moore: "Become a planner. Make short- and long-term objectives. Practice patience when evaluating your progress toward these objectives. You may have to adjust your timetables. Be a self-starter and don't be afraid to make mistakes. It's through learning from the results of your decisions that your experience base is formulated. Be willing to accept criticism, it is part of your learning cycle. Be aggressive toward achieving your goals. Don't expect your employer to carry you through your career.

Many young people just starting out find themselves in new environments and, naturally, want to make friends with their employees. Don't get caught in this trap. Remember, you will be supervising and perhaps disciplining them in the future."

Jim Tye: "Do your homework; it will probably take more honest work to match your priorities (personal and professional) with the right company culture than anything else you will ever attempt. Be flexible; a still-frame picture of our world no longer exists. Recognize that continuing education is an absolute; there is always something to learn in our business."

Regynald G. Washington: "Thoroughly understand and educate yourself regarding all areas of any collective bargaining agreement governing the organization in which you function as management. Additionally, always exercise consistency in the way that you conduct your day to day management affairs."

Conclusion

Human resources management is assuming a larger role in the organizational effectiveness of the hospitality enterprise. We can no longer afford to give lip service to the importance of our people. The 1980s verbalized the importance of human resources. In "the next chapter" we must act upon our knowledge. Labor is our partner, not our enemy.

Your biggest challenge as you leave the classroom and assume human resources responsibilities will be the severe labor shortage. Each of the human resources functions discussed in this text plays a vital role in either attracting or retaining a motivated work force. We will continue to seek new and innovative approaches to the challenges we face in the management of our human resources. Solutions, instead of theories, will be needed if we are to succeed. It is our sincere hope that this text, with the input and advice of hundreds of years of hospitality experience, will provide you with at least some of those solutions. Despite the challenges, the rewards prevail!

"If you can dream it, you can do it."—WALT DISNEY

RECOMMENDED READING

Albrecht, K. and Zemke, R. 1985. *Service America!* Homewood, Illinois: Dow Jones-Irwing.

Arthur, D. 1987. The human resources function and the growing company. *Personnel* 64, (11): 18–24.

Butler, J. E. 1988/89. Human resources management as a driving force in business strategy. *Journal of General Management* 13, (4): 88–101.

Driver, M. J.; Coffey, R. E.; and Bowen, D. E. 1988. Where is HR management going? *Personnel* 65, (1): 28–31.

Galagan, P. 1987. Here's the situation. *Training and Development Journal* 41, (7): 20–22.

Kamerman, S. B. and Kahn, A. J. 1987. *The Responsive Workplace Employers and a Changing Labor Force.* New York: Columbia University Press.

Minor, R. S. and Fetridge, C. W. (Eds.). 1984. *The Dartnell Office Administration Handbook.* Chicago: Dartnell.

National Restaurant Association. 1989. *Foodservice Employment 2000: Exemplary Industry Programs.* Washington, D.C.: National Restaurant Association.

Walker, A. J. 1987. Human resources: preparing for the next century. *Personnel Journal* 66, (11): 107–112.

Wolfe, P. R. 1988. Personnel issues for the 1980s and beyond. *Lodging Hospitality* 44, (3): 56–57.

END NOTES

1. Frazee, Joan and Harrington-Kuller, Janet, "Money Matters: Selling HRIS to Management," *Personnel Journal* 66, (1987, 8): 98–107.
2. Myers, Charles A., "New Frontiers for Personnel Management," *Personnel* 41, (1964, 3): 31–38.
3. Bakke, E. Wright, "The Human Resources Function," In Bakke, E. Wright; Kerr, Clark; and Anrod, Charles W. (Eds.) *Unions, Management and the Public,* New York: Harcourt, Brace and World, Inc., (1960): 198.
4. Tomeski, Edward A. and Lazarus, Harold, "The Computer and the Personnel Department," *Business Horizons* XVI, (1973, 3): 62.
5. Vittolino, Sal, "Taking the Reins," *Human Resource Executive* 2, (1988, 8): 1, 18–20.

406

BIBLIOGRAPHY

Chapter 2

Bartholomew, D. J. and Forbes, A. F. (1979). *Statistical Techniques for Manpower Planning*. New York: John Wiley & Sons.

National Restaurant Association. (1988). The Foodservice Industry 1986: A Brief Review. *Restaurants USA,* 8, (6), 39–41.

Chapter 4

Field, H. S. and Gatewood, R. D. (1987). Matching Talent with the Task. *Personnel Administrator,* 32, (4), 113–114, 116–117, 119–120, 122, 124–126.

Kennedy, W. R. (1987). Train Managers to Write Winning Job Descriptions. *Training and Development Journal,* 41, (4), 62–64.

McCormick, E. J. (1979). *Job Analysis: Methods and Applications*. New York: AMACOM.

Plachy, R. J. (1987). Writing Job Descriptions That Get Results. *Personnel,* 64, (10), 56–63.

Chapter 5

Bacas, H. (1988). Fire Them All? *Nation's Business,* 76, (2), 62–63.

Bader, M. (1988). Attitudes Harden Before Arteries When Hiring the Elderly. *Wall Street Journal,* CCXI, (109), 22.

Birger, L. (1988). Teens The Incredible Shrinking Work Force. *Miami Herald,* March 21, 1, 12–13, 15.

Lodging (1989). A Recruiting Guide for Alternative Labor Sources. *Lodging,* 14, (5), 30, 36.

National Restaurant Association. (1988). *Foodservice Industry 2000*. Washington D.C.: National Restaurant Association.

National Restaurant Association. (1988). *A 1988 Update: Foodservice and the Labor Shortage*. Washington D.C.: National Restaurant Association.

VanDyke, T. and Strick, S. (1988). New Concepts to Old Topics: Employee Recruitment, Selection and Retention. *Hospitality Education and Research Journal,* 12, (2), 347–360.

Villano, D. (1988). The Big Kahuna of Headhunters. *South Florida,* 41, (12), 32, 34.

Chapter 6

Hunsaker, J. and Hunsaker, P. (1989). How to Hire the Right Person for the Job. *Working Woman,* 14, (1), 28, 31.

Karr, A. R. (1988). Law Limiting Use of Lie Detectors Is Seen Having Widespread Effect. *Wall Street Journal,* CCXII, (1), 19.

Karren, R. J. and Nkomo, S. M. (1988). "So, You Want to Work for Us. . .". *Personnel Administrator,* 33, (4), 88–90, 91.

Paunonen, S. V., Jackson, D. N. and Oberman, S. M. (1987). Personnel Selection Decisions: Effects of Applicant Personality and the Letter of Reference. *Organizational Behavior and Human Decision Processes,* 40, 96–114.

Smart, B. D. (1987). Progressive Approaches for Hiring the Best People. *Training and Development Journal,* 41 (9), 46–53.

Susser, P. A. and Jett, D. H. (1987). Negligent Hiring: What You Don't Know **Can** Hurt You. *Employment Relations Today,* 14, (3), 279–285.

Chapter 7

Steinmetz, C. S. (1976). The History of Training. In Craig, L. C. (Ed.) *Training and Development Handbook.* New York: McGraw-Hill.

Rackham, N. and Morgan, T. (1977). *Behaviour Analysis in Training,* London: McGraw-Hill.

Chapter 8

Simonsen, P. (1986). Concepts of Career Development. *Training and Development Journal,* 40, (11), 70–74.

Chapter 9

Feiertag, H. (1988). Proper Performance Appraisals Can Boost Productivity. *H&MM,* 203, (12), 28.

Girard, R. (1988). Is There a Need For Performance Appraisals? *Personnel Journal,* 67, (8), 89–90.

Levinson, H. (1976). Appraisal of What Performance? *Harvard Business Review,* 54, 30–36.

Martin, D. C. (1986). Performance Appraisal, 2: Improving the Rater's Effectiveness. *Personnel,* 63, (8), 28–33.

Meyer, H. H., Kay, E. and French, J. R. P. (1965). Split Roles in Performance Appraisal. *Harvard Business Review,* 43, 123–129.

Prince, J. B. and Lawler, E. E. (1986). Does Salary Discussion Hurt the Developmental Performance Appraisal? *Organizational Behavior and Human Decision Processes,* 37, 357–375.

Smith, M. (1987). Putting Their Performance in Writing. *Management Solutions,* 32, (3), 4–11.

Chapter 10

Basile, R. E. (1985). Beware of Compensatory Time! *Restaurant Hospitality,* 69, (10), 46–51.

Cleaver, J. Y. (1987). Incentive Programs Light Productive Fires. *Advertising Age,* 58, (18), 22–23.

Garcia, A. and Peters, T. (1989). A Piece of the Action. *Success,* 36, (1), 14.

Gethman, B. R. (1987). The Job Market, Sex Bias, and Comparable Worth. *Public Personnel Management,* 16, (2), 173–180.

Grant, P. C. (1988). Rewards: The Pizzazz Is The Package, Not the Prize. *Personnel Journal,* 67, (3), 76, 78–81.

Halcrow, A. (1988). What's Wrong With HRIS? *Personnel Journal,* 67, (2), 12–13.

Hertzberg, F. (1968). One More Time How Do You Motivate Employees? *Harvard Business Review,* 46, 53–62.

Hills, F. S. (1987). *Compensation Decision Making.* Chicago: The Dryden Press.

Husband, T. M. (1976). *Work Analysis and Pay Structure.* London: McGraw-Hill.

Kanter, R. M. (1987). From Status to Contribution: Some Organizational Implications of the Changing Basis for Pay. *Personnel,* 64, (1), 12–37.

Verespej, M. A. (1988). We'll Have to Earn Our Keep. *Industry Week,* 236, (8), 57.

Walker, C. T. (1987). The Use of Job Evaluation Plans in Salary Administration. *Personnel,* 64, (3), 28–31.

412

413